THE ENDS OF PHILOSOPHY

THE ENDS
OF
PHILOSOPHY

Pragmatism, Foundationalism, and
Postmodernism

Lawrence E. Cahoone

Blackwell Publishers

© 2002 by Lawrence E. Cahoone

Editorial Offices:
108 Cowley Road, Oxford OX4 1JF, UK
Tel: +44 (0)1865 791100
Osney Mead, Oxford OX2 0EL, UK
Tel: +44 (0)1865 206206
Blackwell Publishing USA, 350 Main Street, Malden, MA 02148-5018
Tel: +1 781 388 8250
Iowa State University Press, a Blackwell Publishing Company, 2121 S. State Avenue,
Ames, Iowa 50014-8300, US
Tel: + 1 515 292 0140
Blackwell Munksgaard, Nørre Søgade 35, PO Box 2148, Copenhagen, DK-1016,
Denmark
Tel: + 45 77 33 33 33
Blackwell Publishing Asia, 54 University Street, Carlton, Victoria 3053, Australia
Tel: +61 (0)3 9347 0300
Blackwell Verlag, Kurfürstendamm 57, 10707 Berlin, Germany
Tel: +49 (0)30 32 79 060
Blackwell Publishing, 10 rue Casimir Delavigne, 75006 Paris, France
Tel: +33 1 53 10 33 10

First published 1995 by State University of New York Press, Albany
First published in the United Kingdom 2002 by Blackwell Publishers Ltd, a Blackwell
Publishing company

ISBN 0-631-23405-5

A catalogue record for this title is available from the British Library.

This book has been printed digitally by Lightning Source in association with
Blackwell Publishing Limited

For further information on
Blackwell Publishers, visit our website:
www.blackwellpublishers.co.uk

For my wife,
Elizabeth Baeten

CONTENTS

PREFACE

Participants in the debate between "modernism" and "post-modernism"—myself included—have often combined epistemic and social concerns through a historical treatment to generate a global cultural diagnosis. In this way modernity is sometimes said to exhibit a certain view of knowledge that is linked to a modern form of social organization. While preparing a sequel to an earlier book on modernity, I came to the conclusion that this syncretic approach was inadequate, that epistemic and social concerns had to be addressed separately. I decided that I had first to write a book on knowledge and philosophy, a book of an entirely different nature than I had anticipated, and to put off social theory and cultural diagnosis until later.

The decision was also a personal one. It meant a return to the issues that led me to become a philosopher, namely, how ought we to view our world, and derivatively, what can we know? I have always been a "first philosopher" at heart, even if that heart has been repeatedly broken. The decision to write the present book was a decision to narrow my interests to the more purely philosophical, rather than expand to the interdisciplinary, a narrowing that risks irrelevance, indecisiveness, and uselessness.

But neither can I claim for this project the virtues of narrowness, namely, competence and precision. For also at play was my desire to engage the twentieth century philosophers I found most interesting, regardless of philosophical tradition, hence, regardless of my level of competence. Each of the issues and philosophers I treat deserves book-length study. My comparative task must appear superficial to specialists, and to this kind of superficiality I readily confess. Nevertheless, the book seems its own kind of philosophical depth.

ix

This work exhibits the influence of many inquirers, living and dead. Chief among the living are my colleagues of the Department of Philosophy at Boston University. Of particular help have been Robert Cohen, Charles Griswold, Victor Kestenbaum, Alan Olson, and Leroy Rouner. I thank colleagues generous enough with their time to read and comment on drafts of various chapters: Elizabeth Baeten, Robert Bernasconi, Burton Dreben, Charles Griswold, Jaakko Hintikka, Len Lawlor, Michael Naas, Robert Neville, Abner Shimony, Thomas Thorp, and Kathleen Wallace. I have benefited from the views of Steven Gerrard and Sahotra Sarkar. I am specially indebted to Burton Dreben for his philosophical inspiration and generosity. Last, I am grateful to Robert Neville for his continuing encouragement.

I would no more want to philosophize without teaching than to teach without philosophizing. Excellent students, like those I have had at Boston University, make this combination possible. In a real sense, this book is theirs.

The late Justus Buchler has had a profound and continuing influence on my thinking, despite the difference in our aims and philosophical associations. Buchler refused either to follow others, which would have granted him reassurance through an appeal to authority, or to drape his work in grandiose costume, the better to befuddle critics and fascinate converts. I hope these refusals have found some minor echo here.

I wish to thank the Director of the State University of New York Press, William Eastman, and Production Editor, Diane Ganeles, for their help.

An earlier version of part of Chapter Nine appeared in *Philosophy Today* 38, no. 2 (Summer 1994): 204–224.

Without the support of my wife and colleague, Elizabeth Baeten, and my mother, Mary Candelet, this book could not have been written. Whether that is to their ultimate credit or discredit is up to God or Nature. To me, though, they are swell.

ABBREVIATIONS

Buchler

CM: *The Concept of Method* (Lanham, Md.: University Press of America, 1985).

ML: *The Main of Light: On the Concept of Poetry* (New York: Oxford University Press, 1974).

MNC: *Metaphysics of Natural Complexes* (New York: Columbia University Press, 1966).

NJ: *Nature and Judgment* (New York: Grosset and Dunlap, 1966).

OCW: "On the Concept of 'The World'," *The Review of Metaphysics*, 31, no. 4 (June 1978): 555–579.

PN: 'Probing the Idea of Nature," *Process Studies* 8 no. 3 (Fall 1978): 157–168.

TGT: *Toward a General Theory of Human Judgment* (New York: Dover Press, 1979).

Derrida

D: "Différence," in SP, pp. 129–160.

DS: *Dissemination*, trans. Barbara Johnson (Chicago: University of Chicago Press, 1981).

E: *The Ear of the Other*, trans. Peggy Kamuf (Lincoln: University of Nebraska Press, 1985).

L: *Limited, Inc.*, trans. Sam Weber (Baltimore: Johns Hopkins University Press, 1977).

M: *Margins*, trans. Alan Bass (Chicago: University of Chicago Press, 1982).

NO: 1983 interview with *Le Nouvel Observateur*, English trans. in David Wood and Robert Bernasconi, *Derrida and Différance* (Evanston, Ill.: Northwestern University Press, 1988).

OG: *Of Grammatology*, trans. G. C. Spivak (Baltimore: Johns Hopkins University Press, 1976).

P: *Positions*, trans. Alan Bass (Chicago: University of Chicago Press, 1981).

PR: "The Principle of Reason: The University in the Eyes of its Pupils," trans. Catherine Porter and Edward P. Morris, *Diacritics* 13 (Fall 1983): 3–20.

S: *Spurs*, trans. Barbara Harlow (Chicago: University of Chicago Press, 1978).

SP: *Speech and Phenomena*, trans. David Allison (Evanston, Ill.: Northwestern University Press, 1973).

WD: *Writing and Difference*, trans. Alan Bass (Chicago: University of Chicago Press, 1978).

Nietzsche

A: *The Antichrist*, in PN, pp. 568–656

BGE: *Beyond Good and Evil*, trans. Walter Kaufman (New York: Vintage Books, 1966).

BT: *The Birth of Tragedy*, trans. Walter Kaufman (New York: Vintage Books, 1966).

EH: *Ecce Homo*, trans. Walter Kaufman (New York: Vintage Books, 1967).

GH: *The Genealogy of Morals*, trans. Francis Golffing (Garden City, N.Y.: Anchor Books, 1956).

GS: *The Gay Science*, trans. Walter Kaufman (New York: Vintage Books, 1974).

H: *Human, All Too Human*, trans. R. J. Hollingdale (Cambridge: Cambridge University Press, 1986).

PN: *The Portable Nietzsche*, ed. Walter Kaufman (New York: Viking Books, 1968).

PT: *Philosophy and Truth: Selections from Nietzsche's Notebooks of the Early 1870's*, trans. Daniel Brazeale (Atlantic Highlands, N.J.: Humanities Press, 1979).

SL: *Selected Letters*, trans. A. N. Ludovici (London: Soho, 1985).

TI: *Twilight of the Idols*, trans. Walter Kaufman, in PN, pp. 464–563.

TL: "On the Truth and Lies in a Nonmoral Sense," in PT.

WP: *The Will to Power*, trans. Walter Kaufman and R. J. Hollingdale (New York: Vintage Books, 1986).

TSZ: *Thus Spoke Zarathustra*, trans. Walter Kaufman, in PN, pp. 112–439.

Peirce

CP: *Collected Papers of Charles Sanders Peirce*, 8 vols., ed. Charles Hartshorne and Paul Weiss (Cambridge, Mass.: Harvard University Press, 1931–1958); vols. 7 and 8 ed. by Arthur Burks.

Rorty

COP: *Consequences of Pragmatism* (Minneapolis: University of Minnesota Press, 1982).
CIS: *Contingency, Irony, and Solidarity* (Cambridge: Cambridge University Press, 1989).
EHO: *Essays on Heidegger and Others* (Cambridge: Cambridge University Press, 1991).
PMN: *Philosophy and the Mirror of Nature* (Princeton, N.J.: Princeton University Press, 1979).
ORT *Objectivity, Relativism, and Truth* (Cambridge: Cambridge University Press, 1991).

Wittgenstein

LE: "Lecture on Ethics," *The Philosophical Review*, 74, no. 1 (January 1965): 3–12.
LT: *Letters to Russell, Keynes and Moore*, ed. G. H. von Wright and B. F. McGuinness (Oxford: Basil Blackwell, 1974).
N: *Notebooks: 1914–1916*, trans. G. E. M. Anscombe (London: University of Chicago Press, 1979).
OC: *On Certainty*, trans. by Denis Paul and G. E. M. Anscombe (New York: Harper Books, 1969).
PI: *Philosophical Investigations*, trans. G. E. M. Anscombe (New York: Macmillan, 1958).
RFM: *Remarks on the Foundations of Mathematics*, trans. G. E. M. Anscombe (Cambridge: MIT Press, 1983).
RPP: *Remarks on the Philosophy of Psychology*, I, ed. G. E. M. Anscombe and G. H. vonWright, trans. G. E. M. Anscombe (Chicago: University of Chicago Press, 1980).
T: *Tractatus Logico-Philosophicus*, trans. D. F. Pears and B. F. McGuinness (London: Routledge, 1961).
VC: *Ludwig Wittgenstein and the Vienna Circle: Conversations with Friedrich Waisman*, ed. Brian F. McGuinness (Oxford: Basil Blackwell, 1967).

Z: *Zettel*, trans. G. E. M. Anscombe (Berkeley and Los Angeles: University of California Press, 1970).

Whatever the consequences may be for "intelligence," the philosopher is unable to adjust means to ends with any semblance of the definitiveness attained in other forms of discipline. Much of this travail of imbalance and insecurity he can spare himself, by lowering his sights, purging his discipline of its extravagant hopes, and confining himself to problems not more docile, perhaps, but more bountiful of reward. The alternative is to endure his identity, which is molded by his deeper feelings, and to accept the methodic lameness he has inherited, since he must perceive sooner or later that the beauty and the meaning of his query are unimpaired.

Justus Buchler
The Main of Light

INTRODUCTION

Construed modestly, the tasks of philosophy are eminently achievable, making its justification unnecessary. Philosophers increase our knowledge of our ideas and theories. They clarify our views and reveal inconsistencies. They suggest new possibilities for conception and interpretation. They teach us the great ideas of the past. Gnawing on their work sharpens our intellectual teeth: philosophy makes us smarter. Philosophy is an important part of what we regard as a liberal education, a significant limb of the body of knowledge society wishes to bequeath to subsequent generations. Occasionally, philosophical ideas make their way into cabinet meetings, boardrooms, and political rallies. Philosophy is a respectable citizen, whose membership in the cultural community is not in question.

But only as long as we do not take it too seriously. For, immodestly construed, the tasks of philosophy are so monumental that no justification of it seems possible. Philosophy in the sense of an attempt to know not just some truths but the whole truth, the most comprehensive or fundamental truth, seems quixotic, absurd, and dangerously arrogant. In a world where we are tossed from the comic to the tragic, from the joys of animal satisfactions and the simplicity of unreflective life to the responsibility to make choices in the knowledge of approaching death, a world where, in Whitehead's phrase, "the fairies dance, and Christ is nailed to the cross," how can the philosopher fancy an understanding of the whole, even in its most abstract, barest outlines? How can we achieve a comprehensive vision of the endless passing enormity in which the inquirer is a momentary participant, according to the Venerable Bede's figure, a bird flying from darkness through a lighted room and out into darkness again? How can we hope to *know*, and not merely to opine, what is fundamental or ultimate or primary? How indeed, when the deep-

1

est and most comprehensive attempt at understanding must necessarily put itself in the balance to be weighed with everything else, must open itself to its own questionability.

What is this foolishness called *philosophy*? Whatever it may be, it is not just a professional foolery. Philosophy is an expression of the urge to comprehend the highest and lowest, the fundamental and the final. Philosophy is inquiry at its most ultimate and comprehensive, hence its most indefinite and uncertain. If philosophy is absurd, then inquiry, the urge to know, is touched with absurdity, as is the human spirit it serves. Inquiry has, for almost as long as we can remember, pushed its search beyond the familiar, the local, and the determinable, beyond the reach of its supply lines. Philosophy is inquiry trying to transcend its medium, like a jet airplane trying to climb beyond the atmosphere. In reaction, some have tried to draw a line that inquiry ought not cross, to prohibit inquiry from trying to go too far, for its own good. But how to draw a line in the air? That is no less daunting a task than what it tries to prohibit. The sensible ones who want to limit philosophy are as unsensible as the rest. They are, after all, philosophers, too.

Of course, knowing is the most common thing in the world. It is part of life. There is no mystery about it, there is no living without it. Our problem is not, how do we know, but rather what happens when knowing, in an expansion that seems natural to it, climbs higher or digs deeper? When we push knowing far enough, when we want to know, not what caused this or that, but what caused everything or what is a cause, we find ourselves outside the well-worn paths of our community life, in a lawless territory. There are travelers there, and have always been; there are charts and maps they have left behind. But there is no law, few institutions, little domesticity. There are individuals making their way in an unsubdued country. This is where, should he or she choose to accept it, the philosopher lives.

The adventure is only a mental one, to be sure. Philosophers in our culture are professors, working for the state or for private non-profit corporations, utterly domesticated in their behavior. There is nothing wrong with this. Some few geniuses may thrive on isolation or bohemian independence of institutions, but most of us would disintegrate without the borders of community and socialized work, or at least drift into useless eccentricity. Teaching helps to humanize the philosopher. So, the domestication of the philosopher's daily life is probably beneficial. This is not true of the domestication of the philosopher's *thought*, however. Philosophical thinking needs to be free, which is to say, devoid of guidance, lonely—freedom being, in the words of the songstress, "just another word for nothing left to lose."[1] Mentally, philosophers are cut adrift to make their own way, even if they eventually conclude that all thinking is social. That was the irony of Charles Peirce, America's philosophical genius, who defined truth in terms of the community that exiled him.[2]

The invention of philosophy within what is misleadingly but conveniently labeled "the West" is habitually credited to the ancient Greeks. It is to that time and people that we trace the expansion of the use of inquiry from its earlier home in the domain of practical concerns, like engineering, to include ultimate matters such as the nature and origin of all things, which had earlier been the sole province of art and religion. The Greeks encouraged inquiry to muscle in on more exalted turf, and there has been a battle ever since. Philosophy is that exalted inquiry, hence basically the same process of judgment we use to find water, quarks, or our keys, albeit extended to *ultimate* questions.

To doubt the purpose and validity of philosophy is to wonder whether this expansion was a mistake, a foolhardy venture into which inquiry was seduced by the overconfident Greeks. It is to wonder if inquiry may be constitutionally unable to serve exalted purposes. Should inquiry now, more than two millennia wiser about its incapacity, retreat from the higher ground and leave ultimate matters to other cultural media, like religion or art or politics? In short, should philosophy as inquiry come to an end?

The nonhistorical way to approach this question would be to ask, What is the value or validity of philosophy? But this is still too wide a net. The traditional valuation of philosophy is that it aims to gain knowledge of what is true, and more precisely, to *say what* is true and *say why* it is true. It will be a sufficiently overwhelming task to try to decide whether that traditional valuation is plausible. The question my book will address is then, Is characteristically philosophical knowledge possible?

Clearly philosophers know many things: when Kant was born, that Husserl influenced Heidegger, that mechanism is a kind of materialism, that Descartes's arguments for the existence of God are problematic. These are not examples of the kind of knowledge in question here. Among the many things philosophers seek to know there is one kind of knowledge, the search for which defines philosophy as different from intellectual history and science. This characteristically philosophical knowledge would be represented by answers to questions like these: Does God exist? What is the meaning of human life? Is science true? Is morality solely conventional? Is democracy right? Questions like these mark philosophy's special function. My question is, Can philosophical inquiry yield knowledge in this sense? If not, why not?

Although philosophy has ever been suspect, the twentieth century has witnessed an unprecedented series of charges brought against philosophy by philosophers. Remarkably, some of the most important philosophical movements of the century—analytic philosophy of language, logical positivism, existentialism, phenomenology, Marxism (in a sense), pragmatism, and what is today called 'postmodernism'—have alleged that most pre-twentieth century philosophy globally exhibits some crucial misunderstanding. The deepest attacks have come, not from marginal cranks, but from the very first rank of the century's philosophers, like Wittgenstein and Heidegger, who suggested that Western philosophy is the history of a mistake, an illness or an illusion, that philosophy as usually understood is at or should be at an end.

The current debate over philosophy has been given impetus by the French criticism born in the 1960s (e.g., Michel Foucault, Jean-Francois Lyotard, Gilles Deleuze), especially by the work of Jacques Derrida. In America Richard Rorty has famously synthesized this with earlier critical currents. These developments have in effect created a new genre of philosophy that I will call *antiphilosophy*. By this I mean not the avoidance or simple rejection of philosophy, but a philosophical undermining of philosophy that puts philosophy, so to speak, in brackets. This movement has been associated, however rightly or wrongly, with postmodernism, hence with American academic "multiculturalism," and the critique of traditionalist and "modernist" intellectual habits in philosophy, literature, and social theory.[3] My description is purposely vague; later on we will examine Rorty and Derrida at some length. Suffice it to say that they are widely viewed as part of a new and virulent attack on traditionally pervasive philosophical beliefs and methods and, indirectly at least, on historically associated academic, cultural, and political institutions. They are seen as the new wave in the century-long critique of the legacy of the Enlightenment and hence of the search for objectivity and truth. At any rate, they put philosophy as inquiry in question. This newest of antiphilosophical storms takes some of its thunder from earlier tempests whipped up by Nietzsche, Heidegger, Wittgenstein, and John Dewey.[4]

The question of the validity of philosophy ought to be the most radical and interesting, the deepest and most vital discussion philosophers could have. It is, after all, a continuation of Socrates's defense of his philosophic (and nonphilosophic) life at his trial, immortalized in Plato's *Apology*. For those philosophers who believe we have but one life on earth, the stakes remain only slightly less high than for Socrates. For if philosophy cannot do or be what it claims, if it cannot serve the ends for which we choose to practice it, then our lives are threatened too, not with death, which must befall everyone, but with *waste*, a fate Socrates would have thought considerably worse than hemlock.

The contemporary debate, however, is marked by more evasion than engagement. Each side seems skilled at avoiding the deepest questions of the interlocutor, at shifting the burden of proof to its opponent, at attacking the weaknesses of the other's rhetoric while dodging the strengths of the other's logic. Evasive maneuvers multiply. Common strategies are the uncritical resort to common sense to block skepticism; the use of "the method of avoidance," which turns the failure to answer philosophical questions into an achievement;[5] the simplification and reification of terms like 'metaphysical' and 'foundational' by philosophy's defenders and critics, so as to create a straw man on whose illegitimacy all can agree without need of argument or analysis; the implicit message that philosophers before the 1870s are of merely historical interest as the material for the application of contemporary methods, not as methodological competitors; and the coupling of radically antiphilosophical posturing with an uncritical valorization of scholarship, pedagogy, and hermeneutical esoterica that somehow escapes the otherwise ubiquitous charges of traditionalism and elitism. These responses reveal the desire to have done with the issue, to dismiss it without reflection. They avoid facing the primary question: What is the validity of what we philosophers do?

It is clear that some of the defenders of philosophy simply refuse to take antiphilosophical queries seriously. But taking questions seriously, even the most outlandish or unattractive questions, is one of the few differentia of the philosophical vocation. For good or ill, *it is what we do*. Failing that, we are just killing trees; to paraphrase a colleague, a philosopher who fails to take questions seriously is a waste of good firewood.[6] Indignation and smug incredulity ill-suit the philosopher. The aim of the present study is to accept and not avoid the blows of antiphilosophy, then carefully assess the damage.

Nevertheless, I will be critical of antiphilosophy. A personal remark might help to make my perspective more clear. During my graduate school years, in the late 1970s and early 1980s, the air was already thick with Derrida and Foucault, and the excitement over Rorty's *Philosophy and the Mirror of Nature* (published 1979) was at its peak. The zeitgeist in which my peers and I began our education as professional philosophers was one that largely assumed traditional philosophy was an anachronism, except perhaps as retrieved by interpretive iconoclasts. We *began* philosophizing at the *end* of philosophy. Our problem was to philosophize in and about this twilight. Today I would avoid the eschatological metaphors, having recognized that the status of philosophy remains profoundly unsettled; but the spirit of philosophy's questionability remains with me. Whatever the costs of coming to philosophical age within that end-of-philosophy zeitgeist, we acquired a willingness to put everything into question, including ourselves. We were rendered permanently skeptical of any philosophy that saw itself as a *defense* of anything.

My admiration for Rorty's work has always been tempered by a feeling of anachronism, a feeling I imagine Rorty must have regarding the philosophical battles of earlier generations; for example, the debate between Darwinism and religion. I cannot escape the feeling that Rorty is like a boxer who holds his opponent up with one hand while beating him with the other. If, as he claims, philosophy is literature, fine; then foundationalism and metaphysics are literary phenomena too, no more invalid than any other fictive genre. Their claim to nonfictive truth is just a part of their charm. Why not let them be, just as most Darwinists let religious fundamentalism be? But Rorty will not let them be; he is concerned to oppose them, to sway the philosophical community to reject them. This very concern seems to me to betray a continuity with his opponent deeper than Rorty would like to admit. Of course, such continuity would not prove his opponent *right*, only inescapable.

Philosophy, as we shall see, can be conceived in a variety of ways. It may, for example, be conceived as inquiry into truth, understood as the attempt to say what is true and why it is true. I will later call this the notion of philosophy as *episteme*. Philosophy may, on the other hand, be conceived as an attempt to do something: for example, to improve the world or reconstruct experience. This is philosophy as *praxis*. Last, it may be understood as a construction with its own qualitative value, as, for example, a mode of experiencing the world. This is philosophy as *poiesis*.

For the Western tradition philosophy has been primarily, although not exclusively, inquiry into truth. The possibility of attaining this truth has always been in question. A particularly influential way of justifying philosophy's hope for truth, especially in the modern tradition, might be called *foundational realism*, or foundationalism for short. Defining realism is a tricky matter that we will take up in Chapter Two, but for the moment we can say that realism is the view that at least some of our judgments are valid with respect to what they judge, where what they judge obtains independent of judgment. As it is usually put, for the realist our knowledge reflects the way the world really is. Foundationalism is the view that what philosophy seeks is a kind of knowledge that is ultimate, hence different from other kinds of knowledge. As an approach to justifying realism, foundationalism often implies that some ultimate knowledge "grounds" all other knowledge.

Foundational realism has been under prolonged and deadly attack for over a century. Its greatest vulnerability is its belief that foundational or unquestionable knowledge is available. For many twentieth century philosophers such knowledge is not even imaginable. It appears that we have no nontrivial philosophical knowledge that, once stated clearly and precisely, cannot be doubted. The notion that some special class of judgments of the world are immediately determined by the world, hence uncriticizable or "privileged," be they a priori metaphysical claims or theory-free sense data or eidetic intuitions, is no longer plausible. This critique of *privilege* or *presence*, of immediate incorrigible judgment, is the most fundamental and widespread form of the attack on foundational realism.

Two families of related approaches have responded to the implausibility of foundational realism. *Nonfoundational realism* is an attempt to retain realism while abandoning the prospect of foundational knowledge. Its most prominent form limits philosophical aims through reducing the kind of validation required for justifying philosophical claims; this can be seen especially in the philosophy of science and epistemology. A related approach seeks to revive systematic or metaphysical philosophy while accepting that the validation of such a system can be only hypothetical, never certain. Hence it too limits the kind of validation that foundationalist philosophy traditionally sought. Nonfoundationalist philosophers insist that there is a third option for philosophical method that avoids both the Scylla of traditional foundationalism and the Charybdis of postmodernism and antiphilosophy.

That Charybdis, the second family, seeks not to preserve but to critique philosophy's capacity to say what is true. It is *antifoundationalist*, and with respect to philosophical knowledge, it is *antirealist*; that is, it denies that the enterprise of philosophy can attain anything deserving the name of realist knowledge.[7] This is antiphilosophical in the sense that it undermines the traditional notion of philosophy; that is, the kind of knowledge philosophy has traditionally sought is rendered implausible. Such critics might seem to paint themselves into a self-contradictory position, since they are apparently engaging in philosophy in order to undermine it. We will see that the antifoundationalists have given sophisticated attention to this problem.

It should be noted that these radical philosophies, although generally eschewing any traditional epistemological discussion, must at least implicitly engage in epistemology in order to criticize realism. Consequently, we will have to explore realism and antirealism to understand their new criticisms of philosophy. There are, I will suggest, three forms of antirealism prominent among the relevant philosophers: relativism, pragmatism, and naturalism. (It may seem odd to include the last of these. However, we will see that naturalism can be antirealist under some applications.)

Pragmatism, the long-neglected fruit of classical American thought, has become a remarkably pervasive and flexible player in recent philosophy. Traditionally, pragmatism has been linked to the nonfoundationalist program for maintaining belief in the possibility of philosophical knowledge. We will see that nonfoundationalism almost always includes a pragmatic element. Pragmatism was arguably created for just this purpose by that great defender of nonfoundationalist speculative philosophy, Charles Peirce. However, I will show that by itself pragmatism is antirealist, indeed, radically so. Under the right circumstances, it is entirely capable of betraying nonfoundational philosophy and embracing its antiphilosophical opponent. This pragmatic antiphilosophy is precisely Richard Rorty's unique contribution.[8]

So, as I will try to show, those who would retain the notion of philosophy as inquiry while avoiding a discredited foundational realism must choose between nonfoundational realism, on the one hand, or antifoundationalism and antirealism, on the other. There is, however, a more fundamental alternative. Convinced of an intrinsic connection between philosophy as inquiry and foundational realism, or otherwise unhappy with the afore-mentioned options, one can reject philosophy as inquiry altogether and understand philosophy instead as poiesis or praxis. Such a full commitment to praxis is difficult to find in contemporary philosophy. To be a pragmatist *in inquiry* is to believe that the criterion of truth is found in activity; to adopt a complete metaphilosophical pragmatism is to replace *episteme* with *praxis*, hence to believe that the aim of philosophy is goodness or success, not truth, or that truth is nothing but goodness or success. Most pragmatists stop short of this conclusion. There is, however, a philosopher who abandons *episteme* in favor of *poiesis*: Heidegger. In his later work Heidegger rejects philosophy as inquiry into truth, where truth is correct or adequate representation. This makes him the most radical critic of philosophy as inquiry. Yet, however interesting are philosophy as praxis and poiesis—and they will be briefly discussed later—the aim of this volume is an understanding of the implications of philosophy as inquiry (hence, the virtual absence of Heidegger from this volume).

The major chapters in the present study will consider exemplars of the various forms of thought I have just sketched. Charles Peirce is the root figure. While arguing for a kind of nonfoundationalist realism, Peirce provides a virtual cornucopia of antirealisms. He makes the classical formulation of the critique of presence; endorses naturalism; uses various kinds of relativism, most notably conventionalism; and, of course, invents pragmatism. After surveying Peirce's virtually "anti"-realism (Chapter Three) and various non-foundational realisms akin to Peirce's intentions (Chapter Four), we will in Chapters Five through Nine examine various attempts to supersede foundational realism through recourse to antirealism.

First, we will examine antiphilosophy based primarily in naturalism, in the work of Friedrich Nietzsche (Chapter Five).

Second, we will turn to the most influential form of antirealism, relativism, which is the view that the validity of our judgments is significantly determined by a relation to something other than its objects. Relativism is often confused with subjectivism, or the granting of epistemic priority to the individual subject. The most interesting and powerful forms of relativism escape this connection, however; they make validity relative to factors not intrinsic to individual subjects. We will examine three distinct types of nonsubjective relativism in three very different philosophers. First we will see that Ludwig Wittgenstein's critique of philosophical knowledge is based on a *social relativism*, or *conventionalism*, that makes the validity of judgment relative to community, an approach linked to pragmatism (Chapter Six). Justus Buchler, a lesser known philosopher who, like Peirce, hoped to form a nonfoundational basis for systematic philosophy, offers us the most consistent version of *objective relativism*, in which objective, natural contexts determine the validity of judgment (Chapter Seven). Last, in the work of Jacques Derrida we will find a *semiotic relativism*, for which the validity of judgment is dependent on the dynamic relations among signs (Chapter Eight).

Although there are strands of pragmatism in these thinkers, it is Richard Rorty who uses pragmatism as the primary basis for an antifoundationalist critique of philosophy, as we will see in Chapter Nine. Hence Chapters Three, Four, and Seven constitute my answer to current non-foundationalist defenses of philosophy, whereas Chapters Five, Six, Eight, and Nine constitute a response to the sources for antiphilosophy.

There are intriguing connections among these thinkers. The eclectic thought of Peirce acts as a comparative thread. Wittgenstein adopts a kind of pragmatism. Nietzsche and Wittgenstein share the common influence of Schopenhauer, whose revision of Kant through the notion of the primacy of the will bears comparison to Peirce's pragmatic revision of Kant. Derrida is familiar with Peirce, and their work exhibits a remarkable consonance. Buchler is a student of Peirce and radicalizes the Peircean tradition in the same sense that Derrida radicalizes phenomenology and Wittgenstein, analytic philosophy. Buchler, Wittgenstein, and Derrida do not so much *represent* their traditions as they *test* them. Rorty, the most famous contemporary critic of foundationalism and traditional philosophy, is indebted to Peirce, Nietzsche, Wittgenstein, and Derrida.

All these thinkers push against the bounds of philosophy, and in doing so must extend their philosophical languages as far as possible. We must see how they did this, and what happened to them when they did. Toward this end, I will ask three questions of each philosopher: What is the validity of judgment in general? What is the validity of philosophical judgments in particular? What is the status of *his own* discourse, given the answers to the first two questions?

The point of this largely historical discussion will be to establish my own conclusions negatively. I will show that each of these responses to the question of the validity of philosophical knowledge is problematic, leading by process of elimination to my conclusion. *Neither* the nonfoundational, pragmatic, limited approach to philosophy—of Peirce, Buchler, and others—*nor t*he antiphilosophical escape from philosophy—of Nietzsche, Wittgenstein, Derrida, and Rorty—can be accepted as philosophically valid. Simply put, one may address the problem of the possibility of philosophical knowledge by seeking to *solve* it, *resolve* it, or *dissolve* it. Nonfoundational attempts to resolve it are inadequate. Antiphilosophical attempts to dissolve it fail to do so. Resolution and dissolution put aside, the question will be whether solution is possible. Possible or not, it is the avenue to which, I suggest, philosophy by its very nature commits us.

Hence I will argue, on the one hand, that the defense of meliorism, of common sense, of a nonfoundational or limited or humbled or chastened philosophy fails to appreciate the depth of the antiphilosophical critique. It underestimates the ubiquity of what we blithely encapsulate with the term 'foundationalism.' I will suggest that foundationalism of a kind cannot be abandoned on pain of self-inconsistency or of ceasing to do philosophy at all. Attempts to limit philosophy, however sophisticated, violate philosophy's nature. If philosophy is primarily *ultimate inquiry*, then philosophy cannot accept limited validation as sufficient, nor can it accept the validation of judgments in terms of some norm other than truth (e.g., practical necessity or goodness).

On the other hand, I will show that the radical antifoundational critics of philosophy fail to escape the problematic philosophizing they criticize. They remain within philosophy and so are subject to self-reflexive inconsistencies, despite the sophisticated strategies they deploy to avoid them. There is, I will claim, no *principled* escape from philosophy; that is, no escape from the burdens of philosophical validation that can legitimately regard itself as achieving a validity philosophy ought to recognize. Of course, one can anytime abandon philosophy without claiming validity for the abandonment. There is no obligation to philosophize. I deny only that antiphilosophy can claim a valid escape from the philosophical problems it diagnoses. Consequently, what follows is no "defense" of philosophy, or of foundationalism, or of realism, in the sense of defending their truth or validity. It argues only that philosophy as inquiry is unavoidable and that philosophy as inquiry is inherently foundationalist and realist. It is an attempt to judge philosophy radically, yet by its own standards, thereby to discern its limits from within.

The book thus has two main burdens. The first is to make the point that inquiry aimed at truth is distinct from action aimed at success or goodness, and from constructions aimed at achieving aesthetic quality. If philosophy is primarily inquiry, then the only question relevant to deciding that a philosophical judgment is acceptable or valid is the question, Do we have evidence that it is true of what it judges? A great deal of contemporary philosophy, in effect if not in aim, treats the moral, political, or aesthetic impact of a philosophical judgment as a desideratum of validity or truth. In the twentieth century objections have been made against the single-minded pursuit of truth, but the implications of alternative conceptions are rarely explored. The result is often a putatively philosophical discourse that is haphazardly governed by several different norms (e.g., truth, goodness, beauty). This book is an attempt to distinguish what is often conflated without argument.

In a sense, this implies that my book is a critique of the widespread influence of pragmatism in contemporary philosophy. This influence is particularly evident in what could be called the *new commonsensism*, the attempt to protect the possibility of philosophical knowledge through a dismissal of postmodernism, antiphilosophy and traditional skepticism. The latter two seem frequently to meet with impatient or even indignant dismissals; impatient when it is implied that what the doubters of philosophical knowledge have missed is obvious, indignant when it is implied that their inquiry has violated moral concerns. Against these dismissals I must say that if philosophy is primarily inquiry aimed at truth, then it is not clear why it ought to recognize moral evaluations as relevant, and if philosophy is ultimate inquiry then it is the kind of inquiry for which virtually nothing is obvious.

The second burden is to show what is entailed in making philosophical judgments, to reveal the commitments thereby embodied, the rules invoked, even when such judgments are implicit or avow allegiance to some norm other than truth. The reason is to undercut the, to my mind, overly optimistic strategy that seeks to judge philosophy while claiming an exemption from the normal rules of validation or justification. Such an exemption would make it possible to deny philosophy without doing philosophy, and hence to avoid inconsistency. For example, some philosophers (famously, Wittgenstein) claim to be showing and not saying their point, and some (e.g., Rorty, part of the time) claim beneficial practical effect, not truth, for their arguments. These *metaphilosophical strategies* are rarely evaluated systematically and comparatively; I will try to provide such an evaluation.

Such a discussion requires the use of a special language, one as neutral as possible with respect to the philosophical traditions and issues under examination. Justus Buchler's theory of judgment will serve this purpose. According to Buchler, actions, exhibitions or constructions, and assertions are equally judgmental and so equally open to validation, but validation of different kinds. Truth is the type of validity characteristic of assertive or propositional judgments, not of actions or exhibitions. We will explore this framework more fully in Chapter One. (The reader is hereby reassured that the use of Buchler's theory as a metaphilosophical framework will not lead to the conclusion that Buchler's philosophy is right.)

Mine may seem a narcissistic enterprise: another book by a philosopher about philosophy, rather than about politics, or hunger, or the earth, rather than a book that might *do some good*. Perhaps so; but it may be better to be an honest narcissist than to pretend to have transcended the issue. We must, as Peirce wrote, set out to philosophize where we are, we cannot decide to start from somewhere else. Philosophy is, in David Hiley's phrase, "in question," and there is no sense in gamely trying to ignore the fact that the lights are out and continue trying to read in the dark; better to see if the lights can be fixed. I insist only that this interest is not *solely* narcissistic, that its significance is not restricted to philosophers. Philosophy is an extension of a human occupation, inquiry into truth. Its legitimacy or illegitimacy indicates something about the limits of this human possibility.

What is the value of philosophy? There are many possible values, evident in the many different roles contemporary philosophers actually play. Philosophers may be teachers of morals, encouraging honesty, sincerity, and thoughtful self-questioning in their students; journalists of intellectual culture, reporting on whatever is the current topic of conversation among the scientific, artistic, political, and academic classes of many nations; political activists for whom inquiry is a tool of social change; hermits who wish to be left alone with their contemplation; scientists or scientific fellow travelers, engaged in the collective effort of improving the best current account of the world; aesthetes whose thought is the leading edge of sense, seeking to cultivate an appreciation of the subtleties of experience ignored by bourgeois society; experimental mystics for whom philosophy creates possibilities for the imaginative reconstruction of experience; seekers of a satisfying perspective on the world that will redeem some deep personal loss; erotic conversationalists who have fun talking about ideas with enthusiastic and attractive youths; historians and translators, experts in and conduits for the thoughts of someone else; cynics for whom philosophy is a means of remaining aloof from contemporary culture; guardians of Western civilization, protecting that heritage from the barbarians while transmitting it to them; engineers of *weltanschauungn* that, they think, it will be good for society to accept; and happy white-collar workers with relatively low pay but damned good hours.

Although philosophy can serve many purposes, what purpose should it serve, what is it made for, what is its true function? It is not clear whether philosophy qua philosophy can do any good or whether it ought to try. Certainly individual philosophers exhibit virtues and philosophy has served some good purposes in its long life, but that is not to say that the practice of philosophy in itself is a good. There is little justification for believing that its study improves people morally, and none for believing that philosophy is necessary to moral character or behavior. There is no satisfactory reason for believing that there is something uplifting, high minded, or ennobling in the practice of philosophy or that the contemplative life is superior to other styles of human living. To believe otherwise is partly arrogance, but perhaps due more to a confusion of inquiry with either religion or morality or art or some combination of the three. Philosophy is a demanding intellectual exercise that probably makes us smarter, but advanced mathematics would serve that purpose at least as well. Neither does philosophy seem particularly civilizing in the way that art and good manners sometimes are. On the contrary, the habit of questioning everyone and demanding reasons for everything seems rather uncivilized. Philosophers sometimes write or teach to serve political ends, but do they serve those ends more effectively than if they were full-time political activists? Philosophy is a pleasure for some people, but I must imagine the number of those for whom philosophical thinking and reading are satisfying regardless of outcome or consequence is rather small. Philosophy may have its own kind of beauty, but can it compete with Johann Sebastian Bach or Hound Dog Taylor, or for that matter, with a sunset?

Is it better for the world if a philosopher says, "Following as best I can the method proper to philosophy, I find that philosophy has nothing good to say about anything, and cannot improve the world one bit," or if he or she tries to bend philosophy to the service of a good foreign to its nature? A guiding principle of this book is that, for the sake of improving understanding, it is better for a thing to be what it is and be called by its name than for us to pretend otherwise, even if that pretense makes the thing better. I do not accept this principle in *life*. It is probably better for everyone's safety and happiness (including his own) if a man who, deep in his heart, is a racist, because of timidity or social pressure or good manners acts as if he is not a racist, despite the dishonesty. In social matters I prefer pragmatism to purity. I would happily leave to future generations the job of discerning sincerity and fine-tuning hearts and minds, if in the short-term we could stop slaughtering and humiliating each other. For the sake of learning what is implied in unaided and undiluted philosophy, however, I choose for the duration to be a purist about inquiry.

To paraphrase Derrida's intentionally ambiguous title, the question of the alleged *end* of philosophy depends on the question of the proposed *ends* of philosophy.[9] Is philosophy exclusively and ultimately concerned with truth discoverable through inquiry, with discovering propositions whose truth about their objects can be publicly validated by reasons and evidence; with, that is, saying what is true and saying why it is true? Or is truth itself determined by something else—for example, what is aesthetically satisfying, or what is good, morally or practically—which constitutes philosophy's ultimate goal and standard? For Dewey, philosophy's contribution to social reconstruction, hence, the good, is the ultimate determinant of its truth. For Heidegger, propositional truth is derivative of *aletheia*, unconcealment, the openness to which requires that evidential inquiry give way to a thinking understood as a *poiesis*, a making, that enhances *aisthesis*, perceiving. For these and other thinkers, inquiry's truth is contextualized or determined by, subordinated to, something else. The otherwise single-minded pursuit of assertive or representational truth is thereby compromised.

This book will presuppose that in philosophy considerations of inquiry, propositional truth, and evidence trump all others, at every point. This is not to say that philosophy is devoid of other considerations; no complex human activity can be so reduced that aesthetic and practical considerations have no place in it. Nevertheless, I will take it that what determines the validity of any philosophical judgment is its claimed propositional truth, demonstrated by public evidence and reasons.

This presupposition will, for some, doom my inquiry from the start. For, they will say, and not without reason, that the very ideas of propositional truth and objective inquiry embody deep problems. Indeed, they might continue, it is the great achievement of twentieth century philosophy to show this, to turn philosophical attention away from single-minded concern with propositional truth, objectivity, representation, correspondence, and inquiry free of practical considerations, toward an acceptance of philosophy's inevitable and legitimate determination by other factors.

They may be right, but there are problems with their response nonetheless. Some distinctions must be drawn here. It is one thing to fail to recognize the distinctness of the requirements of inquiry versus other forms of cultural work, a failure that allows an ambiguous equation of truth with goodness or beauty, an equation which may suit the theoretical purpose of the moment. It is another explicitly to reject publicly validated propositional truth as the end of philosophy, in favor of *poiesis* or *praxis*. It is yet another to try, at the limits of one's inquiry, to weave a subtle, dialectical balancing of truth with other norms that are allowed jointly to govern inquiry.

I am critical of the first posture, of those who, unreflectively and without facing the problematic consequences, either poetize or socialize philosophy, who philosophize in the service of a political or pragmatic or moral goal, who conceive philosophy as primarily evocative, literary, or aesthetic in aspiration, or who see philosophy *as an experience*, rather than as an attempt to understand experience. One often finds a philosopher, having rejected some philosophical views on the basis of their inconsistency or lack of supporting evidence—that is, on considerations of truth—go on to endorse an alternative view on the basis of its aesthetic appeal or practical consequences, without a murmur of acknowledgment that the basis of evaluation has shifted, that validation has been allowed to move, unannounced, to the grounds of beauty, theoretical harmony, cleverness, usefulness, or political correctness. The shift is unannounced because no philosopher wants to say, "I believe this because it is beautiful," or "I believe this because it is good to believe it," or "I reject *that* view because there is no evidence for its truth, but accept *this* view regardless of any evidence for or against its truth." To make this unacknowledged change is to fall below the minimum philosophical requirement of public self-consciousness, of recognizing the basis of one's own judgments and announcing that basis to one's interlocutors.

Regarding explicit subordination of truth to goodness or aesthetic quality, I doubt that it can be consistent. First, all philosophers practice philosophy as inquiry at least some of the time; that is, they are at least part of the time concerned to say what is true and why it is true. So, those who make some value other than truth philosophy's norm must admit that their discourse is normatively complex; either all their judgments serve multiple values (e.g., truth, goodness, beauty) or some judgments serve truth and some do not. This has to raise problems. Second, inquiry cannot validate this view *as true*. It makes no sense to pronounce the philosophical judgment, "Philosophy's judgments are governed by something other than truth," with an aim to convince others of its truth. Any view that deposes propositional truth as philosophy's ruler makes its relation to truth and to any discourse still governed by truth problematic.

Now, those who subordinate truth might respond that these objections are compelling only for a truth-governed approach, so that my criticism leaves them unmoved. If this is so, then the only honest response is to distinguish our divergent tasks, give them different names, and go our separate ways. Poetry, engineering, and philosophy do not compete or conflict. If an activity is not governed by the norm of public, propositional truth, then it is a different discourse entirely from one that is so governed. My only caution is that those who reject inquiry cannot then claim to achieve judgments capable of public validation by reasons. If one ceases to do inquiry, then one forfeits inquiry's prize. One cannot claim to win a baseball game with a touchdown.

To the third, more subtle claim that the norms of human judgment—truth, goodness, and beauty—cannot be ultimately divorced, that they are integrally related, that philosophy must strike a dialectical balance among them, I can respond only that this may indeed be right. However, *inquiry cannot know that* it is! Inquiry cannot validate the subordinate place of truth in a larger scheme of values. The distinct nature of inquiry, which all philosophers practice at least part of the time, demands its payment and carries its distinct obligations. There remains a tension among the norms or values of judgment. The rejoinder will be that inquiry is *in fact* contextualized, that inquiry is part of life, and truth is not life's sole concern. This is indeed a fact; the question is, In what sense can that fact be reflected in inquiry's aims and methods? One cannot say that the context that limits inquiry's place is *true* according to inquiry's lights. It will be my goal, not to end this profound discussion by denying the legitimacy of the integrative or dialectical approach, but to contribute to the discussion by clarifying what philosophy as inquiry entails. We will return to an explicit consideration of the integrative approach at the end of this study.

Part of the motivation of this project is the desire to relate divergent schools within twentieth century Western philosophy. Of course, many philosophical perspectives are sufficiently institutionalized to be called "schools," relative to many different problem areas in philosophy. However, there seems good reason for discriminating certain prominent *subcultures* within philosophy, a small number of virtually distinct philosophical languages concerning "first philosophical" issues like the nature of reality, knowledge, and meaning, the proper philosophical method, the aims and prospects for philosophy. The word *prominent* indicates that I mean to refer to those self-defined traditions that have had the greatest impact on the direction or directions of twentieth century philosophy. It may be that a very large number of philosophers in America belong to no coherent, identifiable subculture or tradition at all, except the Western tradition as a whole. For such philosophers, Plato, Aquinas, Nietzsche, Frege, James, and Foucault may be equally and indifferently relevant to the philosophical project. But such work rarely, so to speak, makes the philosophical papers, it rarely determines what will be done by the next generation of philosophers. For good or ill—and it is no doubt both—specialization is characteristic of the leading edge of research in philosophy no less than in other fields, and specialization presupposes fidelity to a single philosophical school and language.

For an American philosopher in the second half of the twentieth century at least three such philosophical subcultures could be distinguished. The dominant subculture—which is to say the language in which most current, non-historical work whose value is confirmed by the largest consensus is being done—belongs to what is called *Anglo-American* or *analytic* philosophy, whose roots lie in Frege and/or Russell and/or Moore and/or the Vienna Circle and/or Wittgenstein. Second, a particularly prominent and well-defined subculture is the "continental" tradition, composed by philosophers whose roots lie in Hegel and/or Marx and/or existentialism and/or phenomenology and/or hermeneutics and/or structuralism and/or post-structuralism.

Here the picture gets more murky. My hunch is that most philosophers in America today stand outside of both of these subcultures, in a region where a larger number of discourses overlap. It is my impression that most philosophers are conscious of inhabiting a single inclusive, intracommunicative discipline of inquiry, whereas, for example, most Heideggerians and most Quineans would deny belonging to whatever discipline houses the other. Out of this vast nonanalytic, noncontinental culture I am most interested in one prominent and identifiable subculture whose members include students of "classic" American philosophy (from Emerson to Dewey), hence pragmatism, and process philosophers (e.g., Whiteheadians). This subculture, like the diverse culture to which it belongs, maintains a greater degree of continuity with pre-nineteenth century philosophy than do either the analytic or continental subcultures.

These cultural differences make an unbiased comparison of Peirce, Nietzsche, Wittgenstein, Buchler, and Derrida difficult.[10] Discussion across philosophical subcultures is hampered by the stereotypical images all cultures have of foreigners. For philosophers outside the American and process tradition, Peirce is either regarded as a brilliant but muddled figure of logical and scientific interest or as an irrelevant nineteenth century metaphysician. Outside of continental philosophy Nietzsche serves as a paradigmatic case of silliness or insanity or evil. Although Wittgenstein is a canonical figure for some analytic philosophers of language, he remains an object of respectful incomprehension for other analysts and philosophers of science, and as the "all-destroyer" of philosophy for many continental philosophers and metaphysicians.[11] To the extent that Buchler is known at all, he is cordially although sometimes suspiciously regarded by pragmatic and process philosophers, and ignored as an anachronistic metaphysician by analysts and continental philosophers. Outside of continental philosophy Derrida is excoriated by pragmatists as an irresponsible revolutionary, and ignored by analysts and scientific philosophers as merely comic.

These attitudes point to a deeper philosophical problem. To pursue a mutually comprehensible and profitable dialogue between what is called analytic philosophy, continental philosophy, and the American pragmatic and process tradition raises the problem of *translation*. Any attempt at comparison across traditions—especially one that seeks to compare each tradition at its most idiosyncratic, that is, as it understands itself and the philosophical task—faces the problem that the language in which the comparison is made may presume the validity of one of the traditions to be compared, to the disadvantage of the others. To compare Peirce, Wittgenstein, and Derrida, for example, requires that we state and contrast their views in a language that does not itself predetermine whose view will be judged valid. To do this, I will employ a language as neutral as possible with respect to the issues being discussed. But this may not be enough. I will treat Peirce, Nietzsche, Wittgenstein, Buchler, and Derrida as if they were commensurable, as if they were engaged, at some level of description, in the same project. But this hypothesis might be false. It is not clear that it is possible or beneficial to discuss them within the bounds of one discourse, as if that discourse could escape the cultural divisions within contemporary philosophy. In short, the task I am undertaking may be impossible.

The fact of the division of contemporary Western philosophy into these different cultures ought to serve as a warning. It is certainly true that today there is significant intercultural discussion in philosophy; no doubt, more than in recent decades.[12] Many philosophers attempt to work in more than one of these cultures; many have, with the best of intentions and reasons, decried this division as harmful to philosophy. But perhaps the existence of these disparate cultures shows us something more than the historically contingent, hence reformable, sociology of contemporary intellectuals. Might these cultures embody principles of knowledge and of the philosophical project that are irreducible and incommensurable? What if it is impossible to do philosophy without at least implicitly endorsing one of these incommensurable principles? That would imply that it is impossible to discuss the work of Peirce, Nietzsche, Wittgenstein, Buchler, and Derrida comparatively and yet with depth, for any discussion would have to presume a notion of philosophy that is accepted by one or more of them and foreign to the rest. My response to this question can be given only in the final chapter. In the meantime, all that can be said is that the present inquiry accepts, and does not dismiss, these dangers. Its goal is less to reduce tensions than to heighten them.

In the process of trying to know whether philosophy can know, we will in effect raise the question, Is philosophy circular? Does the doing of philosophy presuppose certain, at least implicit, substantive ideas, beliefs or aims that philosophy might ultimately want to question? Is philosophy, to call upon the language of our ancestors, like a Greek *kirkos*, 'ring,' from which English gets 'circle,' 'circuit,' and 'circus'?

Is philosophy like a cosmic great circle? Do philosophers live on the surface of a great sphere? This would explain a lot. What a sphere dweller sees as a straight line is actually a circle that returns to itself. Philosophy done on the surface of a sphere would be finite and bounded, but no philosopher's "line" of thought would actually meet these bounds. Inquiry would proceed unimpeded, but would always eventually come upon its starting point. Is philosophy a long and complex way to return to oneself? Is the only kind of knowledge philosophy ultimately achieves a knowledge of the point from which it begins: namely, *self*-knowledge?

Is philosophy like a racecourse, a hippodrome, an intellectual *Circus Maximus*? Is philosophical achievement a question of running around in circles faster than anyone else? Or perhaps with greater rigor? Is philosophy a circumscribed stage, a ring within which performances, exhibitions, take place? Is it a circus, a spectacle of ideas, a menagerie of perspectives, an exhibition of all the exotic possibilities of thought? Would that make the philosopher a semantic ringmaster, a trainer of intellectual beasts, or as some would have it, a dialectical clown? A showman in any case: but *what* does this showman show?

Life in a circle offers the prominent satisfaction of completeness. As Max Weber wrote, the biblical Abraham could die "satiated with life," having exhausted the limited possibilities of an essentially changeless, cyclic world, something impossible in the modern world of linear "progress."[13] Nevertheless, intellectual life in a circle might have its frustrations. Circularity implies that no point is higher or lower than any other, that everything is equidistant from the center. If circles could talk they would presumably be bad at giving directions. But can a philosopher avoid giving directions, that is, norms? Is it not the point of philosophy to point, to be the navigator of the *polis* in Plato's metaphor, to decide on the right direction for the community, to improve the world? Or is a directionless philosophy that leads us to the recognition of necessity, to an intellectual love for our timeless and unchangeable circle, the wisest of all? Krishna, revealing the eternal reality to Arjuna, tells him, "If any man thinks he slays, and if another thinks he is slain, neither knows the ways of truth," so go ahead and kill your relatives.[14] It is not by accident that Nietzsche, the advocate of Eternal Recurrence and the critic of morality and progress, admired Hinduism as a religion of nobility.

Let us presume that philosophy is a search for something, call it *knowledge*. Why philosophy searches is something to be searched into, but not at the moment. We will presume for the time being that philosophy is not circular, that philosophy's aim, like that of modern science and modern society as a whole, is progress, and in philosophy's case, progress in knowledge. We will presuppose the goal, and question only whether philosophy can attain it. Our question will be, Is characteristically philosophical knowledge possible?

But in the very act of asking this question we notice that, although we have abandoned for the time being the idea that philosophy might be a great circle, we immediately face the first of many smaller circles: we are going to try to *know what knowing is.*

Of course, such circles need not be "vicious"; some may even be virtuous. But what are the criteria of virtue and vice in circles? Is it a matter of circumference? If I were to announce with gravity an intention to walk around a circle with a circumference of two meters, everyone would think me eccentric, to say the least. But if I were to walk around the world and return to the very same spot, I would be an admired adventurer.

The current adventure will be a line of inquiry. I have imaginatively set out in a definite direction, toward a point on the horizon. I will try to determine whether those who claim to have solved, resolved or dissolved our deepest philosophical problems are right, whether, as they claim, it is possible to escape from the philosophical *kirkos*. Only after answering this question will I be able to look back and judge whether my own path has been straight or circular.

1

THE QUESTION
OF
PHILOSOPHY

What are we doing when we philosophize? Are we trying to increase our understanding of things, to gain knowledge, to say what is true? Well then, is such knowledge possible? Are the judgments that philosophers most characteristically make open to validation, to being shown to be valid or true? If they are not, what other purpose or value do such philosophical judgments serve?

Recent Western philosophy has raised this nest of fundamental questions with three critiques. It has questioned *foundationalism*, thereby undermining the possibility of the kind of ultimately justified, "foundational" knowledge that philosophy, it is alleged, traditionally sought as a bulwark against skepticism. It has questioned *realism*, the family of accounts of human knowledge that assert that knowledge captures things as they really are, independent of our knowledge of them. Antirealism and antifoundationalism have together paved the way for *antiphilosophy*. Antiphilosophy identifies foundationalism with philosophy so thoroughly as to reject the legitimacy of philosophy altogether or, at least, of anything resembling traditional or pre-twentieth century philosophy.

Other than those stalwarts who defend traditional foundationalism and realism in an unreconstructed form, the main philosophical alternative to antiphilosophy has sought to adapt to the antifoundationalist critique, to defend a nonfoundationalist yet otherwise traditional, realist philosophy. The attempt is to absorb the pounding from recent philosophical radicalism, to bend but not break in the critical wind. It is fueled by a new spirit of common-sensism that draws strength both from the recent renaissance of pragmatism and the reaction against the perceived extravagance of antiphilosophical radicalism.

What follows is based on three convictions that I will try to justify. The first is that the implications of antifoundationalism and antirealism are more radical than is usually supposed. They are too radical to be domesticated by the new common-sensism. When given the respect they deserve they cannot be harmonized with anything like the traditional notion of philosophy as achieving ultimate knowledge. The second is that philosophy is inescapably foundationalist. This is not to say that every philosophy is foundationalist or that every task and problem under the umbrella of philosophy is foundationalist. It is to say that if all vestiges of foundationalism were removed, then philosophy would be unrecognizable. The third conviction will be described shortly.

The critique of philosophy is not new; philosophy has been in question for a long time. The first recorded example of antiphilosophy in what we call the Western tradition occurred sometime in the early sixth century B.C. in the Greek-speaking region of what is now Turkey. Thales, a philosopher of nature who is claimed to have correctly predicted an eclipse in 585 B.C., became the target of ridicule recounted in Plato's *Theaetetus*, when, "a witty and attractive Thracian servant-girl is said to have mocked Thales for falling into a well while he was observing the stars and gazing upwards; declaring that he was eager to know the things in the sky, but that what was behind him and just by his feet escaped his notice."[1]

There have, of course, been worse forms of insult, as the Athenians demonstrated in the case of Socrates. Since the *Apology* of Plato, which presents Socrates's defense at his trial, philosophy has regarded the demonstration of its own legitimacy as part of its work. And, as that first defense of philosophy shows, the job has not gone well.

What is remarkable in our century is the abundance of criticism of philosophy by philosophers and hence, the creation of antiphilosophy as virtually a new philosophical genre. There are certainly varying degrees of comprehensiveness here. Philosophers have always criticized each other. But if a criticism of a philosophical school goes so deep as to deny the legitimacy of a whole area of philosophy, that begins to become an attack on philosophy per se. Such has been commonplace in the twentieth century. But antiphilosophy has gone still further, literally to call for, in the words of Richard Rorty, a "post-Philosophical culture."

The question we will try to answer is straightforward enough: Can characteristically philosophical judgments be validated, and if so, in what sense of *validity*? The reason for the vague term *validity*, as opposed to *truth*, is that, as we will see, it may be possible to claim that philosophical judgments can be valid in some sense other than being true; for example, they may be practically necessary, or beneficial, or beautiful. The practice of philosophy may be valid or cognitively valuable as a negative "edifying" process of undermining belief and promoting creative change. These are possible answers to the question of the validity of philosophy. But, first things first, we must determine whether philosophy can attain validity in the sense of making judgments we can know to be true. (So, unless context indicates otherwise, by *valid* I will mean *true*.)

Contemporary antiphilosophy denies that it can. This denial takes three forms which are not always distinguished. First, it is claimed that characteristically philosophical judgments cannot be known to be true. This is usually argued on the basis of an antirealist account of knowledge that makes truth or validity dependent on certain conditions which philosophical judgments do not meet. An example is contextualism, which makes the validity of judgments dependent on context. Because philosophical judgments, it is alleged, purport to hold for all possible contexts, to be in effect supercontextual, they cannot be valid. Second, it may be claimed, again on an antirealist basis, that philosophical judgments can be true, but only in an antirealist, say, contextualist, sense. Third, it is sometimes claimed that philosophical judgments can be valid only in some sense other than being true. They may be beneficial, unavoidable, pleasing, satisfying, and so forth.

I will treat antiphilosophy as a form of inquiry that raises the most serious questions, questions to which philosophy may in the end have no answer. But I will also insist on a point that may already indicate some difference with those who critique philosophy, and this point is the third guiding conviction of this study. It is that philosophy is continuous with other forms of human judging, in particular, with inquiry. Philosophy represents the possibility of some kind of human knowledge. If we decide that philosophy is illegitimate or fundamentally misguided, then we are in effect deciding that a kind of knowledge to which the human community has traditionally aspired is unavailable. Philosophy is something some people have done. If it ought no longer to be done, then a limitation on legitimate, sensible, or valuable human doings is thereby announced. Perhaps it would be a small loss, perhaps a *good* loss, like the loss of the possibility of smallpox. The point is that antiphilosophy says something about human possibilities in general, to the human community in general, not just to professional philosophers.

The effect of my three convictions, it may be apparent, is to make the status of philosophy as problematic as possible. For if philosophy is continuous with other forms of inquiry, with science and with the various modes of inquiry that occur in common life, then antiphilosophy threatens to spill over into a criticism of any and all inquiry, which raises the stakes substantially. It becomes unclear how we can continue, or reform, or abandon philosophy; each option has a cost that would be hard to bear. But before any of these options can be explored, we must gain some clarity about the thing in question, that is, philosophy.

The Question of Setting Out

In an essay that appeared in *The Monist* in 1905, Charles Sanders Peirce wrote,

> Philosophers of very diverse stripes propose that philosophy shall take its start from one or another state of mind in which no man, least of all a beginner in philosophy, actually is. One proposes that you shall begin by doubting everything. . . . Another proposes that we should begin by observing "the first impressions of sense," forgetting that our very percepts are the results of cognitive elaboration. But in truth, there is but one state of mind from which you can "set out," namely, the very state of mind in which you actually find yourself at the time you do "set out" . . . (CP, 5.416)

So, the journey I now begin, to discover whether there is philosophical knowledge, must begin with an exposition of "the very state of mind" in which I am now. A state of mind is a complex thing. Many beliefs, wishes, hopes, feelings—all presumably related to a surrounding community and world—compose and determine this state. But one set of factors seems most relevant; namely, the kind of questions that I take philosophy to be. Perhaps more than anything, the point from which I set out is constituted by my convictions regarding what is needful of philosophic inquiry, by the questions that drive me to inquire in the first place. There are a set of such questions, which seem so related as to be almost different facets or costumes of a single question. They have always bothered me. Here are some of them.

What is the sense and significance of human life? What is the sense and significance of *my* life? What would give my life meaning, redeem its deficits, satisfy the amorphous sense of absence? What would so redeem or satisfy human life in general? Given that everything is subject to decay and death, that all humans are destined eventually to lose everything they love most dearly, what can make up for that cruel destiny?

In light of this, what ought I do with my life, what should I make of it? What is the most important thing in human life? What should be most important to me? How should human beings live? How should I think about, look at, human life and the world? Is there a purpose to my life, to human life, or to existence in general? Most simply, *what is best*?

And to answer the foregoing I find myself asking, What in experience and thought is real or most real? What is the ultimate, most complete, most fundamental truth about the world and the place of human beings in it? What is the most basic true description of the world? What is the most basic true description of human experience? Which of the many competing views of reality and the place of humanity in it is right?

Now, these are different questions, but they are not unrelated. The answer to any one of them would have implications for the answer to at least some of the others, and perhaps all of them. But more than this, they seem to constitute a kind of family. What makes these questions a family is, at the very least, that their answers would serve a common function. Their answers would be likely candidates to play a certain role in my life, and in the lives of others; namely, the role of giving an ultimate *orientation*, a primary context to which I could always have imaginative recourse. This orientation could guide my actions, form my imaginative picture of the world, be the source of comfort or contemplative enjoyment, or all of these. It might, so to speak, lie dormant in my imagination, until moments of decision between aims, convictions, principles called it forth as the ultimate determinant of decision. Or it might shape my experience at every moment.

For the sake of convenience let us call these questions *uniquely* or *characteristically philosophical* questions. Among all the things that philosophers do and all the kinds of questions they ask, it is from asking this kind of question that philosophy gets its special character. We will see how these philosophical questions lead to a series of other questions. But, before that, we might pause to wonder about the nature and significance of these questions. *What do philosophical questions signify?* This question expands into a host of further questions to which I have no answers; yet they ought to be raised.

Speaking psychologically, are uniquely philosophical questions a sign of ill health? Do they indicate an inability to tolerate uncertainty, a need to certify one's interests as valid, right? Are they the result of a deficiency in the self or ego, a kind of precariousness or feeling of unreality, such that mere living is felt to be insufficient and to require a mythic certification? Are they an attempt to make up for character flaws with intellectual constructs, trying to substitute thoughts for experiences or character traits? Are they symptomatic of a lack of courage, a lack of strong convictions or strong impulses, which seeks social consensus through inquiry to acquire direction in life?

On the other hand, do they manifest special sensitivity or intelligence? Do they indicate an ability to recognize the questionability of things that generally goes unrecognized by others? Are they a response, not to a personal, but to a general human condition? Are they the manifestation of a natural and irreducible human trait, the desire for knowledge? If Aristotle was right that "All men by nature desire to know," are these questions the fulfillment of the human essence? Or are they expressions of the more or less universal need for security, which in the thinker is manifested as the need for secure knowledge? Are they fundamentally soteriological or religious in aim? Would answering these questions serve for the questioner approximately the same function that religious faith serves for others?

Viewed sociologically and historically, are they the secular remnant of an obsolete, ancient tradition that granted social position to the mysterious "wise men," the monks and priests, a tradition that associated book learning and speculation with the supernatural? Have I, for various personal reasons, identified myself with the contemporary vestiges of that tradition, whose real function has been usurped by science, but which has managed to preserve itself in a cozy niche in the modern university? Do I ask these questions because they grant me a special status in society, and the ambiguous respect due a "professor"?

Certainly, regarding their content, the philosophical questions presume certain ideas or beliefs. First is the idea of validity; for example, that there is a difference between having and deserving, between believing and knowing, between what can be done and what ought to be done. Second is the presupposition that my views on the relevant matters are under my control, that I am free to change my views. For if not, what would be the point of asking? Third is the belief that inquiry, or directed and systematic questioning and answering, is viable, legitimate, valid, and that it *matters*. There is a belief that the kind of knowledge represented by answers to the philosophical questions would have a significant effect on the circumstances (both internal and external) that stimulated the questions in the first place.

One way to get at the nature of the philosophical questions is to try to imagine what would answer them. I might conclude that all that we experience was created by a good God who is concerned for each of us and will reward our moral excellence during a continued existence after death; that what is best in human life is autonomy and the pursuit of knowledge because they are inherent in the nature of our rationality; that human life is a purposeless accident created and defined by biophysical events, death is extinction, and life is ruled by pleasure and pain; that, there being no pre- or nonhuman source of significance or knowledge, the conventions of human communities are the only sources of norms and values; that there is an experience, induced by love, religious faith, mystical contact, or psychoactive drugs, whose impact and significance cannot be captured in assertions, that puts these questions to rest in a way that may be considered "answering" them; or that these questions, like all attempts to transcend ordinary language and practice, are unintelligible.

What would be the effect of 'answering' my philosophical questions in these or similar ways? Most likely, I would acquire an imaginative 'picture' that would satisfy something in me. I would know how to think about my life or human life or the cosmos or my society. Having this picture might be felt to be valuable in itself, or it might comfort me in times of difficulty, or it might guide my action in moments of decision. Depending on the kind of society I inhabit, my answer might enable or empower me to teach others what is true or to improve society or to gain a special status or any combination of these. Or the effect might simply be to stop the habit of asking such questions.

One can interpret the value or aim of philosophical questions and answers in a variety of ways. One may engage philosophy as the pursuit of truth valued in itself. One might instead see philosophy as a guide for conduct or practice or as the means to provide an image for the orientation of thought or imagination. It may be that human beings need such images, perhaps to survive or to enforce social conformity or to be creative or to be happy. Philosophy could be seen as a means for the imaginative *reconstruction* of experience, for breaking the hold of the habitual and traditional, and fostering novel experiential possibilities. One could value the *process* of philosophical inquiry, independent of its potential results, for its beneficial effects. Philosophy may be an escape from the pain of life; or it may improve our ability to think about nonphilosophical matters; or it may be an essential component of a complete, cultured, mature personality. All of these views can be combined in various ways.

From what state of mind do I then set out? The present inquirer seems to be under some kind of compulsion to seek philosophical knowledge, to fix philosophical convictions, beliefs, or imaginative representations of the world through validating them as true. The source of the compulsion is unclear, but it is not unlike a religious quest for redemption, except that there is nothing particularly otherworldly about it. It is perhaps best described as an attempt by an individual to determine a most basic orientation through inquiry into what is true. There are many ways to determine an ultimate orientation, including faith in revelation, failure to question one's inherited orientation, and believing what is most pleasing. The philosophical way seeks to know the true orientation or, if there is no such thing, to know *that truth* (that there is none). Hence truth is the primary aim. Its method is inquiry, which involves making publicly accessible claims that are as clear and explicit as possible and subjecting those claims to the test of validation with evidence and inference. In this broad sense of method, the philosophic quest is continuous with science.

I take this to be consonant with the most pervasively expressed aims of Western philosophy. This tentative characterization of our starting point does not, of course, put to rest the many questions raised about philosophy's character. Nothing said here justifies this notion of philosophy, that is, supports the view that philosophy as inquiry makes sense. I am only making the fundamental issue, and the assumptions of this study, explicit. We must assume that philosophy has an aim—truth—and a method—inquiry—if we are to investigate it. At the close of this study we will turn to the question of whether this assumption is valid.

The Circle We Inhabit

The characteristically philosophical questions lead us to other questions. In what follows it will be convenient to refer to those characteristically philosophical questions collectively as *question one*. Question one leads to a new question, *question two*: Can we make judgments of the kind that might answer question one, judgments we can know to be valid, and if so, how and in what sense? The intermediate phrase is crucial. We might already have the answer to any philosophical question we may want to ask. The answer to the question, What is the meaning of my life? may indeed be something like, "To fulfill the purposes assigned me by the Creator" or "To wallow like a pig in the trough of pleasure." But can we *know* that one of these is the answer; that is, can one of these answers be validated? That is the question.

Question two is a second-order epistemological question. It is second-order because it asks a question about the characteristically philosophical questions. It is epistemological because it asks about the conditions of validity of judgments. Question two can be broken down into two component questions:

(a) Can we make any nontrivial judgments that we know are valid? What determines the validity of our nontrivial judgments in general?

(b) Can we make nontrivial judgments *like those in question one* that we know are valid? Can validity be determined for uniquely philosophical judgments? If so, what determines their validity, and what *kind* of validity is open to them?

We may notice something odd about what we have just asked. An answer to question two will probably be a uniquely philosophical judgment. That is, it will probably be the kind of judgment that answers some of the questions included in question one, about whose solvability it (question two) asks. Question two is in effect part of question one.

This brings up *question three*: Does inquiry of the kind we call *epistemological* (of which this study is an instance) make sense, is it legitimate, and if so, what kind of sense does it make? This is an important and natural question to ask. For we have just learned that the epistemological questions we are asking (question two) are of a piece with the uniquely philosophical questions we are asking about. Question three merely makes this explicit.

We are evidently caught up in a circle, although not necessarily a vicious one. The circle is constituted by the fact that any claim we make about the possibility of answering philosophical questions will presumably be a philosophical judgment. If there is something wrong, nonsensical, illegitimate, or just plain pointless about philosophical questions and answers, then our question two is also wrong or nonsensical or illegitimate or pointless.

We will be caught in such a circle throughout this book. The reason lies in trying to inquire into the bounds of inquiry. All the philosophers we will read self-consciously operate, at least part of the time, at the bounds of philosophical assertion. They dance on the edge, if you will. The metaphilosophical strategies they have evolved are the repertoire of special steps required of someone who would do this dance.

The primary aim of this study is to answer question two-b, to determine whether philosophical judgments can be known to be valid. Questions two-a and three will also be addressed, albeit secondarily and incompletely. Question one will be deferred until another time, although we may find that to the extent we answer the other questions, we will thereby gain some advantage with respect to the philosophical questions with which we began.

None of our questions appears to have a claim on logical or conceptual priority. The priority of question one is personal; it is the first-order philosophical questions that bother me. They have *biographical* priority: priority within the order of my life's narrative. But then question two rises up quickly, with three on its heels. As we will see, any attempt to deny the cogency of question one on a principled basis will presuppose an answer to question two or three, even though any answer to two or three will in effect be an answer to question one. The point is that these questions have a circular, not a linear, relationship. Only in a particular order of interpretation, that is, from a particular perspective—whose validity would also be in question—can a priority be established among the three questions.

We must now turn to what will seem an unrelated matter. To engage recent attempts to respond to the problem of the validity of philosophical knowledge, it is necessary to introduce an unfamiliar language. The task of subjecting philosophy to deep criticism has driven some philosophers, cognizant of the self-contradiction entailed in any outright denial of the possibility of philosophical knowledge, to employ sophisticated metaphilosophical strategies. Even to discuss these authors without prejudicing the case requires the use of a special language that is neutral in ways I will describe. The only such language, to my knowledge, is provided by Justus Buchler's theory of judgment. To it we now turn.

Buchler's Theory of Judgment

At the outset of his 1955 book, *Nature and Judgment*, the American philosopher Justus Buchler announced his intention to develop a theory of judgment for which "every product is a judgment" (NJ, p. 8).[2] By *product* he meant any act, contrivance or "verbal combination" rendered by a human being, or to use his synonym for judgment and product, any *utterance* (NJ, p. 10). Propositional assertions are only one type of judgment, product, or utterance. Running for a bus, rearranging furniture, and declaring one's beliefs qualify equally as judgments.

In what follows the relevant portions of Buchler's theory of judgment will be unfolded. But the most significant insight is already present in the preceding paragraph. By changing the reference of the term 'judgment' Buchler has shifted our perspective, such that it will seem natural to ascribe knowledge, comprehension, rationality, creativity, reasonableness, intelligence, and investigation *indifferently* and *equally* to the non-linguistic, non-assertive modes of judgment and the linguistic, assertive mode.[3]

What is involved in judgment in general? According to Buchler, every judgment serves to "embody a policy relating [the judge] to his environment and to his own past history, and characterize the existences among which he is located" (NJ, p. 12). "Each judgment," he suggests, "is the individual's situational recognition of his universe" (NJ, p. 29). To judge is "to bring a natural complex within the orbit of an attitude" (NJ, p. 13). Judging "primarily determine[s] a subject matter . . . and only secondarily disclose[s] an agent" (NJ, p. 16). "To produce," Buchler writes, "is to manifest the natural commitments of a self, and to apply in a fresh instance the cumulative resultant of these commitments" (NJ, p. 11). "A judgment," he insists, "is a pronouncement . . . a commentary . . . a version, a rendition of nature . . ."(TGT, p. 47). Lastly, "Whatever . . . in some possible perspective, can be deemed to *be* made or *be* said or *be* done is legitimately regarded as a judgment" (NJ, p. 18).

Buchler believes that there are three functions of judgment: active, exhibitive, and assertive, or doing, making, and saying (NJ, p. 20). When a judgment functions assertively it is valuable in terms of truth, falsity, probability, and evidence. When a judgment functions exhibitively its relevant achievement is a rearrangement (a "shaping") of materials into a "constellation that is regarded or assimilated as such" (NJ, p. 22) and that manifests a satisfying quality. When a judgment functions actively, it is subject to moral predicates (NJ, p. 28).[4]

The relation of these categories of judgment to the often met cultural trilogy of morality, art, and science is one of whole to part. When judgments are ramified in a way that is directed, systematic or methodical, interrogative and inventive, then the process of judging is an instance of *query*. There can be query in all three modes of judgment. Assertive query is *inquiry* (of which science and philosophy are instances). Active query is organized moral action.[5] Exhibitive query is art.

An important consequence of the process of query is that its product "grows" in the sense of acquiring increasing autonomy from the producer, and this autonomy compels the producer forward in the process of query. In inquiry this compulsion is achieved by evidence, in moral action by the tenable situation, and in art by the quality of the constellation of materials. It is interesting to note that for Buchler, if this autonomy is exhausted, which is to say, if the producer gains complete mastery over the product, query ends, because the source of continued interrogation dries up (NJ, p. 82).

It is in query that the novelty of Buchler's notion of judgment becomes most apparent. For query is the force that establishes human culture, that generates all but the most rudimentary, spontaneous and isolated manifestations of human being. Buchler chides other philosophers for restricting their concept of human achievement to one type of query: "traditionally the tendency has been to identify the processes of reason with the processes of assertive query. . . . the problem of reason has been taken too often as the problem of the limits and forms of discourse. . . . The attribute of reason must be applicable to the whole of human production and not merely to the forms of talk and thought; to inventive communication in all its forms and not merely to that exemplified by assertive query" (NJ, pp. 96–98).

This has interesting results. Fallibilism, for example, is wrong to claim that all legitimate judgments admit of further verification, because "only to assertive judgment does the notion of truth and falsity, and therefore of verification, apply" (NJ, p. 98). Verificationism, we could add, makes the same mistake.

Pragmatism, which was invented by the thinker closest to Buchler, Peirce, suffers from related errors. Buchler writes that, the pragmatists, by "emphasizing the active character of belief, neglect the judicative character of action, and even more, the judicative character of contrivance" (NJ, p. 32).[6] Pragmatism's contribution was to locate assertive judgment in the context of active judgment, to manifest the active character of belief, and to evaluate belief in such contexts. But although its proponents rightly regarded this as a step beyond the "intellectualism" of those who rigidly separated assertive and active judgment, Buchler's view takes a further step. His way of transcending the rigid separation of modes of judgment is not to describe one in terms of the other, but to make the differences between them functional, to expand the concept of judgment to house them all on an equal basis and render them indifferently capable of enjoying the privileged predicates of "validity" and "rationality." Thus "action itself is a mode of judgment rather than a means of bringing us beyond judgment to make it intelligible, valid, or effective" (ML, pp. 148–149).

Buchler claims that all judgments need to be validated. Every judgment, whether act, assertion, or contrivance, is incomplete. As such it implicitly makes a demand on future judgment, a claim that needs to be ratified. A judgment embodies a commitment that needs to be secured and maintained.

Validation, like judgment, comes in three types: assertive, active, and exhibitive. Truth, falsity, and probability hold only for assertive judgments. Assertive validation is also distinguished by three other traits. First, the character of assertive judgments permits an adequate reenactment of their validation conditions by others; the difference between what they are for the producer and for the receiver(s) can be negligible. Second, assertive validation takes the characteristic form of *evidential compulsion*. Third, assertive judgments can oppose or contradict each other, unlike exhibitive judgments (ML, p. 171).[7]

Both active and exhibitive validation can be described in terms of the satisfactoriness, or the degree of assent that results from recognition of the potential for further judgment based on the judgment in question. What is most unique in exhibition is the "gap" between creator and audience; that is, there is likely to be something in the product, by virtue of the process of production, that is "essential" or important in the creator's perception of it, yet cannot be shared by those who assimilate the product (TGT, p. 155). Active validation occupies a kind of middle position in that it shares the possibility of evidential compulsion with assertive validation (TGT, p. 151) and the possibility of a nonshareable component with exhibitive validation (TGT, p. 151). Buchler emphasizes that to validate an act is "to determine its justifiability (in terms of specified ends) under certain conditions" (TGT, p. 152), which he glosses as "moral justification" (TGT, p. 151).

Buchler's account of the distinctive characters of the three functions of judgments remains rudimentary. He was more interested in sketching a general theory of judgment, of which the tripartite categorization is just a part, and in locating judgment in an account of "the human process," than in a rigorous analysis of their differences. Buchler makes this clear in a response to the suggestion that there might actually be more than three modes of judgment.

> Are the three modes of judgment which I distinguish all the modes there are? . . . once judgment is seen not to be limited to assertion, there is no end to the classifications, divisions, and sub-divisions that may be devised. But the essential question is, how useful, how comprehensive, how widely applicable will a classification be? The one I have made . . . is accepted in practice and . . . is as old as man, is universally recognized. . . . Making, saying, and doing . . . are remarkably pervasive. . . . Actually, for me the number of modes of judgment is not nearly so important as the principle that each of them is a mode of *judgment*.[8]

Because his work is poorly known, Buchler's account of the three functions has not yet been developed much further. Consequently, very basic questions about this division have not yet been answered (as we will see in Chapter Seven). The aim of the present study is less to develop Buchler's tripartite view than to use it and so will not help much in addressing this lack. My use of this division does not imply that I endorse all that it may imply. We do not yet know enough about the implications of this powerful theory.

The Metaphilosophical Strategies

It is now time to delineate the various metaphilosophical strategies employed by philosophers concerned with the possibility of philosophical knowledge. The problem to which these strategies respond is this: how to criticize philosophy in a radical and global way *without doing philosophy*? In particular there is the difficulty of asserting antirealism consistently; that is, claiming that the validity of human judgments is not determined by what they judge. If this claim is applied to itself, then this implies that the validity of antirealism is not determined by what *it* judges either, that is, the character of knowledge. Any theorist who tries to make assertions about the bounds of reason or inquiry or philosophy potentially faces this problem.

There are four different ways of trying to avoid the self-referential problem. At the proper moments of inquiry, the inquirer makes only negative assertions, makes assertions that implicitly show or do what cannot be explicitly said, claims that the view in question is invalid according to some norm other than truth; or makes judgments that are supposed to be valid according to some norm other than truth. These strategies are not mutually exclusive; they can be combined. They deserve some explanation.

There are positive and negative philosophical modes of assertion. The former makes claims that purport to characterize whatever is under discussion, whereas the latter makes purely critical claims that deny the validity of other philosophers' characterizations of whatever is under discussion. Given a philosophical position, call it Q, a negative criticism of Q explicitly claims that Q is false or dubious—*dubious* meaning that we cannot know that Q is true, that Q is unsupported—without making positive claims about the phenomena Q concerns. A purely negative approach avoids the burden of justifying knowledge about the phenomena, as well as avoiding the status of a competitor theory to Q. Nevertheless, its point is embodied in explicit truth-claims (e.g., "Q is false or unsupported").

By *implicit* I mean a judgment whose primary function is other than assertion, hence either active or exhibitive. That is, its primary function is to do or show, rather than to say its point or meaning.

A philosopher, while avoiding explicit assertions not only about the phenomena but also about whether a received view of the phenomena is true or false, may still make statements whose effect is a rejection of that view or that exhibit the inadequacy of the view. If a philosopher writes about a view Q, such that the inevitable effect of that writing is to make us abandon Q or treat Q in a way indistinguishable from the way we would treat Q if we thought Q false or unsupportable, then the commentator is implicitly denying Q's adequacy. It is possible to undermine Q without making any positive or negative assertions logically equivalent to the assertion that "Q is false or unsupported." One way to do this is raise doubts about every application of Q to an individual phenomenon, without making any general statements about Q at all. This implicit approach makes assertions, but it uses these assertions to imply something not explicitly stated in them.

It is a different matter to make, in regard to theory Q, the explicit claim that Q is invalid according to some norm or criterion other than truth. This approach avoids the burden of showing Q to be false or unsupported, by asserting that Q is inelegant, useless, unappealing, immoral, impossible to believe, impossible to put into practice, and so on. This is what Rorty has claimed about the entire genre of epistemology. For example, he writes of his "pragmatist" view of truth, "Pragmatists think that the history of attempts to isolate the True or the Good, or to define the word 'true' or 'good,' supports their suspicion that there is no interesting work to be done in this area. . . . This does not mean that they have a new, non-Platonic set of answers to Platonic questions to offer, but rather that they do not think we should ask those questions anymore. . . . They would simply like to change the subject" (COP, pp. xiii–xiv). Notice that the claim being forwarded is a truth-claim; Rorty claims that it is true that epistemology has no *use*. It would be yet another move to offer this very statement as valid in some way other than being true.

The fourth and last strategy makes the latter move. It does not regard its own judgments as governed by truth.[9] Alternatively, these judgments will be governed by practical utility, moral goodness, or aesthetic quality; or the judgments may be offered as nonnormative, as facts that satisfy no norm at all. We will see that this fourth strategy is particularly important in the recent discussion of the possibility of philosophical knowledge. It constitutes what I will call a *method of abstention*, whereby some authors have believed it possible to write in a way that undermines philosophical positions while abstaining from making philosophical truth-claims.

The analysis of this method is difficult. Presumably, to most of our claims, the addition of "It is true that . . ." is redundant, and so claims imply their truth.[10] Yet some may believe that there is a philosophical point to withholding the imputation of truth, to show or exhibit something that cannot be consistently asserted, but that is valid nonetheless. We will see in Chapter Nine that this voice was invoked by Sextus Empiricus, the expositor of Pyrrhonist skepticism. Sextus has been interpreted as avoiding truth-claims, as encouraging his readers to adopt his skeptical "formulae" in order to do something, to affect an abstention from philosophical truthclaims, thereby, in his famous figure, purging our philosophical intestines. He writes of his apparent claim that, regarding any philosophical assertion, the assertion is "no more" true than its contrary, "The formula 'No more,' for instance, even though it exhibits the character of assent or denial, we do not use in this capacity.

Rather, we employ it indifferently and by a misuse of language either in lieu of a question or in lieu of saying, 'I do not know to which alternative I ought to assent, and to which I ought not'" (PH, I.191).[11]

Richard Rorty, whose similarity with Sextus has been pointed out, occasionally makes the same gesture.[12] He sometimes treats his own statements as if they were not claims aimed at truth, but rather actions aimed at producing an effect on the reader. For example: "Conforming to my own precepts, I am not going to offer arguments against the vocabulary I want to replace. Instead, I am going to try to make the vocabulary I favor look attractive by showing how it may be used to describe a variety of topics" (CIS, p. 9). There is nothing illegitimate about this voice. To reject it as insincere or impossible or immoral is, as I suggested in the Introduction, unphilosophical. But, I will argue, neither is it an avenue of escape to some critically invulnerable, indefinable locale.

It is to deal with such strategies that Buchler's terminology was introduced. The Pyrrhonist or Rortyan abstentions may not be truth-claims or assertions, but they certainly are judgments. And Buchler's account of judgmental validity dispels the illusion that the escape from assertiveness is an escape from the demand for validation. If the activity in which a writer is engaged is not inquiry whose norm is truth, but an action aimed at a certain effect, then the legitimate demand for validation does not disappear, it merely shifts to the active. It requires the kind of validation or justification we normally demand of a technique for achieving shared aims, a proposed social policy, a suggested change in our way of life. We may ask, Is this effect good for us, does the author offer any reasons why we ought to accept this action? To take the extreme case, although silence is not an assertion, it is nevertheless a judgment, and so, if offered as valid, compelling, or meaningful, is in need of validation.

On this level Sextus and Rorty will, as we will see, offer some reasons why we ought to accept their views; for example, the Pyrrhonian state of *ataraxia* or tranquility and the enhancement of our "redescriptive" creativity that Rorty envisions. The spirit in which these views are offered dictates that they must be evaluated entirely independent of their possible truth or falsity. For, to the extent that Sextus and Rorty offer their own judgments as non-assertive (not truth functional), considerations of truth are irrelevant. Nevertheless, we are obligated to consider the truth of their reasons for making these judgments; for example, whether it is *true that* abstention from truth-claims is beneficial. So truth has not been circumvented, only relocated to a different level of the discussion.

My point is not that all language is truth governed, still less that it is philosophical. It is that whatever form of query we engage is inevitably evaluative and subject to evaluation. Whatever we do, we must pay the piper; there is no escape from the demand for validation. If utterances are offered as contributions to inquiry, even negative contributions meant to derail inquiry, then they are ipso facto being offered as relevant to truth. If they are not, very well; then they must be validated as good or qualitatively satisfying. Whatever the answer, whatever we are doing at any moment in our discourse, that doing has its own vicissitudes, its own rules, its own evaluative burden. No mode of judgment has any intrinsic superiority, none is intrinsically unsupportable. Truth-governed inquiry is not unconditionally superior to any other mode of judgment, but neither is it unconditionally inferior.

Before leaving the subject of metaphilosophical strategies, something must be said about *irony*. Actually, 'irony' refers to forms of assertion in which what is meant is antithetical to what is "literally" asserted. I have no wish here to engage the very interesting debate over the nature of literal versus tropic (e.g., metaphorical) language. My point is a modest one: if we remain faithful to its dictionary and everyday meaning, then irony is a rather special and limited phenomenon. Not all the cases in which our assertions serve to mean or do more than their literal content indicates are cases of irony. At any rate, that is how I shall conceive of irony. So, the philosophical refusal to answer a question, the answering of a question with another question, the use of metaphorical language or silence as a philosophical option—none of these count as irony in my sense. If, on the other hand, one were to interpret irony more broadly, then much of what will be discussed here would count as ironic.

Philosophy as Ultimate Judgment

The way is now clear to suggest a characterization of the uniquely philosophical questions that were recited earlier and, by extension, the uniquely philosophical judgments that might answer them. It is, as John Herman Randall pointed out, foolish to try to define philosophy.[13] But fools should be honest in their foolery, and if I am to inquire into the validity of philosophical judgments, it is incumbent on me to characterize the distinction between philosophical and nonphilosophical judgment.

It seems inadequate to try to define philosophical judgments in terms of their objects, because many philosophical judgments lack objects that are the sole province of philosophy. Truth is the aim for all inquiry. Philosophy is not alone in its interest in meanings or words or concepts or universals or humanity or God or nature.

Philosophical judgments certainly appear to be general or comprehensive in a way that judgments in other fields of inquiry are not. Philosophy seems to be especially "nonlocal." To ask what is the cause of cancer is not philosophical, but to ask what is a cause, or what is disease, is. There are, however, different ways to be general or nonlocal. Newton's laws of motion were nonlocal, but today we would not call them philosophical. This very example touches on the problem that the bounds of philosophy have fluctuated historically, because Newton did consider himself a philosopher, that is, a *natural* philosopher. Certainly philosophical judgments arise in all walks of life, in indefinitely many contexts. The domain of philosophical questions and judgments is more widespread than the domain of systematic philosophical inquiry.

Our best chance of characterizing uniquely philosophical judgments is in terms of their function, their role, in inquiry or life. That function or role, I suggest, is one of *ultimacy*. Characteristically philosophical judgments are ultimate judgments; characteristically philosophical questions are ultimate questions seeking ultimate judgments.

Ultimate judgments seek priority over other judgments or perspectives, and establish order among perspectives. They establish an orientation for the person or community that utters them. They provide a framework for other judgments. They aspire to be the most comprehensive or most fundamental judgments. I am taking some liberty with Latin etymology of 'ultimacy,' because *ultima* means last or final, and I do not want to restrict myself to final judgments. In my use, 'ultimate' can mean any of the following nonequivalent terms: original, first, last, final, comprehensive, absolute, complete. The implied notion is of judgments in inquiry arranged in a series; not that all judgments are or could be located in one series, but that every judgment has a place in some series. Philosophy characteristically seeks to establish the ultimate judgments in any series of judgments.[14]

Philosophy is, then, ultimate inquiry. But this in effect means that it is unlimited inquiry, inquiry responsible to question any limit placed on any inquiry or on inquiry as a whole. Philosophy is the extension of inquiry beyond any given limit of scope, discipline, or presupposition. This does not mean that any philosopher's work is actually unlimited, but that in principle it must remain open to an unlimited demand for validation.

My intention is to understand what I have called *characteristically* philosophical judgments. Obviously, philosophers make many kinds of judgments in the course of philosophical inquiry. Philosophers discuss when Plato wrote *The Republic* and Kant's relation to Rousseau—but so do intellectual historians. I am concerned with a subset of the totality of judgments made by philosophers whose presence in their inquiry makes the inquiry philosophical. When these judgments appear in other kinds of inquiry they are still philosophical, but their relation to the the aim of the inquiry or discourse is different than it is in philosophical discourse. My interest is solely in those judgments whose defining characteristic, I am suggesting, is this open demand for ultimacy.

My notion of ultimacy is relational. What makes one judgment ultimate is its function or role with respect to other judgments, rather than any nonrelative content of the judgment, say, the occurrence of universal quantifiers or necessity operators or reference to certainty or to the nonempirical world or to what is true "by nature" or what is nonevident, and so forth. We are always open to the possibility of the demand for ultimacy. Given the inferential relation among judgments, any series of judgments implies some judgment or set of judgments that are, relative to the series, ultimate. Philosophy's task is to make these judgments explicit, to articulate, clarify, and validate them. This task will then generate more judgments that are ultimate with respect to the original series of judgments and ultimate with respect to the selected ultimate judgments. What formerly was ultimate may no longer be ultimate.

So, philosophy is that form of inquiry seeking to make valid assertive judgments that are ultimate with respect to the rest of judgment (this is not to say, judgments *about* the rest of judgment, which would mean epistemology solely).[15] Philosophy is that form of inquiry which constantly pushes the boundaries of any inquiry and of inquiry as a whole. Another way to characterize philosophical inquiry is to say that it is *indefinite, indeterminate* inquiry. It is inquiry that cannot state the limits of its task with any precision, because those limits are in question for it.

The pursuit of ultimate principles need not be metaphysical. There seems to have been an expansion of the meaning of 'metaphysical' in some current philosophical circles to cover any and all "foundational" or "superempirical" or "first" principles, regardless of the philosophical subject matter they concern. For me, metaphysical principles can certainly be ultimate, but not all ultimate judgments are metaphysical. Metaphysics is the study of what obtains, in an ultimate sense. There are other inquiries than the inquiry into what obtains, for example, the inquiry into what ought to obtain. Kant's categorical imperative is an ultimate ethical principle, not an ultimate metaphysical principle.

Now, all this talk of ultimacy and unlimited inquiry might seem akin to talk of foundationalism. 'Foundationalism' is the kind of term that carries such a powerful and accessible metaphor, that I would wager most philosophers, upon hearing it for the first time, understood its meaning immediately and without explanation. Although, as in the case of all immediately accessible things, precision regarding this meaning is elusive.

Many elements of the stereotypical notion of philosophy are associated with the foundational metaphor, but two in particular need to be distinguished. The first is that philosophy is in some sense prior to other forms of inquiry, because of its greater comprehensiveness and, in particular, its investigation of the nature of inquiry and truth. The second is the idea that there is available a fund of knowledge—call it *foundational knowledge*—whose validity is unquestionable and self-evident, because it must be independent of all other knowledge. Although foundationalism is often the key term in contemporary criticism of modern philosophy, its lineage goes back to the ancient notion of philosophy as the discoverer of "first principles." Related terms that allegedly characterize "foundational" knowledge are "absolute," "necessary," "immediate," "final," "certain," "essential," "self-evident," knowledge of the "origin," "complete" or "comprehensive" knowledge, "a priori" knowledge, knowledge independent of experience, and so on. The point of mentioning these associations is that it is likely to be believed that 'ultimate' is just another term for absolute, certain, foundational first principles.

My claim that philosophy gains its identity from its discussion of ultimate judgments is an admission that philosophy *cannot* abandon a certain element of foundationalism, *whether that element is legitimate or not*. Philosophy cannot abandon the search for and the attempt to validate those judgments that are, in relation to our other judgments, ultimate; that is, on whose validity the validity of our other judgments seems to us to depend in some sense. The pursuit of ultimacy is intrinsic to philosophy.

This notion of ultimacy does not, however, entail an acceptance of this second element, the notion of immediate, indubitable foundational knowledge, of privilege or "presence." It does not imply that ultimate judgments can ever be validated. It is merely the claim that we cannot eliminate from philosophy the notion of relative ultimacy in the order of our judgments and the attempt to push inquiry and the process of validation to the level of the most ultimate judgments of which we are capable, beyond any limits. The philosophical views that I have grouped under the term nonfoundationalism accept the foundational conception of philosophy, but not the possibility of foundational knowledge. Antifoundationalists on the other hand take the more radical view that the rejection of foundational knowledge implies that the search for ultimate knowledge is impossible as well.

The argument of this study depends entirely on the definition of philosophy as ultimate inquiry. If philosophy is not *primarily*—which is not to say *exclusively*—ultimate inquiry, then my conclusion will not follow. Because any number of questions may be asked about the meaning of *ultimate* and *inquiry*, let me make more clear what I need from these terms. 'Primarily' ultimate inquiry means two things. First, it means primarily inquiry, that is, primarily an interrogative query into what assertions can be publicly validated as true. Second, it is an inquiry open to the demand that its comprehensiveness be unlimited by any conventions or assumptions, that it seeks the ultimate valid judgments of which we are capable.

To deny that philosophy is such is either to deny that it is primarily inquiry into truth or to deny that its aims are ultimate or unlimited. The former must mean either that philosophy does not seek to validate its judgments or that it validates them as good, successful, or aesthetically satisfying rather than as true, or as valid in an undifferentiated sense. The last would be to assert the *omnivalence* of philosophical judgments, that their validity is indifferent and inclusive with respect to the three modes of validity, and would again mean that philosophical judgments do not seek primarily to be true (unless it can be shown that good or beautiful judgments are ipso facto true). The alternative denial of ultimacy must mean that limited or nonultimate validation of philosophical judgments is philosophically adequate or acceptable. As I will argue in Chapter Four, I think this is false. It does not accord with all of philosophical practice, because philosophers act at least part of the time as if limited validation were insufficient. I will argue that to accept such limits is to evade the obligations of philosophy.

My arguments against the alternative notions of limited philosophy or nonassertive philosophy remain, however, either negative or circular. I cannot philosophically show those with an alternate notion of philosophy that my notion of philosophy is preferable. I can only ask that those who do reject philosophy as primarily ultimate inquiry seriously face the implications of their alternate view. We will return to a consideration of such alternatives as the close of this study.

The Validity of Philosophical Judgments

Our problem is, then, the validity of philosophy, which is to say, the validity of ultimate inquiry and of the ultimate judgments it seeks.

I have already suggested a preliminary response to antiphilosophy; namely, that philosophy is continuous with inquiry in general, inquiry being embedded in cultural life. If true, this would mean at least that philosophy cannot be abandoned without affecting the rest of culture. At most my response could indicate that philosophy cannot be abandoned because it is built into reflective human experiencing and inquiry. But the supporters of philosophy must recognize that, even if true, this does nothing to justify or validate philosophy's *truth*.

In general, the practice of criticizing antiphilosophy is of limited value to philosophy's defense. What is needful, from the anti-antiphilosopher's point of view, is a positive account of the validity of potential or actual philosophical knowledge. That is what is so elusive, and it is the strong suit of antiphilosophy that its arguments make it hard to imagine what such a positive account might look like. Of course, there are arguments for the value or validity of philosophy that avoid the question of the truth of philosophical claims. Such arguments have ever been close to the philosopher's heart.

In Plato's dialogue *Meno*, Socrates wanted to discuss whether virtue could be taught. To do so, he began to investigate what virtue is, and so, implicitly or performatively, whether knowledge of virtue could be acquired. But he was immediately threatened with a famous argument from his interlocutor Menon that purported to show that knowledge (or at least ultimate knowledge) could not be sought or discovered at all. The argument is that, if you know what virtue is, you would not look for it, and if you do not know what it is, you would never know what to look for and so could not recognize it if you found it. To answer this objection Socrates offered the famous theory that knowledge is recollection, establishing that, in a sense,

we do have foreknowledge of what virtue is and so will be able to recognize it when it is pointed out by a teacher. Knowledge can be
taught, which clears the way for Socrates to argue that, if virtue is a
kind of knowledge, then virtue can be taught, too.

At the end of the argument for the recollection theory, the
agreeable Menon appeared convinced that the theory had been
proven true, but Socrates responded to his apparent success in an
unexpected way.

> *Menon*: You seem to me to argue well, Socrates. I don't know how
> you do it.
>
> *Socrates*: Yes, I think that I argue well, Menon. I would not be con-
> fident in everything I say about the argument; but one thing I
> would fight for to the end, both in word and deed if I were able—
> that if we believed that we must try to find out what is not known,
> we should be better and braver and less idle than if we believed
> that what we do not know it is impossible to find out and that we
> need not even try.[16]

Admitting to possible argumentative flaws too subtle for his
interlocutor to recognize, speaking beyond him to us readers,
Socrates tells us that he is committed to the validity of his claim
even if he cannot give good reasons for believing it is true! The reason for his commitment is the moral effect of belief on the possibility
of learning.

We might endorse philosophy in just this way. But in doing so,
we ought to recognize the implications. Once the question of practical consequences is opened, it must be pursued. There may then be a
practical argument against philosophy as well as for it, requiring us
to weigh both sides. Socrates' fellow citizens thought the moral cost
of philosophy too great to permit its tenuous benefit. Even if we
retry that case (only mentally, I hope) so that philosophy wins, we
must remember that reasoning from the positive effects of philosophy says nothing about the truth of its claims.

2

REALISM AND
PHILOSOPHICAL
KNOWLEDGE

The business of this chapter is twofold. My main concern is with the accounts of knowledge that must be presupposed if philosophy's claim to knowledge is to be investigated. Hence we must delve a bit into contemporary epistemology, remembering that our aim is eventually to reach a decision about philosophical knowledge in particular, not about the validity of knowledge in general. I cannot solve the problem of realism and antirealism here (or probably anywhere); however, the question of philosophical knowledge requires some provisional formulation of what 'knowledge' implies, and this requires a discussion of realism.

The second task will be to provide some historical background for the work of subsequent chapters through a brief account of the modern problem of knowledge. Peirce, Buchler, Nietzsche, Wittgenstein, and Derrida are part of a modern tradition whose history goes back to Kant and, through Kant, to Hume. That history will perform the additional service of displaying some of the common historical roots of these philosophers, rendering their comparison less implausible. In particular, we can see the extent to which the development of important ideas from Hume to Kant, then to Schopenhauer and Peirce, provides a branching historical tree in which our inquiry may nest.

The philosophical problem of knowledge is rooted in this, that on the one hand we know so much and so well and, on the other hand, all we know, or at least, all of our general and theoretical knowledge, seems to be open to revision or incapable of adequate validation and therefore to be uncertain or false. Differently put, every case of important knowledge, however secure in some respects, appears to be open to real doubt when philosophically examined. What this seems to turn on is not so much the question of *whether* we know, or even *how* we know, but rather *what* we know.[1] That is, when we know, what is it that we know? Do we know something whose character obtains independent of our knowledge of it? Is what we know of a thing its effects on us, a mere phenomenon dependent on the thing's relation to us or even constructed by us? Is the relation between what we know and what exists in the fullest sense a lawful one, it is characterized by "correspondence," so that our knowledge truly "represents" what there is? Or are these very questions unanswerable or even nonsensical?

This issue is what is at stake in the debate between the two warring clans of epistemological positions known as *realism* and *antirealism*. This is a debate about how to think about our knowledge of the world, about how to interpret the validity that we claim for our judgment. To address this controversy we must first define realism and antirealism (in the first two sections), then examine the most prominent contemporary forms of antirealism (in the next three sections), before turning to historical considerations (the last three sections).

My approach in what follows is to assume that truth is a characteristic or norm of judgment and that the truth of judgment implies some notion of representation.[2] Other interpretations of the possibility of valid judgment would reject this approach. Before proceeding, the two most prominent of these must be mentioned.[3]

Heidegger flatly rejects the notion of truth as representation. For him, philosophical knowledge, first of all, is a matter of "seeing," of grasping the preconceptual, preinferential appearances that arise in experience. Furthermore, truth, derived from the Greek word *aletheia*, is to be interpreted as "unconcealment." This implies that truth is primarily a trait of the things themselves or phenomena; truth in the primary or fundamental sense is not a property of judgments at all. Judgments are "true" in the derivative sense of being the occasion for the unconcealment of the things. Consequently, concealment as well as unconcealment, hence falsity and truth in my sense, are equally determined by the objects of judgment. It is impossible for us as inquirers to get rid of all falsity or "errancy," because that is an essential part of what is. Our proper goal is rather to think both truth and falsity together in our consideration of things.

The other approach to philosophical truth is characteristic of a kind of systematic philosophy, which I will call *metaphilosophical monism* later in this chapter. In this view, no account of knowledge, even the limited kind I am concerned to give, can succeed without an adequate metaphysics and philosophical anthropology, in short, outside of the context of a system of philosophy that "closes the circle,"[4] that unites the account of knowing to an account of the nature of the things to be known. Such views are monistic in the sense that they avoid metaphysical dualism, hence the mind-body problem, hence any fundamental discontinuity between the knower and the known.[5] This kind of systematic philosophy is certainly not new; Aristotle, Spinoza, and Leibniz, in short, many of the canonical metaphysicians of the Western tradition, were engaged in this project. In the twentieth century systematic metaphysics has been under a kind of censure; but in the current "postepistemological" Rortyan era, it has returned as an alternative to the now unpopular epistemology that had exiled it. Hegel and Aquinas are the inspiration for some contemporary monists, but others trace their ancestry to Peirce, and especially to Alfred North Whitehead, who has influenced thinkers as different as the theological philosopher Robert Neville and the scientific philosopher Abner Shimony.[6]

Like the Heideggerian perspective, this view would deny that the validity of philosophical knowledge can be understood or justified using my methods. For the Heideggerian, my approach confuses the derivative and narrow mode of truth called *representation* with truth in the primordial or originary sense. For the Whiteheadian, my approach mistakenly tries to decide a question in isolation from the context in which it can rightly be addressed, that is, the context of an account of nature and human nature.

I need not deny the validity of the phenomenological and systematic perspectives to do my work, but I do need to limit it. I will suggest that the Heideggerian and Whiteheadian approaches do not answer my questions, however well they might answer other questions. They do not, and in principle cannot, put to rest the critical questions I am asking. They adopt perspectives on what philosophy is and what it seeks to provide that are different from mine. My interpretation of this dispute, which is really a disagreement about the very nature of philosophy, will be given in Chapter Ten. Nevertheless, it is my intention to craft a conception of realism sufficiently minimal to avoid a premature and unnecessary decision against their approaches.

My final prolusory point is a promise to redeem an apparent inadequacy of the present chapter later on. Much of this chapter's work is the establishment of an epistemological typology, a set of labels: realism, antirealism, relativism, pragmatism, naturalism, and so on. Many philosophers have understandably grown wary of such labels. However, I believe that we cannot help using these or similar terms; we might as well try to clarify them. The real test will come when they are applied in Chapters Three through Nine. There we will see that philosophers may be realist in one respect and anti-realist in another, and so their characterization as one or the other must be tentative. I prefer to be simple and rigid in formulating categories, and flexible in applying them, rather than to dive into the primary texts without polished interpretive tools. I think this is especially necessary when dealing with philosophers from diverse traditions.

Defining Realism

Realism and antirealism are terms used perhaps most often in the philosophy of science and methodology, but they can be and have been imported into epistemological and metaphilosophical discussions easily enough. What is realism? There are a variety of recent definitions. Michael Dummett, in his 1963 essay "Realism," construed it as,

> the belief that statements of the disputed class possess an objective truth-value, independently of our means of knowing it: they are true or false in virtue of a reality existing independently of us. . . . That is, the realist holds that the meanings of statements of the disputed class are not directly tied to the kind of evidence for them that we can have, but consist in the manner of their determination as true or false by states of affairs whose existence is not dependent on our possession of evidence for them.[7]

In contrast, antirealism holds that the meanings of the relevant statements are constituted by what "we count as evidence" for them. The disagreement between realism and antirealism is over "the kind of meaning" possessed by the relevant statements, and this directly affects our judgments about the truth of the statements. The realist believes that statements are determinately true or false "even in the absence of . . . evidence," which is to say, even when we do not presently possess the evidence, whereas for the antirealist "the truth of the statement can consist only in the existence of such evidence," so that, absent evidence, the statement is neither true nor false.[8]

Recent work in the philosophy of science has generated a number of definitions of realism. They generally contain the following three elements (which is not to imply that that the conjunction of these three is either necessary or unproblematic):

1. In Jarrett Leplin's formulation: "The best current scientific theories are at least approximately true."[9]

2. The terms used in these approximately true theories refer to real things.

3. In Richard Boyd's formulation, "The reality which scientific theories describe is largely independent of our thoughts or theoretical commitments."[10]

In addition to these and other characterizations of realism in the philosophy of science,[11] there is a substantially stronger realist claim, one version of which is characteristic of what Hilary Putnam calls *metaphysical realism*, namely, the belief that there is at most one and only one true account of reality. This version of realism has come under the most obvious contemporary disfavor. It is against the background of a retreat from this so-called metaphysical realism that we can understand contemporary antirealism as being determined by two questions. First, how far must we go to renounce the metaphysical version of realism; how deeply rooted is this malignancy, how much conceptual tissue must be cut out to remove it? Can we rest content with a minimal, "relativized" realism, or might this risk recurrence of the foundationalist, metaphysical disease? Second, can the patient live with what will be left after this operation? What is the cost of this surgery and what is the patient's prognosis for recovery? Part of the motivation for my study is the conviction that the costs of the removal of metaphysical or foundational realism have generally been *under*estimated.

Informed by these characterizations, I will try to construct the most general and minimal definition of realism that I can. My first suggestion is that realism is the view that, with respect to the assertive functioning of judgments,[12] they are true if and only if they are *valid with respect to what they judge*. This is meant to oppose the view that judgmental validity obtains solely with respect to other judgments, the condition and nature of the judge, the judge's community, and so forth. This initial characterization of realism takes the determination of judgmental validity to be the issue between realism and antirealism and makes the relation to what is judged the condition of validity. It is my aim to make this formulation progressively more precise, gradually to build a usable notion of realism.

The language of this initial statement is neutral with respect to the nature of that to which the judgment is to be related (the indefinite "what is judged"). The word 'object' is acceptable here as long as it is understood as vaguely as possible. The reason to avoid misleading dualistic talk of "things," "nature," and "the world" as the objects of judgment is that language, mind, and judgment are themselves potential objects of judgment, and the world must include them as its members. There can be no "word-world" dualism at this level, which is not to prejudge the metaphysical issue of dualism versus idealism. The point is simply that if realism is to hold true, then it ought to hold true regardless of type of object, and so hold of judgments about judgmental things—things that happen to be judgments—as well as of judgments about things other than judgments.

Also, although my interest will be in nontrivial or non-analytic judgments, this statement of realism might be able to include analytic judgments, as long as we can say that such judgments judge *something*, for example, themselves, or grammar, or logical structure, or whatever you like. Then they too, under realism, would be valid with respect to their objects.

The task of a definition of realism is to articulate conditions that satisfy the realist's intuitive sense of realism. The challenge lies in determining two things: the nature of the relation that holds between the judgment and its object; and the nature of what is judged. A number of considerations must be addressed here.

First, the relation of the judgment to what is judged may be either distributive or collective, individual or holistic. The realist may hold that there are individual true judgments or, alternately, that only groups or systems of judgments can be true. Concomitantly, the realist may claim that true judgments hold true of individual objects or only of sets of objects or even all objects, the whole world. All can be forms of realism. The intuitive sense of realism is preserved by a holistic approach that assigns validity only to groups of judgments and their relation to groups of objects; holism is not in principle antirealist. Otherwise, our notion of realism is unnecessarily narrowed and disadvantaged.

Consequently, under my definition an interpretation of scientific theories that does not assume that *each* term in such theories individually refers to something with independent existence does *not* disqualify it from being realist, if the interpretation does claim that the theory represents reality in a holistic or structural way. Therefore, my definition is meant to include the kind of approach exemplified by the following remarks of Howard Stein.

> on a certain very deep question Aristotle was entirely wrong, and Plato . . . remarkably right: namely, our science comes closest to comprehending "the real," not in its account of "substances" and their kinds, but in its account of the "Forms" which phenomena "imitate" (for "Forms" read "theoretical structures," for "imitate," "are represented by"). . . . the key to this [scientific] understanding turns out to lie in mathematical structures, and *improved* understanding in *structural "deepening"*. . . . in this structural deepening what tends to persist—to remain, as it were, quasi-invariant through the transformation of theories—is on the whole . . . not the features most conspicuous in referential semantics: the substances or "entities" and their own "basic" properties and relations, but the more abstract mathematical forms.[13]

Second, realism need not presume the absolute determinateness of either valid judgments or their objects. Here I have Peirce's notion of indeterminateness in mind. Imagine that we were able to list all the properties any object might have, which is to say, all possible objective properties (except, for the sake of the argument, the property of not being an objective property). To believe that a thing is absolutely determinate is to believe that, for *every* possible property, the thing objectively possesses either that property or its contrary (e.g., white or nonwhite), whether we know it or not. This is, as Peirce claims, a very strong assumption. It ought not be presumed by a cautious realism. Realism need not presume absolute determinateness of its objects, that every object must have every possible property or its negation. The world need not be entirely definite, but only *partly* definite. That is, for realism it must be true that the objects of valid judgment either have or do not have *some* properties whether we know it or not, but it need not be true that they either have or do not have *every* property whether we know it or not.[14]

This is to deny that *bivalence* holds for all assertions. Bivalence can be understood in two senses. It is one thing to say that truth and falsity are the sole truth-values of propositions, thereby denying values like "true in a perspective." It is another to say that the world is so constructed that every proposition must either correspond to the world or not. The latter entails believing, as Quine has remarked, "that it is either true or false that there was an odd number of blades of grass in Harvard Yard at the dawn of Commencement Day, 1903."[15] Realism in my formulation accepts the former but not the latter. The issue is not the absence of evidence to decide; that is, I do not suggest that lack of evidence determines indeterminacy. It is just that to presume a world determinate in every respect that we can imagine is to presume too much.

Concomitantly, realism need not presume that absolute precision is required for a judgment to be valid. That presumption, which Peirce rejects, is also too strong. It may be that *any* valid judgment can be rendered invalid by demanding indefinitely greater precision from it, and so, if we allow the requirement of absolute precision, we might make judgmental validity impossible. This is a point that, as we will see, Wittgenstein shares with Peirce: the level of precision appropriate for judging the validity of a judgment varies with context. We cannot explore this issue here; suffice to say that we must be wary of letting the urge indefinitely to increase precision, which is a normal and healthy urge among inquirers, enter into the very notion of validity. Even normal and healthy urges need restraint.

Third, realism cannot mean that judgmental validity is determined *solely* by the judgment's relation to what is judged. Obviously, judgmental validity also depends on the meaning of the judgment, on language, and on other beliefs. Realism cannot be put into the position of denying that language, beliefs, theories, culture, or community have any role in the determination of the validity of a judgment. That would be absurd. Realism need claim only that those other sources of determination *do not exhaust* what determines judgmental validity, so that what is judged remains a determining factor. Antirealism must then be construed along the lines of a denial that the relation of judgment to what is judged has any significant role in determining validity independent of language, theory, or culture.

Fourth, and perhaps the most obviously needed condition for realism, is a stipulation regarding the independence of the objects of judgment. Without some such stipulation, the claim that the objects of a judgment are constituted *by* that judgment could count as realist. But this would violate the spirit of realism. Realism must restrict itself to cases in which the character of the validly judged object obtains *independent of judgment*. But here complexities immediately arise.

We are familiar with the various permutations of this problem since the seventeenth century: For John Locke, nature independent of mind causes a mental representation; for David Hume, we cannot know that the object is real beyond its appearance; for Immanuel Kant, the superapparent thing in itself *is* but can never be experienced or known. The nature of the objects as things in themselves has been the stuff of metaphysical debate between materialism or physicalism, dualism, and various forms of idealism. Here realism does not take sides: physicalism, dualism, and idealism can all be realist under the right conditions. George Berkeley, although a metaphysical idealist who makes the objects of knowledge dependent on mind, asserts that the objects of perceptual judgments are independent of all *human* judgment. For Berkeley, mentality is not exhausted by human minds: there remains the mind of God. Thus, although simple mind-independence is impossible, objectivity is independent of all human minds. To make Berkeley an antirealist would be to pack too much metaphysics into our notion of realism.

The point is that "mind-independence"—or in my terms, judgment-independence—is not so simple. Any statement of realism must draw a line indicating the degree and mode of judgment-independence that it demands in its objects. We can imagine several such lines, where the character of what is judged is allowed to be dependent on the judgment in question; independent of the judgment in question, but dependent on some specifiable collection of judgments (e.g., a theory); dependent on the totality of assertive judgments at any given time, but independent of any smaller collection of judgments; or dependent on some collection of judgments in the future (as, we will see, in Peirce).

Realism must exclude the first of these. A realist must hold the object of valid judgment to be independent of the particular judgment in question. The realist must deny the second option, too. The character of what is judged cannot be relative to, for example, a theory held by the judge. But suppose we ask whether the object may be dependent on a framework that holds for all judges or will hold in the indefinite future? This is a delicate matter. To make the realist insist on the object's independence of universal or future frameworks would significantly narrow realism. Because I do not want to prejudge the metaphysical issue, our minimal realism will only require that the character of objects be independent of any *specifiable* set of judgments (e.g. a theory, perspective, paradigm, culture, etc.)

Fifth, must realism include some idea of correspondence or representation in its definition? Is there a more substantive interpretation of our original "valid with respect to," a more particular *kind* of relation, that is required by a realist reading of the relation of valid judgment and its object? Must the validity of the judgment be *determined* by the object? Must a valid judgment have a causal relation to its object, such that the object is the cause of the judgment (or of its validity)? Must the valid judgment correspond to or agree with or adequately represent, or picture or resemble its objects? To ask these questions is to ask for a characterization of truth, however minimal. Must a valid assertion, to use Aristotelian terms, say of what is that it is, or in Tarskian terms, say "snow is white," if and only if snow is white?[16]

A complete explication of realism perhaps ought to describe the special nature of the relation that realism claims to obtain between valid assertions and their objects, but my goals are more modest. Regarding this very subtle matter I will offer only the following. Realism must understand the truth of judgment as a correspondence to or representation of its objects in some minimal sense. For realism, true assertions are true of their objects, and by correspondence or representation I mean nothing more that what must be implied by this "being true of." True assertions represent or correspond to or are more faithful to their objects, whereas false assertions do not or are less so. How correspondence or representation is to be conceived is too complex a matter to be decided here; suffice to say that it need not be interpreted as "picturing" or "resembling." Of course, this correspondence may be holistic and may hold only between all of reality and an integrated set of judgments. It may be that true representations are caused by their objects, or that representation can be understood as unconcealment, or as actualizing real possibilities; one can treat these possible interpretations as subsequent matters.[17]

Now, are the foregoing stipulations enough to characterize realism, or could a view satisfy the conditions stated and still be antirealist, that is, still not satisfy our intuition of what we mean by realism? Up until now it might appear that my realism has little "bite," thereby reducing antirealism to the status of an extremist party. One more condition will reverse this impression.

Let us imagine a philosophy according to which the objects of judgment exhibit indefinitely many distinct characters, so that, although the truth of judgment obtains with respect to its object— hence realism as heretofore construed is fulfilled—inconsistent true judgments with respect to the same object are possible, depending on the real, objective relationships in which the object is embedded. Under such a philosophy, a claim about an object may be true with respect to some one of that object's plural characters. That contrary judgments of the same object can be true in different perspectives, that truth is relative to perspective, has already been excluded from realism as a form of relativism; but the current example applies relativism to the objects of judgment. Such a radically pluralist view would pass our prior realist tests. (This is the problem Buchler confronts us with, as we will see in Chapter Seven.)

Consequently, a sixth element must be added to my definition of realism. The additional parameter for realism is that *all true judgments must be consistent*. Within the totality of assertive judgments, contrary judgments cannot both be true. Another way of saying this is that some version of what Hilary Putnam calls *metaphysical realism*—that there is at most one true account of the world—must be captured by realism.[18] This is a strong and controversial claim, which makes realism significantly riskier. It imputes to the object of a true judgment a single identity or a single character, embodied in determinate characteristics or traits, such that only one set of consistent judgments can be true of it. This is not to deny that objects exhibit traits that obtain relatively, with respect to other objects. But it affirms that making a true judgment of something requires that there be *a* something, and to be a something is to have a single or unified character. I am claiming that our intuitive sense of realism requires something like the condition that there is but one real world, and that only one possible consistent system of judgments can ultimately be true of it. If one accepts that there are alternative, equally true judgments or systems of judgments that are contrary in meaning, then one has given up realism.

The only way for the objective pluralist to avoid admitting the truth of contraries is to espouse relativism of *meaning* as well. For if holism is accepted (as it can be by realist and antirealist alike) and the system of judgments in question is large enough (e.g., a "conceptual framework," an "ontology," a "language"), it may be claimed that the meaning of any judgment is relative to the system to which it belongs and that these systems are incomparable. If this were true, then, because judgments in different frameworks could not be compared as to their meaning, they could not be claimed to be inconsistent. Of course, the relativist must deny that contrary judgments *within* a single system may be true. This relativism of meaning is a version of the famous claim of *incommensurability*. But this alternative has its own problems, as famously shown by Donald Davidson.[19]

We do not need to decide the issue of incommensurability here. We need only say that, if there is intertranslatability or sameness of meaning among systems of judgments, then to accept the possibility of contrary true judgments is to reject realism. Consequently, realism in my interpretation requires a restriction on pluralism, a rather conservative insistence on the unity of valid assertive judgments. Of course, this says nothing about the kind of unity or the level of abstraction at which unity must obtain.

There is one last issue. Realists expect knowledge to be *decisive*. This means that it must be capable of being stated in the form of a yes or no answer to a question. Realists conceive of successfull inquiry as being able to decide, in response to proposed claims, which are true and which false, and so which can be added to cumulative knowledge.

This need not imply rigidity or lack of subtlety, for any intelligent realist recognizes that some questions do not admit of a yes/no decision as stated, but must be broken down into smaller or more precise or more clear questions before a yes/no decision can be given. And of course every realist admits the vast number of claims regarding which we cannot yet, and may never, know whether to say yes or no. The realist is smart enough to accept that some questions might be undecidable. Further, decisiveness need not be distributive or piecemeal; a realist may happily reserve decision for comparison of systems of judgments. And, I might add, this decisiveness is no less characteristic of falsificationist approaches, in which *yes* means "provisionally accepted" or "has survived criticism thus far" and *no* means "disconfirmed."

If a view were to satisfy all the foregoing requirements for realism while rendering all matters undecidable, so that we could not, in principle, hope to get yes or no answers to any important questions into which we inquire, ought we allow that view to qualify as a realism? The question is whether to call such a view realist but skeptical, because it accepts the realist account of true judgment while doubting that such true judgments have been or can be achieved, or to call it antirealist, because it denies realist truth to our actual judgments. To choose the latter is to build yet another qualification into realism; namely, the claim that we do have true knowledge in a realist sense (as do those who define realism as the view that our best current science is approximately true). I will not add this to my intentionally minimal realism; I only flag the issue for future reference.

In summary, then, realism is the view that the validity of assertive judgments holds with respect to what is judged, where the character of what is judged obtains independent of any specifiable collection of judgments, and where contrary judgments cannot be valid, because there is but one real world to which true judgments correspond.

As we will see, the main problem of realism is the difficulty of justifying it, especially given the reality of theory change and the dubiousness of any resort to certainty and immediacy in knowledge. Nevertheless, antirealism, we will see, faces the equally thorny problem of coherence; that is, of its apparent inconsistency with our usual understanding of our pursuit of, and claims to, knowledge, even on the part of those claiming to know the truth of antirealism. Consequently, statements of antirealism face the problem of self-contradiction.

Although this chapter has aimed only to raise and not to resolve epistemological problems, it is only fair that I state my view on the question of realism, despite my inability to justify that view in this context. I claim that some minimal sense of realism is *indubitable*. I suggest that our minimal notion of truth as the norm that governs inquiry implies an at least minimal realism. To say that a judgment is *true of something* is to say at least that the judgment bears a kind of relation, for which 'correspondence' is an admirable but imperfect term, to an object (of whatever existential status) whose character obtains independent of any specifiable set of assertive judgments. To give up all trace of realism would mean to give up either that our assertions can be true of something or that the somethings of which they can be true obtain independent of judgment. To assert the former leaves the guidance of inquiry entirely unclear, whereas to assert the latter is to present a substantive claim about the metaphysical status of the objects of inquiry.

That realism is ineliminable does not mean, however, that it can be known to be *true*. Not only can I not attempt to justify realism here, I do not believe that realism can be adequately justified as true, as I will try to show. All the terms in the preceding statement ('relation,' 'correspondence,' 'object,' 'character,' 'independent') will, as soon as greater precision is demanded, become problematic. That realism is indubitable does not mean that we can show that our assertive judgments are true in a realist sense or that true assertive judgments in a realist sense are possible. Realism could be validated after a fashion through recourse to some kind of pragmatism, as we will see. But I will question whether this kind of validation can be philosophically adequate. In short, realism is implicit in the search for truth, even if its truth cannot be justified.

Defining Antirealism

I will define antirealism in a very broad way as the *principled abstention from assent to realism*. The effect of such a definition is calculated. Many philosophers who otherwise would not be antirealists will, in my definition, be corralled into antirealism. This procedure directly contradicts a widespread tendency to define antirealism more narrowly, in particular, to define it in such a way that an opponent of philosophical realism need not be an antirealist. This tendency carves out a possible space for a "minimal," "everyday," "commonsense," nonfoundational or nonphilosophical realism. My wider definition is, I believe, legitimate as long as I avoid indiscriminately lumping together all versions of what I consider antirealism and ascribing the problems of one version to another. I must distinguish the different ways of being an antirealist.

If, as I have suggested, philosophical arguments and positions are amplifications, articulations, and modifications of arguments and positions that occur in nonphilosophic discourse, then philosophical realism must be continuous with nonphilosophical realism. A kind of realism occurs outside of philosophic discussion, and philosophic realism is continuous with it. If this is so, then to fail to assent to philosophical realism has implications outside of philosophy, implications for other forms of inquiry and for everyday discourse and belief. This claim is the basis for everything that follows. It is in direct contradiction to the most common forms of contemporary antiphilosophy, which try to insulate common sense and science from the critique they aim at philosophic inquiry, for to fail to do so would allow their criticism to threaten the legitimacy of nonphilosophical inquiry and truth.

What are the ways that a philosopher might abstain, on principle, from realism? There are two general approaches. First, one might indicate that realism is dubious or false. This I call the *negative* approach. Second, one might indicate that some alternative to realism is valid. This is the *positive* approach. In each case, the "indication" may be achieved through explicit assertion or *saying* or through an implicit exhibition or *showing*. Let us take the positive approach first.

There is a positive *metaphysical* approach, that is, an attempt to state an alternative to realism through a characterization of the objects of judgment, the things judged. This is most prominently represented by some forms of idealism, the view that the objects of judgment are mental, but includes any claim that what is judged in valid assertive judgments is not independent of judgment, at whatever level required.

The positive *epistemological* approach is to state an alternative to realism by characterizing the validity of judgments as determined by the relation of the judgment in question to something other than what is judged. This is typically done either by defining truth in terms of some such relation (e.g., "true in a perspective") or characterizing truth as conditioned or determined by some such relation (e.g. by making convention the criterion of truth). Consequently, all forms of positive epistemological antirealism are forms of *relativism* in the widest sense of this term. Both pragmatism and naturalism, insofar as they are antirealist, are relativistic in this sense.

We must admit that the term *relativism* is literally misleading. Realism and most positive forms of antirealism take the validity of judgment to depend on the relation of the judgment to *something*.[20] In a literal sense, we are almost all relativists; that is, whoever accepts an account of judgmental validity at all, probably accepts a relational account of validity. However, tradition dictates that *relativism* refers to the dependence of judgmental validity on all relations other than the judgment's relation to its object. In the broad sense, then, pragmatism and naturalism, insofar as they are antirealist, are forms of relativism. I will, however, use *relativism* in the usual and restricted sense (relativism *proper*) to mean the claim that judgmental validity is determined by the judgment's relation to its judge, to other judgments, or the judge's community. Hence, pragmatism and naturalism, which place the judgment in somewhat different contexts, will be alternatives to relativism proper.

Negative antirealism is more complex. There are at least as many ways to show or say that realism is dubious or false as there are components or presuppositions of realism. One can say or show the dubiety or falsity of realism by saying or showing the dubiety or falsity of the claim

1. That assertive judgments can be true at all in the relevant sense of the word *true*. This is the effect of Heidegger's nonpropositional notion of truth.

2. That anything determines the truth or validity of assertive judgments. This is a denial that the truth of judgments can be accounted for by reference either to the objects of judgment or to anything else (e.g., mind, a framework of beliefs, the community).

This is what Richard Rorty has recently called "antirepresentationalism."(ORT, p. 2).

3. That judgmental validity is determined by a relation to what is judged. This is the heart of the antirealist position.

4. That judgmental validity is determined by a relation of correspondence or representation with what is judged. This objection to realism focuses on these traditional interpretations of the realist relation to the object.

5. That the objects of valid assertive judgments are independent of those judgments. This is, so to speak, a negative version of metaphysical idealism.

6. That all true judgments must be consistent. Pluralism denies this by allowing alternative, contrary sets of true judgments.

It will be necessary for us, when discussing philosophers, to distinguish what kind of realism they wish to rebuff, and hence what kind of antirealism they accept.

There are three prominent forms of positive epistemological antirealism (that is, three prominent antirealist accounts of the validity of judgment), namely, relativism, pragmatism, and naturalism. These will now be explored a little more fully.

Any discussion of antirealism must, however, begin with the critique of immediacy or, as it is sometimes called, the critique of *privilege*. This is the gateway to antirealism. The denial of a certain kind of immediacy is a necessary but not sufficient condition for antirealism; every form of antirealism must deny it, but this denial may be compatible with a nuanced or sophisticated realism (e.g., as in Peirce, as we will see). By immediacy I mean that characteristic of an assertive judgment by which it is said to be rendered true through an immediate relation to what it judges. Immediacy implies insusceptibility to criticism. Immediacy is irrefragability ascribed to a judgment's validity with respect to the object of the judgment. Immediate judgments are given "privileged" status over all other synthetic judgments.[21] Remember that what is at issue here is judgment of real objects, that is, objects whose character obtains independent of any specifiable set of judgments. Immediacy refers to judgments of real things that *cannot* be wrong.

Antirealism must deny that there can be such judgments. If there were immediate assertive judgments of independent objects whose significance could be taken up without possible error into our conscious perception of and thought about the world, then epistemological security would be won, and the messy game of antirealist doubt and realist response would be finished. Antirealism of any stripe therefore requires a rejection of any significant form of privilege. Moderate forms of antirealism may accept an attenuated form of privilege.[22] The more complete the antirealism, the more complete is the denial of immediacy.[23]

Relativism is the most important and comprehensive contemporary form of antirealism. Relativism claims that the validity of a judgment is or is determined by the relation of the judgment to something other than what is judged, such as other judgments, perspectives, the judge, semiotic systems, objective contexts, or the judge's community. What is at issue is what can be said to determine the validity of judgment. Almost everyone would say that the validity of a judgment depends both on what is judged and on characteristics of the judgment and the judge; for example, language, theory, perspective, culture. The issue is, Can the relation of the judgment to what is judged be the determining factor in establishing the validity of the judgment? The relativist denies this. *Contextualism* is simply an appealing metaphorical expression for relativism, namely, the claim that the validity of judgment is relative to some context. 'Contextualism' is a perfectly respectable term, and I will sometimes use it interchangeably with 'relativism.' However, one must be careful not to take the prepositional metaphor that naturally attends contextualism too seriously or, better, not to take it seriously at the wrong times. The metaphor is that judgments take place "in" contexts, as if contexts were containers or locations. The image of spatial inclusion can be misleading. A more austere and accurate image, given our need for images, is provided by relativism itself through the idea of relation or reference. For relativism and contextualism, judgment takes place in reference to a perspective, a theory, a language, a community, a context.

Conventionalism is a species of relativism or contextualism. For conventionalism, what determines judgmental validity is the relation of judgment to convention, which I will take to mean a social or cultural norm or rule. As we will see, attempts have been made to add to this interpretation, making conventionalism imply that validity is relative to social agreement and choice. But this is too much. It is unlikely that social conventions are often products of agreement or choice. The attempt to interpret convention in this way appears to be motivated by a desire to dismiss conventionalism by making it a straw man. I will return to this issue in my discussion of Wittgenstein.

As mentioned in the Introduction, relativism need not be "subjectivist." A human subject is only one of the indefinitely large number of items to which judgmental validity could be claimed to be relative. In recent years the attack on subjectivism, which makes the individual human subject or consciousness prior to all other considerations in inquiry, has humbled subjectivist versions of relativism.[24] But this does nothing to discourage nonsubjectivist forms of relativism, which may make judgmental validity relative to social action, orders of objective relatedness, or the dynamics of semiotic systems. The first of these three makes validity relative to something human, to be sure, but not something subjective in the sense of something internal to consciousness or experience. The second relates validity to things entirely nonhuman or objective. The third relates validity to the dynamics of a human artifact (signs), but one that, once created, operates under rules that are mostly independent of human will.

The reason that relativism and its various versions are important in the discussion of the possibility of philosophical knowledge is simple enough. If the validity of judgment is always relative to, for example, context, then what is the validity of philosophical judgments? Either philosophical judgments are, like other judgments, valid only in a contextual sense or they are judgments that seek to be super- or noncontextual. Contextualism makes the latter impossible; judgments attempting to transcend context cannot be valid. So relativism either makes the validity of philosophical judgments contextual—hence nonrealist—or denies that philosophical 'judgments' are legitimate, meaningful judgments in the first place.

Pragmatism has been defined in a number of ways. It was invented to be a theory of the meaning of words, concepts, and beliefs. But even its inventor, Peirce, immediately used it to clarify a particularly important concept: truth. Ever since, pragmatism has entailed an account of judgmental validity.

Pragmatism can be formulated as the claim that the validity of assertive judgments is relative to contexts of action. Pragmatism interprets judgments as having an active function and judges their validity in terms of some context of, or established by, purposeful conduct. The sense in which such an interpretation is antirealist is obvious: It makes the validity of an assertion relative to some active purpose. If the validity of judgments is determined by the fact that the judgments serve an active purpose, then, absent that purpose, the judgments are not valid; so the validity ceases to be understandable as holding in relation to the object of such judgments. Of course, there are interpretive options that might seem to make pragmatism realist. Whether such attempts can be successful we will see later. The simple point is that pragmatism will be antirealist unless special steps are taken. And, in fact, pragmatism is one of the most prominent forms of antirealism today.

Naturalism can be variously defined, as we will see, but the most useful preliminary characterization is the claim that everything, and in particular everything human, is natural or within the order of nature. Hence perception, cognition, interpretation, and philosophical speculation are natural events, obeying natural laws, subject to a natural scientific analysis. What this could have to do with antirealism we will see in the next section.

Some recent philosophers have claimed that relativism is impossible to believe, others that it has been proven false. If these claims are true, there would be little point in proceeding with my examination. Likewise, some pragmatists deny that there is anything antirealist about pragmatism. Naturalism might seem even less likely to be antirealist. In the next three sections I will, respectively, define naturalism and clarify the sense in which it is antirealist, explain the sense in which pragmatism remains antirealist, and suggest that, despite recent denials, relativism remains viable. The second of these sections will be truncated, because Chapter Four will deal more extensively with pragmatic realism.

Naturalism and Monism

Naturalism, generally speaking, is the view that everything is "in" nature, that everything is natural. Most significant, it means that human experience and judgment are located in the order of natural phenomena. Human knowledge, experience, and judgment are natural events that must obey at least some principles that hold for all other natural events. Note that I have just given a circular definition by including the term 'natural' in the preceding sentences. The reason is that the attempt to define nature sufficiently comprehensively, hence sufficiently abstractly, leads to a problem.

To understand the problem we need to define *metaphilosophical monism*. We could define monism negatively as the denial of dualism, that is, the denial that whatever is under discussion may be understood as divided into absolutely different kinds of things. Applying this vague sense of monism as widely as possible, hence metaphilosophically, implies that all orders of being are continuous with each other or that no orders are absolutely discontinuous with all other orders.[25] Naturalism and materialism, which deny that anything is supernatural or immaterial, and idealism, which denies that anything is nonmental, would all be instances of monism. But there could be yet other monisms. The ultimate reality may be regarded as simultaneously mental and physical, as in Spinoza. Or presumably one could attempt to derive reality from something, some category, that exhibits neither the properties we traditionally call mental or physical.

The problem we face is that if we seek to formulate a definition of either naturalism or idealism sufficiently general that no particular, hence controversial, notion of nature or mind is presupposed, then the terms 'nature' and 'mind' threaten to become meaningless. For if, under naturalism, the *idea* of democracy is to be as "natural" an event as photosynthesis, then the meaning of 'natural' must be so abstract as to seem almost contentless. Likewise, if all reality is mental in a strong sense, so that a stone and my idea of a stone are equally mental, then what does 'mental' mean? This is a problem with any term that aspires to refer to everything collectively (e.g., "all reality is . . . ").[26] The problem is as old as Thales, who claimed that everything is water. How then to explain fire, which destroys (evaporates) water and is destroyed (extinguished) by it? The only way to make the explanation work is to strip the concept of water of virtually all its content, so that the "water" which is everything (including fire) will not much resemble what falls at Niagara.

Some have tried to define naturalism as the view that nothing is wholly discontinuous with anything else.[27] This is an interesting definition. But notice the result: *Idealism* could be defined in the same way, making naturalism and idealism identical. The reason this violates our intuitions is that we normally give more concrete content, fuller imaginative meaning, to our notions of idealism and naturalism. We normally conceive of the mentality that idealism ascribes to everything as an extension of what we prephilosophically associate with our human minds. Likewise we conceive of the naturalness that naturalism ascribes to everything as an extension of the processes we normally ascribe to the physico-chemical-biotic universe. But it is not clear that the primary or ordinary meanings of these terms will suffice for their respective extensions. It seems that modifications would be required, that the respective notions of mind and nature would have to be expanded, or at least be understood in a subtle and complex way. That is why I will (unless otherwise noted) use idealism and naturalism in their ordinary connotations as a mentalistic and a physicalistic monism, respectively.

Naturalism can have antirealist implications under certain conditions. This may seem odd, because we associate naturalism with the natural sciences, which we often take as a powerful force for promoting realism. Whether most naturalists are realists or not, there is one respect in which naturalism is antirealist. That is when naturalism in a biophysicalist sense is applied to human experience and knowledge. For if human judgment is explained using categories common to biology, the validity of cognition may be interpreted in terms of survival, adaptive success, or some causal determinism (this obviously depends on the biophysical theory used). Then, that a judgment is valid may be construed as meaning, or as being determined by, not its representation of objects, but, for example, its satisfaction of a biological or psychological need. Indeed, a question arises as to whether norms of validity, like truth, can have any meaning in such a system.

The attempt to give an account of human knowing on the basis of naturalism, and specifically, through recourse to the resources of the best current physical theories, is *naturalistic epistemology*. Naturalistic epistemology has perhaps most famously been championed by W. V. O. Quine and by Karl Popper. In this view, human knowing is a natural phenomenon to be studied like any other. The scientific study of knowing will replace the old epistemology, which tried to justify all knowledge, including science. Acceptance of naturalistic epistemology entails abandonment of the foundationalist project of reconstructing all knowledge, of proving that there is knowledge at all, because naturalistic epistemology presumes the validity of science. Hence it is admittedly circular, although, it is claimed, in a nonvicious way.

In the 1967 lecture, "Natural Kinds," Quine argues that, once we have given up the epistemological project of showing the possibility of knowledge, the circularity becomes entirely natural. Quine suggests that natural selection can explain the happy fact that the human "innate subjective spacing of qualities"—that is, our disposition to accept certain "natural kinds" of things, which disposition accounts for our remarkable inductive success—exhibits a correspondence to or "special purchase" on the natural world. He responds to an anticipated objection:

> I shall not be impressed by protests that I am using inductive generalizations, Darwin's and others, to justify induction, and thus reasoning in a circle. The reason I shall not be impressed by this is

that my position is a naturalistic one; I see philosophy not as *a priori* propaedeutic or groundwork for science, but as continuous with
science. I see philosophy and science as in the same boat—a boat
which, to revert to Neurath's figure as I so often do, we can rebuild
only at sea while staying afloat in it. There is no external vantage
point, no first philosophy.[28]

Other philosophers have similarly encouraged the abandonment of foundationalist epistemology on various grounds, some of
them arguing with Quine that metaphilosophical circularity is not
vicious.[29] The circularity with which we are more immediately concerned is different, however. If naturalistic epistemology, in the
process of studying human knowledge as a phenomenon, conceives
of knowledge as serving biotic functions in a way that implies that
the validity of judgment is determined by the judgment's relation to
biological need or survival, and not determined by a relation to the
independent character of the object, then naturalistic epistemology
is antirealist. But if this is so, then the assertions of naturalistic
epistemology must themselves be interpreted in this way, for example, as valid in the sense of serving organismic needs. Any attempt
on the part of naturalistic epistemologists to ascribe to their own
utterances a realist validity would then generate a self-contradiction. (This self-reflexive problem arises, as we will see, for all
explicit assertions of positive antirealism, not just for naturalistic
varieties.)
    Now, naturalism becomes antirealist in this way only if two
conditions are fulfilled. First, *all* judgment must be interpreted naturalistically, implying that theorizing serves biological needs just as
perception does. Here some naturalistic epistemologists make their
escape from the self-referential circle, although it is not clear that
the exemption of part of the cognitive apparatus from a functional
description can be justified.[30] Second, the biological functions that
cognition serves must be such that a realist interpretation of validity is blocked. Simply put, it must be that in some cases it is better
for the organism to accept a belief that is not valid with respect to its
object, or whose validity with respect to its object cannot be known,
than not to accept it.[31]
    This second point hides complexities. The naturalistic
epistemologist may allow that judgmental validity serves the organism's needs, many of which may be subsumed under the need to survive. But it may be claimed that the organism needs, at least much
of the time, to make judgments that are true in a realist sense to
survive. So, rather than truth being reduced to survival value, real-

ist truth explains survival value. This is not problematic as long as the naturalist makes clear distinctions among kinds of judgments and restricts the range of this explanation. This explanation—of survival value by truth—although highly plausible in the case of perceptions, would raise problems if applied to more abstract cognitions. Is the survival value of *all* human beliefs to be explained by the truth of those beliefs? Is it always "good" for the organism to believe what is true in a realist sense? Would it be beneficial to survival to believe that there is no God, that morality is a changeable human convention, or that the quantum mechanical description of the world is in principle complete? There certainly appear to be truths, belief in which is survival irrelevant, and others that are actually harmful, at least in the short run.

This point can be pushed further to open up the thorny problem of how the naturalistic epistemologist can conceive of truth at all. For if naturalism seeks to apply to all human judgment, then it must account for the norms of judgment, which are, after all, phenomena appearing in human judgment. This raises the question of how naturalism can adequately and consistently conceive of any norms, e.g. truth, goodness, rightness, validity. This is the classical problem afflicting materialism back to the ancient Greek Democritus or, among the moderns, Hobbes, and it remains a difficulty even for our vastly more complex scientific naturalism. Must the naturalistic epistemologist ultimately identify the validity of judgment with the efficacy of judgment, with survival value, with utility with respect to certain needs? This question is troubling as well for naturalistic process philosophers like John Dewey. The problem can be put this way: How can the norm by which a process is to be judged, itself be a product of that process?

Now, some naturalists have developed more complex approaches that avoid this problem by restricting the scope of their naturalistic explanations. Abner Shimony has urged that naturalistic epistemology be augmented with analytic epistemology and a dialectical method, which he calls "integral epistemology," thereby removing the self-referential problem.[32] Nor does the foregoing discussion speak to the adequacy of other forms of monism or "closing the circle," which employ either a mentalistic or other nonphysicalistic metaphysics, because their accounts of judgment are not constrained by what we traditionally think of as biological categories. The most prominent examples of this attempt to harmonize the natural scientific worldview and mentalistic considerations trace their lineage back to Alfred North Whitehead and Peirce, as we will see.

However, to the extent that an epistemology is entirely naturalistic, this antirealist circularity remains. Interestingly, a wide bed is thereby made, in which odd bedfellows find themselves; namely, "scientific" naturalists like Quine, on the one hand, and "postmodernists" like Michel Foucault and Jean-François Lyotard, on the other. For Foucault's analysis of norms of validity (e.g., of knowledge) within the context of power, and Lyotard's description of validity as "performativity," hence as "legitimation by power," are characteristically *naturalist* accounts.[33] Descriptively at least, they refuse to permit an idealized category—the normative, the prescriptive, the ratified, justified, valid, true, right, and so on—to be established outside the realm of the observable, the palpable, the social, the political, the realm of force, power, change, and so forth. Norms like the true, good, and the valid are thus denied their special status and brought back into nature, or flux, or experience, or social relations, or semiosis. Although the habit of thinking of postmodernism in relation to the traditionally anti-naturalistic movements of phenomenology and German idealism makes this comparison with naturalism seem outlandish, it should not. For the primary inspiration for postmodernism, and the source of its critique of norms, was himself a naturalist; that is, Friedrich Nietzsche.[34]

Pragmatism

My sole concern at this juncture is to point out the antirealist nature of pragmatism. This is not to say that any philosophy which incorporates pragmatism is antirealist, because doctrines can be combined in ways that mitigate their individual tendencies. But pragmatism itself, independent of other doctrines, is antirealist, and when combined with other, realist conceptions, will continue to exert an antirealist force.

As we will see in discussing Peirce, pragmatism can be defined as a theory of meaning; namely, the theory that the meaning of a sign or concept is its role in the guidance of conduct. More precisely, pragmatism makes a sign's meaning equivalent to the set of conditional predictions, whose antecedents are experimental and whose consequents are observations, that results from the acceptance of the sign. For example, to predicate "alive" of a man is to predict that if we hold a mirror under his nose, it will fog up; if we listen to his chest, we will hear a heartbeat; if we reach for his wallet, he will flinch; and so forth. Such a theory of meaning inevitably leads to a theory of knowledge and truth, for 'knowledge' and 'truth' are them-selves signs whose meaning pragmatism serves to determine.

William James, who first popularized the term and the doc-trine "pragmatism," has given us one of its most obviously an-tirealist interpretations. In his 1906 lectures published as the book *Pragmatism*, he presents what he takes to be the pragmatist theory of truth: "Purely objective truth, truth in whose establishment the function of giving human satisfaction in marrying previous parts of experience with newer parts played no role whatever, is nowhere to be found. The reasons why we call things true is the reason why they *are* true, for 'to be true' *means* only to perform this marriage-function. The trail of the human serpent is thus over everything."[35] Because truth dwells in the order of human activity and human activity is governed by what is "good," truth is "one species of the good. . . . The true is whatever proves itself to be good in the way of belief, and good, too, for definite, assignable reasons."[36] James allows that truth is agreement between idea and reality. So in a sense, he is a realist. However, he continues, "To 'agree' in the widest sense with a reality *can only mean to be guided either straight up to it or into its surroundings, or to be put into such work-ing touch with it as to handle either it or something connected with it better than if we disagree.* Better either intellectually or practi-cally!"[37] Last, James literally collapses the norm "true" into efficacy or expediency. He writes, "'The true,' to put it very briefly, is only the expedient in the way of our thinking, just as 'the right' is only the expedient in the way of our behaving. Expedient in almost any fashion; and expedient in the long run and on the whole of course. . . ."[38]

Peirce was at pains to distance himself from what he regarded as James's antirealist tendency. This is not to say that James intended antirealism and all its consequences; he certainly did not. There is more to his pragmatism than indicated in the preceding quotations. Like Peirce, he regarded verification and usefulness in the long, not the short, run, as essential to the pragmatic notion of truth. For all the pragmatists, the relatedness of truth to purpose is subtle and complex and must be distinguished from the mere "satis-faction" of needs. Not to mention that they did not intend pragma-tism as a comprehensive doctrine, but a component of a systematic philosophy, to be supported and framed by other ideas. This is espe-cially true for Dewey and Peirce, who employed a process meta-physics to augment pragmatism.

In a similar vein, Dewey characterized knowledge as "war-ranted assertibility,"[39] a characterization that is apparently antirealist. Yet he could at the same time conceive of knowing as the leading edge of an active process of actualizing the possibilities of known objects. The former is a, so to speak, "subjective" formulation of knowledge in terms of what we count as evidence, the latter is an "objective" characterization in terms of the nature of the objects of our knowledge. The latter follows Peirce's definition of pragmatism as the interpretation of ideas through their contribution to the "development of concrete reasonableness," the evolutionary "becoming continuous" of the world (CP, 5.4) So, the pragmatist account of truth and knowledge can be formulated in objectivist as well as subjectivist terms.

It is in this objectivist spirit that Dewey claims in *Experience and Nature* that human culture, in the form of art, actually fulfills nature. Encouraging us to adopt the modern, anti-Greek notion that creation is prior to and higher than mere contemplation, he writes,

> It would then be seen that science is an art, that art is practice. . . .
> When this perception dawns, it will be a commonplace that art . . .
> is the complete culmination of nature, and that "science" is properly a handmaiden that conducts natural events to this happy issue. . . . Thought, intelligence, science is the intentional direction of natural events to meanings capable of immediate possession and enjoyment; this direction—which is operative in art—is itself a natural event in which nature otherwise partial and incomplete comes fully to itself; so that objects of conscious experience when reflectively chosen, form the "end" of nature.[40]

Here we see a philosophy that incorporates an apparently antirealist pragmatism into a broader naturalism that seeks to leave behind all relativism and subjectivism. However, although this incorporative view of Dewey's may be beautiful and immensely satisfying, what reason is there for believing that it is *true*? We have a right to be deeply skeptical of Dewey's claim, which expresses the virtually mythical view that nature lacks something human art and science can provide, as if nature, like the god of some theologies, needed the mirror of worship and created human beings for the purpose.[41]

Dewey is making recourse to a monistic metaphysics as a context for his pragmatism; we will see that Peirce does the same. The various ways of augmenting, framing, and using the pragmatist notion of judgmental validity in a putatively realist system can save pragmatism from the charge of antirealism only if the resulting system can stand the test of truth. That is, to use pragmatic coin, do these various systematic employments of pragmatism *work*? Do Peirce's and Dewey's systems make any sense? If they do not, then it may be because their pragmatism exerts an antirealist pressure that they cannot, however they try, successfully ameliorate. If a philosopher employs a doctrine that would appear to have certain problematic implications, but claims that it does not have those implications because of its incorporation in a whole system of fantastic ideas, then it seems that we have a right to disagree with that philosopher's sanguine attitude toward the doctrine in question. The stakes in this discussion are high, for a true pragmatic realism *would solve the problem of knowledge.* That is what the classical pragmatists thought they achieved. But, if that union of pragmatism and realism is bought at the price of our accepting other conceptions of mind, truth, or of the universe that are implausible or unsupportable, then there is a problem in the original program of uniting the two.

All other things being equal, pragmatism is antirealist. Pragmatism makes the validity of judgment relative to contexts established by action, by action's means or ends. Even if, as Peirce claimed, the "nominal" definition of truth remains the agreement of idea with reality, the criterion of that agreement for the pragmatist is the role of the idea in the guidance of conduct or the realization of purpose. Peirce will make the point quite clearly: the notion of a belief's being true of an object without the possibility of our knowing its truth is, from the pragmatist viewpoint, absurd.

Pragmatism has the interesting role among our three prominent antirealisms of being often united with the other two. Sometimes pragmatism is combined with relativism, so that the validity of judgment is made relative to the purposes of the actions of some community. Other times pragmatism becomes the natural ally of naturalism, as when it is claimed that judgments are valid when they satisfy needs that human beings naturally have. In Chapters Three and Four we will see the limits of pragmatism's prospects as an ally of realism in the task of justifying philosophical knowledge. In its role as ally of antirealism, we will follow pragmatism throughout the rest of this study.

Relativism

Relativism is the most important form of contemporary antirealism. I will argue that some recent attempts to show that relativism is nonsensical, or that consistent adherence to it is impossible, are insufficient to discredit it. Relativism remains a potent, undomesticated antirealist force.

There are many versions of relativism. I will present what seems to me the most fundamental and influential. Let us assume, as the relativist argument does, that the validity of every judgment, J, is dependent on or *relative* to the validity of some other judgment or set of judgments or perspective, P. If so, then the validity of the set of judgments or perspective, P, is also relative to the validity of some other set of judgments or perspective, Q, which is likewise dependent on the validity of another set of judgments or perspective, R, and so on. If so, then we can never complete our validation of the original judgment, J. So, the relational character of judgmental validity leads to one of two conclusions: either we cannot validate any judgment or we accept a relativistic notion of validity so that J is "valid with respect to P."

One way to formulate this problem has been dubbed the "Münchhausen Trilemma" by Hans Albert, in which the quest for complete validation seems to lead to an unhappy choice between three options.[42] The first is that there is an infinite regress of judgments and perspectives, so that we can never judge any judgment as adequately validated. The second is that the trail of validation terminates in a first principle or set of first principles, which, because they are first, cannot in principle be validated. The third appears to terminate in first principles that are valid, but this appearance is due to the fact that the principles presume the validity of the judgments whose validation is sought, and so the apparent validation begs the question or is circular.

Note that the trilemma presupposes a fundamental relativist point.[43] The point is that the validity of a belief can be established only by reference to other beliefs. Of course there is a difference between claiming that the validity of a belief is relative to other beliefs and that *our knowledge of* the validity of a belief is relative to other beliefs; one can claim that we know validity through, so to speak, coherence of beliefs, but the validity holds independent of that coherence.

Two very interesting recent attacks on relativism deserve mention here. A long-standing antirelativist strategy is to show that relativism would undercut beliefs in certain things that nobody, including antirealists, can afford to abandon, in particular certain indispensable norms, like truth or goodness. This argument attempts to show that no one is in fact a consistent relativist. As teachers of philosophy we presumably have all tried to show students expressing a facile moral relativism that they themselves abandon relativism when it comes to judging crimes either directed at themselves or especially heinous. I imagine that Hitler, Stalin, Pol Pot, and Idi Amin have made many an exemplary classroom appearance in service of this point.

One version of this antirelativist strategy is the attempt to catch the antirealist in a "performative contradiction," to show that the antirealist's intellectual activities imply a realist adherence to norms of argument. This has been made famous by Karl-Otto Apel and Jürgen Habermas.[44] Without going into the details of this very interesting argument, its principle is that certain forms of human communication presuppose an implicit commitment of all participants to certain beliefs and ethical norms. For example, participation in argumentative discourse presupposes that all parties accept that there is a difference between reason and force, and that only the former counts within the bounds of the argument. Therefore, within such an argument the assertion of any antirealist view that precludes or effaces such commitments is in effect a self-contradiction, hence irrational. So, it would seem that relativism is irrational.

The problem with this argument is the scope of its conclusion. First, it affects only explicit denials of realist norms. But many forms of relativism or antirealism try to avoid any explicit positive assertion. The Apel-Habermas argument does not affect such strategies. Second, as Habermas himself recognizes, this contradiction does not prove the truth of realism, but only its indubitability. It shows that certain norms are indispensable—which is certainly significant—but not that they are valid or true.[45] Third, it serves as no argument against any form of antirealism aiming to question the very principles of argumentation that, Habermas claims, provide the structure of discourse. It may be, of course, that such questioning can never issue in an explicit, positive, and consistent statement about the invalid nature of those principles. To the project of questioning those very principles, however, this is no disqualification. In other words, I take the Apel-Habermas argument to be a very instructive exposition of the presuppositions of inquiry, an exposition that, in principle, cannot validate those presuppositions. It helps to define the circle in which it dwells, but it does not demonstrate that relativism is false and realism is true.

A different, but not unrelated view, is that the notion of fundamentally different perspectives presumed by the most radical forms of relativism is incoherent in principle. The most famous exponent of this view is Donald Davidson. Davidson argues, in his now classic essay, "On the Very Idea of a Conceptual Scheme"(1974), that, "Given the underlying methodology of interpretation, we could not be in a position to judge that others had concepts or beliefs radically different from our own."[46] The project of sensibly interpreting the expressions of a speaker demands that we maximize agreement between that speaker and ourselves, that we ascribe most of our beliefs about the world to our interlocutor. In other words, "charity is not an option," it is a necessity. This does not preclude disagreement, but it necessitates that disagreements occur in the context of broader and more fundamental agreements. So, we could never have sufficient reason to ascribe to another person a set of fundamental concepts—a "conceptual scheme"—that radically differs from our own.

In another essay, Davidson augments this reasoning to make it clear not only that we must believe that we and any speaker share beliefs, but that those beliefs must actually be mostly true. He employs the idea of an "omniscient interpreter"—an idea about which, Davidson believes, there is "nothing absurd"—who could know the truth about the objects of belief and correctly interpret the beliefs of believers.[47] Because it cannot be that such an interpreter could know ("correctly interpret") that someone is massively wrong about the world, we must be mostly right in our beliefs. We all must ascribe our beliefs to a speaker to interpret him or her. The same is true of the omniscient interpreter, with the additional consequence that those ascribed beliefs must be actually true, because this interpreter is omniscient. The result is Davidson's famous claim that most of our beliefs are true, that "Belief is by nature veridical."[48] It is conceivable that "*each* of our beliefs may be false," but not *most* or *all* of our beliefs.[49] Error makes sense only against a background of shared beliefs that we must take to be true. Massive error would deprive a person "of things to go wrong about."

This argument is part of a larger strategy simultaneously to affirm realism and a coherence theory of knowledge, or as Davidson says, "correspondence without confrontation."[50] On the one hand, he asserts that truth is the correspondence of belief to reality and that beliefs are caused by their objects, yielding a "non-relativized, non-internal form of realism."[51] On the other hand, he insists that "coherence yields correspondence," that the only evidence for the truth of a belief is other beliefs. If he can maintain this combination, he would indeed have a coherentist realism, a synthesis as desirable as the pragmatic realism sought by Peirce. The standard objection to this combination, made especially by skeptical relativists, is that it would be possible for someone to have a system of coherent beliefs that is nevertheless false in a realist, correspondence sense. If so, then coherence cannot yield correspondence. It is this possibility, the possibility of a coherent but fundamentally false system of belief, which Davidson's argument is meant to deny.

Much is to be learned from this powerful line of argument. Nevertheless, I have one objection relevant to my purposes in this chapter.[52] Davidson's argument does indeed point out the senselessness of claims like, "Everything a person believes might be wrong" or "We cannot even understand their beliefs because they have a conceptual scheme unlike ours," or questions like, "What if the framework on which all our beliefs are dependent is wrong?" For we cannot understand what it would mean to be wrong about everything or almost everything, nor what it would mean for an interlocutor to share none or almost none of our beliefs. But the skeptical relativist's question need not be formulated in this objectionable way. That question is, Can it be possible that *any* belief (not *all* belief, collectively), despite being supported by coherence with other beliefs, might nevertheless be false in a realist, correspondence sense? The skeptic's answer is affirmative, and, I believe, Davidson must agree. He admits that any one of our beliefs may be false. Because, in his account, we hold beliefs true only on the basis of coherence with other beliefs, beliefs that cohere can nevertheless be false. This will be judged, of course, on the basis of yet other beliefs. Nevertheless, it is a rather powerful point for skepticism that *any* of our beliefs may be wrong, especially because this must also mean that *any set of beliefs* might be wrong, as long as the set numbers less than "most" of our beliefs.

Davidson's argument also points out the inadequacy of the metaphors often used to describe the relations among our cognitive elements or beliefs. Attempting to deal generally or globally with all such elements, we often speak of "frameworks" (for Rorty, "final vocabularies") of fundamental beliefs on which all others are epistemically dependent and of "bodies" or "systems" of beliefs. But are there such things as bodies or systems of beliefs, that is, are all of a person's beliefs somehow related? Do these bodies exhibit frameworks on which all beliefs are dependent? To what extent are beliefs epistemically dependent on other beliefs?

Suppose that two women, one who says that all reality is spiritual and evolving toward an objective perfection, another who says that that reality is material and all values are conventional, argue over coffee. One drops her spoon, the other catches it. As Davidson would indicate, the area of background agreement in their beliefs is enormous: Each believes the spoon will fall, that coffee is for drinking, that they are human beings, and so on. Lacking a way of counting beliefs, we cannot even begin to estimate the quantity of what they share. Nor is it clear how to compare the relative importance of their areas of agreement with their areas of disagreement. One might expect that metaphysical beliefs about reality, due to their extreme generality, ought to affect many other beliefs and so be particularly important. A disagreement over the nature of reality ought to weigh heavily toward making their respective belief "systems" different. That is, because spoons and people and houses are all members of reality, a difference in their beliefs about reality ought to mean that the two women believe very different things about spoons and people and houses.

But I think we would rightly guess that this is not in fact so, that the two women probably share most of the same beliefs about spoons and people and houses. Thus, in what sense are their beliefs about spoons and people and houses "dependent" on other more "fundamental" beliefs about reality per se? Could we make any general statements about which beliefs—presuming we could distinguish them in the first place, which we cannot—are so primary that disagreement over them makes for virtual *systemic* incompatibility, that is, incommensurability? I think we cannot do this.

The metaphor of a belief "framework" to which all other beliefs are relative, or a "body" of belief that can be wrong as a whole, is indeed problematic. But that does not derail the skeptical-relativist claim about the distributive vulnerability of all our beliefs, because this claim need not be formulated in the objectionable way. For the relativist need claim only that the validity of a person's beliefs is relative to some class of items, such as other beliefs or conventions, and not that they are *all* relative to *a single* item, such as *a* framework. At any rate, the possibility that any given chunk of beliefs, hence any belief, might be wrong with respect to reality despite coherence with other beliefs has not been ruled out. That leaves significant room for skepticism based on a limited but substantial relativism. This means that the difficulties inherent in the synthesis of coherentism and realism, which Davidson's argument was intended to eliminate, remain. If I am right, Davidson has not so much ruled out that we can be powerfully and deeply wrong about the world (despite the coherence of our beliefs), as he has thrown out the unity implicit in the very idea of a "system" or "framework" of beliefs.

The point of the forgoing discussions of Apel, Habermas and Davidson is to suggest that relativism is not dead. It remains a powerful, if problematic, philosophical force. The dynamic of the debate between realism and antirealism appears to be determined by the inability of the realist to justify, or perhaps even to give a sufficiently clear account of, his or her position in the face of antirealist criticism. Hence the realist tendency to retreat first from the attempted demonstration of realism's truth to the attempted demonstration of its indispensability, and then even further, to the purely negative task of showing that antirealism is incoherent or inconsistent. The defense of realism becomes a largely negative affair in which the strategy is to shift the burden of proof.

Antirealism, on the other hand, has a number of problems, one of which seems especially intractable. It is not clear how any statement of positive antirealism can fail to compromise its own validity. Some statements of positive antirealism are actually self-contradictory, like the claim that "It is absolutely true that all truths are relative." But such self-contradiction is rare. More commonly, positive antirealisms compromise or limit their own validity. For example, the claim that "The validity of all judgments is relative to communal convention" ought to be subject to itself and so be valid relative to convention. This is not a self-contradiction, but it does limit its own validity, thereby implying that it is *possible* that there are judgments whose validity is not conventional. Once the conventionalist claim is applied to itself, it is *not* contradicted by the claim that, "There is some judgment whose validity is not relative to convention." It is the point of such relativism to make it possible to eliminate the contradiction between a claim and its denial by replacing the bivalent truth values 'true' and 'false' with 'true-' and 'false-relative to a convention.' Hence the positive statement of relativism ("validity is relative to convention") and the realist denial of relativism ("there can be judgments whose validity is nonconventional") *fail to contradict on relativist grounds*. This is certainly not what the relativist intended.

So, the inability of realism to find a justification of its truth, as opposed to a vindication of its ineliminability, is matched by antirealism's inability not only to convince that realism is dispensable, but to state its own position consistently. The effect of the latter problem has been the increasing appeal to antirealists of negative and nonassertive metaphilosophical approaches, which avoid positive general claims. Nietzsche, Wittgenstein, Derrida, and Rorty represent this attempt, albeit in very different forms. But before turning to my major chapters, some historical orientation will be helpful. The following three sections will trace the recent problem of knowledge as it relates to the question of philosophical knowledge in its formulation by Hume, the alternative responses of Reid and Kant, and the alternative readings of Kant given by Schopenhauer and Peirce, which readings set the stage for pragmatism, Nietzsche, and Wittgenstein.

The Historical Background: Hume

If we want to discover a common perspective on Peirce, Nietzsche, Wittgenstein, Buchler, Derrida, and Rorty we have to return to a point in the history of philosophy preceding the divergence of the philosophical traditions to which these thinkers belong. The philosophy of Immanuel Kant is such a point.[53] But Kant's epistemology is itself a reaction to Hume. So we must go back to Hume. We will see that Kant's answer to the dilemma posed by Hume set the stage for what was to follow. For Kant begat not only Peirce, who begat Buchler, but also Schopenhauer, who begat both Nietzsche and (with assistance) Wittgenstein. Between the two giants of the late Enlightenment, Hume and Kant, it will be instructive to examine a relevant non-Kantian response to Hume, that of Thomas Reid. Reid is important for several reasons. A brief review of his philosophy of common sense will show that, despite his disagreement with Hume, the roots of that philosophy are in Hume himself. Hume is in an important sense a commonsense philosopher. Second, Reid influenced Peirce. In a 1905 exposition of his own "critical common-sensism," Peirce admitted to adhering, with "inevitable modification," to the views of ". . . that subtle but well-balanced intellect, Thomas Reid. . . ." (CP, 5.444) Peirce noted that there are "two rival ways of answering Hume," the "Critical Philosophy," represented principally by Kant, and "the Philosophy of Common-Sense" (CP, 5.505) Peirce makes it apparent that his critical commonsensism combines the two.

David Hume (1711–1776) is the most famous skeptic in modern European philosophy. His skepticism is rooted in an acceptance of the division of knowledge into two types, knowledge of the "relations of ideas" and knowledge of "matters of fact." This dualism was already present, in a different form, in the philosophy of John Locke. Hume, however, made the dualism the centerpiece of his view. His argument regarding knowledge can be seen in his *An Inquiry Concerning Human Understanding* (1748).[54]

For Hume all knowledge is either experiential knowledge of existing states of affairs, "matters of fact," or purely rational, non-empirical knowledge of the relations of concepts to one another, "relations of ideas." The latter can attain absolute certainty, but can give no information about anything that exists. It is Hume's analysis of the former, however, which is so profound and leads to his deep skepticism. All knowledge of matters of fact, hence all experiential or empirical knowledge, is based on causal inference. But our knowledge of the connection of cause with effect, and hence all predictive knowledge of the future and of the lawfulness of natural events, must also be either known through the logical relations of the ideas involved or through the experience of matters of fact. Upon analysis, we see that causal knowledge is not merely logical ("analytic" as Kant will later call it). Neither can it be known experientially, because knowledge of causal relations was introduced precisely to explain experiential knowledge! Differently put, the belief that the future will resemble the past is what allows us to get knowledge *from* experience and so cannot be validated *by* experience.

How then is this belief validated? It is not. For Hume, there is no rational justification of our knowledge of matters of fact, or of the belief that the future will resemble the past, hence of induction, hence of scientific knowledge. All such knowledge is based on habit or custom. The repetitive mental association of two ideas from past experience leads us, upon experiencing one, to expect the other. He concludes, "All inferences from experience, therefore, are effects of custom, not of reasoning."[55]

The most bleak, and most interesting, presentation of the implications of this view occurs in Hume's *A Treatise of Human Nature* (1739).[56] Rarely has such an intimate despair been publicly aired by a great philosopher. This passionate epistemological discussion immediately precedes Book II of the *Treatise*, "Of the Passions."

Hume reiterates his skeptical thesis. Our search for the "ultimate" principle of human understanding, the "tie" connecting cause and effect, disappointingly terminates in something that "lies merely in ourselves"; namely, habit.[57] This leaves us with a profound anthropocentrism: the ultimate principle lies not in "the external object," but in us. This principle is not, however, subjective in the sense of being personal or subject to our control. For habit is "nothing but one of the principles of nature," like "instinct" in animals.[58] Indeed, Hume says, "To consider the matter aright, reason is nothing but a wonderful and unintelligible instinct in our souls, which carries us along a certain train of ideas. . . . This instinct, 'tis true, arises from past observation and experience; but can any one give the ultimate reason, why past experience and observation produces such an effect, any more than why nature alone shou'd produce it? Nature may certainly produce whatever can arise from habit. . . ."[59]

If we accept this conclusion, then the understanding, at least in its epistemological attempt to understand itself, "entirely subverts itself." The understanding removes all reason for confidence in the work of the understanding. This leaves us in a truly abysmal dilemma. Either we engage in the "refin'd and elaborate reasoning" that seeks the ultimate justification for knowledge, that is, either we engage in philosophy and be led thereby to Hume's skeptical conclusions, or we "condemn all refin'd reasoning," contenting ourselves with the level of understanding characteristic of common life. The latter, Hume claims, means the end of philosophy and science, not to mention that this choice to condemn inquiry, because it is itself the consequence of the refined reasonings that it condemns, contradicts itself.[60] "We have, therefore, no choice left but betwixt a false reason and none at all." This is Hume's lowest point. He laments, "Where am I, or what? From what causes do I derive my existence, and to what condition shall I return? . . . I am confounded with all these questions, and begin to fancy myself in the most deplorable condition imaginable, inviron'd with the deepest darkness, and utterly depriv'd of the use of every member and faculty."[61]

But the unbearable gloom breaks: "Most fortunately it happens, that since reason is incapable of dispelling these clouds, nature herself suffices to that purpose. . . ." Events and needs invade the philosophical melancholy and return Hume to life. He continues, "I dine, I play a game of back-gammon, I converse, and am merry with my friends; and when after three or four fours' amusement, I wou'd return to these speculations, they appear so cold, and strain'd, and ridiculous, that I cannot find in my heart to enter into them any farther. Here then I find myself absolutely and necessarily determin'd to live, and talk, and act like other people in the common affairs of life."[62]

Hume makes the same point in the concluding chapter of his *Inquiry*. There he contrasts the "academical" or "mitigated" skepticism that he favors with Pyrrhonism, which in his account is an impractical skepticism that throws doubt on all reasonings and abstains from drawing any conclusion from experience or inquiry. Hume writes, "The great subverter of *Pyrrhonism* is action, and employment, and the occupations of common life. These principles may flourish and triumph in the schools. . . . But as soon as they . . . are put in opposition to the more powerful principles of our nature, they vanish like smoke. . . ."[63] The greatest objection to excessive skepticism is,

> that no durable good can ever result from it. . . . We need only ask such a skeptic, *What his meaning is? And what he proposes by all these curious researches?* . . . a Pyrrhonian cannot expect that his philosophy will have any constant influence on the mind: Or if it had, that its influence would be beneficial to society. On the contrary, he must acknowledge, if he will acknowledge any thing, that all human life must perish were his principles universally and steadily to prevail. . . . It is true; so fatal an event is very little to be dreaded. Nature is always too strong for principle.[64]

This is a form of pragmatism. The meaning and value of philosophical principles is to be found in the effect those principles have on life or action. If they have no effect, they are meaningless; if they have a bad effect, they are to be rejected.

To return to the *Treatise*, this pragmatic and commonsense abandonment of skeptical philosophy is actually its fulfillment. For, Hume tells us, "in this blind submission [to nature] I shew most perfectly my skeptical disposition and principles"![65] A radical doubt doubts its own project and its criteria for adequate knowing, thereby returning itself, momentarily at least, to ordinary, nonskeptical belief. Skepticism regarding our knowledge of nature has led us to accept the dictates of nature.

Because each alternative view is unjustified, because he must in any case be a fool, "as all those who reason or believe any thing *certainly* are," Hume decides he will be a fool for natural inclination, modifying it by critical reasoning only on occasions of practical necessity.[66] Yet, with another turn in the dialectic, Hume recognizes that philosophy itself is natural, at least for him. He finds himself, at certain times, "naturally inclined" to its reasonings. He feels an "ambition" to contribute to humankind's knowledge. He concludes: "Since therefore 'tis almost impossible for the mind of man to rest, like those of beasts, in that narrow circle of objects, which are the subject of daily conversation and action, we ought only to deliberate concerning the choice of our guide, and ought to prefer that which is safest and most agreeable."[67]

Using this standard, philosophy is a safer guide than "superstition" or religion. For, "the errors in religion are dangerous; those in philosophy only ridiculous."[68] Here Hume lets the matter rest in his *Treatise*. But the *Inquiry* adds that when, through these reasonings, the Pyrrhonian "awakes from his dream he will be the first to join in the laugh against himself and to confess that all his objections are mere amusement, and can have no other tendency than to show the whimsical condition of mankind, who must act and reason and believe, though they are not able, by their most diligent inquiry, to satisfy themselves concerning the foundation of these operations or to remove the objections which may be raised against them."[69] The impossible situation to which human judgment is condemned, pulled between the judgments of common practical life and the refined reasonings to which they inevitably lead, is not tragic but *comic*. Here Hume can rest.

This is the beginning of the modern commonsensist objection to philosophy. Philosophical inquiry is to be abandoned at the point where it contradicts mature, which is to say, *socialized natural instinct*. This is quite literally an antiphilosophical conclusion, albeit a mitigated or moderate one. Philosophy is illegitimate when it goes too far. When it does not, it can perform the beneficial service of pointing out to us the proper appreciation of the forms of knowledge, that is, of empirical or scientific knowledge of matters of fact and a priori knowledge of relations of ideas.

We may also mention that Hume thereby triggers the self-reflexive problems of any naturalistic epistemology. He began with a putatively internal, Cartesian or phenomenological analysis of whatever appears to the mind. This analysis turns up no possible justification of human knowledge. He then leaps out of this perspective to give a naturalistic account of human knowledge in terms of habit and instinct. This second-order account, he well recognizes, gives no justification of reasoning's truth, only an explanation of its existence. Yet the question remains, What is the justification of this second-order naturalism, which presumes a substantive view of nature and the mind's natural processes, a view that is unjustifiable and unknowable at the first-order level?

The famous last lines of the *Inquiry* epitomize the Humean division of knowledge that Kant would later seek to bridge. They also embody a problem with which Hume failed to come to terms. Hume concludes, "When we run over libraries, persuaded of these principles, what havoc must we make? If we take in our hand any volume of divinity or school metaphysics; let us ask, *Does it contain any abstract reasoning concerning quantity or number?* No. *Does it contain any experimental reasoning concerning matter of fact and existence?* No. Commit it then to the flames: For it can contain nothing but sophistry and illusion."[70] The problem Hume ignores is that, if we accept this imperative, we ought to torch the *Inquiry* and the *Treatise* as well. They concern neither empirical nor logico-mathematical reasoning. We will see that Kant tries to take this self-reflexive problem into account, but only up to a point. The self-immolation that Hume spares himself will be fully preformed only 170 years later by Wittgenstein at the end of his *Tractatus Logico-Philosophicus*, where Wittgenstein explicitly recognizes that, according to his own criteria of sense, the *Tractatus* itself must be nonsensical.

Answering Hume: Reid and Kant

We now turn to the work of David Hume's contemporary and fellow Scotsman, the Reverend Thomas Reid (1710–1796), the inventor of the modern philosophy of "common sense." Reid presents an important answer to Humean skepticism that anticipates subsequent and more fully appreciated philosophical work. This, despite Hume's response to Reid that "parsons" ought to leave philosophy to philosophers.[71]

In Hume, according to Reid, modern epistemology has come to the absurd conclusion of doubting the validity of virtually all human beliefs, for example, the beliefs in the existence of matter and in natural causation. "Poor untaught mortals," Reid ironically laments, who still believe "that there is a sun, moon, and stars; an earth, which we inhabit; country, friends, and relations. . . ."[72]

Reid's objection to this skepticism is that in it philosophy has overstepped its proper boundaries. He offers a striking figure: "the votaries of . . . Philosophy, from a natural prejudice in her favour, have endeavoured to extend her jurisdiction beyond its just limits, and to call to her bar the dictates of Common Sense. *But these decline this jurisdiction*; they disdain the trial of reasoning, and disown its authority; they neither claim its aid, nor dread its attacks"[73] (my emphasis). Furthermore, philosophy is no match for common sense, because it, "has no other root but the principles of Common Sense; it grows out of them, and draws its nourishment from them. Severed from this root, its honours wither, its sap is dried up, it dies and rots."[74]

Reid insists that there are principles which human beings are "under a necessity to take for granted," principles which cannot be proven or justified, and cannot be doubted without absurdity. Such principles are part of our "natural constitution," they are "instinctive beliefs," and function as the first principles of all our reasoning. "To reason against. . . ." these principles, he insists, "is absurd; nay, to reason for them is absurd. They are first principles; and such fall not within the province of reason, but of common sense."[75]

Like our contemporary Richard Rorty, Reid saw Descartes, Locke, Berkeley, and Hume as part of a single mistaken philosophical system; Reid called it the *Cartesian* system.[76] The errors of the Cartesian-Lockean representationalist epistemology inevitably lead to the skepticism of Berkeley and Hume. The Cartesian philosophy effectively denies the validity of all commonsense beliefs, including, ultimately, beliefs in the existence of matter and in natural causation. To the adherents of this philosophy, such common beliefs testify to the credulity of the "vulgar." To Reid they testify to philosophy's bankruptcy. His remarks seem to be a direct response to Hume.

> This opposition betwixt philosophy and common sense, is apt to have a very unhappy influence upon the philosopher. . . . He considers himself, and the rest of his species, as born under a necessity of believing 10,000 absurdities and contradictions, and endowed with such a pittance of reason as is just sufficient to make this unhappy discovery: and this is all the fruit of his profound speculations. Such notions of human nature tend to slacken every nerve of the soul, to put every noble purpose and sentiment out of countenance, and spread a melancholy gloom over the whole face of things. If this is wisdom, let me be deluded with the vulgar.[77]

Philosophy has made an error. It has overstepped its proper boundaries: It has tried to evaluate the validity of that on which it is based. Reid's answer to Hume is that the belief that the future will resemble the past is an instinctive belief of common sense and so is true but cannot be justified by reason.[78] Also instinctive are the beliefs that nature is uniform;[79] that two times two is four; that we have beliefs (although belief is both indefinable and inexplicable); that the sensation of heat indicates ("suggests" or signifies, as a "natural sign") that the quality of heat is present and independent of the sensation;[80] that a heavy object must fall; and that objects continue to exist when unperceived. To produce philosophical reasons to doubt these principles of common sense is "metaphysical lunacy."[81] It is philosophy's choice either to work with common sense, investigating and clarifying it, or to oppose it and be subjugated by force. Philosophy can be instinct's servant or its slave.[82] There is no third option.

Immanuel Kant's (1724–1804) answer to Hume's epistemic dilemma is more than familiar. Kant's new approach in his *Critique of Pure Reason* (1781) was to ask what are the necessary subjective conditions for any possible experience, thereby undercutting the empiricist tradition from which he otherwise drew so much. By 'subjective' I mean that Kant is interested in the conditions characteristic of the cognition of any rational creature; these conditions are not idiosyncratic or private, and it turns out, they constitute objectivity. Without denying the limited validity of naturalistic explanations of the possibility of experience given by Locke (and to some extent by Hume), Kant claimed that such explanations are not sufficient, that the subject, the experiencer, has its own requirements that must be satisfied by any potential object of human experience. Naturalistic conditions cannot suffice to explain how experience is possible.

This transcendental turn necessitated a distinction between objects as they are experienced, or appearances, and objects as they obtain independent of experience, or as Kant called them, *things in themselves*. This distinction has three great implications for Kant. First, our knowledge of objects can indeed be certain yet nontrivial, that is, our knowledge of objects as appearances can be a priori and yet synthetic. Hume is thereby defeated. Second, of things in themselves we can have neither experience nor knowledge. Thus Kant rejects all "dogmatic" metaphysics and accepts a kind of skepticism. But this very skepticism serves the master's purpose. Third, because knowledge and hence science cannot determine the things in themselves, including the will in itself of any rational being, science is prohibited from determining that the will in itself cannot be free. Thus morality remains possible. We can believe in a free will, a Supreme Intelligence, and an intelligible, moral world without fear of contradiction by the encroaching determinism of science. We can never know that these things are, but neither can science know that they are not. Kant has, as he says, "found it necessary to deny knowledge, in order to make room for faith."[83]

We need to remind ourselves of some of the elements of Kant's philosophy that are most relevant for the story we will be telling.

Most obviously important is his critical or transcendental *idealism*, in which the objects of knowledge and experience are shown to conform to the subjective conditions of the possibility of knowledge and experience. The reality we know is in some sense mental, that is, dependent on us. Hence the world we know is *our* world. This is a kind of anthropocentrism, a notion Kant himself evokes.[84] That of which we are conscious as experience, the phenomenon or appearance, is already mediated, is already the product of a synthesis. Because this synthesis is accomplished by us, in a sense we construct the world. Of course this construction is not conscious, it is not under our control. Nevertheless, it is our product. Knowledge, the known world, is dependent on our intellectual activity. The concomitant diremption of the object as thing in itself from the object as appearance leads to: (a) a kind of *phenomenalism*, that is, the view that what we experience and know are phenomena whose existence depends on us; (b) the belief that we do have unquestionably valid knowledge of phenomena (because they belong to us); and (c) skepticism regarding any judgments of the things in themselves.

The last point indicates the basis of Kant's critique of metaphysics and his limitation of philosophy and reason. Metaphysics, if conceived as a priori knowledge of what exists independent of experience, is illegitimate, even though it is the ultimate work of human reason. Kant is the spiritual father of all those movements of twentieth century philosophy that declare large chunks of philosophy to be senseless or incapable of attaining knowledge. Certainly, this was not new with Kant; it was the conclusion of empiricists back to Ockham, and skeptics from Pyrrho to Hume. But many of these had criticized much of what ordinary people and scientists would say is irreplaceably knowledge. Kant, on the other hand, left everyday knowledge and science standing, more or less; it was that pride of the philosophical district, metaphysics, that he wanted to raze. Differently put, Kant was the most famous practitioner of the modern art of discerning the limits of the intelligible or the cognizable in such a way that science and everyday knowledge largely fell inside those limits, whereas a large part of philosophy fell outside.

At the same time, Kant insists that we cannot stop doing metaphysics. Human inquiry is intrinsically dialectical or tragic. It is compelled to try to transcend its own limits, inevitably resulting in confusion. This compulsion cannot be denied.

In "The Antinomy of Pure Reason" in the *Critique of Pure Reason*, Kant attempts to show the dialectical results of seeking metaphysical knowledge of the natural world. He considers the questions of whether the world did or did not have a beginning in time, whether the world is or is not composed of simples, and most important, whether all events in the world are absolutely necessary or some are free. These "cosmical" metaphysical ideas (absolute beginning, simples, necessity, freedom) refer to the "absolute totality in the synthesis of appearances," or the "unconditioned totality" of the "world-whole."[85] The only way that reason can complete the series of conditions of any phenomenon is to carry the series back to the "unconditioned." Kant argues, "For a given conditioned, reason demands on the side of the conditions . . . absolute totality. . . . Reason makes this demand in accordance with the principle that if *the conditioned is given, the entire sum of conditions, and consequently the absolutely unconditioned* (through which alone the conditioned has been possible) *is also given.*"[86]

Reason wants to imagine the totality or completion of the series of conditions. This completion *is* the idea of the unconditioned.[87] But because appearances are given only through a "successive synthesis of the manifold of intuition," the unconditioned, or that which "will dispense with the need of presupposing other premisses," is not possible. The only way to hope to perform an imaginative regressive synthesis of the entire series of conditions is to determine a first member of the series (the beginning, the limit, the simple, etc.).[88] But doing so generates metaphysical illusion. This is an interesting way for Kant to determine the difference between rational inquiry that can increase knowledge, or science, and rational inquiry that can only generate confusion, or dogmatic metaphysics. The imagination of a completion of the series of conditions in experience is, in effect, to imagine an outside, something not contained in the series, something *un*conditioned.

A related point is made in Kant's fascinating Conclusion to his *Prolegomena to Any Future Metaphysics*, a brief presentation of the main argument of the *Critique* published in 1783.[89] Here Kant distinguishes between "bounds" (*Grenzen*) and "limits" (*Schranken*). Limitation implies mere incompleteness, a failure to exhaust one's project. To have bounds means to be able to confront or contact a stopping point, to run up against an outside space. Science can never finish its task, it will never find "completion in its internal progress," and so is limited. These limits exist because there is an outside, an other, which science cannot know, namely, things in themselves. But this fact does not constitute a bound for science because science *never meets up with* the things in themselves; they are entirely outside of its sphere.

> Natural science will never reveal to us the internal constitution of things, which . . . can serve as the ultimate ground for explaining appearances. Nor does that science need this for its physical explanations. Nay, even if such grounds should be offered from other sources (for instance, the influence of immaterial beings), they must be rejected and not used in the progress of its explanations. For these explanations must only be grounded upon that which . . .

can . . . be brought into connection with our actual perceptions according to empirical laws.[90]

Another way to put this is that, "Experience . . . does not bound it-self; it only proceeds . . . from the conditioned to some other equally conditioned thing. Its boundary must lie quite without it. . . ."[91]

However, reason, in metaphysics, seeks to determine the bounds of experience and reason itself. The transcendental ideas (soul, the cosmical ideas, God) "mark" these bounds. This boundary, Kant says, belongs both to the sensible and to the purely intelligible: "For this boundary belongs to the field of experience as well as to that of the beings of thought. . . ."[92] It is the "spot where the occupied space (viz., experience) touches the void, that of which we can know nothing (viz., noumena). . . ."[93] Although we cannot know anything of the beings signified by these ideas *in themselves*, we can know or determine what and how they are *for us*, that is, in relation to the world of appearance. With reference to the idea of God, Kant labels this approach "symbolic anthropomorphism," in contradistinction to traditional "dogmatic anthropomorphism."[94]

According to Kant we not only can, we must think these tran-scendental ideas. Reason cannot help but seek to determine the in-determinable. For *appearances are incomplete*.

> Reason . . . finds for itself no satisfaction because ever-recurring questions deprive us of all hope of their complete solution. . . . But [reason] sees clearly that the sensible world cannot contain this completion. . . . The sensible world is nothing but a chain of appear-ances connected according to universal laws; it has therefore no subsistence by itself; it is not the thing in itself, and consequently *must point to that which contains the basis of this appearance. . . .* In the cognition of [that] alone can reason hope to satisfy its desire for completeness in proceeding from the conditioned to its condi-tions.[95](my emphasis)

This point deserves some attention. At times Kant writes as if reason's search for the unconditioned were the result of the exten-sion of the goal of all inquiry—that goal being to find a condition for every phenomenon—to its maximum, the totality or completion of the series. Experience does not contain its bounds, but reason, in its regressive synthesis, seeks those bounds. Kant's metaphor here is the attempt to pass from the parts to encompass the whole. Inquiry, Icarus-like, fails to be content with its world of limitations and tries to fly too high, to go too far.

At other times, as in the preceding passage, Kant implies something different. He implies that appearances are intrinsically incomplete and so "point" beyond themselves. Here inquiry has not overstepped its bounds, rather it is responding to an insubstantiality, a privation or lack, *within* its normal sphere. Metaphysics is not merely inquiry gone too far, it is not merely a *"casual* enlargement in the progress of experience"(my emphasis). Rather it is reason's response to a condition that obtains within the sphere of normal inquiry.[96]

Returning to Kant's central aim, the transcendental ideas are also necessary because they alone keep us from the materialism, naturalism, and fatalism that would result from the identification of appearances with all of reality. This distinction serves two of reason's purposes: it encourages speculative or cognitive reason to seek to know more than it presently knows; and it leaves open the space for practical reason to determine the will, making moral life possible. In moral experience, in the practical employment of reason, we may grasp the thing in itself, because the apparent choice of the will *is* the will itself. There is a breakthrough, a transcendence, in willing that is not available in cognition. This must be taken very seriously: There is noncognitive transcendence in willing, although our *knowledge of* this transcendence must be limited and *not* transcendent.

Before leaving Kant, the parallel with common-sensism and the traces of naturalism in his work must be noted. Like Reid and Hume, Kant claims that our knowledge of the world of experience incorporates and depends on certain principles whose validity is not dependent on how things are independent of our knowing. These principles are not justifiable in the sense of realism, nor are they dispensable. Whence their validity, and their hold on us? For both Hume and Reid they are part of our natural constitution; for Hume they cannot be known to be true, for Reid they must be true.

For Kant the answer is more complex. These principles are the transcendental subjective principles of rational creatures. But this leaves Kant very close to saying, with Hume and Reid, that they are part of the *nature of reason*, part of the natural constitution of rational creatures. The principles in question, for Kant as for Hume and Reid, are indispensable, out of our control, and justified only in the sense that we cannot imagine human life or the objective world without them.

Kant is not a naturalist per se. The opposition of reason and nature is fundamental in his system; this is especially apparent in his moral philosophy. Nevertheless, like most modern philosophers he lapses into naturalism at certain points. For example, the concept of empirical sensation in the *Critique* is a naturalistic concept. For experience to occur there must be an effect of the object—the object independent of our experience—on our intuition. Hence, there must be a relation of the system of experience to an outside, a relationship that must itself be located in the natural order.[97] In the Conclusion to the *Prolegomena*, referring to reason's compulsion to transcend experience, Kant writes,

> "Such is the end and the use of this natural predisposition of our reason...whose generation, like every other in the world, is not to be ascribed to blind chance but to an original germ, wisely organized for great ends. For metaphysics, in its fundamental features, perhaps more than any other science, is placed in us by nature itself. . . ."[98]

And, as he writes a few pages later, "everything that lies in nature must be originally intended for some useful purpose."[99] The "natural end" of metaphysics is, ultimately, moral. Thus, the capacity of our faculty of knowing to extend itself where knowledge is impossible—which is to say, beyond nature—is part of our natural endowment, and receives its justification by serving a purpose designed by this nature. The apparent transcendence of nature is a natural purpose encoded in us by nature. (We will see the same idea in Nietzsche.)

To recapitulate partly, science, which investigates the series of appearances, cannot bound or justify itself. It is a self-contained series that knows no bounds. Only reason can think the bounds of experience and knowledge by means of its metaphysical markers. It thereby accomplishes important purposes, both cognitive and, especially, moral. If it assumes that these markers determine things in themselves, then reason is dogmatic (and wrong). If it recognizes them as its own necessary presuppositions, as determining how the series of conditions must be completed *for us*, and not in itself, then it is critical, that is, Kantian. And, of course, through writing and reading Kant's work, reason has somehow come to know all of this.

Reformulating Kant: Schopenhauer and Peirce

Arthur Schopenhauer (1788–1860), in *The World as Will and Representation* (1844), produced a reinterpretation of Kant that on one hand simplified and clarified Kant's system and on the other hand pushed Kant in a new direction.[100] He simplified Kant by reducing Kant's two forms of intuition and twelve categories of understanding to one principle, the principle of sufficient reason, applied in four different spheres. He did away with the transcendental machinery of the *Critique of Pure Reason* (the transcendental unity of apperception, modes of synthesis, schematism, etc.) He criticized Kant's notions of intuition and understanding—in which all experience of objects presumes thought, and all concepts concern objects of experience—substituting for them his own notion of perception, which alone has objects, and thought, which is the province of reason. Last, he called attention to Kant's inconsistency in making things in themselves the cause of sensations. Because causality obtains only within the realm of appearances, it cannot be a condition *of* appearances; causality is therefore applicable only to the objects of perception.

Schopenhauer's reformulated Kantian picture is one of the "world as my representation," the perceived world as constituted by the subject's principle of sufficient reason. This world is a "closed whole." Within it, all is relational, hence intelligible. The world as a whole has no explanation, no intelligible relation to anything outside it and unrepresented in it, because all intelligibility rests on the principle of sufficient reason. Intelligibility is, so to speak, "intraworldly."[101] Yet this intelligible world "mirrors" noumenal reality.

Here Schopenhauer takes his boldest and most famous steps. First, because plurality is a condition holding for representations only, the superrepresentational reality must not be subject to number, and hence must be one. There are no "things in themselves," there is only *the* thing in itself. Second, Schopenhauer identifies the thing in itself as the will, that is, unintelligible, unconscious, purposeless, endless striving, incapable of representation, and expressed most immediately in my embodiment, but also in the forces of nature. That my body is in space and time and that its movements are predictable is a matter of representation, but that what happens to my body *matters to me*, has overwhelming meaning for me, indicates that *representation does not exhaust existence*. The meaning of anything in the world, its importance, the command it has on our feeling—including the meaning of the world as a whole, which metaphysics seeks—rests on a relation to the will. Thus the meaning of the world, to cite a Schopenhauerian claim that Wittgenstein will repeat in his *Tractatus*, lies outside the world of representation, in its relation to the will.

We must be careful in trying to classify Schopenhauer as an idealist: He is both an idealist and a naturalist, and he is neither. The real world of experience is a subjective representation, as for Kant. But everything represented in it is also will, which, embodied, is nature. Everything is in nature.[102] Schopenhauer takes on characteristically naturalist elements: an evolutionary account of the relation of human to nonhuman functions that places human traits in a phylogenetic series; a denial of immortality; a philosophically rare attention to the meaning of the body and bodily experiences (e.g., sex); and a Hobbesian definition of goodness in terms of the passions.[103] His naturalism has an impact on his account of knowledge. Schopenhauer claims that "rational knowledge" is "a means for preserving the individual and the species, just like any organ of the body."[104] "The will is first and original," he writes, "knowledge is merely added to it as an instrument belonging to the phenomenon of the will."[105] In a sense, Schopenhauer has produced a naturalized version of Kant by applying what Kant says of human beings to all phenomena, namely, that their essence is "something absolutely free, in other words, a will."[106] And what after all is the will? It is not cognition, not consciousness, not perception. Neither is it matter. In other words, the ultimate reality for Schopenhauer does not answer to the usual philosophical predicates of mind or nature, hence idealism or naturalism. The most accurate description of Schopenhauer is that he is a metaphysical monist for whom ultimate reality is a nonmaterial, nonphysical force that embodies itself in nature. Human cognition is, however, utterly within nature, and so in this sense Schopenhauer is indeed a naturalist.

Schopenhauer had a strong influence on both Nietzsche and Wittgenstein. What is most relevant to my purpose is to see how Kant, via Schopenhauer, has shaped their thought.

For Nietzsche, Schopenhauer is both a great thinker and a severely limited one. His greatness lies in his rebellion against the main currents of German idealism by giving priority to the will and, thereby, to nature. In his 1874 essay "Schopenhauer as Educator," Nietzsche is critical of Kant's "skepticism and relativism," and all the more admiring of Schopenhauer for escaping the fatalistic effect of Kantianism, for turning from "skeptical gloom" to "tragic contemplation," to the greatness in suffering.[107] Schopenhauer's great limitation, of which Nietzsche became increasingly critical, was his asceticism, in which Nietzsche saw Schopenhauer's inability to liberate himself from Christianity and its inevitable nihilism. It is for this "negation of life" that Nietzsche eventually refers to

Schopenhauer as one of his "antipodes" (the other being Richard Wagner).

One of the Kantian notions, modified by Schopenhauer, that shows up in Nietzsche, is the conception of the natural world as a closed whole, a series of appearances with respect to which the mind is capable of thinking (although not of knowing) an outside, of asking what determines this whole. For Kant, the outside is populated by thinkable but unknowable things in themselves, including the ground of being, God. For Schopenhauer, it is the will that lies outside. For Nietzsche it is controversial whether one ought to say that the will to power is outside appearance (hence "metaphysical") or rather that the will to power constitutes or is identical to the collection of appearances.[108] Either way, the kinship with Schopenhauer is strong.

His protestations to the contrary notwithstanding, Nietzsche retains much of the idealism of Kant and Schopenhauer. He utterly rejects their moral idealism, of course, the idealism by which nature is conceived as embodying a moral order or as encouraging a moral response. But he retains the view that the world of human experience and knowledge is in some significant sense a human construction, which is a kind of epistemological idealism. At the same time, Nietzsche is a naturalist. This he inherits from Schopenhauer, who had shown how, given the right perspective, the Kantian system could be made partly compatible with naturalism. One could argue that this is the achievement of Peirce's reconstruction of Kant as well, hence that pragmatism and Nietzschean existentialism are both the result of a *naturalization of Kant*.

To see the Kantian influence in Wittgenstein we must distinguish between Wittgenstein's early and late works. The project of Wittgenstein's early *Tractatus* can accurately be described in Kantian terms as an inquiry into the conditions of the possibility of representation.[109] Schopenhauer's influence is strong in Wittgenstein's discussion of ethics and the meaning of the world at the end of that text. There we can see the Schopenhauerian idea of the world of representation as a closed whole, within which representational truth is possible and outside which the whole is grasped and evaluated by the will, never known by thought. Wittgenstein's denial that we can speak sensibly of ethics or of anything outside the factual world is a descendent of the Kantian project of drawing limits to human knowledge, with two especially significant differences: Wittgenstein is drawing limits to meaning, not knowledge, and unlike Kant, he admits that the act of drawing the limits of sense is itself nonsense.

The perhaps more intriguing question is the continuing influence of Schopenhauerian, and less directly of Kantian, ideas in Wittgenstein's later work. Here more controversial matters of interpretation are at stake which can be addressed only later. For the moment, the point can be expressed in two hypotheses. If Wittgenstein is in his late work a kind of relativist or contextualist, then there is a plausible connection to the idealism of Schopenhauer and Kant. *If* Wittgenstein is in his late work a kind of pragmatist, then there is a plausible connection to Schopenhauer's naturalistic pragmatism and to the primacy he gave the will. We will return to these big 'ifs' later.

Although the presentation of Peirce's philosophy must wait until the next chapter, some of the ways in which his work is a response to Kant may be described here.[110] As mentioned, there is historical reason for associating Schopenhauer and Peirce, despite their great philosophical differences. They are arguably the two greatest Kantians of the nineteenth century. Their reformulations of Kant altered the course of twentieth century philosophy, Schopenhauer's by influencing Nietzschean existentialism, and through it Heidegger, Sartre, Merleau-Ponty, and Derrida, not to mention Wittgenstein, and Peirce's by creating pragmatism and hence a crucial part of the "classic" American philosophical tradition.[111]

Peirce retained and reconstructed important features of the Kantian approach. He accepts the basic Kantian strategy for circumventing the Humean dilemma, namely, the idealization of the objects of knowledge. Common sense and science really do know, because the objects of knowledge are the product of a mental synthesis that is the same for all inquirers and experiencers. Yet, Peirce denies that anything that is real is unknowable, hence, he eliminates the distinction between the apparent object and the thing in itself. He does this by becoming, in one sense, more of an idealist than Kant, by making the thing in itself, the ultimately real, the eventual object of the agreement of all inquirers. Kant limited his idealism or constructivism to appearances; Peirce extends it to all realities by means of the community and the future.

At the very moments of sameness Peirce alters Kant. What Kant regarded as subjective conditions of experience are for Peirce characteristics of the things we know.[112] Kant's transcendental subjective conditions of knowledge are reduced by Peirce to the sign function.[113] All that is intrinsic to our way of knowing are the three modes of the sign and the three modes of inference. Peirce criticized Kant for believing that things in themselves are particular, thereby restricting generality to appearances, which are the product of an a priori synthesis. This restriction of generality to phenomena is what Peirce calls "nominalism" and it is for him the greatest sin of modern philosophy. Throughout his career, Peirce insisted on a Scotistic realism, and eventually on a metaphysical "synechism," both of which ascribed generality to things themselves. Peirce regarded this as absolutely necessary to an adequate account of knowledge and reality.

Finally, as we will see, what we might call *Kantian hope* remains essential to Peirce. That is, in attempting to justify scientific and philosophical inquiry we are led to certain ultimate presuppositions that inquiry must believe and that are incapable of validation as true. We can show only that they are not impossible, not contradictory, which leaves us free to believe in their validity. Consequently, for Peirce as for Kant, the ultimate justification for the answer to the question, "What can I know?" lies in the answer to the question, "What may I hope?"[114]

3

PEIRCE'S
(ANTI)REALISM

"He who would not sacrifice his own soul to save the whole world is . . . illogical in all his inferences. . . ."

—"The Doctrine of Chances"

Peirce cannot be adequately summarized at less than book length.[1] The volume of his published and unpublished writing is enormous,[2] a body of work all the more remarkable for the extremely difficult circumstances under which Peirce labored for much of his life.[3] More problematic for the interpreter is that Peirce wrote no magnum opus that announces its centrality to us as the proper focal point of his thought. Rather, there are essays, reviews, and notes covering many fields in philosophy and science scattered over six decades, a career containing many inconsistent and changed views. Justus Buchler commented that "we can find [Peirce] to say almost anything somewhere or other."[4] Peirce rightly referred to himself as "a mere table of contents, a very snarl of twine"(CP, 6.184). The interpreter is left to decide which texts constitute the "real" Peirce. Last, Peirce is particularly refractory to labels. He is a naturalist and an idealist, a pragmatist, a relativist in some respects, even a conventionalist, yet a realist in others, a common-sense philosopher and a neo-Kantian, a "prope-positivist" and a panpsychist. He is a major source for nonfoundational realism. Hence all the themes of the other philosophers in this volume are represented in Peirce's cornucopia.

A brief essay of interpretation can pick out only a small set of considerations organized about a central theme, woven through a few selected texts. I will focus on two moments in Peirce's history. The first and most important is the extremely fruitful decade from

1868 to 1878, when Peirce wrote some of his greatest essays, including the initial exposition of pragmatism. This period is bounded by two series of essays, one in 1868 and the other in 1877–1878, roughly bisected by an important 1871 review. Second, I will refer to his late clarifications of pragmatism, by that time renamed "pragmaticism," from 1902–1906.

Our theme will be Peirce's maximally attenuated realism. Peirce claims to be a realist even though his writings are a reservoir of antirealist doctrines, especially the critique of immediacy (of which Peirce gives, in my view, the canonical formulation), relativism, pragmatism, and a kind of skepticism he called "fallibilism." Peirce razes the traditional havens of realism, forcing realism into a more Spartan home.[5] His is a most "anti" realism. His subtlety, his refusal to rely on the usual forms of foundationalism, forces Peirce to turn to deeper supports for his synthesis of realism and antirealism, famously, to pragmatism. But we will see that Peirce's pragmatism is tied to conventionalism. Hence Peirce's pragmatic realism, and with it his philosophical system, whatever its intrinsic satisfactions, cannot succeed in justifying the possibility of realist philosophical knowledge.

After reviewing Peirce's early theory of cognition, the critique of immediacy, and the fallibilism to which they led in the first section, we will examine in the following four sections Peirce's pragmatism, his naturalism, his theory of truth as convergence, and his conception of philosophy and the foundations of inquiry.

The Semiotic Theory and Fallibilism

Peirce's 1867–1878 writings are based in part on his semiotic theory of cognition, which he began to develop in the 1867 essay, "On a New List of Categories." There he formulated his triadic notion of the sign. Peirce accepts the Kantian claim that the function of concepts is to "reduce the manifold of sensuous impressions to unity and that the validity of a conception consists in the impossibility" of doing so without that concept (CP, 1.545). The concept of the present, rendered by the word *IT*, which is simply the given manifold, is what philosophers normally indicate by the word *substance*. The task of the understanding is then to reduce the IT to unity by means of a proposition, that is, by joining a predicate to the IT-subject. This is accomplished through the concept of *being*, here understood only as the copula, hence "empty" of content. Being is the reduction to unity, the accomplishment of the work of the proposition. The predicate is some determinate concept by means of which the unity of being is applied to the indeterminate IT.

The predicate is of three types: reference to a ground or quality; reference to a correlate or an other; and reference to an interpretant, which represents the ground or quality *as representing* the same correlate that the interpretant represents. "Such a mediating representation," Peirce writes, "may be termed an *interpretant*, because it fulfils the office of an interpreter, who says that a foreigner says the same thing which he himself says" (CP, 1.553). Thus, to use Peirce's example, in a French-English dictionary next to *homme* we find "man." *Man* represents the word *homme* as representing the same entity that *man* itself represents. Interpretants establish synonymy.

This analysis is the basis of Peirce's triadic conception of the sign: A sign is *something* that stands *for* something *to* someone. Peirce bases all cognition on this structure. As he will say in a subsequent essay, "all thought is in signs" (CP, 5.253). This is crucial for what is to follow, for if a cognition is a sign, then it is complex, relational, and can function only in a series of signs. There can be no such thing as a lone meaningful sign.[6]

But the sign structure has even wider significance for Peirce. Although Peirce agrees with Kant that the "fundamental categories of thought" must come from formal logic (CP, 1.561), he characteristically changes the significance of this position, claiming that, "logic has for its subject-genus all symbols" or, more precisely, the "reference of all symbols to their objects . . ." (CP, 1.559). Decades latter, in commenting on his discussion of 1867, Peirce wrote,

> I came to see that Kant ought not to have confined himself to divisions of propositions . . . but ought to have taken account of all elementary and significant differences of form among signs of all sorts, and that, above all, he ought not to have left out of account fundamental forms of reasonings. At last, after the hardest two years' mental work that I have ever done in my life, I found myself with but a single assured result of any positive importance. This was that there are but three elementary forms of predication or signification, which as I originally named them . . . were *qualities* (of feeling), (dyadic) *relations, and* (predications of) *representations*. (CP, 1.561)

Everything is to be interpreted through this triadic scheme, which remained the guiding thought of Peirce's career to the very end. Developed out of his notion of the sign, it was eventually given a general formulation in his "phenomenology," for which all phenomena are taken to exhibit Firstness or sheer quality, Secondness or resistance or otherness, and Thirdness or relation or representation.

The 1868 essay, "Questions Concerning Certain Faculties Claimed for Man," is arguably Peirce's first great work. Its aim is to deny that we have intuitions. An intuition would be a cognition or thought of an object that is determined solely by that object and not at all by any preceding cognition or thought. Intuitions would be, in my language, cognitions immediately related to and determined by what they cognize, privileged cognitions. Peirce tries to show that, in the process by which an object initiates a series of cognitions, prior to any cognition we might try to designate as the first cognition of the series, we could always find an earlier cognition. There is no discriminable first cognition, undetermined by earlier cognitions.

We must be clear about what Peirce is *not* denying. He is not denying the fact that mental events are themselves facts, specifically, that cognitions have a "feeling" or a "material quality." Peirce distinguishes the material quality or feeling of a cognition from its meaning. Second, he is not denying that there is a given "in" consciousness. On the contrary, he assumes there is, and later rests his notion of "perceptual judgments" on it. Last, he is not denying that external objects affect cognition and that series of cognitions begin with some perceptual response to something outside of consciousness. His point is that the perceptual given is a product of a process whose nature we cannot discern. He is denying that the beginning of that process is discrete, that there is a discriminable first moment of the series determined solely by the object without interference from earlier cognition, that is, from semiosis.[7] Thought is a continuum, that is, something all of whose parts have parts. Continua do not have discrete, simple, unanalyzable members. Although mental elements "in themselves," taken as facts or qualities, are simple and unanalyzable, as meanings or elements of consciousness they are not. We are conscious of individual cognitions only in their connection with subsequent cognitions (CP, 5.289). As Peirce will later write, the continuum of inference is driven by "a real effective force behind consciousness" (CP, 5.289), of which we have no knowledge.[8] Therefore there is no discrete first member of a perceptual process (CP, 5.181).

Peirce makes other important denials in "Questions." One to which he will repeatedly return is that there is no concept of the absolutely incognizable. We cannot understand or cognize the meaning of something claimed to be incognizable under all conditions for all time. If all thoughts are signs, there can be no meaningful sign representing "that which is incapable of being represented." Connected with this is that we cannot explain anything through a concept of the inexplicable. As he wrote in a subsequent essay, Peirce denies any elements of knowledge that are "ultimate, independent of aught else, and utterly inexplicable—not so much from any defect in our knowing as because there is nothing beneath it to know." He makes this denial because the sole justification for the introduction of a concept is its ability to explain experience; this is the meaning of "abductive" inference, the inference from a fact to a condition that would explain it. If so, then, "It is, however, no explanation at all of a fact to pronounce it *inexplicable*. That, therefore, is a conclusion which no reasoning can ever justify or excuse" (CP, 1.139).

Peirce also denies that we are conscious of images, meaning absolutely determinate images or cognitions (CP, 5.312). Because all cognition is a continuum of signs, and nothing continuous can be wholly determinate, cognition is always partly indeterminate. The *meaning* of every thought and every sign (as opposed to the signs' material quality), is partly indeterminate. It is, of course, not *wholly* indeterminate.

Indeterminacy can be of two kinds, vagueness and generality. For Peirce every sign, every cognition, must be both vague and general. Generality means that the sign is predicable of more than one individual. As described in Chapter Two, vagueness means that the sign is not determinate with respect to all possible traits or predicates. If a cognition were absolutely precise it would have to represent its object as either having or not having every one of all possible objective traits, so that no possible trait would be left undecided. But, Peirce claims, it is clear that our cognitions are never like this. Cognitions represent their objects as having or not having *some* traits, but they never exhaust the possibilities. We are, for example, perfectly capable of identifying an acquaintance without being able to list all his or her visible traits. The cognition is left indeterminate in respect to the remaining possibilities.

Last, we have no power of inner intuition or introspection. Our knowledge of our selves is inferential and semiotic, like our knowledge of everything else. This is connected to Peirce's denial that signs can be private and idiosyncratic in their meaning. Hence Buchler's name for Peirce's epistemology: "public empiricism."[9] This theme reappears most famously in Wittgenstein's attack on the

notion of a private language in the *Philosophical Investigations*.
Long before Wittgenstein and Heidegger, and even before Frege,
Peirce objected to the subjectivism of grounding meaning in private
mental experience and introspection.[10]

The striking implications of Peirce's denial of intuition and his
semiotic theory of cognition are drawn in the next essay in the 1868
series, "Some Consequences of Four Incapacities." There Peirce concludes that "the mind is a sign developing according to the laws of
inference" (CP, 5.313). He explains that since man is thought and
thought is signs, "There is no element whatever of man's consciousness which has not something corresponding to it in the word . . . the
word or sign which man uses is the man himself . . . that every
thought is an external sign, proves that man is an external sign. . . .
Thus my language is the sum total of myself; for the man is the
thought" (CP, 5.314).[11] So Peirce's theory of cognition is also an
incipient semiotic theory of the self.[12]

This semiotic conception forms the background for Peirce's fallibilism. A personal statement about fallibilism from an unpublished
manuscript of 1897 is useful to keep in mind.

> Only once, as far as I remember, in all my lifetime have I experi-
> enced the pleasure of praise . . . and . . . it was meant for blame. It
> was that a critic said of me that I did not seem to be *absolutely sure
> of my own conclusions*. Never, if I can help it, shall that critic's eye
> ever rest on what I am now writing; for I owe a great pleasure to
> him. . . . For years . . . I used for myself to collect my ideas under the
> designation *fallibilism*. . . . Indeed, out of a contrite fallibilism,
> combined with a high faith in the reality of knowledge, and an
> intense desire to find things out, all my philosophy has always
> seemed to grow. (CP, 1.10–11)

Peirce claims that, "an absolute termination of all increase of
knowledge is absolutely incognizable, and therefore does not exist . . .
no one can maintain, that it is possible to cognize everything, that is,
that at some time all things will be known" (CP, 5.330). Indeed, it is
worse than that: "in no possible state of knowledge can any number
be great enough to express the relation between the amount of what
rests unknown to the amount of the known . . ." (CP, 5.409).

Peirce's fallibilism has at least three components. First, none of
our beliefs is precisely true, if precision is taken in an absolute sense
as the absence of indeterminateness (CP, 5.382, n. 1). Second, nothing is certain, even a priori knowledge, such as mathematics,
because mistakes in reasoning can never be ruled out.[13] Third, to

claim that some belief is known to be true a priori is simply to assert that whatever I have a very strong inclination to believe must be true. The resort to *a priori* truth is, for Peirce, nothing more than the canonization of instinctual belief, that is, of belief toward which I am instinctively inclined!

This fallibilism is epitomized in Peirce's famous dictum, "Do not block the way of inquiry" (CP, 1.135). This injunction puts the preceding claims in the form of a normative principle. According to Peirce, inquiry is blocked by belief in certainty, unknowable or incognizable real things, ultimate and inexplicable things and precise and inviolable law. We block inquiry whenever we believe that knowledge is complete, either collectively or distributively, or unattainable. By collective (or extensive) completeness of knowledge, I mean a state in which all things are known. By distributive completeness, or completeness in depth, I mean a state in which any thing we know is known finally, that is, completely or certainly. Peirce is saying not only that we can never know all things collectively, but that we can never know everything about *any individual thing*. To claim that any area, any subject matter, no matter how small, has been exhausted by inquiry is unacceptable to Peirce.

We ought not regard this Peircean imperative as an ennobling but innocuous counsel of intellectual virtue. It is an extremely powerful theoretical injunction. If we accept it we are prohibited from ever asserting certainty, for example, by claiming that a given result is impossible; from asserting a claim's truth while admitting that it can never be justified; from admitting the existence of anything that is in principle inexplicable or unknowable; from accepting any portion of our knowledge as settled or complete; from regarding any claim as precisely true; or from accepting that the first principles of our theories are first in the sense of being beyond the reach of explanation and derivation. Peirce's injunction requires nothing less than that we regard nothing as settled, admit that nothing can ever be regarded as settled, *and yet* devote ourselves to trying to settle all! We will return to this rigorous conception of the vocation of inquiry later.

The most telling metaphor for fallibilism is relevant here. Peirce writes, "For fallibilism is the doctrine that our knowledge is never absolute but always swims, as it were, in a continuum of uncertainty and of indeterminacy" (CP, 1.171). This is an antifoundationalist metaphor if there ever was one.[14] Knowledge exists, but floats on a sea of uncertainty and indeterminacy. It has an articulate structure. It can grow and expand. But not only is there an expanse of watery surface yet unknown, there are the depths. Even if our knowledge were to someday cover the entire surface of the epistemic waters, to every point in our floating structure would correspond an unknown depth of indeterminateness, imprecision, uncertainty.[15]

Peirce's denial of intuition, his semiotic theory of cognition, and his fallibilism are already severe blows against all but a very lean realism. They, so to speak, pull the stopper out of the bottle in which inquiry hoped to contain itself. For what Peirce has outlawed is an inquiry that believes it can cease. Belief in the possibility of intuitive judgments, utter determinacy, complete precision, certainty, uncognizability, and the inexplicable were all ways to limit inquiry without truncating its validity, to give inquiry a resting place, a self-satisfying sense of accomplishment, an anticipated "end" in the sense not of a goal but a termination. Peirce has put this in question.

Our question is, How radical are the implications of this fallibilism?

The Invention of Pragmatism

Peirce created pragmatism.[16] He claims to have got the name from Kant's distinction in the *Critique of Pure Reason* between the practical and the pragmatic use of reason.[17] The "practical" (*praktisch*) refers to the moral law reason gives a priori to the will as an end in itself; the "pragmatic" (*pragmatisch*) refers to the empirical laws reason gives to the will to attain some end "commended to us by the senses," for example, happiness. Kant calls the latter "hypothetically necessary," connecting them to the "hypothetical imperatives" of his moral writings, rational rules whose obligation is relative to the value of some end given by our nature or inclination, as opposed to ends given by reason alone. According to Kant, all these "pragmatic beliefs" are indexed by a "specific degree" of confidence, the "touchstone" or exemplar of which is betting.[18] Peirce's pragmatism bears comparison to Kant in a number of ways; Peirce maintained that Kant was "nothing but a somewhat confused pragmatist" (CP, 5.525).

Although the name is Kant's, Peirce credits the inspiration for formulating pragmatism to the discussions of "The Metaphysical Club," a group that met in Cambridge in the early 1870s, including Peirce, William James, Nicholas St. John Green, Chauncey Wright, Oliver Wendell Holmes, Jr., and Joseph Warner.[19] Green is singled out for introducing Alexander Bain's gloss of *belief* as "that on which a man is prepared to act."[20] Peirce tells us that he "drew up a little paper expressing some of the opinions that I had been urging all along under the name of pragmatism" and delivered it to the club around 1871–1872. This paper became the basis for two published essays, "The Fixation of Belief" (November 1877) and "How to Make Our Ideas Clear" (January 1878), in which the doctrine of pragmatism was formulated but not named.

The name *pragmatism* attached to Peirce's doctrine did not appear publicly until William James's 1898 lecture "Philosophical Conceptions and Practical Results," delivered in Berkeley, California.[21] James attributed the doctrine to Peirce, specifically to the discussions of the 1870s, and refers to "How to Make Our Idea Clear."[22] Peirce first used the term in print in his entry on "Pragmatic and Pragmatism" in Baldwin's 1902 *Dictionary of Philosophy and Psychology*. He gave an important series of lectures on pragmatism in the Spring of 1903 at Harvard. Then, in the 1905 essay, "What Pragmatism Is," Peirce announced that the extant use of the term 'pragmatism' by others (e.g. James) had so deviated from his original definition that it was necessary to "kiss his child good-bye" and invent a new name for his old doctrine, that being *pragmaticism*, a name "which is ugly enough to be safe from kidnappers" (CP, 5.414). Remarkably, the term most famously associated with American philosophy was publicly disowned by its father almost immediately upon stepping out into public life.

Peirce defined and described pragmatism-pragmaticism in many different ways over the years.[23] The importance of pragmatism for the present study makes it necessary to chronicle the development of Peirce's conception is some detail. Much of the later history of the problems of pragmatism was prefigured in Peirce's struggle to understand and define his own doctrine.

In "How to Make Our Ideas Clear" Peirce declares that thought is a system of relations among sensations, a system whose "sole motive, idea, and function is to produce belief" (CP, 5.396). "The essence of belief," he continues, "is the establishment of a habit," or a rule of action" (CP, 5.398). Consequently, the meaning of a thought is "simply what habits it involves" (CP, 5.400).[24] The "identity" of a habit is subjunctive, it depends on how the rule of action might or would lead us to act under whatever circumstances "as might possibly occur, no matter how improbable they may be." Peirce concludes that "our idea of anything *is* our idea of its sensible effects" (CP, 5.401) and that "there is no distinction of meaning so fine as to consist in anything but a possible difference of practice"

(CP, 5.400). Or, again, "Consider what effects, that might conceivably have practical bearings, we conceive the object of our conception to have. Then, our conception of the these effects is the whole conception of the object" (CP, 5.402).

An example of how Peirce intends to use this principle is his objection to a scientific text where,

> it is stated that we understand precisely the effect of force, but what force itself is we do not understand! This is simply a self-contradiction. The idea which the word force excites in our minds has no other function than to affect our actions, and these actions can have no reference to force otherwise than through its effects. Consequently, if we know what the effects of force are, we are acquainted with every fact which is implied in saying that a force exists, and there is nothing more to know. (CP, 5.404)

Peirce applies this notion to the concept of reality. Reality, like every other "quality," "consists" in sensible effects. The sensible effects of reality are beliefs (CP, 5.406). Reality causes true beliefs, which is to say, causes those beliefs on which the scientific community is fated to agree eventually. "The opinion which is fated to be ultimately agreed to by all who investigate, is what we mean by the truth, and the object represented in this opinion is the real" (CP, 5.407).

It is instructive to note the emendations that Peirce later intended to make to his essay.[25] These additions point out that the meaning of any conception lies in its conceivable effects not for the individual actor, but for the development of our entire civilization, and that the pragmatic rule means that the "intellectual purport" of a sign lies not its effects but in *our conception of* its effects. Continuing the latter point, pragmatism (by this time, pragmaticism) makes "thought ultimately apply to action exclusively," but it does not make thought "consist in acts, or [in] saying that the true ultimate purpose of thinking is action. . . ." Rather, "Pragmaticism makes thinking to consist in the living inferential metaboly of symbols whose purport lies in conditional general resolutions to act" (CP, 5.402).

In the 1902 entry in Baldwin's dictionary, Peirce repeated elements of the 1878 definition, adding that a natural extension of the pragmatic maxim, gaining for pragmatism even greater "clearness of thought," is to see the meaning of concepts, not in "individual reactions," but "in the manner in which those reactions contribute" to the "development of concrete reasonableness. . . ." (CP, 5.4).

Around the time of this entry Peirce formulated a set of ideas that produced a new perspective on pragmatism. He determined that logic is a species of ethics and both are dependent upon aesthetics; the three compose the set of "normative sciences," one of the three branches of philosophy (with metaphysics and phenomenology) (CP, 1.186). Aesthetics studies what is best, what is valuable for its own sake. Ethics studies the conditions for attaining what is best in the realm of self-controlled activity. Logic studies the conditions for attaining what is best in self-controlled thinking. Consequently, "that truth the conditions of which the logician endeavors to analyze, and which is the goal of the reasoner's aspirations, is nothing but a phase of the *summum bonum* which forms the subject of pure ethics . . ." (CP, 1.575).

In a letter to William James from November 1902, Peirce connects this to pragmatism. He writes that it was not until after founding logic in ethics and then ethics in aesthetics that he "got to the bottom" of his own doctrine of pragmatism. "These three normative sciences," he wrote, "correspond to my three categories, which in their psychological aspect, appear as Feeling, Reaction, Thought. . . . The true nature of pragmatism cannot be understood without them. It does not, as I seem to have thought at first, take Reaction as the be-all, but it takes the end-all as the be-all, and the End is something that gives its sanction to action. It is of the third category. . . . This then leads to synechism, which the keystone of the arch" (CP, 8.256–57). Synechism is Peirce's cosmological doctrine, according to which continua are real. Four years later, Peirce remarked in a letter to James that, for pragmatism, "the end of thought is action only in so far as the end of action is another thought" (CP, 8.272).

In 1903, Peirce announced that pragmatism is "nothing else than the question of the logic of abduction." The "end" of any abductive hypothesis is,

> to lead to the avoidance of all surprise and to the establishment of a habit of positive expectation that shall not be disappointed. Any hypothesis, therefore, may be admissible . . . provided it be capable of experimental verification, and only insofar as it is capable of such verification. This is approximately the doctrine of pragmatism. But just here a broad question opens out before us. What are we to understand by experimental verification? The answer to that involves the whole logic of induction. (CP, 5.197)

Here Peirce repeats his 1878 point that the "logical import" of two conceptions cannot differ unless they "might conceivably modify our practical conduct differently . . ." (CP, 5.196). He expands on the significance of pragmatism by opposing it to the doctrine that a term can be defined only by listing its "universal predicates," each being more abstract or general than the term to be defined, implying that there are ultimately abstract, simple indefinable terms. Pragmatism, on the other hand, inspired by the "logic of relations," holds that "all conceptions ought to be defined, with the sole exception of the familiar concrete conceptions of everyday life . . . " (CP, 5.207).

In a 1903 lecture Peirce refers to Kant in a way that is particularly important for understanding pragmatism and its implications for realism. Having recounted two other Kantian doctrines, Peirce turns to a third.

> It is really a most luminous and central element of Kant's thought. I may say that it is the very sun round which all the rest revolves. This third moment consists in the flat denial that the metaphysical conceptions do not apply to things in themselves. Kant *never* said that. What he said is that these conceptions do not apply beyond the limits of possible experience. But we have *direct experience of things in themselves.* . . . Our knowledge of things in themselves is entirely *relative*, it is true; but all experience and all knowledge is knowledge of that which is, independently of being represented. (CP, 6.95)

The Kantian limitation of knowledge to the objects of possible experience is recaptured by pragmatism's limitation of the meaning of concepts to their role in possible conduct. But, Peirce wishes to say, these limitations do not deny the objects of experience the status of existing independent of representation, they merely situate and concretize that status. We will return to this later.

For Peirce's final descriptions of pragmaticism we must turn to his 1905–1906 essays. In "What Pragmatism Is," Peirce emphasizes that pragmatism makes explicit the natural methods of an experimental scientist. It holds that the rational meaning of a word or expression "lies exclusively in its conceivable bearing upon the conduct of life . . ." (CP, 5.412). And because it is "obvious" that only what could result from experiment "can have any direct bearing on conduct," "if one can define accurately all the conceivable experimental phenomena which the affirmation or denial of a concept could imply, one will have therein a complete definition of the concept, and *there is absolutely nothing more in it*" (CP, 5.412). Pragmatism's "most striking feature" is its "recognition of an in-

separable connection between rational cognition and rational purpose . . ." (CP, 5.412). Both are observational or empirical, active or
operational, and hypothetical or conditional.

An important and potentially very misleading passage occurs
here that deserves to be quoted at length. Pragmaticism (by now
Peirce has renamed his doctrine),

> will serve to show that almost every proposition of ontological
> metaphysics is either meaningless gibberish—one word being
> defined by other words, and they by still others, without any real
> conception ever being reached—or else is downright absurd; so
> that all such rubbish being swept away, what will remain of philos
> ophy will be a series of problems capable of investigation by the ob
> servational methods of the true sciences. . . . In this regard,
> pragmatism is a species of prope-positivism. But what distin
> guishes it from other species is, first, its retention of a purified phi
> losophy; secondly, its full acceptance of the main body of our
> instinctive beliefs; and thirdly its strenuous insistence upon the
> truth of scholastic realism . . . (CP, 5.423).

The "purified" philosophy Peirce wishes to retain will presumably be cleansed of concepts judged meaningless by pragmaticism. This will leave philosophy with only "real" conceptions. But as
we will see, these real conceptions are real by virtue of being implicit
in the nature of human thought and action, and imply a panpsychist
cosmology and an idealist metaphysics. Throughout his career
Peirce maintained allegiance to Scholastic realism (in the tradition
of Duns Scotus), insisting that reality cannot be conceived as solely
composed of particulars, and so that generals are real.[26] This realism is incorporated into Peirce's doctrine of synechism. Peirce considered these metaphysical doctrines to be tied to pragmatism,
declaring at one point that synechism proves pragmatism to be true
(CP, 5.415). In short, Peirce's "positivism" is not like any other positivism (e.g., of August Comte, Ernst Mach, or the Vienna Circle).

An important aspect of pragmatism is that it puts the "rational
meaning of every proposition" into "the future" (CP, 5.427). For,
"future conduct is the only conduct that is subject to self-control . . ."
Thus, the pragmaticist, "does not make the *summum bonum* to consist in action, but makes it to consist in that process of evolution
whereby the existent comes more and more to embody those generals which were just now said to be *destined*, which is what we strive
to express in calling them *reasonable*" (CP, 5.433). It is in this sense
that pragmaticism "is closely allied to the Hegelian absolute ideal-

ism." The difference, according to Peirce, is that Hegel makes generality or relation (Thirdness) the self-sufficient essence of the world, whereas pragmaticism regards quality (Firstness) and otherness (Secondness) as "independent and distinct elements of a triune Reality . . ." (CP, 5.436).

In "Issues of Pragmaticism"(1905), Peirce characterizes pragmatism as the assertion that, "The entire intellectual purport of any symbol consists in the total of all general modes of rational conduct which, conditionally upon all the possible different circumstances and desires, would ensue upon the acceptance of the symbol" (CP, 5.438). Also in this essay Peirce claims that pragmaticism implies a corollary doctrine, "critical commonsensism," the view that our thinking is based on propositions and inferences that are not under our self-control, hence are uncriticizable ("acritical") and indubitable. Pragmatism is "based...upon a study of that experience of the phenomena of self-control which is common to all grown men and women . . ." (CP, 5.442).

Critical commonsensism is a pivotal doctrine for understanding Peirce. He claims that he had "defended [it] . . . about nine years before the formulation of pragmaticism," hence in 1868 (CP, 5.439). So Peirce regards the doctrine as implicit in his great early essays, "Questions" and "Some Consequences." Its name makes clear the extent to which Peirce seeks to combine the views of Kant's "critical" philosophy and Reid's "commonsense" philosophy—which Peirce had claimed were the two possible answers to Hume (CP, 5.505). What distinguishes Peirce's "critical" commonsensism from that of the Scottish school is that Peirce holds that the "acritical" or uncriticizable beliefs are intrinsically vague (CP, 5.446) and that their indubitability does not imply their *truth*.

In a very helpful 1906 manuscript Peirce gives perhaps his clearest definition of pragmatism. He begins by insisting that pragmatism is "in itself no doctrine of metaphysics, no attempt to determine any truth of things. It is merely a method of ascertaining the meanings of hard words and of abstract concepts." The "ulterior and indirect effects" of pragmatism are another matter (CP, 5.464).

Pragmatism is a method of clarifying the meanings of "intellectual concepts"; that is, concepts concerning objective facts, not feelings or sensations. Whether that which excites in us the sensation we now call blue always did so, or once made us feel redness, has nothing to do with objective fact, but solely with "subjective" feeling. Pragmatism has "nothing to do with qualities of feeling." In a passage that bears comparison with Wittgenstein, Peirce remarks,

"Hence could two qualities of feeling everywhere be interchanged, nothing but feelings could be affected" (CP, 5.467).[27]

For Peirce a sign may have three types of "significate effects": a feeling or "emotional interpretant"; an active or "dynamic interpretant"; and a "logical interpretant," which is itself a sign (CP, 5.475–476). A sign that has a logical interpretant is an "intellectual concept," and these are "all either generals or intimately connected with generals . . ." (CP, 5.482). Pragmatism is a method for determining the cognitive meaning—the logical interpretant—of intellectual or general signs.[28] It asserts that, "the *total* meaning of the predication of an intellectual concept is contained in an affirmation that, under all conceivable circumstances of a given kind . . . the subject of predication would behave in a certain general way" (CP, 5.467). Alternately put, "to predicate any [intellectual] concept of a real or imaginary object is equivalent to declaring that a certain operation, corresponding to the concept, if performed upon that object, would (certainly, or probably, or possibly, depending on the mode of predication), be followed by a result of a definite general description" (CP, 5.483). Pragmatism defines the meaning of intellectual concepts through a list of hypothetical "would-dos" and "would-bes," such that, given condition A, X would be observed, given B, Y would be observed, and so forth. And these conditions (A, B, . . .) include our actions, our experimental manipulations. This is Peirce's clearest statement of pragmatism.

Peirce adds a new conception at this point. In any chain of meanings there must be an "ultimate" or "final" logical interpretant, which must be a habit.

> The real and living logical conclusion *is* that habit; the verbal formulation merely expresses it. I do not deny that a concept...may be a logical interpretant. I only insist that it cannot be the final logical interpretant. . . . The deliberately formed, self-analyzing habit . . . is the living definition, the veritable and final logical interpretant. Consequently, the most perfect account of a concept that words can convey will consist in a description of the habit which that concept is calculated to produce. (CP, 5.491).

This notion may seem to contradict Peirce's fallibilism, for which nothing is final. Justus Buchler faults Peirce for introducing the final interpretant and suggests that it is unnecessary to his system.[29] It seems to me that the fault is in the terms 'ultimate' and 'final,' and not in what Peirce seeks to express by them. It is not entirely clear that he means there is a temporally last interpretant,

that there can be no more interpretants after the habit is reached—
which would be queer indeed. He seems instead to mean that every
sign must, at some point, have implications in the realm of action,
must produce a habit, for it to mean at all. But this is just what
pragmatism says: The sign must translate into a rule, or a component of a rule, for action. We must also remember that for Peirce the
term *habit* means a conditional rule of action and not the acts themselves; hence a description of a habit is not a mere description of
action.[30]

Last, another 1906 manuscript contains Peirce's exposition of
the pragmaticist notion of truth. That truth is the correspondence of
a representation with its object is, Peirce agrees with Kant, "merely
the nominal definition" (CP, 5.553). The question is, In what does
that correspondence consist? First, truth belongs "exclusively" to
propositions, and indicates that the predicate is a sign of that of
which the subject is a sign. Second, the meaning of correspondence
must "be something that thought can compass." The idea of a truth
that humans could not know is pragmatically meaningless. Peirce
suggests that "if we can find out the right method of thinking,"
which is to say, the right method of "transforming signs," then the
truth "can be nothing more nor less than the last result to which the
following out of [the right] method would ultimately carry us." That
result must itself be a sign. Third, there must be an "action of the
object upon the sign" to make the sign true, the latter must be "compelled" by its object.[31] We will return to this notion of truth later.

Before moving to the next section a few points of clarification
might be helpful. First, there may seem to be an ambiguity in that
Peirce defines pragmatism sometimes in terms of action and sometimes in terms of sensible results or observations.[32] It seems to me
that this is resolvable: the definition in terms of action is primary,
the other serves to clarify it.

According to Peirce, the function of thought is to eliminate
doubt and establish belief, which is to say, to establish a habit, a
conditional rule of action. The meaning of any sign is equivalent to
the rule that determines its role in the guidance of possible action
or, more loosely, its connection with rational, purposeful conduct. If
the sign is a belief or a proposition, then its meaning is equivalent to
a nexus of habits. If the sign is a concept, then its meaning is equivalent to its role in the determination of the habits entailed by the
acceptance of the concept. In either case, meaning is expressible as a
hypothetical or conditional contribution to action. Again, meaning is

not action, but it is *related to* action. Peirce understands this to be the experimental scientist's notion of meaning.

Peirce defines the "identity" of habit through the twin notions of stimulus and sensible result. In 1878 he wrote, "What the habit is depends on *when* and *how* it causes us to act. As for the *when*, every stimulus to action is derived from perception; as for the *how*, every purpose of action is to produce some sensible result" (CP, 5.400). This is echoed in Peirce's claim that the rational meaning of an expression lies "exclusively in its conceivable bearing on the conduct of life; so that, since obviously nothing that might not result from experiment can have any direct bearing upon conduct . . .," the conceivable experimental phenomena can define its meaning (CP, 5.412). Peirce reminds us in the same paragraph that the reason for choosing the term *pragmatism* for this view is that it expresses a "relation to some definite human purpose." The point is that pragmatism defines meaning primarily in terms of contribution to rational or controlled or rule-governed action; secondarily, action can be defined in terms of the connection between an observable circumstance (stimulus) and the production of observable consequences.

Second, Peirce derives the famous convergence theory of 'truth' and 'reality' directly from an application of the pragmatic doctrine of meaning to these terms. They refer, respectively, to the opinion fated to be ultimately agreed to by the community of inquirers in the indefinite future and to the object of that belief.

Surprisingly, in the most famous passages explicating the convergence theory of truth, Peirce does not explicitly take the additional step, fully justified by his doctrine, of making truth equivalent in meaning to the *habit* of the scientific community in the indefinite future, the habit whose establishment is the meaning of that ultimate opinion. Again, habit here is not a set of actions; it is a hypothetical rule of action, so it is still an intellectual matter. But without this step, Peirce has defined the meaning of the term 'truth,' or the adjective 'true' attached to, say, a belief, in terms of yet other beliefs. This must be an incomplete explication by Peirce's own standards. For the difference between a true belief and a false belief must entail, like all other meaningful differences, a difference in practice. So on Peircean grounds a true belief ought to be the rule of actions that would characterize the community of inquirers in the long run.

There is another possible interpretation of convergence that Peirce avoids. Why is the pragmatic meaning of truth not equivalent to the "satisfactory"? If action aims to satisfy and truth is definable in terms of action, why not say that the true belief is one that satisfies our aims? In a 1906 manuscript Peirce admits that, "It is . . . no doubt true that men act, especially in the action of inquiry, as if their sole purpose were to produce a certain state of feeling, in the sense that when that state of feeling is attained, there is no further effort" (CP, 5.563). Peirce nevertheless rejects the claim that truth *is* satisfaction; to believe so is a logical error. Satisfaction is not an aim, but a feeling that accompanies the accomplishment of an aim. We act *as if* satisfaction were our aim. The pragmatist notion of truth cannot, in Peirce's analysis, be reduced to feeling or to those conditions that produce a certain feeling.

Third, pragmatism would appear to entail voluntarism, that is, the primacy of the will, the view that action is the basic currency of human life. But this is not quite right. What is fundamental is not will or action, but *mediated* will or *rationalized* action. For Peirce, the greatest good is the evolution of a rationalized existent or rationalized action. Peirce wrote in a letter to James in 1897, "In my later papers, I have seen more thoroughly than I used to do that it is not mere action as brute exercise of strength that is the purpose of all, but say generalization, such action as tends toward regularization, and the actualization of the thought which without action remains unthought . . . (CP, 8.250).

In 1906 Peirce wrote that, "As the for the ultimate purpose of thought, which must be the purpose of everything, it is beyond human comprehension; but according to the stage of approach which my thought has made to it . . . it is by the indefinite replication of self-control upon self-control that the *vir* |man| is begotten, and by action, through thought, he grows an esthetic ideal . . . as the share which God permits him to have in the work of creation" (CP, 5.402, n. 3). Pragmatism thus makes the end of human existence the synthesis of action and thought, that is, meaningful, self-regulated action, validated as an aesthetic construction.

For Peirce, the goal of inquiry is the collective regulation of conduct. Truth is the eventual collective agreement of inquirers, and agreement or shared belief must be collective acceptance of rules of action, and reality is the hypothesized common independent *object* of such belief, *cause* of the stimuli and *bearer* of the consequences of the common habits. The ultimate community, now evolving, is the condition of truth and reality. Its validation is the aesthetic ideal it thereby embodies through its cumulative self-control. This notion was, I believe, in Peirce's mind when he wrote of his notion of God in a 1905 letter to James, in a passage that shows how unpositivistic his pragmatism is, "our ideas of the infinite are necessarily extremely vague and become contradictory the moment we attempt to make them precise. But still they are not utterly unmeaning, though they can only be interpreted in our religious adoration and the consequent effects upon conduct. This I think is good sound solid strong pragmatism" (CP, 8.262).

Peirce's Monism

Peirce rejects metaphysical dualism for a form of monism in which mind and matter are not fundamentally discontinuous. The way he does this can occasion misunderstanding, for he is in some respects a naturalist and in others an idealist. But if we arrange Peirce's doctrines in the right logical order, and remember that naturalism can be variously interpreted, Peirce's view is straightforward. He locates human cognition within the natural world, going so far as to develop a naturalist theory of inquiry and truth. He explicitly makes inquiry obey natural laws. But his conception of nature is fundamentally idealist, that is, he believes that matter is "effete mind." This is Peirce's "panpsychist" cosmology. So, the nature whose laws our minds must obey is itself mental in a fundamental sense. In this section we will begin by examining Peirce's naturalism, then turn briefly to his cosmological essays of 1891–1892.

Peirce remarks in his fascinating 1877 essay, "The Fixation of Belief," that, "We are logical animals, but we are not perfectly so." For "logicality" or good reasoning, he writes, "in regard to practical matters . . . is the most useful quality an animal can possess, and might, therefore, result from the action of natural selection; but outside of these [matters] it is probably of more advantage to the animal to have his mind filled with pleasing and encouraging visions, independently of their truth; and thus, upon unpractical subjects, natural selection might occasion a fallacious tendency of thought" (CP, 5.366).[33] The restriction of a possible beneficial fallaciousness to "unpractical" matters evidently refers to matters regarding which there is no experiential evidence, leaving thought free to conclude as it will.[34]

What determines us to draw one inference rather than another is habit. For Peirce, "belief is of the nature of a habit . . ." (CP, 5.377). Doubt is "an uneasy and dissatisfied state from which we struggle to free ourselves and pass into the state of belief" (CP, 5.372). Doubt "stimulates us to inquiry", that is, to a "struggle" whose only resolution is the destruction of the doubt. This is, Peirce says, like a reflex action stimulated by the irritation of a nerve; differently put, Peirce accepts a tension-reduction model of the formation of belief. This is Peirce's famous "doubt-belief" theory of inquiry. He writes, "Hence, the sole object of inquiry is the settlement of opinion. We may fancy that this is not enough for us, and that we seek, not merely an opinion, but a true opinion. But . . . this fancy . . . proves groundless; for as soon as a firm belief is reached we are entirely satisfied, whether the belief be true of false. . . . The most that can be maintained is, that we seek for a belief that we shall *think* to be true. But...it is mere tautology to say so" (CP, 5.375). This implies that doubt requires real struggle between competing beliefs, hence one cannot decide to doubt; that the premises of a satisfactory argument need to be, not insusceptible of possible doubt, but only not actually doubted; and that inquiry without a real doubt would be "without a purpose."

If this is so, if the sole purpose of investigation is to fix belief and not to discover true belief, then why not satisfy our purpose by simply holding to any old belief? Well, Peirce tells us, that is one way. There are in fact four methods of fixing belief. Peirce proposes to compare these methods, weighing benefits and costs, without imposing a normative rule regarding which is the 'right' or 'true' way.

For example, in discussing the first method, the method of sheer "tenacity," Peirce refuses to condemn it. "When an ostrich buries its head in the sand as danger approaches," he writes, "it very likely takes the happiest course." If a human being takes this approach, insisting that "I hold steadfastly to the truth, and the truth is always wholesome," Peirce responds, "I do not see what can be said against his doing so." To call such a person irrational "only amounts to saying that his method of settling belief is not ours" (CP, 5.377).

The problem with tenacity is one of efficacy, not truth. Once the individual realizes that others in the community disagree with him or her, there arises a strong impulse to regard the beliefs of others as equally valid, and this will diminish confidence in the tenaciously held view. Because we are social animals tenacity fails to be adequate, on the whole. The problem becomes, "how to fix belief, not in the individual merely, but in the community."

The next method is authority, which nicely takes account of what tenacity ignored: society. Some institution will enforce fixity of belief in the individual and the community. Peirce recognizes the "mental and moral superiority" of this method to tenacity. It is perhaps the dominant method in human history, and "for the mass of mankind, then, there is perhaps no better method than this" (CP, 5.380).

Once again the failing of the method is its relative ineffectiveness. Not all beliefs can be regulated in this way, so there will be a large part of life in which beliefs vary. Special individuals will eventually notice these inconsistencies, as well as the different beliefs of foreign communities and, again, will be unable to find any reason why the official beliefs are superior. Doubt inevitably creeps in.

A new method is devised that not only fixes belief, but "shall also decide what proposition it is which is to be believed." Peirce implies that for tenacity and authority the *content* of the belief is more or less irrelevant. For the third method, however, content determines fixity. People, guided by their own "natural preferences . . . conversing together . . . gradually develop beliefs in harmony with natural causes." This method is similar to that of art. The beliefs fixed are those deemed "agreeable to reason." But for Peirce this means those beliefs "that we find ourselves inclined to believe." This "method of inclinations," also called the "a priori method," or the appeal to "conscience," and which is exhibited most clearly in the history of metaphysics, makes inquiry a matter of *taste*. Here we have one of Peirce's most remarkable insults to the history of philosophy. He is claiming that the very concept enshrined by modern philosophy as the condition of absolute knowledge and hence the goal of inquiry—the a priori—is nothing but taste and instinct.

The a priori method differs not too much from that of authority. Peirce imagines that "there are some people" who will find it unsatisfactory. They will notice that sentiments, tastes, inclinations to believe, vary with culture, and again, they will wonder what makes one set of instinctive beliefs superior. They will seek a method by which belief is fixed by the relation of its content to "nothing human," but to an "external permanency—something upon which our thinking has no effect" (CP, 5.384). Their doubt needs a stronger tonic.

That tonic is science, the last method. Science rests on the following hypothesis: "There are Real things, whose characters are entirely independent of our opinions about them; those Reals affect our senses according to regular laws, and...we can ascertain by reasoning how things really and truly are; and any man, if he have sufficient experience and he reason enough about it, will be led to the one True conclusion" (CP, 5.384). This is the only method that distinguishes between a "right and a wrong way" of acquiring beliefs, that is, it is properly normative.

This method requires a new belief on our part, the belief in reality. What is the justification of this belief? Peirce gives an interesting answer. First, although inquiry cannot confirm the existence of real things (because it presumes them), it cannot disconfirm them either. Second, everyone in fact uses this method wherever he or she can see how to apply it. Third, experience of the method does not show any limitations that would encourage doubt. Fourth, doubt itself implies that "there is some one thing which a proposition should represent." If one really doubted reals, doubt would not be dissatisfying. Therefore, nobody really doubts reality.

Notice that Peirce has defined both science and the problem it solves in realist terms. The only way to fix belief adequately is to determine belief through reference to an independent reality, an "external permanency" (CP, 5.384). We shall fix beliefs by the property of their being true, which means that they are determined by reals, whose nature we will infer from experience, the true beliefs being the ones to which collective inference will (or would) eventually lead.

Peirce admits that the other methods have some advantages over science. The a priori method flatters our vanity. Authority will always rule the mass of people, and this brings peace. "Most of all" he admires the tenacity characteristic of all persons of success. Although science, the sole method that seeks to fix belief through its coincidence with facts (CP, 5.387), should be "loved and reverenced as [man's] bride," the other methods may still be honored.

The question arises, Is Peirce's account of the superiority of science really adequate? Does it allow for a normative obligation to choose the method of truth, reality, and science? Or if the choice is governed solely by efficacy in fixing belief, is there any obligation to assent to science? Why ought we do science or seek truth, rather than fix belief by the other methods? To quote a philosopher writing at the same time as Peirce, *"What does all will to truth signify?"*[35] If there is no normative obligation, but only an expeditious advantage for the naturalistic aims of the human organism, then the empirical or predictive question of the veridicality of that advantage becomes all-important. Is it really true that science brings more fixity and stability and that it will continue to do so in the future? It certainly does not always seem so; as we will see, Peirce himself admits in another context that science aims as *destabilizing* belief, at least in the short-run.[36]

Before addressing the problems raised by his naturalistic theory of inquiry, we must take note of the cosmology in which Peirce's naturalism is located. His cosmology was formulated in an important series of essays in *The Monist* (1891–1892). Here we have space only for the briefest indication of their general orientation. Rejecting metaphysical dualism, Peirce turns to "hylomorphism" or "monism." Of the options within this family, "The one intelligible theory of the universe is that of objective idealism, that matter is effete mind, inveterate habits becoming physical laws" (CP, 6.25). The other crucial cosmological doctrine is synechism, the claim that continua, hence generalities, are real.

The relationship between the mental and the material is a complex one for Peirce. He writes,

> It may be well here to reflect that if matter has no existence except as a specialization of mind, it follows that whatever affects matter according to regular laws is itself matter. . . . Hence, it would be a mistake to conceive of the psychical and the physical aspects of matter as two aspects absolutely distinct. Viewing a thing from the outside, considering its relations of action and reaction with other things, it appears as matter. Viewing it from the inside, looking at its immediate character as feeling, it appears as consciousness. These two views are combined when we remember that mechanical laws are nothing but acquired habits, like all the regularities of mind, including the tendency to take habits, itself; and that this action of habit is nothing but generalization, and generalization is nothing but the spread of feelings. (CP, 6.268)

Mind must be more fundamental for Peirce because mental elements exhibit continuity and the tendency to spread or generalize. Feeling cannot be explained by matter, whereas matter can be explained as habituated feeling. Mind is matter from the inside, as feeling, as chance, and as qualities in themselves. Matter is mind from the outside in action and reaction, in determinacy and hence necessity. The two states are related by growth, which is the spread of relation and the development of habit. There are thus three elements in the world for Peirce: chance, law or necessity, and habit taking (the tendency to take on habits). Differently put, they are mind, matter, and evolution (CP, 6.32).

Now, the question is, Does Peirce's naturalism, and more particularly his naturalistic theory of inquiry, generate any antirealist problems? I suggest that it does and that whatever the metaphysical merit of Peirce's panpsychist cosmology, there is no reason to believe that it alleviates those problems. What the cosmology does for Peirce is make the location of mind in an apparently material universe conceivable. But the antirealist problems caused by naturalism are more local. Naturalism puts us wholly in nature, whether that nature is idealistic or physicalistic, and this location generates the epistemological problems. It dictates that nothing human is super- or nonnatural. Consequently, human norms (e.g. truth, goodness, beauty) must be compatible with natural principles. Nothing about Peirce's objective idealism explains how the principles of animal behavior manifest themselves *both* in human phenomena that are apparently consonant with the nonhuman (e.g. the need to acquire information that helps survival) *and* in normative human phenomena that appear to be uniquely human (e.g. the desire to know what is true regardless of needs or consequences).

Peirce says that the sole function of thought and belief is to transform and establish rules of action, whether the beliefs are true or false. The reason science and belief in reals were adopted by human society is their efficiency in establishing beliefs and preventing or circumventing doubt. Why ought we believe that this happy confluence of efficacy and our usual notion of truth will continue forever? What if science someday fails to be efficient, while still corresponding to reality? Would the doubt-belief theory then dictate that some other method be used? Not to mention that science constantly changes its beliefs, not in all respects, to be sure, but in some. Even if one could plausibly argue that, despite the scientist's revision of some beliefs, the areas of constant belief in science that are unlikely to be overturned make belief as a whole more stable than the other methods—which is dubious—it must still be asked how the scientist's *aim* can be an impractical truth, when the doubt-belief theory says the aim is sheer stability?

The oddest fact about Peirce's view is that elsewhere he makes the scientific and practical temperaments antithetical, declaring that the scientist's whole aim is to shake belief! (CP, 6.3). In an 1898 manuscript, Peirce insists that science is utterly impractical: "But nothing can be more unscientific than the attitude of minds who are trying to confirm themselves in early beliefs. The struggle of the scientific man is to try to see the errors of his beliefs—if he can be said to have any beliefs" (CP, 6.3). Peirce distinguishes philosophy that is interested in knowing the truth or "laboratory" philosophy from philosophy which has a practical interest, including the practical interest of moral improvement, or "seminary" philosophy, and declares himself for the former (CP, 6.3). The "temperaments requisite" for the two are "altogether contrary to one another." Whereas the practical individual stakes "everything he cares for" on certain beliefs, and so must believe that he or she already has the ultimate truth, the scientific individual "ardently desires to have his present provisional beliefs . . . swept away."

In the same year, he writes of science that, unlike the concerns of practice, it "has nothing at stake on any temporal venture but is in pursuit of eternal verities (not semblances to truth) . . ." (CP, 5.589). He goes even further in his 1898 lectures, "Detached Ideas on Vitally Important Topics,"

> Hence, I hold that what is properly and usually called *belief* . . . has no place in science at all. We *believe* the proposition we are ready to act upon. *Full belief* is willingness to act upon the proposition in vital crises, *opinion* is willingness to act upon it in relatively insignificant affairs. But pure science has nothing at all to do with *action*. The propositions it accepts, it merely writes in the list of premises it proposes to use . . . the whole list is provisional. . . . The scientific man risks nothing upon them. . . . There is thus no proposition at all in science which answers to the conception of belief. (CP, 1.635)

Peirce makes it clear that reasoning and inquiry are poor guides to practical living. Instinct, common sense, and cultural convictions are far superior when the issue is "vital." Religion, poetry, and ethics are based, and should be based, in sentiment. How then can science be defined as the great stabilizer of habits of action?

Another problem is Peirce's claim that no one can fail to believe in reals because otherwise doubt would not be dissatisfying. If this were so, then the doubt-belief theory inherently must ascribe belief in reality to all human beings. But then all are scientists, and so no one can follow the other methods.[37]

Furthermore, which method is Peirce using to propose the doubt-belief theory, the superiority of science and the indispensability of belief in reals? Is Peirce's theory more effective in stabilizing belief than alternative theories of knowledge? It would seem not, because it makes the belief in reals an hypothesis, a belief whose validity is a matter of relative effectiveness. Like all naturalistic epistemologists, Peirce is giving us an account of the norms (truth, reality) we use to judge a process (of belief production and acceptance) that makes those norms a product of that process. And *his account* is also a product of that process.

In other words, deep problems are raised by the doubt-belief theory, the locus of naturalistic epistemology in Peirce. It is difficult to see how the implications of a naturalistic doubt-belief theory can be made consistent with Peirce's realism, his commitment to truth above all else, and his fallibilism. Naturalism is not the only internal threat to Peirce's realism. But before examining the other threats, we must more fully explore the realism they threaten.

Peirce's Convergence Realism

Peirce apparently accepts a realist view of knowledge in my sense of the term.[38] True or valid assertive judgments are those whose validity is determined by the judgments' relations to the things judged. The things known thereby are real in the full sense of that term. They are real things, "whose characters are entirely independent of our opinions about them" (CP, 5.384). Things known by mind, although related to mind, "doubtless are, apart from that relation . . ." (CP, 5.311). Peirce insists on this again and again. We know the reals, not merely their phenomenal effects. He connects reality to his category of Secondness. Secondness is fact, force, the experience or phenomenon of resistance. The independence of the objects of knowledge embodies this Secondness, which *compels* our cognition to conform to its object. For Peirce; "Nothing can be more completely false than that we can experience only our own ideas . . . all experience and all knowledge is knowledge of that which is, independently of being represented" (CP, 6.95).

What allows Peirce to insist that we do in fact have such knowledge of reals is his unique description of reality in terms of the convergence of inquiry. The real is the object of true opinion, and the true opinion is the opinion on which the indefinitely large community of inquirers is fated to converge in the indefinitely long run. He writes, "Thus, the very origin of the conception of reality shows that this conception essentially involves the notion of a COMMUNITY, without definite limits . . ." (CP, 5.311). If inquiry—that is, science— could proceed unimpeded long enough, thought would be in perfect accord with reality.

It is important to see that Peirce is giving us on the one hand a *definition* of truth and reality and on the other hand a *characterization* of them. These may seem not to cohere, but it is his view that they do cohere. The "nominal" or "abstract" definition of truth is the correspondence of a representation to its object (CP, 5.553). Likewise, the real is defined as that whose character obtains independent of representation (although this needs clarification, as we will see). But these definitions do not make the concepts of truth and reality "perfectly clear" (CP, 5.406) or "usable" (CP, 5.553). Pragmatism must be called in to characterize reality and truth more fully. In light of pragmatism, "The opinion which is fated to be ultimately agreed to by all who investigate, is what we mean by the truth, and the object represented in this opinion is the real" (CP, 5.407). The convergence theory is nothing more than a pragmatic clarification of the unclear concept, 'truth.'

Peirce admits that this pragmatic characterization may seem to violate the realism of the nominal or abstract definitions of those terms, because pragmatism "makes the characters of the real depend on what is ultimately thought about them" (CP, 5.408). Indeed, it might appear to introduce conventionalism, because it makes the truth relative to community opinion. But Peirce believes he has a way out of the apparently antirealist implications of pragmatism. It is that the real is dependent on mind *in general*, on the eventual convergence of possible minds in the possible future, and not dependent on any *specifiable* community of minds or inquirers.[39] As he writes in 1878, "reality is independent, not necessarily of thought in general, but only of what you or I or any finite number of men may think about it . . ." (CP, 5.408). This in effect means that truth and reality are determined not by what is cogniz*ed* at any particular time, but by what is cogniz*able*.

This is the strategy Peirce will pursue for reconciling the incipient conventionalism of his pragmatic approach with realism. We will trace his various presentations of the convergence theory and try to determine whether he can maintain his realism. In passing, we must remember that Peirce's objective idealism is presumed throughout. Because reality is ultimately mental, a Peircean realism could never hold that the characters of real things obtain independent of mind simpliciter. They must, however, obtain independent of any specifiable set of minds and judgments that represent them. That is the yardstick of realism against which we must measure Peirce.

The pragmatic interpretation of reality appears quite early in Peirce's career. In 1868, regarding the issue of whether there is a concept of the absolutely incognizable, Peirce writes, "Over against any cognition, there is an unknown but knowable reality; but over against all possible cognition, there is only the self-contradictory. In short, *cognizability* (in its widest sense) and *being* are not merely metaphysically the same, but are synonymous terms" (CP, 5.257).

The first full formulation of the convergence view of reality appears in "Some Consequences." Because there is no meaningful concept of the absolutely incognizable, the 'real' must be cognizable. Cognitions are signs that develop through inference. The concept of the real developed along with the unreal as an explanation for error. The possibility of self-correction required a distinction between "an *ens* relative to private inward determinations," or the "idiosyncratic," and "an *ens* such as would stand in the long run." Peirce argues,

> The real, then, is that which, sooner or later, information and reasoning would finally result in, and which is therefore independent of the vagaries of me and you. Thus, the very origin of the conception of reality shows that this conception essentially involves the notion of a COMMUNITY, without definite limits, and capable of a definite increase of knowledge. And so . . . the real . . . consist[s] of those [cognitions] which, at a time sufficiently future, the community will always continue to re-affirm . . . (CP, 5.311)

The most controversial part of this theory is the claim that opinion is in fact converging, and will converge, over the long run. Peirce expresses this idea in a number of ways. He gives it a regulative cast when he writes that, even though the unknown will always be far greater than the known, "yet it is unphilosophical to suppose that, with regard to any given question . . . investigation would not bring forth a solution of it, if it were carried far enough" (CP, 5.409). On the homely side, Peirce wrote that, "practically, we know that questions do generally get settled in time, when they come to be scientifically investigated; and that is practically and pragmatically enough" (CP, 5.494). In the same paragraph, however, he goes beyond this homely observation to say that, "truth's independence of individual opinions is due (so far as there is any 'truth') to its being the predestined result to which sufficient inquiry *would* ultimately lead. I only object that . . . there is not the smallest scintilla of logical justification for any assertion that a given sort of result will, as a matter of fact, either *always* or *never* come to pass . . ." (CP, 5.494). Indeed, Peirce goes as far as to say that, regarding any given question, "we cannot know that there *is* any truth," which can mean only that we cannot know that inquiry will converge regarding any specific question or phenomenon.

possibility of striving for an end higher than one's individual
satisfaction. He closes his review with the remark that, "The question whether the *genus homo* has any existence except as individuals, is the question whether there is anything of any more dignity,
worth, and importance than individual happiness. . . . [of] whether
men really have anything in common, so that the community is to be
considered as an end in itself . . ." (CP, 8.38).

So the appearance of conventionalism in Peirce is neither accidental nor unintentional. Conventionalism is nothing other than
the doctrine that the validity of our judgments is relative to the community, whether it be a definite, actual, and local community, or an
indefinite, possible and universal community. Pragmatism implies
conventionalism because pragmatism dictates that the idea of a real
thing that the community of inquirers will never know is nonsensical. That reality is knowable means that the community must be
capable of knowing it in the long run. Peirce believes this conventionalism is entirely compatible with realism. If the term had not
been appropriated by a now defunct aesthetic theory, his view ought
to be named *socialist realism*.[41]

The ascription of conventionalism, hence relativism, to Peirce
may seem to ignore, not only his claimed realism, but his naturalism, his ascription of Secondness to phenomena, and other doctrines. My argument does not ignore these, but asks whether these
elements can survive the antirealist presure of pragmatism and
conventionalism? Take the example of reality. On the one hand,
reality is resistance or Secondness, hence independent of what anybody thinks, and it compels cognition. On the other hand, reality is
defined idealistically as the object of the community's opinion. John
Smith distinguishes these as "the real" and "reality" in Peirce. The
real, or what is real, is Secondness, force, independence from
thought, whereas reality is "a matter of Thirdness or of thought, and
this involves something more than the ability to react with other
things."[42] Buchler points out that this distinction is problematic
unless the real is understood pragmatically, as Peirce insists it
should be.[43] An independent real cannot mean an unknowable real,
in principle unrelated to mind.

Peirce says that truth is by definition the correspondence of
proposition to object. But what is *correspondence* and what are the
objects? Peirce, as a pragmatist, claims that any realism that insists
on the independence of the object of judgment from *all* possible
human judgment makes no sense. Absent that unrealistic realism,
Peirce takes the next most realist position, that the real objects are

dependent on the totality of scientific (that is, truth-seeking) human judgment, not on any specifiable theory, culture, or set of judgments. Correspondence with these objects means correspondence with the scientific community's ultimate opinion. But, as we have seen, how science or truth-seeking can be explained and justified within the bounds of Peirce's pragmatist and naturalist assumptions is not clear either.

The question is, Does a pragmatic realism make sense, does it cohere, can it be justified? Peirce's affirmative answer to this question is based on his notion of *community*, which he makes carry a heavy burden. We can weigh that burden if we explore the root of Peirce's foundationalism, his justification of the validity of inquiry. Peirce, like Kant, has an answer to Hume.

Foundations and Foundationalism

Despite Peirce's fallibilism, pragmatism, and commonsensism, elements of his thought are foundationalist in a quite traditional sense. These bear some examination.

Peirce was a system builder. He wanted "To erect a philosophical edifice that shall outlast the vicissitudes of time . . ." (CP, 1.1). His aim was to build a system of knowledge in which all the sciences would have a place. Philosophy is a science for Peirce and ought to "imitate" the method of the sciences (CP, 5.265). It is, with mathematics on the one hand and "idioscopy" or the "special sciences" on the other, a science of "discovery." Philosophy alone can decide the proper relations among these special sciences. Of the three branches of philosophy (phenomenology, metaphysics, and normative science), phenomenology, because it provides the categories through which everything is to be described, can claim priority to all other forms of inquiry.

Among its tasks, philosophy must investigate first principles. Peirce writes,

> the special sciences are obliged to take for granted a number of most important propositions. . . . In short, they always rest on metaphysics. . . . The philosopher alone is equipped with the facilities for examining such "axioms." . . . Find a scientific man who proposes to get along without any metaphysics . . . and you have found one whose doctrines are thoroughly vitiated by the crude and uncriticized metaphysics with which they are packed. We must philosophize, said the great naturalist Aristotle—if only to

> avoid philosophizing. . . . In short, there is no escape from the need
> of a critical examination of "first principles." (CP, 1.130)

On the other hand, Peirce explicitly rejects the search for *foundational knowledge*. No first principle, no foundation, is certainly true. No successful inquiry is unilinear in its argumentation: that is, advances without presuppositions or inferences external to a single deductive series of inferences, as in the Cartesian model (CP, 5.264–265). Philosophy ought, like the sciences, to "trust rather to the multitude and variety of its arguments than to the conclusiveness of any one." Last, because thought is never justified in introducing some claim that is itself inexplicable as an explanation, any foundational claim must itself be capable of explanation.[44] There is neither a beginning nor an end to inference. The most important point is that for Peirce foundations do not legitimate or justify or legislate to inquiry, so much as they explain inquiry to itself. The aim of first or foundational philosophy is to explain inquiry, not to make it possible.

We must separate the question of first principles and philosophical foundations from the question of indubitable beliefs. With Reid and the other members of the Scottish common sense school, Peirce accepts that we have indubitable beliefs. But, consonant with the "critical" character of his common-sensism, he denies that we know these beliefs to be true. We simply are not free to doubt them, because the inferences that led to them are unconscious and not under our control. Perceptual judgments are examples of such beliefs, as are certain very general beliefs; for example, that nature is orderly. Peirce had written as early as "Some Consequences" that, "At any moment we are in possession of certain information, that is, of cognitions which have been logically derived by induction and hypothesis from previous cognitions which are less general, less distinct, and of which we have a less lively consciousness. These in their turn have been derived from others . . . and so on back to the ideal first, which is quite singular, and quite out of consciousness" (CP, 5.311). Thus, there are cognitions, even propositions, whose validity cannot be questioned in any real sense. We are bound to act as if they are true, although we cannot know they are true; that is, we are not conscious of an inference that would make them true.[45]

In the third of Peirce's remarkable 1868 essays, "Grounds of Validity of the Laws of Logic," Peirce tried to give a foundation for inquiry; the essay constitutes, in effect, Peirce's answer to Hume. There is no argument, Peirce says, against someone who would doubt the validity of all inference. But, because all cognitive process is inferential, no such person exists. There might, however, be persons who doubt the validity of all *principles* of inference, such as the established laws of logic. Peirce's carefully phrased aim is to show how "the laws of logic can be other than inexplicable" (CP, 5.318).

Peirce's main question is, How is it that, given the present experience of part of a class of things, we can know something about the future experience of the rest of the class?[46] This is the problem of induction, Hume's problem, to which the transcendental philosophy of Kant and the commonsensism of Reid were proposed as answers. Peirce gave this question great importance. Whereas Kant asked, how synthetic a priori judgments are possible, Peirce remarked, "But antecedently to this comes the question how synthetical judgments in general, and still more generally, how synthetical reasoning is possible at all. . . . This is the lock on the door of philosophy" (CP, 5.348).

"Intellectual intuition," which Peirce says is the Kantian answer, is no answer at all. It is like, Peirce says, explaining opium's sleep-producing capacity by reference to its "somnific virtue." Natural selection, another possible answer, "no doubt" accounts for the existence of this faculty, but that still does not explain its "possibility" or, I would say, its validity. Another candidate is the claim that nature is orderly. Peirce denies that this order is a fact. Nature is not merely regular, it is partly regular and partly irregular: "No order could be less orderly than the existing arrangement" (CP, 5.342). We cannot imagine a universe in which probable inference would be valid less often than it is in this one. No fact about things can validate probable argument, just as no non-factual, purely deductive argument can (CP, 5.347).

According to Peirce, the validity of probable inference, for example, the inference from the proportion of black and white beans in a sample to the proportion in the collection from which the sample was drawn, rests on one fact: "in the long run, any one bean would be taken out as often as any other" (CP, 5.349). But the "real" character of the collection, Peirce says, is simply what is asserted of the collection by that judgment about the collection that holds true in the long run. The continuous or general nature of inference and reality explains and validates induction. No one inference is valid. Thus, "the validity of induction depends simply upon the fact that the parts make up . . . the whole" (CP, 5.349). Peirce in effect justifies induction with his convergence theory of reality. He writes,

> Upon our theory of reality and of logic, it can be shown that no
> inference of any individual can be thoroughly logical without cer-
> tain determinations of his mind which do not concern any one
> inference immediately; for we have seen that that mode of in-
> ference which alone can teach us anything, or carry us at all
> beyond what was implied in our premises—in fact, does not give
> us to know any more than we knew before; only, we know that, by
> faithfully adhering to that mode of inference, we shall, on the
> whole, approximate to the truth. Each of us is an insurance com-
> pany, in short. (CP, 5.354)

This leads to an interesting claim. Validity is in the collection of
inferences. Someone who has a "transcendent personal interest"
that outweighs all others, Peirce says, "can make no valid inference
whatever." In other words, "logic rigidly requires, before all else,
that no determinate fact, nothing which can happen to a man's self,
should be of more consequence to him than everything else. . . . So
the social principle is rooted intrinsically in logic" (CP, 5.354).[47]

The individual thinker and the individual datum cannot outweigh the many. Indeed, the "ideal perfection of knowledge," which
"constitutes" reality for Peirce, presumes a community in which the
complete identification of each individual with the interests of the
community has been achieved (CP, 5.356). Logic is thought identified with the whole.

Ten years later, in "The Doctrine of Chances," Peirce explicated
this social theory of logic with an intriguing example. Imagine someone faced with the following choice. There are two packs of cards,
one containing twenty-five black cards and one red card, and
another containing twenty-five red cards and one black card. One
card must be picked from one of the two packs. If a red card is
drawn, "eternal felicity" will be the chooser's fate; if a black card,
"everlasting woe."

According to Peirce's analysis of probable reasoning, neither
choice is rational, because the case is unrepeatable. For a probable
inference, like "if A, then B," to be true, there must be some "real
fact" such that "*whenever* such an event as A happens such an event
as B happens," a fact to which the inference corresponds. But there
is no such real fact in this case; there is no "whenever," because the
case is unrepeatable. As Hilary Putnam remarks on Peirce's example, "a person can have eternal felicity or everlasting woe only
once!"[48]

Yet, Peirce admits, in reality we would all choose a card from
the mostly red pack. How can Peirce explain our choice? Peirce

pushes the problem further. The same predicament holds regarding all the choices or "chances" of a person's life taken collectively as one unrepeatable choice. Not only is our success in life uncertain; it is worse than that. Peirce claims, "It is an indubitable result of the theory of probabilities that every gambler, if he continues long enough, must ultimately be ruined" (CP, 2.653). For, given finite resources, eventually the gambler must lose enough to lack sufficient remaining resources to win back everything (actually, everything lost plus $1) on the next bet. "The same thing is true," Peirce says, "of an insurance company," whose losses must eventually ruin it. The gambling that constitutes human life must end in loss. Peirce writes, "All human affairs rest upon probabilities, and the same thing is true everywhere. If man were immortal he could be perfectly sure of seeing the day when everything in which he had trusted should betray his trust, and, in short, of coming eventually to hopeless misery. He would break down, at last, as every great fortune, as every dynasty, as every civilization does. In place of this we have death" (CP, 2.653). For individuals death limits the series of bets, making it uncertain whether the individual's final bet will be a losing one. We are saved from inevitable ruin by death—so much for Peircean optimism.

How, then, to explain our gamble on the mostly red pack, or on life, even though the choice is unrepeatable? The only explanation, Peirce says, is that we must *in fact* identify "our interests with those of an unlimited community." He writes,

> It seems to me that we are driven to this, that logicality inexorably requires that our interests shall *not* be limited. They must not stop at our own fate, but must embrace the whole community. This community, again, must not be limited, but must extend to all races of beings with whom we can come into immediate or mediate intellectual relation. It must reach, however vaguely, beyond this geological epoch, beyond all bounds. He who would not sacrifice his own soul to save the whole world, is, as it seems to me, illogical in all his inferences, collectively. Logic is rooted in the social principle. (CP, 2.654)

Peirce admits in both essays that there is no evidence whatsoever for the assumption that the community will "ever arrive at a state of information greater than some definite finite information . . ." (CP, 5.357) or that the human community "will exist forever" (CP, 2.654). There is no "scintilla" of evidence to show that intelligent life will exist at any future moment. Neither is there any reason or evidence against it (CP, 2.654). Hence, our belief in the indefinitely extensive and enduring community is a necessary "hope," in the Kantian spirit. Peirce says of the belief that the community's search for knowledge will be completed, that it

> involves a transcendent and supreme interest, and therefore from its very nature is unsusceptible of any support from reasons. This infinite hope which we all have . . . is something so august and momentous, *that all reasoning in reference to it is a trifling impertinence*. We do not want to know what are the weights of reasons *pro* and *con*—that is, how much *odds* we should wish to receive on such a venture in the long run—because there is no long run in the case; the question is single and supreme, and ALL is at stake upon it (CP, 5.357; long emphasis is mine)

The question of the inevitability of the completion, hence the convergence, of knowledge is an issue whose valid resolution *cannot be imagined via the notion of the long run*. It is an issue that stands outside the series of inferences, the progress of inquiry, because it concerns a condition of that series and its progress. We must believe convergence *in order to* inquire. Peirce seems close to founding reason on an irrational, or at least non-rational, leap of faith. But he continues, "We are in the condition of a man in a life and death struggle; if he have not sufficient strength, it is wholly indifferent to him how he acts, so that the only assumption upon which he can act rationally is the hope of success. So this sentiment is rigidly demanded by logic . . . it is always a hypothesis . . . justified by its indispensableness for making any action rational" (CP, 5.357).

In this remarkable passage, in terms reminiscent of James's essay, "The Will to Believe," Peirce seeks to close the circle, to *make the choice to be rational a rational choice*; indeed, a "rigidly" logical one. To accomplish this his rhetoric has shifted to the practical and naturalistic. The "logical" justification for the choice to be logical is logic's practical indispensability, which increases our chances of success in the "life and death struggle." As he wrote in 1890 of the necessity of believing that all facts are explicable, "This is what Kant calls a regulative principle, that is to say, an intellectual hope. . . . Despair is insanity. . . . We must therefore be guided by the rule of hope" (CP, 1.405).

The Community of Hope

Peirce's realism and his justification of inquiry are in the end based on three related commitments: to community, to convergence, and to inquiry. The first is the idea of a particular, methodologically homogeneous community. Its unity is essential; only the unified nature of that society saves truth in Peirce from pluralist disintegration. Its members share a method, science, and a purpose, truth. One of the necessary conditions of convergence is that the community wants to converge, that it shares the notion that truth is one, that it is devoted, ethically and aesthetically, to inquiry. We can see how logic and science are connected to ethics, not only in the sense that logical thought is a species of ethical self-control, but in that both are built on communal identification. We can also see Peirce at his most transcendental here, for the community we must identify with transcends time and place.[49] Convergence is dependent on a transcendental community.

At the same time, community presumes convergence. The community is held together by belief in truth, which is the eventual convergence of belief. Convergence is the hope that unifies the community. We must affirm this hope, which is to say, we must pledge allegiance to the community of inquirers, as a matter of practical necessity, just as, for Kant, we must accept membership in the ideal "kingdom of ends."[50] Because convergence is the justification of realism, Peirce's position is in effect that *we must believe that realism is justified in order to live*. A kind of foundationalism, in the sense of the justification of realism, is both a naturalistic and a pragmatic necessity. The validity of truth as the end of philosophy and inquiry is established by the fact that truth serves the *end* of life against the *end* of life; it serves the aim of life against insanity and death.

If a conventionalist believes that there is only one epistemically relevant community, characterized by a common goal and in substantial agreement, then conventionalism converges on realism. It asymptotically approaches realism, as it were; in practice, they become indistinguishable. For what makes conventionalism antithetical to realism is the possibility of multiple and discordant communities and conventions. Peirce's belief in the singularity and unity of the relevant community is what restricts the antirealist implications of his otherwise frankly conventionalist epistemology.

The third leg of the triadic basis of Peirce's thought is his pragmatic command: encourage inquiry! Inquiry is for Peirce a moral and aesthetic quest. It rationalizes the world, thereby embodying an aesthetic ideal with religious significance; in his marvelous phrase, it "grows" an ideal. This is, in a way, the last word on Peirce. He placed the ultimate value on inquiry, the hypothesis and pursuit of truth. This pursuit will lead to the greatest community of self-controlled conduct, to the actualization of the highest moral, aesthetic, and religious ideal.

Peirce's system hangs together if one accepts his community, his hope, his love of inquiry. But we need not accept them, and he can produce no noncircular reasoning to support them. The Peircean attempt to justify a maximally attenuated realism, a pragmatic realism, has not avoided the problems of its antirealism. It has not and cannot succeed in justifying either realism or the possibility of philosophical knowledge. All it can do is map out what the world must be like if inquiry's hope is to be justified, if the inquirer's despair is to be avoided. Peirce explains what the world must be for inquiry to be what it is. One might ask Peirce, "Why ought I step into your circle?" He would presumably reply, "Are you not already in it? Are you not already an inquirer? Can you inquire, or live, without the community of hope?"

4

NONFOUNDATIONAL
REALISM

Before proceeding with the examination of our major figures, we must address a systematic question. As we have seen, Peirce raised the possibility of justifying philosophical knowledge without foundational or immediately certain cognitions, of philosophy as systematizing and extending the work of the sciences and of a pragmatic realism based in experimental method. Today these ideas are prominent among a family of current philosophical methods that I have called the *nonfoundationalist* response to the crisis of philosophy, which seeks to reform traditional, foundationalist philosophy rather than reject it. It will be useful to discuss these approaches at this point, in Peirce's wake, because they in effect extend the metaphilosophical possibilities raised by Peirce. In that sense, this brief chapter will serve as a long footnote to its predecessor.

There are several ways to try to justify the truth of philosophical inquiry without recourse to foundational knowledge and without intentionally abandoning realism, but all involve an alteration of the type or degree of validation traditionally required for philosophical judgments so that something less than ultimate justification is required. In particular, one may accept that all philosophical validation is hypothetical or abductive or vindicatory or comparative or pragmatic. This chapter will suggest that this approach is philosophically inadequate, because it seeks to satisfy unlimited inquiry either with *limits* or with something *other than truth*. The attempt to justify philosophy by reducing its traditional, Promethean intentions, cannot be justified within the bounds of ultimate inquiry. This is not to deny the reasonableness of the nonfoundational response to the crisis of philosophy, but it is to question *whether philosophy ought to be reasonable*. That too would have to be established by argument. Reasonableness or prudence is no doubt one plausible

philosophical impulse among others, but to equate it with the philosophical spirit as a whole, to insist that philosophy must be prudent
to be legitimate, is another matter. And to justify such a claim one
would have to offer nonprudential reasons.To say that a certain
philosophical option is true because no other option coheres with the
requirements of practice, or because accepting it enriches human
life, or because it seems intuitively satisfying, or because some theory must be believed and the option in question is the best current
theory, or because the effects of accepting the theory are good—and
these are certainly different claims—is to accept a certain view of
what constitutes justification. That view itself, if we are to subject it
to philosophical inquiry as to its truth, demands a noncircular justification. If, as I believe, none is forthcoming, then to accept it as true
is to make a decision about the aim or end of philosophy, namely,
that truth is subordinate to some other end, that philosophy is not
primarily inquiry into truth.

Limiting Philosophy

There are three ways of avoiding the demands of ultimacy,
hence foundationalism, while yet justifying philosophical knowledge. They are to accept some philosophical judgments as indubitable; a limited, hence comparative, notion of validation; or some
kind of pragmatism, for which the demands of practice justify philosophical judgments as valid or true. These three are not necessarily
independent; whether they are independent depends on the kinds of
questions we may legitimately ask about their meaning. Suffice to
say that they are often combined. One could for example hold that
certain judgments are indubitable, or that limited, comparative validation is philosophically acceptable, because of the demands of
practical activity. It could be argued that some kind of pragmatism
lies behind all the attempts to limit the demands of philosophical
validation.

One method of limiting inquiry would be to introduce some
notion of indubilitability, to claim that some knowledge is unquestionably valid. There is a version of this notion that does not assume
privilege or presence—that is, immediate, unquestionable truth—
and that we have met before. There may be indubitable assertions
whose validity cannot be shown but cannot be doubted either. So,
one might propose to limit inquiry by asserting certain principles
that are indubitable, and perhaps true, although unsupportable.
This is the positive claim made by commonsensism, exemplified by

The notion of destiny appears in a more famous presentation of the convergence theory in "How To Make Our Ideas Clear." Having already defined the real as "that whose characters are independent of what anybody may think them to be . . ." (CP, 5.405), Peirce writes,

> all the followers of science are animated by a cheerful hope that the processes of investigation, if only pushed far enough, will give one certain solution to each question to which they apply it . . . the progress of investigation carries them by a force outside of themselves to one and the same conclusion. This activity of thought by which we are carried, not where we wish, but to a fore-ordained goal, is like the operation of destiny. . . . This great hope is embodied in the conception of truth and reality. The opinion which is fated to be ultimately agreed to by all who investigate, is what we mean by the truth, and the object represented in this opinion is the real. That is the way I would explain reality. (CP, 5.407)

A famous exposition of his theory of reality occurs in Peirce's 1871 review of A. C. Fraser's *Works of Berkeley*. The real, he says, "is that which is not whatever we happen to think it, but is unaffected by what we may think of it" (CP, 8.12). Peirce repeats that there must be real things, because our opinions are constrained by something other than ourselves, and that human opinion converges on the truth about them. He asks, "What is the POWER of external things, to affect the senses? . . . [It] is nothing different from . . . a general drift in the history of human thought which will lead it to one general agreement. . . . And any truth more perfect than this...any reality more absolute than what is thought in it, is a fiction of metaphysics" (CP, 8.12).[40]

In the midst of presenting his vaunted realism, Peirce is also willing to face the conventionalism implicit in his view. He writes, "Wherever universal agreement prevails, the realist will not be the one to disturb the general belief by idle and fictitious doubts. For according to him it is a consensus . . . which constitutes reality. . . . And if a general belief, which is perfectly stable and immovable, can in any way be produced, *though it be by the fagot and the rack*, to talk of any error in such belief is utterly absurd" (CP, 8.16; my emphasis).

Despite the chilling tone of this remark, conventionalism has for Peirce an important moral significance. Nominalism, the view that reality is composed entirely of individuals, means the unreality of community. Pragmatic realism saves community, and with it the

Thomas Reid; its negative claim being the denial that certain principles are open to philosophical doubt. Reid asserts the existence, and
the truth, of indubitable principles, but denies that they can be justified.

This use of indubitables is open to some obvious objections.
First, how are we to be sure that some belief is really indubitable?
Mistakes about this are common. Further, as Peirce claimed, the
assertion of indubitables is tantamount to asserting that whatever
we have a very great inclination to believe must be true.
Indubitability would seem to be a psychological condition, subject to
historical change and interpersonal variation. What is indubitable
to one community at one point in history may not be to another at
another time. And last, what is the justification for making indubitability a justification for the truth of belief? Why ought we believe
that what we must believe is true? The point is either that there is
no justification and none is required or that there is the practical
necessity of basing inquiry on what we cannot help believing. This is
not to say that the use of indubitables is wrong, but that their use
cannot be shown to be right.

A second and more common method is to deny that completeness of validation is necessary, and accept that *incomplete* validation legitimately determines philosophical assent. This approach
constitutes a wide avenue with many different philosophical travelers. According to them, we push the process of validation as far as
we can, but the absence of a completion to the process does not disqualify the principles we are investigating from being held to be
valid. For, this view continues, we are able to give partial validation
to many principles; that is, we find evidence for them and reasons to
believe them. Our failure to find adequate reasons for the reasons
for the reasons for, and so on, ought not erase the value of the limited validation we have provided. Connected with this is the strong
tendency to believe that our aim is to improve our beliefs with
respect to their truth, improvement being a fundamentally historical and comparative notion. Inquiry is melioristic in practice, if not
in its ultimate goals and transcendent hopes. And, at any rate, if we
are doomed to think and question, to guide our actions by beliefs, so
that the inhibition of belief is not an option, then a reasonable and
common-sense metaphilosophy would seem to accept as true the
best currently available theory, 'best' being determined according to
our 'best' current methods. This may mean that 'truth' is equivalent
to 'rational acceptability,' the latter being indicated by whatever
view best survives rational criticism. One may regard philosophies

as hypotheses, never certain, but not for that reason incapable of being asserted as true. What makes one consistent explanatorily adequate hypothesis acceptably true is that it is superior to others. Philosophy must accept justification via vindicatory arguments, which justify a theory by claiming that if any theory is adequate, the theory in question is. This family of related ideas shares the notion, implicitly or explicitly expressed, that a true view is the one that is better than the alternatives, hence that *validity is ultimately comparative*.

Let us briefly survey some of these related ways of avoiding foundationalism. We have already discussed one of the most famous versions, namely, naturalistic epistemology. In Chapter Two we saw the potentially antirealist self-reflexive inconsistency of naturalistic epistemology. What is relevant here is naturalistic epistemology's abandonment of foundationalism.

In his 1968 lecture "Epistemology Naturalized," Quine argues that, because it has proven impossible to demonstrate the validity of the foundations of science or even to provide a rational reconstruction of science out of sense experience (due to the underdetermination of scientific theories by sense data), there is no longer any reason to avoid the inclusion of epistemology *in* science. He writes, "Epistemology, or something like it, simply falls into place as a chapter of psychology and hence of natural science. It studies a natural phenomenon, viz., a physical human subject. This human subject is accorded a certain experimentally controlled input . . . and in the fullness of time the subject delivers as output a description of the three-dimensional external world and its history."[1]

The apparent circularity of this way of conceiving epistemology is that science is an instance of that whose genesis and validity it seeks to study. Quine recognizes the circularity, but he does not consider it vicious.

> The old epistemology aspired to contain, in a sense, natural science. . . . Epistemology in its new setting, conversely, is contained in natural science. . . . But the old containment remains valid too, in its way. . . . There is thus reciprocal containment, though containment in different senses: epistemology in natural science and natural science in epistemology.
>
> This interplay is reminiscent again of the old threat of circularity, but it is all right now that we have stopped dreaming of deducing science from sense data. We are after an understanding of science as an institution or process in the world, and we do not

intend that understanding to be any better than the science which
is its object.[2]

In effect, Quine is basing the validity of philosophical knowledge on the claim that science is essentially indubitable. Science,
hence philosophy, is one seamless methodological fabric of inquiry,
and we have no other. It would make no sense to doubt the validity
of philosophy or science, since we have no other method that could
issue in that judgment. Quine is happy to live with the limited validation implied.

A more complex, yet similarly naturalistic context for philosophical inquiry is offered by Abner Shimony's "dialectical" approach to the foundations of knowledge. Like Quine, Shimony has
urged that naturalistic epistemology admit its circularity. But
unlike Quine, he argues that it be augmented with analytic epistemology and a dialectical metaepistemological approach, which he
calls "integral epistemology."[3] Shimony's circularity involves the
acceptance that our knowledge is dependent on several fundamental points or bodies of knowledge, none of which can be ultimately
validated separately, but that can be used to validate each other.
The system of scientific and philosophical knowledge is, as Peirce
recommended, built on multiple supports that are mutually rein-
forcing.

However, it would seem that to accept this approach is either to
admit these pockets of fundamental knowledge as irreducible
indubitables or to validate them on the grounds that together they
make the best available comprehensive account of the world. These
two interpretations are not incompatible, for one could claim that
we cannot doubt the truth of either the best current modern scientific theory or common sense, and so the comprehensive philosophical construction that best harmonizes these indubitables is
valid. We are, so to speak, inside the circle determined by several
bodies of data and propositions whose collective validity we cannot
doubt. We cannot determine whether our circle is the *right* circle,
but only clarify, coordinate, and improve it from within.

Shimony's is not the only attempt to provide a theory of the
world that dovetails with epistemology to give the latter intelligibility and a more complete validation. The very different philosophical
view of Robert Neville is another example of this monistic attempt
to "close the circle." Strikingly, both are indebted to Peirce, as well
as to the author of perhaps the most remarkable twenieth century
attempt to harmonize the natural scientific world view with idealistic considerations in a single metaphysical system: Whitehead.

Among contemporary philosophers Neville has laid out perhaps the most articulate case for the plausibility and necessity of this kind of systematic philosophy. For Neville, philosophical systems are hypotheses. As such their adequacy with respect to their truth is provided by a complex set of criteria: internal consistency; compatibility with accepted "less vague" (such as lower level and empirical) theories; specifiability by less vague propositions; and the unavailability of a better system.[4] The truth of such an hypothesis is constituted by the absence of specifications that turn out to be false according to our less vague true propositions. Neville rightly admits that truth in this sense is only one of the criteria or aims that an adequate philosophical system seeks to satisfy as a pragmatic and aesthetic project of civilization.

My response is simple. To regard a philosophical system as true or valid in a hypothetical sense does indeed abjure a kind of foundationalism. But it also fails to answer deeper questions about the validation of the system's truth, such as what reason is there to believe that the best current hypothesis is true or what if *no* theory about the subject matter in question is true? The temptation is to turn to a pragmatic metaphilosophical position, namely, that we must believe one of the current theories in order to guide our imaginations and actions. But this returns us to the metaphilosophical question, Why should we believe that what we must believe is true or, more simply, what is the relation of utility or goodness and truth?

Another, less ambitious, and more purely epistemological example is the attempt to reinterpret or replace the notion of a belief's justification with its survival of a process of rational criticism. Sir Karl Popper's falsificationism and W. W. Bartley III's comprehensive critical rationalism oppose the "justificational" approach, for which an assertion can be accepted as valid or true only if it is justified in a positive sense.[5] Recognizing that the attempt to accept only justified beliefs condemns us to either an endless search in which no belief is sufficiently justified or the adoption of first principles that are themselves unjustifiable, Bartley proposes a "nonjustificational" alternative, which he calls, a "critical rationalist" or "comprehensively critical" approach.[6] That inquiry be rational requires only that all beliefs be subject to criticism and that accepted beliefs be those that best survive criticism. Bartley asserts, "Our approach . . . denies that justifications must be given for something to be rational. . . . For we contend that nothing at all can be justified rationally. *Not only do we not attempt to justify the standards* [of rationality]; *we do not attempt to justify anything else in terms of the standards. . . .* Rather we locate rationality in criticism. A rationalist is, for us, one who holds all his positions . . . open to criticism."[7]

This approach might seem to avoid my problem of validation or justification altogether. However, I mean assertive validation in a broad sense that includes what Peirce would call abductive as well as inductive and deductive inference. A theory that best survives criticism is to be accepted because it is claimed to be the best available explanation of phenomena. So, the claim that such a theory ought to be accepted as true, for whatever reasons, comes under my notion of validation, albeit in a limited and comparative sense. That a belief is to be accepted, however provisionally, on Bartley's or Popper's grounds must mean either that the belief is more successful than any other candidates or superior in some equivalent way.

For these philosophers limited validation is adequate. This is, perhaps, a reasonable view, but its validity is not unquestionable. There are things in this world that are valuable when incomplete. Half a loaf of bread is far better than none to a hungry human being. But when trying to vault across an abyss, is reaching halfway across appreciably better than reaching a quarter of the way, or better even than falling straight off the edge? The question is, From the perspective of inquiry into truth, is incomplete validation more like half a loaf of bread or half the way across an abyss?

If all validation of philosophical judgments is incomplete, how do we know when our incomplete validation is sufficient to warrant assent? For example, if I am trying to see if the belief that there is an omnipotent God is valid or true, and the reason is offered that such a God would explain the existence of the world, shall I now accept the belief? For if all validation is incomplete anyway, so that no amount of inquiry will produce a complete validation, why not stop with this first, entirely plausible reason for assent? Suppose criticism of this proposed validation is given—for example, there are other adequate, nontheistic explanations of the universe—eliciting another validating reason—for example, that those other accounts do not explain the objectivity of moral values and give no meaning to my life. Why not stop now? Why, indeed; many people do stop there. The philosophical community, on the other hand, evidently feels the obligation to continue the process of inquiry. But how far must a philosopher continue to inquire? When may we legitimately decide that enough validation has been given? If the incompleteness of the validation does not make assent unphilosophical (does not constitute a cessation of inquiry that is illegitimate from the point of view of ultimate inquiry), then how is one incomplete set of validations superior to another incomplete set?

Nor is indeterminacy merely a quantitative matter, a matter of how many validating steps are taken or how much evidence there is. It is also a qualitative question of the kinds of evidence, the character of the reasons given. People differ as to what kind of reason is decisive. This happens even in science. For Einstein, the absence of a certain kind of reason for believing in the completeness of the quantum mechanical description of reality outweighed all the weight of evidence in its favor. The theist and atheistic typically disagree over the kinds of evidence that are decisive. How then to adjudicate that issue?

Abstractly put, my point is that the renunciation of the possibility of completing the process of validation changes the meaning of any incomplete step within the process, because it eliminates the meaningfulness of imaginatively adopting the perspective of the completed process. Absent a belief in the cogency of completion, that is, of ultimate validation, we cannot know that the validation of *any* judgment will not be overturned later. I believe that many philosophers, out of an understandable and perhaps mature desire to limit extravagance and expectation, have underestimated what is implied in denying the possibility of achieving complete validation. It is as if people who once believed they were engaged in a process of inevitable progress that would end in the achievement of an ideal state, having been epistemically chastened, ceased to believe in inevitability or the attainability of the ideal, but remained steadfastly confident about the *fact of* progress. This might possibly make sense if we were speaking of social progress, but if the subject is progress in knowledge, then that confidence is misplaced. For if the achievement of an ideal knowledge that cannot later be falsified is impossible, then our belief that our current knowledge is more true than our previous knowledge is also uncertain. That is, the validity of the assertion that we are engaged in a process of improvement is no more justifiable than the assertion that we will attain completion. The fact of melioristic progress is as uncertain as achievement of the ideal.

Of course, with respect to nonphilosophic inquiry the answer will immediately be given that we confirm this knowledge of improvement with practical tests. I have no desire to dispute that claim; my concern is with philosophical knowledge, not all knowledge. In the case of philosophy the very idea that practical tests can validate claims is in question, so to use pragmatic criteria is to give a controversial philosophical answer. The justification of the claim that practical benefit or practical necessity validates truth is elusive.

Because many competing beliefs are presumably capable of varying degrees of limited validation, belief acceptance on these grounds is inevitably comparative. What justifies assent to the truth of belief is the superiority of one belief to other candidates for belief in terms of their relative validation. (This does not by itself imply that the *truth* of such belief is relative.)

Despite the apparent reasonableness of the comparative approach, we must still ask whether it is justified to claim that the *best* of all candidate theories is *true*. At virtually all times in history with respect to most important issues there has been a "best" theory, but presumably most of those "best" theories have been false, indeed, for us, laughably false. Every prehistoric tribe of animists no doubt contained within it some reasonable persons who claimed that skepticism was wrong, and that the most reasonable theory, the best theory at the current time, was valid. But were they right?

Imagine three ancient competing beliefs: one says the earth rests on the back of a great tortoise, the second that the earth rests on the back of a great squirrel, the third doubts that any extant theory is approximately true. Imagine that the view that the world is supported by a tortoise, with its strong, stubby legs and broad back, eventually defeats both the view that the world is on the back of a large squirrel, as well as the skeptical view that what kind of animal wears the world is unknowable. The tortoise theory was the best theory available at the time. Today we think both the tortoise theory and the squirrel theory about as absurdly far from the truth as it is possible to get, and that the tribal skeptics were right at least about the limits of physical knowledge in their day, if not for all time. The best physical theory was not only false, it was laughably false. Hence we may still wonder whether *our* best theory is true, however reasonable it is to believe it, relative to its competitors.

One may, of course, still say that we ought to believe or assert the best current view. But we must ask about the justification of this 'ought.' Either it is based on a belief in the view's truth after all, whose validity I am questioning, or it is based in the belief that it is *practically* beneficial, or even practically necessary, to believe that the best current theory is true. That may or may not be. Certainly it is commonly beneficial to believe the best current theory. Frequently it is necessary to do so. Perhaps it is often "wise." Sometimes, however, it is neither wise nor beneficial. One might say that modern science proves its truth by its practical, technological success, hence it is wise for modern people to believe the best current theory. But, to repeat, ought the practical benefit of accepting a belief be our criterion of its truth? What does *utility* have to do with *truth*, if truth is understood in a realist sense?

Further, the various proposed limitations on inquiry cannot be justified without recourse to the kind of ultimate inquiry they seek to make irrelevant. If we seek to validate or justify those limits, we are thrown back into the kind of discussion those limits seek to avoid; namely, an open-ended philosophical discussion about ultimate justification. And this is, I suggest, what usually happens when arguments for limitation are made in philosophical company. This indicates something important: *it is not possible to justify the cessation of ultimate inquiry by reasons that will be acceptable to ultimate inquiry.*

Now, this fact does not falsify the project of limitation. It only indicates that, even when philosophers try to limit ultimate inquiry, they feel obliged to engage in ultimate inquiry to justify those limits. If this were not true, then the advocates of limitation would simply avoid giving any further validation for their proposals; and of course, such avoidance remains a possibility. The way to avoid my argument is not to define philosophy as ultimate inquiry. Practically, that would require that we not ask certain kinds of questions, that when such questions are asked we do not try to give an answer. The question is, Would such a philosophy be what most of us philosophers expect and want? I believe that, at least part of the time, it would not be.

Does this mean that science and everyday experience are not true, or do not produce knowledge of reality? No, it means that once we think *philosophically* we cannot be sure that they do, that whether they do remains an open question for us. The incompleteness of validation does not render their judgments invalid nor need it impair or inhibit inquiry. But once we open ourselves to the questionability of all judgments and the continuous demand for validation, we lose the ability to assent to judgments of reality without recognizing their provisional nature ('provisional' being understood in a strong sense).

My analysis may inspire a basic criticism. One might say that because it is the point of these philosophical positions to deny the possibility and the necessity of validation beyond a certain limit, there is no point in my claiming that they cannot be validated beyond that very limit! This criticism raises a deep issue. My response to it is twofold. First, if a philosopher believes that it is senseless to question the validity of a certain metaphilosophical view—that is, the view that validation is limited—then I must question whether it is sensible to assert the validity or truth of that view. If the view cannot be sensibly regarded or treated as invalid, then how can it be sensibly regarded or treated as valid, rather than merely as a fact without normative sanctification? Second, to accept this limited alternative is to make an important claim about the nature of philosophy; namely, that a range of questions philosophy has variously asked, consonant with its role as ultimate inquiry, cannot be sensibly asked. Here I would ask only for consistency. If philosophy is limited inquiry, whose nature requires nothing more than limited validation, then the search for deeper and wider validation must, at some point, be irrelevant and unnecessary. The search ought simply to stop. But what is that point, how would we know it, and how would we justify our claimed knowledge of it?

Pragmatic Realism

Pragmatism is currently enjoying a kind of renaissance. Hilary Putnam, Richard Rorty, and Joseph Margolis, to name but a few, have sought to recapture the philosophical tradition of Peirce, James, and Dewey as a tonic for the apparent exhaustion of other philosophical resources. Peirce in particular has been the subject of a renewed interest made all the more striking by his virtual absence from earlier philosophical conversation.

It seems to many that a pragmatic realism is the royal road through the collapse of foundationalism and the crisis of philosophy. If it can be said that we know things as they are, yet within the context of human activity, with the validity of knowledge either guaranteed by practical success or interpreted as melioristic improvement, a kind of nonfoundational validation of inquiry would seem possible. What better home could we find for philosophy, for all inquiry, than to be contextualized by human activity in the real world? Carnap, Habermas, Quine, Putnam, Rorty, perhaps even Wittgenstein and Heidegger, not to mention the classical pragmatists themselves, appear in differing senses to make recourse to this convenient way home.

But it is my claim that this way is not valid in the eyes of ultimate inquiry. As I have argued earlier, all other things being equal, pragmatism is antirealist. Pragmatism makes the validity of judgment relative to contexts established by action, by action's means or ends. Even if, as Peirce admitted, the nominal definition of truth remains the agreement of idea with reality, the criterion of that agreement for the pragmatist is the role of the idea in the guidance of conduct or the realization of purpose. The notion of a belief's being true of an object without the possibility of our knowing its truth is, from the pragmatist viewpoint, absurd.

The attempt to justify the possibility or actuality of philosophical knowledge via pragmatism can succeed only if success is made the goal of philosophizing. Only if philosophy already accepts that it is primarily an attempt to improve the world or serve human interests, to do something valuable rather than to *say what is true*, can philosophy regard pragmatism as a justification of philosophical knowledge. A philosophy that hews close to the notion of philosophy as primarily inquiry cannot regard pragmatism as providing that justification.

We shall briefly examine two recent versions of pragmatism, the first of which could with equal justification be considered a kind of relativism and the second of which employs a kind of naturalism. My argument will be that in each case, albeit for different reasons, the pragmatic realist approach cannot adequately justify the possibility of philosophical knowledge.

Hilary Putnam's current view, called *internal realism* or *pragmatic realism*,[8] is that all truth is relative to conceptual schemes, yet realism can be preserved, for "realism is *not* incompatible with conceptual relativity."[9] Conceptual relativism does not imply that conceptual schemes are incommensurable or are all equally good.[10] The question "What does the world consist of?" makes sense and can be answered only "*within* a theory or description. . . ."[11] "Metaphysical" realism, which claims that there is at most one true or approximately true account of the world, is thereby rejected. With it goes the "nonsensical" idea of things in themselves.[12] We cannot occupy a "God's Eye point of view" on the world.[13] Putnam believes that the rejection of metaphysical realism works to save common sense or everyday realism, with which the former appeared to be allied, but was actually incompatible.

For Putnam, the meanings of all fundamental terms (object, existence, individual, real) are relative to conceptual scheme; which is to say, meaning and truth are not "legislated" by the situation being described. Yet this is not a form of relativism, according to Putnam, because once the choice of conceptual scheme is made the answers to our questions are dictated by objective necessity. Comparing two possible descriptions of a hypothetical world of three individuals

(Carnap's and a Polish logician's), one of which counts every subset of individuals as an object in the world, Putnam claims, "If I choose Carnap's language, I must say there are three objects because *that is how many there are.* If I choose the Polish logician's language ... I must say there are seven objects, because *that is how many objects ... there are.* There are 'external facts', and *we can say what they are.* What we *cannot* say—because it makes no sense—is what the facts are *independent of all conceptual choices.*"[14]

Relativism, which Putnam more or less equates with the incommensurability thesis, is self-refuting because it claims that "every person (or, in a modern 'sociological' formulation, every culture, or sometimes every 'discourse') has his (its) own views, standards, presuppositions, and that truth (and also justification) are relative to *these.*"[15] This makes it impossible to draw a distinction necessary for rational inquiry, namely, the distinction between *being* right and *thinking* one is right.[16]

Putnam draws much from the pragmatist tradition, in particular from Peirce. He defines truth as an "idealization of the notion of a statement that it is rational to believe."[17] Putnam makes fact and rationality "interdependent notions," in good pragmatist fashion. He writes, "The notion of truth itself depends for its content on our standards of rational acceptability, and these in turn rest on and presuppose our values. Put schematically and too briefly, I am saying that theory of truth presupposes theory of rationality which in turn presupposes our theory of the good."[18]

Putnam tries to maintain a subtle balance that will avoid either metaphysical realism or relativism. Some of his claims are problematic. For example, nothing in relativism denies necessity; to claim that, given a perspective, certain consequences are necessary is entirely compatible with relativism. Neither must relativism make validity relative to individual judges; that would be only one version of relativism. Also, it is not clear how Putnam can at one point deny that any conceptual scheme can be "more the 'right'" view than any other, yet hold at another point that conceptual schemes are not equally good. Despite this, his view is subtle enough that my basic criticism must be stated hypothetically. If Putnam means that our true judgments are true with respect to the character of their objects, which character obtains independent of conceptual scheme or language, then he is a realist under my definition. Putnam evidently denies this, making him an explicit antirealist in my terms. Furthermore, I have claimed that realism additionally requires that there be a single system of reality, which the realist hopes to know.

Putnam certainly wants to deny this, making him an antirealist in aspiration at least, but it is not clear that he can. It will be instructive to see how it is unclear.

Putnam uses an example, referred to previously, to make the double point that conceptual relativity is ineliminable and that what he calls the "cookie cutter metaphor"—a form of metaphysical realism—is an inadequate response to that relativity. The example is meant to show that even to count the number of objects in some array presumes a principle of individuation that determines what is to count as an object. Giving one version of the example Putnam writes, "Consider a 'world with three individuals' . . . x_1, x_2, x_3. How many *objects* are there in this world?"[19] In another, he offers, "Suppose I take someone into a room with a chair, a table on which there are a lamp and a notebook and a ballpoint pen, and nothing else, and I ask, 'How many objects are there in this room?' "[20] The answers might seem to be three and five, respectively. But in each case, one could count as objects not only the individuals mentioned (x_1, x_2, x_3, or the lamp, the notebook, etc.), but any part or any combination of those individuals (e.g., $x_1 + x_2$, or each page in the notebook). Consequently there are many possible enumerations of objects in each example, each enumeration being determined by a different meaning or criterion of 'object,' hence by a different conceptual scheme. It is the point of Putnam's pragmatic realism to say that none of these enumerations or schemes is more right than the others.

The "cookie cutter" view says that "there is a single world (think of this as a piece of dough) which we can slice into pieces in different ways."[21] Elsewhere Putnam writes, "The things independent of all conceptual choices are the dough; our conceptual contribution is the shape of the cookie cutter."[22] Putnam's point is that, although this is ostensibly an acceptance of conceptual relativity, it is still metaphysical realism. For if we ask what are the parts of this dough—or, I take it, ask for any further description of the dough—every possible answer will be one of the "partisan" descriptions that presumes a conceptual scheme.

> The cookie-cutter metaphor *denies* (rather than explains) the phenomenon of conceptual relativity. The internal realist suggestion is quite different. . . . [It] is that what is (by commonsense standards) the same situation can be described in many different ways. . . . The situation does not itself legislate how words like "object," "entity," and "exist" must be used. . . . What the cookie-cutter metaphor tries to preserve is the naive idea that at least one

Category—the ancient category of Object or Substance—has an absolute interpretation.[23]

Now, Putnam is right that the metaphysical realist is in trouble if he or she tries to describe the "dough" in any substantive way, for this could be done only using a partisan description. But what if the metaphysical realist does not try to describe the dough? What if he or she maintains only that there is a single real system of which there are various descriptions, and that the truth of judgment must presuppose some relation of judgment to that real system? Does Putnam mean to deny the cogency of *this*? It appears that he does. If it is metaphysically realist, if it is a case of cookie cutting, to say that "there is a single world" that we can describe in nonequivalent but equally legitimate ways, then Putnam's pragmatic realism is *more antirealist than it may seem*. For, given it, how could we say that alternate descriptions are descriptions of the "same situation"? How could we, for example, deny religious and artistic imaginations the status of competitors with science over reality?[24] In other words, if Putnam is denying realism at this level, then he no longer straddles the fence, but falls into a strong relativistic antirealism.

And, as we have seen, positive relativism is self-undermining. This fact shows up in Putnam's examples. Putnam introduced his first example by saying, "Consider 'a world with three individuals'." Is the meaning of 'individual' less conceptually relative than that of 'object'? If not, then this description is already a partisan one, even if it does not determine how 'object' must be used. In his second example, Putnam supposes a room with "a chair, a table, . . . a lamp and a notebook and a ballpoint pen, and *nothing else* . . ." (my emphasis). After his companion counts five objects, Putnam responds "How about you and me? Aren't we in the room?" If Putnam were to ask this of me, I would have to answer, "No we are not, for you just said there was *nothing else* in the room."[25] It is true that his a priori description of the situation is not determinate with respect to whether the notebook or each of its pages or the notebook-and-table count as objects. We do not know how many objects there are until *object* is defined. But we do know a lot about the contents of that room, independent of and prior to any alternative conceptual schemes that Putnam may want to distinguish. We know it contains a chair, a table, a pen, and so forth, and we know that pens are for writing, chairs for sitting, and so forth, in other words, we know all about these Xs, even though we do not know what general term to substitute for X (e.g., "object," "part of object," "set of objects"). We know all this because Putnam has told us as much in setting up the example.

Putnam's examples do exemplify that situations can be indeterminate with respect to concepts, absent the definition of those concepts. We do not know how many *livres* there are in a room if we are unfamiliar with the French word *livre*. It is, in other words, true that we cannot *know* without partly determinate meanings. But the question is, Does the character of what we know obtain independent of our judgment? Putnam's examples do not serve to show that we cannot know anything independent of conceptual scheme. No such example could be given, because we cannot formulate an example without presuming our ability to give a neutral description of a situation, that is, neutral with respect to the conceptual schemes we wish to compare. No one can give an example to show that conceptual relativity is ubiquitous, just as no one can consistently formulate a positive relativism.

Putnam is right that anyone who says that our knowledge is relative to conceptual schemes cannot go on to say that these schemes are windows on a reality that can be known independent of a conceptual scheme. But if Putnam is denying that it makes sense to say that there is one reality, or that the objects we know obtain independent of our language—a position to which, I have claimed, his examples fail to speak—then he must face the problems of relativist antirealism.

Joseph Margolis's view bears comparison to Putnam's. Margolis wants to avoid metaphysical realism on the one hand, which is linked with "foundationalism" and "privilege," and incommensurability, on the other, which is linked with Protagoreanism and skepticism. Margolis criticizes Putnam and others for failing to accept that their movements away from metaphysical realism are movements toward relativism. Relativism is not the enemy of science or philosophy; only the most radical forms of relativism defeat the minimal realist intuition required by inquiry. Margolis argues that a minimal realism is compatible with an "internal relativism" on pragmatic grounds.

Margolis' parameters are straightforward. A minimal realism requires that we know a real world that is mind independent.[26] A minimal relativism requires that the bipolarity of truth-values be weakened, so that propositions that would, in a strictly bipolar model, be unacceptably contradictory can be accepted as true relative to some body of evidence or justification, hence as "nondetachable" from evidence.[27] These two constraints can be satisfied by a combination of pragmatism and holism. Realism can be justified only on the basis that: (a) the whole of science or inquiry has a valid relation to the whole of the world, implying an *en bloc* rather than a "distributive" correspondence; (b) this holistic correspondence is evidenced by the ("second-order") success of the practical, survival-oriented, inquiry-guided activities of the human community. For Margolis, "realism cannot—once freed from foundationalist assumptions—remain directly accessible epistemically. We can remain realists, but the only defense possible pretty well requires that we turn to pragmatist or biological grounds and obliges us to refuse to draw a sharp demarcation between realist and idealist theories."[28] So, realism ultimately rests on what Margolis calls the pragmatist (for me, naturalist) claim, "that human inquiry is continuous with, and develops out of, the biological and precognitive interaction between organism and environment. . . ."[29]

This second-order justification of realism, a reflective rationale for positively appraising our knowledge of the real world, does not, however, efface relativism. It merely envelopes it. For the second-order pragmatic justification, and the holism of our knowledge's validity, provides no "distributive" or "epistemic" guidance, nor does it help us adjudicate among particular claims. This leaves us with a minimal relativism, with truth relative to evidence *within* science or inquiry.

Margolis makes another important point: *"There is . . . no first-order inquiry without second-order inquiry,"*[30] hence, "no first-level theories without second-level theories or second-level theories without first-level theories."[31] There is a "conceptual symbiosis" of first and second, or reflective, orders. It makes little sense to accept the legitimacy of inquiry, everyday discourse and the truth-claims therein, while denying the legitimacy of the reflective philosophical inquiry into those truth-claims and their status. The attempt to sever the line of inquiry just when it begins to ask about itself seems highly artificial, especially given that, as Margolis notes, "science itself . . . quite naturally generates its own second-order questions."[32]

Whatever its virtues, it is important to see what Margolis's approach does not do. First, he has not offered—nor does he claim to offer—a justification of realism, or pragmatic realism, or a relativized realism, except in hypothetical terms. He offers as limits on his inquiry these "boundary intuitions," that, "We cannot seriously believe that science utterly misrepresents the way the world is; and we cannot accurately determine the fit between the two."[33] His aim is not to question these, but to find a way of reconciling them. So, he attempts no justification of his second-order pragmatism.

Second, Margolis's reconciliation does not escape antirealism. On the first-order level, as he admits, we are in a relativist position, where truth-values are evidence-relative. This, he believes, could be redeemed at the second-order level, where a naturalistic pragmatism is offered as the justification of the holistic realism of science or inquiry. But Margolis does not face the antirealist implications of naturalism at this level and the self-referential problems of any positive assertion of it. So we are left, in effect, with a kind of vindicatory argument that, if realism is to justified at all, if our realist boundary intuitions are to be redeemed, then this is the only kind of justification available. But it is these big 'ifs' that I am questioning.

My point with respect to Putnam and Margolis is that attempts to domesticate relativism, to render it harmonious with a minimal realism, are problematic. They either take an antirelativist position at a higher level, and so are not truly relativistic, or are authentically relativistic and leave realism in peril. Pragmatic realism has internal problems of self-inconsistency due to the incipient antirealism of pragmatism, as we saw in Putnam. It can avoid these problems in two ways. It may limit its aims to producing a reconstruction of epistemology within certain limits, as Joseph Margolis does. But to do so avoids questioning the possibility of philosophical knowledge. Or it may explicitly abandon truth as the norm of inquiry in favor of success or goodness, making the question of realism moot. Despite the appeal of pragmatism it is hard to find philosophers willing to take that leap, at least explicitly.

Philosophy Without Foundations

My point is not that the attempt to continue the philosophical search for knowledge, to claim that philosophy has achieved such knowledge, or to justify the possibility of such knowledge, without recourse to foundationalism, is wrong. Foundational knowledge, knowledge of reality that is not open to question, is inaccessible. On this I am in agreement with nonfoundationalists and antiphilosophers alike. The question is whether, absent such knowledge, philosophical knowledge can be justified through the strategy of abandoning that element of foundationalism that I earlier claimed was inexpugnable, namely, ultimacy. Can a turn toward common sense—of a sophisticated sort, to be sure—and away from the skep-

ticism engendered by ultimate questions and the search for ultimate validation resolve the crisis of philosophy?

I have argued that it cannot, with one possible exception. The
cost of rejecting foundationalism, the unity of knowledge, the belief
in the possibility of attaining ultimate knowledge is higher than is
usually believed. The claim that we may simply abandon philosophy's extravagant hopes and relax in a reasonable, critical commonsensism may seem obvious to many. But its obviousness rests on a
failure to ask deep questions about the validity of this approach.

The one possible exception is that one might change the very
aim of philosophy. In this way, pragmatism could resolve the problem of the possibility of philosophical knowledge. Pragmatism has a
ready response to the question, Can philosophical judgments be
valid? The response is they *can* be valid in the sense of goodness or
success, or, as Peirce said, they can evolve "concrete reasonableness." By stipulating that the *end* of philosophy is not truth but
goodness, criticism is short-circuited, because potential critics are
disallowed from asking the pragmatist whether *it is true*, in the
sense of correspondence, *that* the aim of philosophy is goodness or
utility. But this pragmatism is not an option for me, since I have
assumed from the outset that philosophy is primarily inquiry aimed
at truth. To the validity of that assumption we will return in the
final chapter. For the moment it must suffice to say that those who
interpret the end of philosophy pragmatically must at least be consistent in their replacement of correspondence truth by success or
goodness and not simultaneously regard their view as true in the
traditional sense.

We have seen the limitations on the work of the inventor of
pragmatism, who saw the necessity of a speculative philosophical
system to harmonize that doctrine with realism. In Chapter Seven
we will see one more case of a philosopher seeking to avoid foundationalism, at least in the sense of a recourse to foundational knowledge, while preserving what at least appear to be traditional
philosophical hopes. Buchler will seek to do so without recourse to
pragmatism. Whether he is successful in this avoidance, or in
achieving his hopes, we shall see. But, following our chronology, we
must first turn to the labyrinthine heart of one of the great sources
for contemporary antiphilosophy. We must consider Nietzsche on
the question of truth.

5

NIETZSCHE'S NATURALISTIC EPISTEMOLOGY

I, Zarathustra, the advocate of life, the advocate of suffering, the advocate of the circle . . .

—*Thus Spoke Zarathustra*

Less than nineteen years from the time that Nietzsche began work on his first book, *The Birth of Tragedy*, he became insane.[1] The legacy of this short career is a body of work devoted, more than any other in the history of Western philosophy, to the question of the relationship of inquiry and knowledge to life.[2] We will pursue this theme in Nietzsche's work. In what respects does knowledge contribute to life and to culture, and in what respects does it undermine them? Can knowledge and art be harmonized? The obvious self-referential problem that we will have to face is that we are now engaged in knowing, that is, in inquiry. Can we gain an insight into the disadvantages of inquiry through inquiry? Could Nietzsche?

Nietzsche famously encompassed his inquiry in an apparent self-contradiction, that truth itself is an error, an illusion, a lie. Sympathetic commentators have read this judgment either as a rhetorical extravagence, a mistake later corrected, or as evidence that Nietzsche's work is an exhibitive, artistic effort ultimately not intended to be 'true' at all. I will argue that Nietzsche's greatness is diminished by any attempt thus to reduce the tensions embodied in his judgment. Just as it is important not to amalgamate Nietzsche to stock positions, it is important not to subject him to an overrefinement or to a negative theology that denies his participation in the normal aims of inquiry. I will take him at his word. Nietzsche was passionately and quite traditionally devoted to the search for truth

157

and he undercut the value of truth. He pursued the ends of philosophy recklessly into contradiction. The question is then, What are we to learn from this predicament, this labyrinth, as he called it, into which Nietzsche invites us?

Before turning to the vexing problem of the status of truth in Nietzsche, we need to acquire some perspective on his interests and concerns. Nietzsche wanted to understand the vicissitudes of the achievement and maintenance of excellence in cultures and personalities. This also requires an understanding of the conditions of degenerate and decadent qualities in culture and personality. There are no universal rules here; what is needful for the creation of greatness in a particular culture depends on the internal constitution of that culture. He wrote in 1872, "My task: to comprehend the internal coherence and necessity of every true culture; to comprehend a culture's preservatives and restoratives and their relationship to the genius of the people . . ." (PT, p. 10).

He was especially concerned to understand his own culture, modern German and European culture. He found it sorely lacking. The cause of its degeneration was particularly Christianity, but also morality in general and the idealism that justified morality. Morality, idealism and Christianity are the preeminent targets of the polemical writings of Nietzsche's last years.

On the other hand, Nietzsche did not fail to appreciate modernity's strengths. In the notes published after his death as *The Will to Power*, Nietzsche praised the "humanness" of modernity (WP, 63), its scientific rationality, its realism (in the everyday sense), and its secularism. European humanity had become "less ashamed" of its instincts and stronger (WP, 120), so that "the barbarian in each one of us is affirmed" (WP, 127). Of course, for every one of these compliments there are condemnations elsewhere in his writings. For Nietzsche modern European culture had a fundamentally "*ambiguous* character" (WP, 110).[3]

Within the historical analysis of culture there lay a systematic problem. Nietzsche believed that the pre-Socratic Greeks had found a way to achieve cultural unity out of the conflict between knowledge and art. Their way was the spirit of tragedy, which Nietzsche understood as a thisworldly pessimism, a rejection of otherworldly solutions to the pain of life, from which the Greeks managed to wring a joyous intensification of life. Nietzsche's aim was to understand the conditions of that "courageous" pessimism, in order to oppose the otherworldly, "renunciating" or "Romantic" pessimism of his age (H, pp. 210–214). He wrote in 1875, "My general task: to show how life, philosophy, and art can have a more profound and congenial relationship to each other, in such a way that philosophy is not superficial and the life of the philosopher does not become mendacious" (PT, p. 134).

This project presumed that the search for philosophic or ultimate knowledge leads inevitably to skepticism. Nietzsche believed that Kant had shown knowledge to be a dead end in regard to the deepest intellectual needs of humanity. Knowledge is severely limited, and even within its limits, is an anthropomorphic construction. The will and knowledge are in opposition, Kant had said, so that we must "limit knowledge to make room for faith," which is in effect to say, to make room for the will. What can be known through inquiry is not the sole, nor the highest, rightful determinant of thought. Thus this negative conclusion had a positive significance. Kant and Schopenhauer had, Nietzsche claimed in *The Birth of Tragedy*, destroyed "intellectual Socratism" in favor of a "Dionysiac wisdom" (BT, p. 120).[4]

The conflict of knowledge with life was not only a philosophical but a personal quandary. Nietzsche wrote in 1872, "no one can live in this skepticism . . ." (PT, p. 32). What is the sense of human existence? What is the sense of *Nietzsche's* existence? He was threatened by nihilism, by a "disgust for life." He wrote in 1875 to Von Gersdorff, "My conviction about the worthlessness of life and the delusiveness of all aims frequently oppresses me . . ." (SL, p. 106).

Nietzsche nevertheless believed that he was destined for greatness, destined to achieve or embody something "high," and that the struggle to do so in the face of an immobilizing skepticism would be the story of his life. We must, he wrote to his friend Rohde in 1870, "strain every nerve to raise ourselves out of the atmosphere of these times and by being not only wiser but above all better men," and that this would require "a thoroughly radically truthful existence . . ." (SL, p. 73). In 1882 he announced to Rohde,

> Now I have my own plan of study and behind it my own secret goal to which the remaining years of my life are *consecrated*. I find it *too hard* to live if I cannot do so in the *grand style*. . . . Without a goal that I could regard as inexpressibly important I should not have been able to hold myself aloft in the light above the black floods. This is really my only excuse for the sort of literature I have been producing ever since 1875; it is my recipe, my self-concocted medicine against the disgust of life. (SL, p. 146)

Nietzsche was devoted to the search for knowledge. When contemplating the resignation of his professorship in 1875, Nietzsche wrote to Von Gersdorff that once his official duties were resolved, "then my health will be more settled—a condition I shall not attain before I thoroughly deserve it, before, that is to say, I have discovered that state of my soul which is . . . my destiny, that healthy state in which it has retained but one of all its instincts—the will to know" (SL, p. 107).

Four sections and a conclusion follow. In the first we will examine Nietzsche's texts relevant to the question of truth and begin the task of interpreting his view. There will be a detailed discussion of the posthumously published essay, "On the Truth and Lies in a Nonmoral Sense." The second section will respond to an important recent work on Nietzsche's notion of truth, Maudemarie Clark's *Nietzsche on Truth and Philosophy*. The third section will explore the extent to which Nietzsche is a naturalist and a pragmatist. The fourth section will present my response to the thorniest question relating to Nietzsche's critique of truth; namely, How can he avoid the apparent self-contradiction implied in asserting that truth is deceptive? In so doing, this section will also explore Nietzsche's conception of philosophy and of his own discourse.

The Status of Truth

Virtually all of Nietzsche's written works address the problem of the evaluation of knowledge and its role in life and culture. Our scope must be narrowed to only the most relevant texts.[5]

Before proceeding, we must recognize that, throughout his career, Nietzsche insisted on the value of truth and truthfulness. He remained, at least at one level of his discourse, an Enlightenment thinker whose aim was to clear away comfortable superstition. In 1888, in his Preface to *The Antichrist*, he insists that, "One must have become indifferent; one must never ask if the truth is useful or if it may prove our undoing" (A, p. 568). In that book he excoriates modern people for lacking the honesty to admit that they no longer accept Christian superstitions. Although Nietzsche often distances himself from skepticism, here he speaks highly of it: "One should not be deceived: great spirits are skeptics. Zarathustra is a skeptic. Strength, *freedom* which is born of the strength and overstrength of the spirit, proves itself by skepticism" (A, p. 638). The need for faith is a "weakness." The "last and most valuable of all the senses" is the *"sense for facts"* which is expressed in science and suppressed by

Christianity (A, p. 650). Later in the same year, in *Ecce Homo*, Nietzsche begins by announcing that the sign of his philosophy ought to be, "We strive for the forbidden," and the forbidden is "truth alone" (EH, p. 219). He claims to be "the first to discover the truth by being the first to experience lies as lies . . ." (EH, p. 325). Zarathustra "is more truthful than any other thinker. His doctrine, and his alone, posits truthfulness as the highest virtue . . ." (EH, p. 328). Nietzsche ends the book with the Voltairean slogan, "Ecrasez l'infame!"[6]

My point here is not to decide the question of the status of truth in Nietzsche prematurely. It is to prevent any simplistic impression that Nietzsche does not believe in truth, or inquiry, or science. On the contrary, Nietzsche believed that inquiry, respect for the scientific method, and a ruthless devotion to truth are prerequisites for his work. They are the weapons against superstition, Christianity, morality, and idealism. Nietzsche's problem was at a higher level. Once we have shown these delusions to be delusions, then what? In particular, what happens if we apply this skeptical and rigorous inquiry to itself and the perspective it embodies? Whatever the results of that investigation, they cannot be taken to imply that inquiry, science, and truth are dispensable. Far from abandoning them, Nietzsche is attempting to push inquiry and truth to a new level.

We must also keep in mind that, because of his reading of Kant and Schopenhauer, the idea that human knowledge is illusion was familiar to Nietzsche from the outset of his career. This is evident in *The Birth of Tragedy* (1872) and in Nietzsche's notebooks from the same period. Nietzsche accepted the Kantian position that human knowledge cannot truly represent the things themselves and that the knowledge we do have is the product of our own construction. This is where Nietzsche begins.

He translated this Kantian-Schopenhauerian point into his own language. The "optimism" and "cheerfulness of the theoretical man" (BT, p. 109), like Socrates, according to which knowledge can solve the pain and contradiction of life, is both false and impoverishing: false, because as Kant had shown, it cannot achieve its aims; impoverishing, because that disappointment ultimately leads to skepticism, hence inaction and loss of confidence. Thus the search for knowledge threatens to undermine art, culture, even life itself.

On the other hand, if the human construction called knowledge is illusion, then it too is art. Nietzsche wrote of Socratic optimism, "there is, to be sure, a profound *illusion* that first saw the light of the world in the person of Socrates: the unshakable faith that thought . . . can penetrate the deepest abysses of being, and that thought is capable not only of knowing being but even of *correcting* it. This sublime metaphysical illusion accompanies science as an instinct and leads science again and again to its limits at which it must turn into *art— which is really the aim of this mechanism*" (BT, pp. 95–96).

For Nietzsche, nature is artistic in that it generates and requires illusion. He wrote further that "both art and life depend wholly on the laws of optics, on perspective and illusion; both, to be blunt, depend on the necessity of error" (BT, p. 10). Hence for us, the only fulfillment is aesthetic: "for it is only as an *aesthetic phenomenon* that existence and the world are eternally *justified*" (BT, p. 52). Nature produces illusion, we need illusion, the search for knowledge is itself a kind of illusion which proves inadequate and must be replaced or supplemented by other artistic illusions. So, we see how complex is Nietzsche's web, in which art and knowledge are opposed but intertwined.

Nietzsche begins the fascinating unpublished essay, "On the Truth and Lies in a Nonmoral Sense" (1872), by claiming that knowledge is anthropocentric. Human knowledge presupposes a human perspective on reality, just as a gnat's knowledge presupposes a gnat's perspective. Nietzsche wants to deflate our "pride" in the unique truth of what we know.

His main point follows quickly. Perception and cognition are fundamentally dissimulative. This is true not only of humans, for dissimulation is a means of preservation for all "weaker" creatures. Nevertheless, "This art of dissimulation reaches its peak in man" (TL, p. 80). Why does Nietzsche say this? Negatively, we can see that knowledge fails to penetrate to the things themselves. The very nature of our senses limits them to surface "forms." The inner essence of things, the "bowels," are hidden by nature from view. Positively, human social existence demands lies. It requires the establishment of an accepted, normal illusion, that is, the illusion that will count as "truth." The drive to know truth—in order to obtain the "pleasant, life-preserving consequences" of truth—is born of this social need (TL, p. 81). And, of course, this very process and the conformist reason for believing in the truth must be forgotten. We must believe that what is held to be true is true of reality in itself.

Nietzsche gives an account of the genesis of this "knowledge" by our cognitive apparatus. First, the objects of our knowledge are not things, but nerve stimuli. Our inference from a nerve stimulus to its

ness, and no expression; there is, at most, an *aesthetic* relation: I mean a suggestive transference, a stammering translation into a completely foreign tongue—for which there is required, in any case, a freely inventive intermediate sphere and mediating force" (TL, p. 86). Thus there can be no "adequate" or "correct" expression or representation of object in subject, and certainly no resemblance or 'picturing'.[9] The only sense in which an element of one medium (e.g., a word) may substitute for an element of another (e.g., an image) is as a metaphor of it. A perceptual image "represents" a nerve stimulus in the way the image of a rose represents love in poetry, not the way an effect represents a cause or a photograph represents its subject. Cognitive representation is an *aesthetic* relation.

Nietzsche is here accepting a kind of semiotic Kantianism, not unlike that of Peirce. Metaphors are, after all, signs. Perception is the translation of a preconscious stimulus into metaphorical sign; cognition is fundamentally semiotic. The translation itself is preconscious, hence uncontrollable, and the sign-image cannot be compared with its nonsemiotic referent. To be sure, Nietzsche differs from Peirce in regarding this, first, as an aesthetic creation and, second, as dissimulative. We will return to these two most characteristic marks of Nietzschean radicalism later.

In Part Two of the essay, Nietzsche distinguishes between the new metaphors that humans are constantly driven to produce ("The drive toward the formation of metaphors is the fundamental human drive") and the existing, socially accepted framework of concepts that have precipitated out of earlier metaphors. He represents these as two opposed impulses: the "intuitive" impulse, like an active volcano spontaneously erupting with novel metaphors, which are channeled by the "rational" impulse into the stable, hardened frameworks of myth and art. Each of the two impulses waxes and wanes in its domination of a culture; each wishes to "rule." So long as the creative, intuitive impulse can do its work without injuring, it is allowed freely to reform the rational "scaffolding" of concepts, free to be openly deceptive or dissimulating. But it is the rational spirit that knows how to "meet [man's] principle needs by means of foresight, prudence, and regularity . . ." The artistic impulse creates not out of practical need, but by "playing with seriousness." The rational spirit seeks to avoid injury and suffering, but it cannot produce happiness. The intuitive spirit seeks to avoid pain, but by producing "illumination, cheer, and redemption . . ." When the latter does suffer, the suffering is greater; and this happens more often because the intuitive spirit cannot learn from experience and so "keeps falling over and over again into the same ditch" (TL, p. 91).[10] Culture must achieve a balance of the two. Nevertheless, the two forces are not equals. For the rational is constituted by metaphors, of which the intuitive is the only source. The rational is the system of old, "useful," shared metaphors, the formerly hot lava now hardened into rock. The dialectical relationship of the two impulses is complex. We will return to the problems raised by this very interesting essay later.

Nietzsche continued to address the question of truth and knowledge.[11] In an important passage from *Human, All Too Human* (completed in 1878), Nietzsche asked, "But will our philosophy not thus become a tragedy? Will truth not become inimical to life, to the better man? . . . The whole of human life is sunk deeply in untruth. . . . Is it true, is all that remains a mode of thought whose outcome on a personal level is despair and on a theoretical level a philosophy of destruction?—I believe that the nature of the after-effect of knowledge is determined by a man's *temperament* . . ." (H, p. 30). Whether inquiry, hence skepticism, improves or destroys a human being depends on the character of the individual, or collectively, of the culture in question.

Nietzsche claims in 1882 in *The Gay Science* that humans instinctively accept "life-preserving errors" as truth. But gradually, partly through demonstration of its *utility*, a further need or impulse for truth itself, independent of utility, became differentiated: "Thus knowledge became a piece of life itself." Consequently, the impulse for truth itself is capable of *opposing* the original life-preserving errors. He writes that, "A thinker is now that being in whom the impulse for truth and those life-preserving errors clash for their first fight, after the impulse for truth has proved to be also a life-preserving power. Compared to the significance of this fight, everything else is a matter of indifference: the ultimate question about the conditions of life has been posed here, and we confront the first attempt to answer this question by experiment. To what extent can truth endure incorporation?" (GS, 110).[12]

The "unconditional will to truth," a conviction that "*Nothing* is needed *more* than truth . . ." (GS, 344), is not practically useful, on the contrary it is dangerous. It is a moral conviction, a refusal to deceive anyone, including oneself. But life itself aims at "semblance . . . error, deception, simulation, delusion, self-delusion. . . ." So the will to truth seems to oppose life, to be a will to death. Those who oppose life do so on the basis of the affirmation of another world. Thus, science still rests on a "metaphysical faith." But not just science, "even we . . . godless anti-metaphysicians still take our fire, too, from the flame lit by a faith that is thousands of years old, that Christian faith which was also the faith of Plato, that God is the truth, that truth is divine . . ." (GS, 344). We must wonder, is this the sole source of fire for Nietzsche? Is the idealist, metaphysical impulse embodied in the will to truth, that Nietzsche seeks to question, the sole source of creative passion for Nietzsche and other "free spirits"? Differently put, is this illusion not only the child but the mother of creativity? Once we ask this question we realize that we are simply repeating Nietzsche's own question about truth, and that he has already answered it in the affirmative. For truth is an illusion born of a will to illusion, yet Nietzsche remains a seeker after truth.

In *Beyond Good And Evil* (written 1885) Nietzsche reiterates that untruth is a "condition of life" (BGE, 4) as seen, for example, in the need to simplify, to narrow perspective (BGE, 188). Life requires "perspective estimates and appearances" (BGE, 34). This impulse toward simplification or "falsification" is countered by another impulse.

> *This* will to mere appearance, to simplification, to masks, to cloaks, in short, to the surface . . . is *countered* by that sublime inclination of the seeker after knowledge who insists on profundity, multiplicity, and thoroughness, with a will which is a kind of cruelty of the intellectual conscience and taste. . . . Why did we choose this insane task? Or, putting it differently: "why have knowledge at all?" Everybody will ask us that. And we, pressed this way, we who have put the same question to ourselves a hundred times, we have found and find no better answer— (BGE, 230)

In the conclusion of *The Genealogy of Morals* (written 1887), Nietzsche connects the will to truth with the *ascetic ideal*, the otherworldly ideal that rejects life. He writes that contemporary atheists are themselves the heirs of the ascetic ideal: "it is they who are its most subtle exponents, its scouts and advance guard, its most dangerous and elusive temptation. . . . These men are a long way from being *free* spirits, because they still believe in truth . . ." (GM, p. 287). Real freedom requires that the "notion of truth itself has been disposed of," for example, in the saying—which Nietzsche ascribes to the medieval Shiite sect, the Society of Assassins—"Nothing is true; everything is permitted." Skepticism is renunciation born of the "absolute will to truth," which is really a belief in the metaphysical value of truth. Earlier philosophies failed to examine this value. But once the ascetic ideal is questioned, the "problem of the value of truth" arises, and with it, the problem of the justification of inquiry itself. Of course, one must remember that Nietzsche's condemnations are never absolute, but always relative. He admits that he has "great respect for the ascetic ideal so long as it really believes in itself and is not merely a masquerade" (GM, p. 294).

Nietzsche explains that Christian truthfulness has "triumphed over the Christian god," Christian ethics over Christian metaphysics. The rigorous pursuit of truth is what "makes us good Europeans and the heirs of Europe's longest, most courageous self-conquest." But the yet unfulfilled destiny of this pursuit is the self-examination of Christian truthfulness, the attempt to answer the question, "What does all will to truth signify?" The ascetic ideal gave human existence meaning. But that ideal, "like all great things," has led to its own destruction. The last vestige of the ideal is the will to truth. He writes, "what would our existence amount to were it not for this, that the will to truth has been forced to examine itself? It is by this dawning self-consciousness of the will to truth that ethics must now perish. This is the great spectacle of a hundred acts that will occupy Europe for the next two centuries, the most terrible and problematical but also the most hopeful of spectacles . . ." (GM, pp. 297–298).

Nietzsche's notebooks, excerpted in the published text *The Will to Power*, contain some very important passages related to the question of truth, knowledge, and their relation to art and life. During 1887–1888, while writing about nihilism, Nietzsche remarked, "The feeling of valuelessness [or nihilism] was reached with the realization that the overall character of existence may not be interpreted by means of the concept of 'aim,' the concept of 'unity,' or the concept of 'truth.' . . . the character of existence is not 'true,' is false. One simply lacks any reason for convincing oneself that there is a *true* world" (WP, 12).

Here we have an example of one of the interpretive problems we will face. Does Nietzsche mean to deny the truth of our worldly knowledge or only the truth of our alleged knowledge of a nonexperiential or "metaphysical" world? Put in a different way, is Nietzsche objecting to truth or to a *true world*? We will return to this question.

As we will see in section three, Nietzsche accepts some kind of pragmatism and some kind of naturalism. He wrote in 1988 that, "Appearance is an arranged and simplified world . . . it is perfectly true for us; that is to say, we live, we are able to live in it: proof of its truth for us . . ." (WP, 568). To declare something true is a "valuation." The motivation for such valuation is that what is declared 'true' is a condition of "preservation and growth" for the being that declares it (WP, 507). The categories of reason express an expediency: "their utility alone is their 'truth'" (WP, 514). Our need is "not to know" but to "impose upon chaos as much regularity and form as our practical needs require" (WP, 515). Preservation and growth, like life itself, are expressions of the will to power. Consequently, "The criterion of truth resides in the enhancement of the feeling of power" (WP, 534).

This holds even for logic and for the law of noncontradiction. That we cannot simultaneously affirm and deny the same proposition implies only a subjective rule, an incapacity on our part, not a law that holds for reality. The "subjective compulsion" to avoid contradiction is a "biological compulsion: the instinct for the utility of inferring . . . ," and not a "truth in itself" (WP, 515). Logic contains, then, "no *criterion* of truth, but an *imperative* concerning what *should* count as true."[13] The rules of logic and the concept of identity represent a normative reconstruction of things (WP, 516).[14]

Nietzsche famously exhibits a view sometimes called *perspectivism*. He declares that, "the world, apart from our . . . living in it . . . does not exist as a world 'in-itself'; it is essentially a world of relationships . . . it has a different aspect from every point; its being is essentially different from every point . . ." (WP, 568). From 1887 we find the remark, "The most extreme form of nihilism would be the view that *every* belief . . . is necessarily false because there simply is no true world. Thus: a *perspectival appearance* whose origin lies in us . . ." (WP, 15). Likewise, he famously asserts that, "No, facts is precisely what there is not, only interpretations" (WP, 481). He continues, "In so far as the word 'knowledge' has any meaning, the world is knowable; but it is *interpretable* otherwise, it has no meaning behind it, but countless meanings.—'Perspectivism'. . . . Every drive is a kind of lust to rule; each one has its perspective . . ." (WP, 481). Summarizing this theme, Nietzsche writes, "That the value of the world lies in our interpretation . . . that previous interpretations have been . . . for the growth of power; that every elevation of man brings with it the overcoming of narrower interpretations; that every strengthening and increase of power opens up new perspectives . . . this idea permeates my writings" (WP, 616).

Nietzsche claims that, "To impose upon becoming the character of being—that is the supreme will to power" (WP, 617).[15] Becoming, he has told us, is without aim, unity, or truth, and so has no meaning for human beings. But the will to power in humanity must deceive as a means of preserving human life and as a condition for creation. There are many forms of deception, the most important being knowledge and art. The epochal question is, What deception will replace the Christian idealism that is now disappearing?

Last, in a longer section concerning art,[16] Nietzsche writes that science, religion and metaphysics are all products of the artistic will, the "will to lie," a will humanity shares with all natural things (WP, 853). Power and happiness are conditioned by lying. Art makes life possible; its function is "redemption." He then remarks, presumably of *The Birth of Tragedy*, that, "in this book . . . pessimism, or . . . nihilism, counts as 'truth'.[17] But truth does not count as the supreme value. . . ." For the will to illusion is more basic; the will to truth "is . . . merely a form of the will to illusion." The antidote to the pessimism that results from the will to truth is the recognition that there is "something that is stronger than pessimism, 'more divine' than truth: *art* . . . art is *worth more* than truth" (WP, 853). Let us begin to try to make some sense of this wealth of textual material by formulating an initial interpretation of Nietzsche's view of truth.

Nietzsche presents an antirealist view of knowledge. According to him, our judgment cannot reach things as they exist independent of our experience. Judgment is restricted to nerve stimulations or the images produced by them: that is, to a kind of phenomenalism. Further, the objects of our knowledge are constructed by us and so are "anthropomorphic." Each species of life constructs its own apparent world, and what we take to be the real world is no more uniquely real or true than the world as perceived by any other species. What is known is always relational, so that the apparent object is dependent on the relation of the thing to the perceiver. In particular, the validity of judgment is determined by the relation of judgment to the "perspective" of the judge. This is epistemic relativism pure and simple, despite Nietzsche's occasional protestations against relativism (e.g., GS, 345). Furthermore, perspectives vary among different human drives, interests, and cultures. So, there is epistemic pluralism. This is a noteworthy addition because a perspectivism without pluralism would be a fairly toothless antirealism. With pluralism, perspectivism or relativism develops a formidable set of teeth.

Last, Nietzsche certainly rejects the possibility of knowledge beyond nature and experience, or what some might call metaphysical knowledge. He rejects the knowledge of substance, God, atoms, and the unity of the self. As for a general criterion of what are the bounds of knowledge, I know of only one passage that is helpful. In *Twilight of the Idols* (1888) Nietzsche writes, "Judgments . . . of value, concerning life, for it or against it, can, in the end, never be true: they have value only as symptoms . . . *the value of life cannot be estimated*. Not by the living, for they are an interested party . . . not by the dead, for a different reason" (TI, p. 474). In addition, Nietzsche sometimes denies the existence of a supernatural world of "things in themselves." This must mean, at least, that he is denying the existence of unperceiv*able* things.

The foregoing remarks put Nietzsche among antimetaphysicians and antirealists. But there is a more radical side to Nietzsche's view. For Nietzsche appears to say that the *function* of assertive human judgment and inquiry is to deceive. It is important to put the matter in terms of function. It is one thing to claim that the results of inquiry are false, hence deceptive. Anyone who denies the veridicality of judgment could say that judgment is deceptive, that what is called truth is, de facto, a lie. But Nietzsche appears to say that the *function of truth is to lie*, that its aim is deception. This is a de jure attack on truth.

It implies, first, that assertive judgment and inquiry serve something external to themselves. The norm of assertion, that is, truth, is subsumed under some other realm or norm. Assertion represents itself as seeking the opposite of the lie, but in reality what it seeks is, from the point of view of assertion, dissimulation.[18] This is the radical core of Nietzsche's critique, and it takes him beyond skepticism and beyond most antirealist appraisals of knowledge.

What does Nietzsche mean? Does he really intend to destroy truth? Is he denying the validity of what we believe or destroying the very idea of validity? Is he destroying truth under any interpretation of it or only truth as correspondence to reality? Is he destroying some kind of truth—say, "metaphysical" truth—or all truth, including "empirical" truth? What makes Nietzsche doubly difficult to interpret on this issue is that he equivocates the meaning of *true*. He uses it—sometimes in the same sentence—to mean both traditional correspondence with reality and his own revision of the term, or "metaphors that answer needs," "socially accepted beliefs," and so forth.[19]

In the following sections I will argue that Nietzsche is referring not just to metaphysical truth, but to empirical truth as well. Hence, Nietzsche's view is indeed a radical and problematic one. If truth means correspondence of judgment to an independent reality, for Nietzsche there is no such thing as truth. What gets *called* truth in human discourse are metaphors that we produce that are socially stabilized and serve needs for survival and social harmony, judgments that achieve either exhibitive or active validity. But humans also need to regard these metaphors as assertively valid, as true in the sense of correspondence (which is the only interpretation of assertive validity that Nietzsche recognizes). Some humans liberate the notion of truth from its social-pragmatic home and pursue it independent of any recognition of its practical value. These are the inquirers, among whom are philosophers. The creation of metaphors, the satisfaction of needs through stabilized and pragmatic metaphors, the faith in their correspondence, and the pursuit of truth for its own sake, all serve and are manifestations of the will to power or the will to life in different ways.

Nietzsche's Antirealism

We need to be reasonably sure that Nietzsche is making this radical attack on truth before we ask whether his own discourse survives the self-referential problems associated with it. If I am wrong, and Nietzsche is not an antirealist regarding knowledge and truth, then the self-referential problem evaporates.

The most thorough recent treatment of the issue of which I am aware is Maudemarie Clark's study of Nietzsche.[20] Her conclusions are that Nietzsche rejects metaphysical truth, not truth in general and certainly not empirical truth; that he accepts a perspectivist notion of knowledge; and that he opposes, not the will to truth per se or the spirit of inquiry, but the will to truth above all, the claim that truth is the highest value. The motivating principle of her interpretation seems to be that we should make every reasonable attempt to save Nietzsche from the blatant performative self-contradiction inherent in the claim that "Nothing is true." Crucial to her view is the claim that Nietzsche defined truth as correspondence to reality, understood as "things in themselves," until about 1885, but afterward rejected this "representationalist" view in favor of perspectivism. Having done so, Nietzsche could retain a belief in empirical or nonmetaphysical truth, now understood as intrinsically perspectival. So Nietzsche's apparent rejection of all truth is a characteristically early doctrine, abandoned by his mature philosophy.

Clark is, I believe, right to approach Nietzsche conservatively; that is, to take pains not to ascribe to Nietzsche a more radical view than is forced on us by the most consistent interpretation of his texts. Nevertheless, she is, I believe, wrong in her conclusions.

Nietzsche takes a more radical position than Clark allows; he cannot be saved from self-contradiction.

Clark is right to call hers a "neo-Kantian" interpretation of Nietzsche.[21] Nietzsche did imbibe the outlines of his early philosophy from Kant and from Schopenhauer's neo-Kantianism, but he interprets the Kantian position in a quite un-Kantian way. To claim that what counts as true for humans does not correspond to things themselves, but is the product of a reconstruction within the human perspective, is Kantian. But Nietzsche is both more and in a sense, less radical than Kant. He is more radical in that for him perspective can vary, whereas only one perspective, the perspective of rational beings, is relevant to Kant; the construction of knowledge is pluralistic, metaphoric, artistic, cultural, and historical, not one uniform system of intuitions, concepts, and ideals for all rational beings as in Kant; the world of knowledge is illusion and deception (with Schopenhauer) rather than "objective" as for Kant; and this deception serves natural and pragmatic needs (again with Schopenhauer). He is less radical in that he regards the Kantian system as intolerably skeptical and nihilistic (excepting its religious implications), whereas Kant is content to tolerate devotion to a knowledge of limited aims.[22]

My first objection to Clark is that Nietzsche's critique of truth is not restricted to metaphysical truth, but applies to empirical truth as well. Clark's answer is that my claim is true of pre-1886 Nietzsche only. But such an interpretation would require us to restrict the scope of Nietzsche's mature view to the last three and a half years of his life. He could still write, in the summer of 1885 in *Beyond Good and Evil*, that truth is necessary errors, that "untruth is a condition of life." His works after this time are mostly polemics against Christianity and morality in which, it could be plausibly said, truth is not the main issue and it would be natural for Nietzsche to focus on metaphysical idealism.

Although it is true that Nietzsche's post-1885 publications rarely refer to the radical antitruth view, there are passages in the unpublished work after 1885 that seem to extend the critique of truth to all truth, not just metaphysical truth, passages that later appeared in *The Will to Power*.[23] During 1887–1888 Nietzsche wrote that it is the "needs for untruth" that give value to life (WP, 5) and that the "criterion of truth lies in the enhancement of the feeling of power" (WP, 534). Nietzsche connects the denial of a "*true* world" with a recognition of the "necessity of lies" (WP, 15).

Last, there is the passage from the conclusion of *The Genealogy of Morals*. As we saw, Nietzsche refers approvingly to the slogan of the Society of Assassins as the criterion of true freedom: "Nothing is true; everything is permitted." Nietzsche comments, "Here we have real freedom, for the notion of truth itself has been disposed of. Has any Christian freethinker ever dared to follow out the labyrinthine consequences of this slogan? Has any of them ever truly experienced the Minotaur inhabiting that maze? . . . I know none has. Nothing could be more foreign to our intransigents than true freedom and detachment; they are securely tied to their belief in truth . . ." (GM, p. 287). The consequences are "labyrinthine" only if Nietzsche means *all* truth, not just metaphysical truth, or if he believes that metaphysical truth cannot be disentangled from truth in general. A page later he writes that, "It appears that today inquiry itself stands in need of justification (by which I do not mean to say that such justification can be found)." If Nietzsche has rejected only metaphysical truth, then it is not clear why inquiry in general should be threatened at all.

There is a philosophical, and not only a hermeneutic, issue between Clark and myself. It concerns two related matters: the implications of perspectivism and the nature of metaphysics.

Clark claims that perspectivism does not generate a self-referential inconsistency for Nietzsche.[24] She argues that perspectivism does not rule out the commensurability of all perspectives, nor the superiority of a perspective (e.g., science) to all others.[25] When perspectives compete, if there is a "neutral" shared third perspective to appeal to, agreement is possible on which perspective is superior. She also suggests that Nietzsche can be interpreted as promoting multiple perspectives for the sake of greater "objectivity."[26]

Clark is right that perspectivism does not deny the possibility of universal agreement. It merely makes validity relative to perspective. How many perspectives there are, whether some perspective is shared by all inquirers, or whether there is a necessary and unavoidable perspective are issues left open by perspectivism per se. What perspectivism does say is that the existence of a truth, and the obligation to admit it, is dependent on a logically prior perspective. Even if all inquirers shared the same perspective, hence the same truth, they could truthfully understand that truth to mean only "true in a perspective." Nietzsche's perspectivism, taken by itself, does not imply the thesis that truths are deceptions; nor does it generate a self-contradiction in Nietzsche's assertion of it.

Perspectivism's implications are nevertheless quite radical. Perspectivism denies that what is to be judged can be said to have a nature that can determine the validity of judgments regardless of perspective. For perspectivism, that different judges make contradictory judgments of a thing is no argument against the validity of those contradictory judgments, nor cause for further inquiry. A given perspectivist or community of perspectivists may decide, on pragmatic grounds, to seek a single, internally coherent, universally acceptable set of judgments. But that set of judgments, if obtained, is no more valid in view of perspectivism than any of the contradictory judgments produced in other perspectives: all are true in a perspective. A particular judgment or theory or perspective could certainly be more true than any other for a perspectivist. That is, the perspectivist need not say, "All perspectives are equally valid" (if he or she did, this judgment would be true relative to perspective). Yet the superiority of any judgment would hold only for some perspective(s). In other words, perspectivism's implications *are antirealist*.

A strong perspectivism, one that holds for all claims, holds also for the claim that nature exists or that there are perspectives and human beings to entertain them. Any attempt to say that our judgments of things can be valid with respect to things independent of perspective, albeit that our judgments are incomplete, that they exhibit different aspects of what they judge, aspects truly characteristic of the independent thing in a super-perspectival sense is *not* perspectivism, but an ordinal or pluralistic conception of the things to be known.[27] One can be a realist and still accept that all judgments are fallible and the totality of true judgments of a thing cannot exhaust the nature of the thing. Perspectivism is another matter.

Furthermore, if the truth of judgment is relative to perspective, then God does exist for Christians, but does not for the atheist. God both exists *and* does not exist. The slaves, the Jews, the anti-Semites, the Christians, the priests, the historians, the idealists— the targets of Nietzsche's violent polemics—are all *right*, valid in the only sense there is, that is, valid in a perspective. I see little evidence that Nietzsche held this view. My point is that even the perspectivism Clark ascribes to Nietzsche would generate deep antirealist problems, including the self-referential dilemma she seeks to avoid. This is especially true because Nietzsche claims that there are multiple perspectives, that each instinct has its own perspective.

alleged cause is "a false and unjustifiable application of the principle of sufficient reason" (TL, p. 81). Truly, our knowledge can represent only "subjective" stimulations.

We then transfer or translate the nerve stimulus into a perceptual image, which is itself a "metaphor" for the original stimulus. This image is subsequently transferred into a sound or word, a "copy of the nerve stimulus in sound," which is a second metaphor. The word represents an arbitrary and subjective representation of the metaphor of the stimulus. On its basis we then form a concept by taking the word to represent many things in some respect. This step involves significant abstraction or selection. "Every concept arises from the equation of unequal things," through "overlooking what is individual and actual; whereas nature is acquainted with no forms and no concepts, and likewise with no species . . ." (TL, p. 83). This is another anthropomorphization. The final step is the creation of hierarchies of concepts to form the systems of distinctions that characterize human society and inquiry. It is the ability to transform perceptual metaphors first into conceptual abstractions and then to systematize them that distinguishes human from animal.[7] Yet any concept remains the mere "residue of a metaphor."[8]

The result is that in "knowledge" we actually possess nothing but *metaphors*. Nietzsche summarizes the point in the most famous passage from the essay: "What then is truth? A movable host of metaphors, metonymies, and anthropomorphisms: in short, a sum of human relations which have been poetically and rhetorically intensified, transferred, and embellished, and which, after long usage, seem to a people to be fixed, canonical, and binding. Truths are illusions which we have forgotten are illusions . . ." (TL, p. 84). And consequently, to be "truthful" is "to lie according to a fixed convention . . ." In forgetting the process of formation and taking the perceptual metaphors or images to be the things themselves the sense of truth arises.

Nietzsche calls the metaphor-making process artistic, and writes that, "only by forgetting that he himself is an *artistically creating* subject does man live with any repose, security, and consistency." The reason for his use of 'metaphor' to describe the status of successive representations (image, word, etc.) is that each representation belongs to an utterly different medium. How can a sound "represent" a visual image, or a visual image represent a neural stimulus? The media of stimuli, images, language, and concepts, are all "absolutely different" from each other and from the things to be represented. Between them there can be, "no causality, no correct-

To look at the problem from another perspective: what does it mean to deny that there are "things in themselves"? It all depends, to be sure, on whether and in what sense we ascribe mind- or judgment independence to the things in themselves. To say that the relational character of whatever we judge prohibits judgment of things as they are independent of our judgment is to beg the question. In the realist's account, judgment is intrinsically relational; in fact, it is a relation. The question is, *To what* are we related in a valid act of judgment? Are we related to something whose character obtains independent of our judgment or something whose character is dependent on us?

One senses in some contemporary attempts to domesticate relativism and perspectivism, to deny their antirealist implications, a tendency to conflate two different meanings of 'metaphysics.' One traditional meaning refers to a realm of reality, to a set of reals, whose nature is unlike anything in the experiential world. Traditionally, this means higher or supernatural things, like God. Here metaphysics is something beyond the world of experience. Another meaning refers to whatever there is. Metaphysics, as the most general account of reality, includes the experienced world as a part.

In Kant's usage, objects exist in two senses, as appearances and as things in themselves. My foot in itself is not in a separate realm from my foot as appearance, it is only that my experience—indeed, all possible human experience—of my foot does not, for Kant, exhaust its being. The character of the foot obtains independent of that totality of experience. My foot in itself is not ideal in the way that God is ideal, except in the sense that neither is reducible to the totality of experienced characters.

The point is that the denial that things in themselves exist can be far more than a mere denial of a transcendent realm; it can be a strongly antirealist move. It can be the assertion that the objects of judgment do not exist independent of judgment, that they are dependent on us. Some forms of realism can tolerate this denial through an idealist view of the being of the objects of judgment and claim to retain realism thereby. But this option cannot be open to Nietzsche, the great critic of idealism!

Consequently, although Clark believes that she has found a safe passage for Nietzsche between the Charybdis of metaphysics and correspondence and the Scylla of antirealism and the destruction of truth, I think her route is already within the precincts of the latter. Nietzsche offers no realist alternative to correspondence realism; perspectivism will not do.

Now I still have not answered the basic motivation of Clark's interpretation. My antirealist interpretation of Nietzsche would seem to make him blatantly inconsistent. For first of all, there are his many statements about the importance of the ruthless pursuit of truth. Second, there is the self-contradiction involved in asserting that there is no truth. Ought we not drop the imputation of antirealism in the face of these two facts?

The fact that a certain interpretation of Nietzsche would make him inconsistent need not convince us that the interpretation is wrong. Such an inconsistency would not necessarily make Nietzsche silly or ridiculous. We are dealing here with such difficult questions at the outer reaches of inquiry that it may plausibly be argued that an inconsistency at this point is either unavoidable or instructive. I will argue that Nietzsche cannot be saved, nor does he want to be saved, from self-contradiction. Neither does he contradict himself blithely, nor does he mean to imply that self-contradiction is acceptable in normal inquiry. I believe he regarded his inquiry as historically and systematically unique and as requiring a form of expression that violated the intrinsic (and perfectly acceptable) rules of inquiry. But before trying to determine this any further, we need to clarify Nietzsche's naturalism and pragmatism.

Nietzsche's Aesthetic Naturalism

Nietzsche is a true naturalist, that is, he insists that there is nothing outside of nature, hence everything is natural. The hesitation, common among philosophers, to apply this label to Nietzsche has two sources. One is the doubt that any philosophical position, any "ism," can be ascribed to Nietzsche. I empathize with this caution and will address it later. The other is based on a narrow view of naturalism, which equates it not only with a scientific view of nature, but with nineteenth century determinism and mechanism. This is a mistake. There are many different ideas of nature, hence many naturalisms: scientific, vitalistic, Romantic, pluralistic, contextualist, and so on. Only if we retain an anachronistic and simplistic conception of naturalism can we remain blind to Nietzsche's naturalism.[28]

To deny naturalism is to exempt something from subjection to natural processes (whatever these are). What is usually exempted is some feature of human being, which is homologous to the ground of being, which is also exempted. Idealism is the canonical form of this exemption. Idealism is perhaps Nietzsche's greatest polemical target. But here we must be careful, for Nietzsche was strongly influenced by two partial idealists, Kant and Schopenhauer, and his philosophy can sometimes appear idealist. Nietzsche's acquaintance and correspondent Malwida von Meysenbug could, in writing to Nietzsche, call his philosophy a "practical idealism," albeit one without "metaphysical preconceptions."[29] What Nietzsche opposes is any attempt to affirm a higher, supernatural reality. What Nietzsche has in common with idealism is his belief that the world we know is a mental construction in some significant sense—a belief shared by Kant, Schopenhauer, and Peirce.

The nature of this nature is less clear. Nietzsche's is not the nature of modern science, but this is not because the latter is material and nonteleological. Nietzsche emphasizes the materiality, and purposelessness of nature. Rather, Nietzsche's nature is nonscientific in that it is not determinable by discoverable laws; it cannot be exhausted by knowledge. We may be tempted to call his a Dionysian nature, as he suggested (WP, 1067). Perhaps the best label for Nietzsche's philosophy would be *aesthetic naturalism*. As we saw in *The Birth of Tragedy*, Nietzsche makes nature itself artistic in the sense of producing illusion.

What is most clear in Nietzsche's naturalism is that it makes us subject to nature in all respects. But even this sense of naturalism is, in Nietzsche, complex. For it is natural for us to fight against what is natural. In *Beyond Good and Evil* he wrote,

> "According to nature" you want to *live*? O you noble Stoics, what deceptive words these are! Imagine a being like nature, wasteful beyond measure, indifferent beyond measure, without purposes and consideration, without mercy and justice, fertile and desolate and uncertain at the same time; imagine indifference itself as a power—how could you live according to this indifference? . . . Is not living—estimating, preferring being unjust, being limited, wanting to be different [than this nature]? (BGE, 9)

Here we can already see the dialectical implications of Nietzsche's naturalism. Although the will to power—which is "after all, the will of life" (BGE, 259)—and nature constitute reality, human life naturally must seek to exempt itself from the conditions of that natural life. In other words, it is *natural* for human beings to seek to be *unnatural*.

Nietzsche's most famous description of the natural world, written in 1885 and published as the last entry in *The Will to Power*, deserves to be quoted at some length.

> And do you know what "the world" is to me? . . . a monster of energy, without beginning, without end . . . a sea of forces flowing and rushing together, eternally changing, eternally flooding back, with tremendous years of recurrence . . . out of the simplest forms striving toward the most complex, out of the stillest, most rigid, coldest forms toward the hottest, most turbulent, most self-contradictory, and then returning home to the simple . . . back to the joy of concord . . . blessing itself as that which must return eternally, as a becoming that knows no satiety, no disgust, no weariness: this, my *Dionysian* world . . . without goal, unless the joy of the circle is itself a goal . . . do you want a *name* for this world? . . . *This world is the will to power—and nothing besides!* And you yourselves are this will to power—and nothing besides! (WP, 1067)

This view of nature as the will to power embodies what Nietzsche regarded as his most important thought, the eternal recurrence. This idea has been subjected to much discussion, which cannot be explored here. Very briefly, it is the idea that, given infinite time and finite matter, every possible combination of matter will not only occur, but must be repeated endlessly. All events, in every detail, will eventually recur, again and again. The key to the notion is the denial of creativity to a natural universe without a Creator or a goal. There is a limit to the possible states and events of the universe; it cannot create indefinitely many new possibilities. It is *finite*. Hence all states must repeat. The eternal recurrence, which Nietzsche first thought in August 1881, first described in *The Gay Science* (GS, 341), and which is central to *Zarathustra*, is Nietzsche's criterion of world-affirmation. To say "yes" to an eternally recurring world is to say "yes" to a purely natural world, without supernatural myth.[30] Nietzsche remarks in a note from 1883–1885 that his notion of the eternal recurrence "is the closest *approximation of a world of becoming to a world of being:*—high point of the mediation" (WP, 617). It is the measure of the "this-worldly" pessimism, the joyful or courageous pessimism that Nietzsche had been seeking from the beginning of this career.

Near the end of *Zarathustra*, Nietzsche wrote that beneath the agony of life, there is joy. It is possible to see the world without transcendence and yet with joy, to say "yes" even to the agony. "Joy . . . does not want heirs, or children—joy wants itself, wants eternity, wants recurrence, wants everything eternally the same. . . . Have you ever said Yes to a single joy? O my friends, then you said Yes too to *all* woe. All things are entangled . . . if ever you wanted one thing twice . . . then you wanted *all* back . . . oh, then you *loved* the world. Eternal ones, love it eternally and evermore; and to woe too, you say: go, but return! *For all joy wants—eternity"* (TSZ, pp. 434–435). This is a *naturalistic transcendence*, if you will. The human spirit, Nietzsche included, craves eternity. Nietzsche's myth, the eternal return, grants us a naturalistic eternity, without purpose, ideality, or progress: an eternal existence in nature.

If nature includes all, then it includes what we normally regard as unnatural; namely, artificial, artistic human constructions. In 1872 he wrote that, "advanced physiology will . . . comprehend the artistic powers already present in our development—and . . . also in that of animals. Advanced physiology will declare that the *artistic* begins with the *organic"* (PT, p. 18).[31] So, again the human realm is entirely within nature.

Most relevant to our purposes, Nietzsche applies his naturalism to account for consciousness, perception, intelligence, knowledge, and inquiry. In other words, Nietzsche *naturalizes epistemology*. The faculty of knowledge evolved in natural history as a trait of the human species. Perception, cognition, even inquiry, serve the biological needs of the organism, needs that may be quite complex. Knowing is a natural capacity like any other; it is limited and fallible, anthropocentric, and serves precognitive purposes or interests.

Nietzsche wrote in 1872 that, "The inviolability of the laws of nature surely means that sensation and memory are part of the essence of things" (PT, p. 36). Regarding evolution, he claimed, "Now man has evolved slowly, and knowledge is still evolving. . . . Naturally it is only a clearer and clearer mirroring. But the mirror itself is nothing entirely foreign and apart from the nature of things. On the contrary, it too slowly arose as [part of] the nature of things" (PT, pp. 37-38). Nietzsche accepts the Darwinian account of the evolution of species by natural selection (PT, p. 43). He criticizes Darwinism only for making survival and not the expression of power the ultimate goal of natural creatures (TI, pp. 522–523).

For Nietzsche this naturalism implied a kind of pragmatism, a belief that knowledge must be located in the context of action and success. Naturalizing human cognitive processes means that those processes must—at least most of the time—serve precognitive needs, needs which are satisfied through action. Arthur Danto correctly sees the traces of a "pragmatic theory of truth" in Nietzsche.[32] Nietzsche claims that what gets accepted as true are generally judgments that serve needs or interests, usually the needs of society.[33] Sometimes, as we have seen, he says that the truth *is* what is useful or socially accepted. This is prima facie a kind of pragmatism: It is a claim that what determines the validity of judgment for us is the role of the judgment in action or in achieving purpose. (This is not to say that it is *Peirce's* kind of pragmatism.)

Nietzsche does make some statements that seem to distance himself from pragmatism. For example, "Happiness and virtue are no arguments . . . making unhappy and evil are no counterarguments. Something might be true while being harmful and dangerous in the highest degree. Indeed, it may be a basic characteristic of existence that those who would know it completely would perish . . ." (BGE, 39). Here we see Nietzsche equivocating on 'truth'. What is accepted as true is what is beneficial, but that may not be what is *really true*, meaning what corresponds to reality. Indeed, correspondence may be deadly! This passage, and the few others like it, testify to Nietzsche's apparent inconsistency, to which we will return in the next section. It does *not* mean that he failed to apply pragmatism to *most* of human judgment. In terms of weight, the naturalistic-pragmatic view tips the interpretive scale in Nietzsche's estimation of truth.

As mentioned, Nietzsche's notion of the will to power is dialectical. That which apparently opposes the will to power is itself an expression of the will to power. The ascetic ideal, the "last" expression of which is the will to truth, is antilife. Yet, Nietzsche believes that even its prima facie nihilistic, antilife function serves life in another sense. It gives meaning to life by opposing life. As he writes in the ultimate passage of *The Genealogy of Morals*, "man would sooner have the void for his purpose than be void of purpose . . ." (GM, p. 299).

This is the same dialectic that appears in Schopenhauer. In his conception the metaphysical One (the will) manifests itself in an Other (representation) that appears to oppose the One and yet ultimately serves the One.[34] Every monistic metaphysics must face the problem of deriving from the origin that whose character apparently contradicts the character of the origin. Dialectic is a means of solving this problem, by using a historical dimension of internal development to locate the apparent division. In the diachronic or historical dimension there is opposition, but in the synchronic or metaphysical dimension the Other is just a manifestation of the original One. Thus for Schopenhauer the will is reality, manifesting itself in real human consciousness, which represents the will in its own system. Consciousness represents itself and its knowledge in opposition to what it represents as will and nature; yet, in fact, this knowledge serves will and nature. The element in Schopenhauer that does not appear in Nietzsche is the element of escape, the belief that it is possible for the product of the origin to transcend the origin, or in the human case, possible for us to will nothing, for the mind to achieve a purely negative independence from natural striving. Nevertheless, Schopenhauer's simultaneous opposition of representation and will and reduction of representation to will, is central to Nietzsche.

How can we make sense of this dialectical view, that the ascetic ideal has, in our age, come to question itself in its final and most fundamental form; namely, the will to truth? There is a relatively straightforward naturalistic way. In nature, life is fed by death. Nature is a collection of beings that are distinct, and the continuation and growth of each distinct existence is bought at the price of some other.[35] The ascetic ideal devalues life. It is the impulse to depict life as subordinate to a supernatural sphere. This impulse, it turns out, serves as a condition for the life, continuation, and growth of human beings. It is natural for humans to be unnatural. This is a paradoxical way of expressing the point; but is the point really so paradoxical? Is it any more paradoxical than the fact that the urge to continue and grow leads some creatures to expend all their energy in the task of reproduction and so die?

The combination of naturalism with the supremacy of aesthetic values is very rare among philosophers; Nietzsche has drawn them into a circle.[36] Art, the creation of a style, culture, are so many masks and illusions that serve our natural needs, and so have pragmatic value for us. This is a value for nature as well, for these illusions keep us alive, keep us from melancholy and suicide, so that we can continue as part of becoming. But in drawing this circle it was inevitable that the artist be caught inside. It is to the consideration of the implications of the circle in which Nietzsche is apparently caught that we now turn.

The Self-Referential Problem

How does Nietzsche's work on truth, given my antirealist reading of it, fare with respect to the self-referential problems it raises? There are two such problems. First, if there is no truth, how can

Nietzsche know that our beliefs are false—as opposed to being merely unsupportable—because to do so would seem to imply that he must know the truth? Second, if there is no truth, how can Nietzsche propose his own view as true? The latter is the more fundamental problem and will lead to an appraisal of Nietzsche's view of philosophy and his own discourse. We will begin with the former.

How can Nietzsche *know* that our beliefs do not correspond to reality?[37] It appears that Nietzsche believed the very nature of human representation precluded correspondence, allowing him to deny correspondence without comparing our completed picture of the world against the world as it really is. His reasons for believing this seem to be twofold.

First, representation of any kind (perception, cognition, etc.) represents objects in relation to the agent of representation. This means that the "thing in itself," the object independent of the relation to the representor is unknown. Second, perceptions, words, and concepts register events outside of experience in their own media. The very nature of these media (nerve stimuli, images, sounds, abstract ideas, signs) precludes correspondence to objects. This implies that Nietzsche, at least early on, held two relatively simplistic notions of correspondence; namely, that the correspondence of a representation to an object is individual and not holistic or collective, and that correspondence depends on the resemblance of representation and object. I can imagine no other reason for denying correspondence on the basis of the nature of the media of representation. For Nietzsche, the structural isomorphism of a system of conventional signs to a system of natural events or objects cannot constitute correspondence.

Nietzsche's other objections do not, however, appear to make these presumptions. That is, they would constitute an attack on even more subtle notions of correspondence. Take, for example, his claim that all perception and cognition are perspectival. Because the divergent perceptions and cognitions of the same reality obtaining in differing perspectives are equally "representative," they cannot be said to correspond to reality in any sense (unless we accept a radically pluralistic view of the objects of judgment).

Now it may be that Nietzsche believed it possible to give a true account of the process of judgment formation. That is, he may have held his theory about the determination of our judgments by perspective, instinct, need, social convention, and metaphor to be a true account; that is, one that corresponds to the actual process of judgment formation. If he did believe this, then he must have distinguished between our ability to know human cognitive processes and our ability to know all other things. This would mean that among all the various subdisciplines of inquiry, epistemology and psychology would be exempt from his critique of truth. Nietzsche would not be the first to grant epistemology this exemption. Kant failed to explain what kind of knowledge was represented by the *Critique of Pure Reason* itself, that is, how his own transcendental knowledge of knowledge could avoid subsumption by the categories he claimed exhausted knowledge—analytic, a posteriori, synthetic a priori[38]—just as Hume neglected to mention whether his *Inquiry* was an example of knowledge of matters of fact or knowledge of the relations of ideas.

But there is little textual evidence that Nietzsche made this exemption. Even if we were to give Nietzsche this leeway, it would remain the case that he cannot conclude the deceptive nature of our judgment without presuming the truth of some, however vague, account of the natural world—a true account to which Nietzsche is denying the bulk of humanity access. His account of the generation of knowledge out of nerve stimuli is already an account of a natural process. He seems to accept the truth of an ontology of natural things, including human beings with sensory organs and objects that result in nerve stimuli. Nietzsche accepts the truth of naturalism to give an account of how truth is deceptive. So, this interpretive strategy would not save him from self-contradiction.

Regarding the more difficult question of whether Nietzsche is putting forth his critique of truth as true, and if so, how to deal with the apparent self-contradiction, there is little textual guidance.[39] We can take three interpretive attitudes toward this problem. First, we can deny that Nietzsche is making a general claim about truth and so deny that there is a self-contradiction. That is Clark's strategy, which I have criticized. Second, we can accept that Nietzsche's view leads to a contradiction, but deny that this contradiction tells us anything positive about Nietzsche's view. It is evidence of a mistake, an oversight, or a limitation on Nietzsche's part. Third, we can accept the apparent self-contradiction as intentional and try to interpret what it means.

If, as I have argued, Nietzsche is making a denial of truth strong enough to apply to his own philosophy and particularly to that very denial itself and if he regards his denial to be true, then there is no alternative but to admit that Nietzsche is contradicting himself. Taking the second attitude mentioned previously, two ways of interpreting Nietzsche would downplay the importance of the contradiction.

The first possibility is that Nietzsche did not notice the contradiction. I think this is very unlikely, partly because it is blatant, that is, blatant to us. The principle of charity dictates that we grant Nietzsche an ability to see it that is equal to ours. There is also some textual evidence, like the remark in *The Genealogy of Morals* about the "labyrinthine consequences" of the idea that nothing is true. It is true, however, that there are not many statements of this kind. Nietzsche does not dwell on the apparent self-contradiction.

Second, it might be that Nietzsche recognized the contradiction but did not know what to do about it. One might feel that Nietzsche was at the limit of his powers and saw no way out of a contradiction he would have preferred to avoid. Arthur Danto seems to adopt this attitude as to whether perspectivism holds true only with respect to some perspective, when he remarks that, "I do not believe that Nietzsche ever worked it out."[40] However, the only reason to accept this kind of interpretation—which essentially denies that the apparent contradiction is interesting—would be our failure to find a better interpretation.

There is a more interesting interpretation to be considered; namely, that Nietzsche *intends* to contradict himself. To admit this is to accept that Nietzsche chose to present us with an assertive contradiction and suggest that the contradiction was intended to function in a nonassertive way. It is to interpret the apparent contradiction as not merely *performative* but also *informative*. It presupposes that although "truth is deception" cannot be assertively valid, it could be valid as either an action or exhibition, valid for what it does or shows.[41]

There are two ways to do this. The first interpretive strategy claims that Nietzsche's discourse is primarily exhibitive in aim and method, hence not intended to be governed by assertive truth. Nietzsche's aim is to construct something—a view, a literature, or even a self—that has exhibitive or aesthetic value. Nietzsche aims to subordinate truth to construction, to power, to aesthetic quality, *and* he accepts that interpretation of his own work. This is the interpretation taken, in different ways, by Gilles Deleuze, Alexander Nehamas, and Alisdair MacIntyre.

Gilles Deleuze, in his very interesting book on Nietzsche, employs a distinction prominent in *The Genealogy of Morals*. Deleuze suggests that knowledge and truth oppose life only when they express a "reactive," rather than an "active," interest. Hence, when Nietzsche, despite his critique of truth, refers to himself and his kindred spirits as seekers after knowledge, Deleuze, identifying himself with Nietzsche's cohort, insists, "But we do not replace the ascetic ideal, we let nothing of the place itself remain . . . we want another ideal in another place, another way of knowing, another concept of truth . . . which is not presupposed in a will to truth but which presupposes a completely different will."[42] Deleuze claims that Nietzsche "takes knowledge to task, not for seeing itself as an end, but for making thought a simple means of serving life."[43] Understood in an affirmative or active way, "truth perhaps takes on a new sense. Truth is appearance. Truth means bringing of power into effect, raising to the highest power. In Nietzsche, 'we the artists' = 'we the seekers after knowledge or truth' = 'we the inventors of new possibilities of life'."[44]

The "new image" of inquiry that Deleuze proposes in a Nietzschean spirit is of thought as governed by a critical, anticonventional sense of what is noble or high, versus what is base and low.[45] Consequently, philosophy's aim becomes the "exposure of all forms of baseness of thought," in service of "creating free men, that is to say men who do not confuse the aims of culture with the benefit of the State, morality or religion."[46] So, in Deleuze's Nietzsche, truth literally becomes what is "high" or "noble," hence an aesthetic and active (and political) property.[47]

In his *Nietzsche: Life as Literature*, Alexander Nehamas reads Nietzsche as constructing his self, his destiny, out of his written work.[48] Nietzsche's denial of truth functions to construct a perspective, a view that is unique to Nietzsche. It serves the task of what he called that "one thing needful"; namely, to "give style" to one's character (GS, 290). Hence, it is not governed by the value 'truth,' but by aesthetic quality or, to the extent that it is also active, by success. Remarks like "Every philosophy also *conceals* a philosophy; every opinion is also a hideout, every word also a mask" (BGE, 289) might be taken as support for this kind of interpretation, in that Nietzsche may be read as admitting that, although he appears to inquire, his work is not subject to the rules of inquiry.

Alisdair MacIntyre's recent reading of Nietzsche as the representative of genealogy, one of the *Three Rival Versions of Moral Enquiry*, follows the same path, if only for a limited distance. Linking his interpretation with those of Foucault and Deleuze, MacIntyre criticizes the attempt to see Nietzsche as a failed antiphilosopher who tried to do the impossible, to say the unsayable, his failure proving the ubiquity of the traditional idiom. MacIntyre writes,

> The objection fails . . . what its attempt to coopt Nietzsche cannot reckon with is his subordination of the elucidatory academic treatise to the poem and the epigram, a subordination designed to enable us finally to dispense with elucidatory treatises altogether in favor of a mode of discourse . . . in which . . . disruptions of sense make use of assertions only in order later to displace them.
>
> Hence the argument that Nietzsche could not have propounded a set of statements which put him at such radical variance with traditional ways of understanding the place of logic and grammar in our discourse, because *any* set of statements *must* presuppose to some large degree just that kind of understanding, misses the point. Nietzsche's final standpoint, that towards rather than from which he speaks, cannot be expressed as a set of statements.[49]

Reading Nietzsche as Deleuze, Nehamas, and MacIntyre do has as a consequence the release of his readers from the obligation of considering the possible truth of his work, by rendering truth in terms of exhibition or action. To the extent that we read Nietzsche's statements as exhibitive, the possibility of self-contradiction disappears,[50] for exhibitive judgments do not contradict. Inquiry requires assertive consistency, but if Nietzsche is not engaged in truth-governed inquiry, then the very problem we are struggling with—his performative self-contradiction—evaporates. What also disappears is our obligation, in order to evaluate their meaning, to consider the truth of his utterances. If Nietzsche is to be interpreted as creating an exhibition, we must then evaluate his work as we would a poem or a novel. If this interpretation is supposed to apply to all of Nietzsche's work, then it means that his critique of Christianity, his genealogy of moral values, and his critique of idealism are not meant to be true.

I suggest that the price of such a consistently aesthetic view of Nietzsche's work is too high. To repeat an earlier point: Nietzsche demands a ruthless devotion to the truth! A consistently aesthetic interpretation would make this side of Nietzsche absurd.

An *ambivalently* aesthetic interpretation would be a different matter. That is the point of the second, and last, interpretive strategy, and it is the approach I suggest. The exhibitive, constructive, self-creative task cannot be the last or ultimate word; indeed, there can be no last word, for Nietzsche has consciously left us in an ambivalent, dichotomous position.

Nietzsche makes the apparent assertion that truth is an illusion, which means that all judgments we regard as true serve natural will, which is inherently dissimulative. But if this statement is true, then it too is a lie, hence false. In the interpretation I am suggesting, this judgment of Nietzsche's would be regarded as functioning assertively, exhibitively and actively. We cannot ignore, nor can we harmonize, the multiple meanings or functions of his judgment.

We have seen what the assertive function of the statement is. It makes a truth-claim, based, I have argued, in Nietzsche's naturalism, which contradicts itself.

Exhibitively, the judgment functions to mark, to show the limits of inquiry, assertion, truth, and hence the will to truth that has motivated much of Western culture (that is, the culture of the Greek and Christian inheritance). As such, it makes a judgment of truth and inquiry from outside the realm of truth and inquiry, by marking the limits of that realm. Putting this exhibitive function together with the assertive function, we may say that the statement *both is and is not true*. Nietzsche's claim marks the end, hence the bounds, of inquiry. It points out that inquiry reaches a boundary when it seeks to justify itself, a boundary that cannot be unambiguously a part of inquiry.[51]

The judgment also serves, as Nehamas points out, to construct Nietzsche's place, his destiny, within the Western tradition. A number of Nietzsche's remarks—especially at the end of the *Genealogy*—confirm this. In our age truth has come to question itself: this is our destiny. And Friedrich Nietzsche is the self-conscious herald of this self-questioning.

In a sense, my suggested interpretation is akin to Heidegger's reading of Nietzsche, with one crucial exception. For Heidegger, Nietzsche's apparently self-contradictory view of truth is determined by his faithfulness to the Western misunderstanding of truth as the correctness of representations of beings, rather than as *aletheia* or "unconcealment." Nietzsche understands truth as "holding to be true." Heidegger reads Nietzsche as presenting the *Aufhebung*, the fulfillment and cancellation, of this notion of truth. Nietzsche interprets truth as one of two human comportments toward primal chaos or Becoming; knowledge fixates the chaos, while art transfigures it. Deeper still, the basis for holding to be true, and for art, for all *homoiosis* or harmony with the actual, is *justice*.[52] Heidegger writes, "Justice as the positing of something right, a positing that constructs—that is, founds, erects, and opens a vista—is the essential origin of the poetizing and commanding nature of all knowing and forming."[53] Justice in this sense is "the essential ground of life" itself. Consequently, "Commanding explaining and poetizing transfiguration are 'right' and just, because life itself at bottom is what Nietzsche calls justice."[54] Hence Heidegger reads Nietzsche as locating assertive truth within the originary exhibitive and active positing that is, for Nietzsche, the basic task of life itself.

With the notion that Nietzsche exhibits the self-cancellation of the pursuit of propositional or representational truth, my interpretation is in agreement. The crucial difference with Heidegger is that I do not take this as emblematic of an error, of Nietzsche's failure to free himself from the Platonic legacy of truth as correctness. I suggest that Nietzsche exhibits the inescapable crisis of philosophy, which is to say, of inquiry into truth extended to its maximum.

Nietzsche's self-contradiction also functions actively in two senses. First, it makes him, or anyone who accepts it, free. Truth is a limit on freedom. To recognize the dissimulative nature of truth, as in the motto of the Society of Assassins, is to eliminate the last vestige of moral-idealist constraint on freedom. Second, this recognition of Nietzsche's must serve the will to life, as everything must. In both these senses, Nietzsche's assertively self-contradictory judgment achieves validity in a active sense: it does something that must be done. And as we have seen throughout Nietzsche's work, there is no contradiction between exhibitive or aesthetic validity and active validity, even within the context of his naturalism. That his judgment shows something valuable is perfectly compatible with its active role in the service of the will to life.

Nothing in my interpretation makes Nietzsche's self-contradiction less problematic within the context of assertion. It is still the case that Nietzsche accepts the truth of his judgments about Christianity, morality, and so on; accepts the truth of naturalism, that all human activity serves natural will; and, accepts the truth of the claim that all our truth-claims serve a fundamentally dissimulative natural will. This is a contradiction. It is the aim of my interpretation to retain this contradiction. For, in my view, if we cease to interpret Nietzsche as holding these three truths, then he ceases to be interesting. We must maintain these truth-claims for Nietzsche to remain a radical critic of inquiry or, indeed, a radical critic of anything. But this makes him self-contradictory. My interpretation keeps him self-contradictory, but finds method in the madness; that is, nonassertive meaning in the self-contradiction.

The point here is that we are in the labyrinth and that *we always were*. We cannot look at assertion as a limited sphere independent of the interests of life. So the assertion that assertion serves life is true and self-compromising. There is no clear ground to stand on here. This implies that Nietzsche is being ironic in the sense that he means more than he says. But there are many forms of irony, and it would be, I believe, a mistake to suggest that Nietzsche is hiding his meaning from us or that he means the opposite of what he says. He is showing us something by making an assertion that violates the norms of assertion.

Nor does this interpretation undermine the extent to which naturalism is the constant background for his Nietzsche's work. Naturalism is the framework within which the contradiction is generated. Nietzsche places all the functions of judgment within the will to power. He treats the will to power or life as more fundamentally tied to exhibition and action than assertion. Assertive validity is derivative, it must serve the will to life, hence active success or exhibitive quality, or both. Truth is the method of limiting belief or metaphor by alleged "correspondence" to reality. It puts the brakes on the drive to create metaphors. Those brakes are indispensable to the drive they control. I claim that Nietzsche believed this to be a true assessment, one that corresponds to the human reality in nature. He saw the inconsistency in this, that in him inquiry was judging itself to be capable of correspondence in its work of denying correspondence.

Yet he also believed that the few seekers and free spirits that question truth occupy an aberrant position within the will to life. Their strange role was to seek truth independent of social convention and the standard metaphors. In the current era, this leads them—that is, him—to question the truth of truth. This Nietzsche regarded as his unique destiny. But inquiry must stop here because it is structured by truth. Nietzsche regards himself as showing, in his own work, the self-overcoming of inquiry governed by truth, which is to say, the self-overcoming of knowledge-culture.

This point suggests one more relevant factor that has been largely absent in our discussion of Nietzsche. It is that Nietzsche accepts the premodern notion of *rank*. Nietzsche believes that human beings differ by nature and that these differences find natural expression in the virtually universal division of premodern societies into classes or castes (usually three, according to

Nietzsche).[55] Nietzsche believes that different norms are appropriate for people of different ranks or natures. This applies to himself and his kindred "free spirits." Thus he writes in *The Gay Science*, "The greatest danger that always hovered over humanity and still hovers over it is the eruption of madness. . . . what is needed is *virtuous stupidity*, stolid metronomes for the slow spirit, to make sure that the faithful of the great shared faith stay together and continue their dance. . . . *We others are the exception and the danger.* . . . there actually are things to be said in favor of the exception, *provided that it never wants to become the rule*" (GS, 76).

This view must apply as well to the norm 'true.' For the masses, truth has most basically indicated whatever beliefs preserve life, benefit the believer, or "work." For the Christians, heirs to a slave morality, truth is what they owe to God or the City of God. For the ancient nobility truth was the sign of good character and good manners, but only relevant in dealing with one's peers. For the free spirit truth is presumably something else, perhaps a tool of liberation. Only the free spirit may know the self-negation of truth. The contradiction is for the few. For them it serves an active function, like a zen koan, encouraging absolute freedom.

"The Advocate of the Circle"

Nietzsche seems to have found his personal answer to life in the eternal recurrence, which allowed him to affirm nature in all its forms. Thus he could accept as his destiny to push inquiry to the point of an informative self-contradiction. I believe at this point he sublated his activity into art, that is, he came to see his activity as a poetic construction and exhibition. But only *at that point*—the point where truth questions its origin and function in nature—because up to that point his aim was to inquire rigorously after the truth, to accept no pragmatic or exhibitive "deception." For Nietzsche, diachronically, in terms of the narrative history of his activity, inquiry must follow its norm of truth to its limits, while synchronically, in terms of his best judgment of things at the end of this inquiry, inquiry and truth are the constructions of the will to life for its various purposes. The distinction between these two perspectives does not in any way resolve Nietzsche's self-contradiction. It merely gives us two ways to look at it.

Therefore the picture with which Nietzsche leaves us is one of the human activity of inquiry, which ought ruthlessly to unmask the deception of idealism, while being located within (and thus serving) the human will to life, which is aimed at producing judgments that, from the point of view of inquiry, are deceptions. And inquiry, in the case of the few, knows all this (that is, can utter the preceding sentence). When inquiry says this it becomes art, an activity whose validity lies not in correspondence but in the quality exhibited by what it constructs. Although synchronically, from the point of view of the will to life, it *always was* art. Hence assertion, pushed to its limits, reveals its active function, and this revelation's value is exhibitive and active. Thus Nietzsche's philosophy must simultaneously function assertively, actively, and exhibitively.

We may wonder, what would Nietzsche think about the current project of clarifying his view? It is, like all inquiry, a religious devotion to the myth of truth. My inquiry has an aim, to make a decision about how we ought to regard Nietzsche, to prescribe how we ought to stand with respect to him, as if this would provide some solution or salvation. For Nietzsche, this marks me, and my ilk, as moralists seeking to redeem life through some objective ideal. Instead of affirming my own values, I ask, "What values ought I have?" But are not all inquirers so? Including Nietzsche himself? Is not Nietzsche caught in the same circle? I think the answer Nietzsche gives is, yes. What marks Nietzsche's uniqueness is that he *affirms* the circle, he "advocates" it. More than anyone, Nietzsche is the philosopher of the *kirkos*, the circle or circus in which inquiry dwells, along with everything else.

6

WITTGENSTEIN'S SOCIAL RELATIVISM

"The facts of the matter are of no importance for me."

—Conversation with Friedrich Waisman

Wittgenstein may be the most influential Western philosopher of the twentieth century.[1] The power of his mind and personality have indelibly marked English and North American philosophy and have influenced continental European thought as well. The intensity with which he pursued his thought and his willingness to subject his own conclusions to criticism are remarkable. He can be read as the most radical critic of traditional philosophy, one who takes no philosophical position himself.[2] We must be careful, however, to avoid making a fetish of philosophy or of Wittgenstein, the former by investing all our moral hopes in the prospect of saving our old discipline, the latter by making Wittgenstein the divinity of a negative theology that allows no term to be adequate to describe him. The real questions are, What is he doing and what can we learn from seeing what he is doing?[3]

I will ask whether we may consider Wittgenstein an antirealist and in particular, a relativist, a conventionalist, and a pragmatist. There can be two reasons for denying these predications: first, that it is more reasonable to believe that Wittgenstein held positions other than these; second, that it is more reasonable to believe that Wittgenstein held no philosophical position at all. For organizational reasons I must put off dealing with the latter issue until the fourth section of this chapter, which will have the unfortunate effect of making it appear in the meantime that I have presumed an answer. But I believe that we must work up to that most radical question gradually, after examining Wittgenstein as if he were a normal philosopher. Hence, my first three sections will operate within the hypothetical, "If Wittgenstein took a philosophical position, what would it be?" Then, in section four we can ask, "Did he take a philosophical position at all?" When we turn to the latter issue, the distinctions among the various metaphilosophical strategies will become important. Above all, the distinction between an explicit or assertive and an implicit or exhibitive approach will be essential. To ascribe to a philosopher an implicit view does not give us the right to regard this as nothing but an explicit view in sheep's clothing. If the philosopher chose to be implicit, there is presumably a reason and that reason presumably matters. If the philosopher is a great philosopher, then it definitely matters.

I will argue that Wittgenstein does have a philosophical view, indeed, that he is a conventionalist and a pragmatist. Wittgenstein's conventionalism and pragmatism, however, cannot be consistently asserted: They are *unspeakable*. The reason is that, once spoken, they would be self-undermining. I will argue that this is part of the reason for the dialectical procedure of Wittgenstein's later work. In 1918, on the final page of the early masterpiece he was later to reject, his *Tractatus*, Wittgenstein famously announced that the *Tractatus* itself was without sense, that it should be kicked away like a ladder whose purpose had been served. I will argue that Wittgenstein's later work is just as nonsensical according to its own pragmatic and relativistic criteria. Wittgenstein was as aware of this in the final days of his life, at the age of sixty-two, as he had been at twenty-nine.

My interpretive aim is not to try to drag, at any cost, an unconventional thinker back into comfortable philosophical categories. It is to open up the usual categories so that what Wittgenstein is doing can be seen as continuous with other philosophy. Of course, this may mean that the wolf is made one of the flock, that the rejection of philosophy becomes a philosophical position. But such is in keeping with time-honored philosophical tradition, as long as the wolf is a good dialectician.

Five sections and a conclusion follow. The first will discuss the project of the *Tractatus*, its Schopenhauerian and Kantian background, the saying-showing distinction, and other themes in Wittgenstein's early work. The second section will explore the question of pragmatism in the *Investigations* and in Wittgenstein's final project, *On Certainty*.[4] The third section will examine the extent to which we can characterize the later Wittgenstein as an antirealist, and particularly as a conventionalist, using primarily *On Certainty*. The fourth will try to answer the question as to whether any philosophical position can be ascribed to the later Wittgenstein, and if not, what that fact signifies about his work. The fifth section investigates Wittgenstein's view of philosophy and his own inquiry.

Saying and Showing in the Early Work

The *Tractatus* aims to determine the limits of representation. It is not clear how much of semiosis Wittgenstein thought could be understood through the kind of theory proposed in the *Tractatus* beyond linguistic and mathematical signs (what Peirce called "symbols"). It might appear that the conventional symbols of natural and artificial languages were all he meant to include; certainly it is the material with which the book overwhelmingly deals. But, if legend be true, the inspiration for the "picture theory" that forms the heart of the book was a physical model of a car accident.[5] Certainly visual pictures themselves come under the picture theory. And Wittgenstein regards thoughts as pictures (hence, like Peirce, as signs). Presumably, whatever can function as a picture, means, and so is to be accounted for, in some sense, by the *Tractatus*.

The book is, in one way, a very Kantian project. Wittgenstein attempts to comprehend the conditions of the possibility of representation, hence also the limits of possible representation. As he says in the Preface, "Thus the aim of the book is to draw a limit to thought, or rather—not to thought, but to the expression of thoughts. . . ." (T, p. 3). What Kant tried to do for knowledge, Wittgenstein is trying to do for representation or meaning.

In one respect the aim of the *Tractatus* is simple: to understand what Frege's *Begriffsschrift* (1879) is and is not, in such a way that its problems, discovered by Russell and others, disappear. The *Begriffsschrift* was Frege's conceptual notation, a system of signs in which the objective meaning (both *Sinn* and *Bedeutung*, sense and reference) of any set of linguistic signs could be expressed and so inference between signs formalized. As such, it was the model for an ideal or logically perspicuous language. The philosophical question for Wittgenstein was, What is the *Begriffsschrift*, or any comparable system. What does it do or signify, if anything?

A number of philosophical innovations allow Wittgenstein to accomplish this; for example, the picture theory of propositions, the concept of logical form, the general form of the proposition, and the metaphysics of atomic facts. But our aim is not to recount the logical apparatus or the philosophy of language that is presented by the *Tractatus*. For my purposes, one element is most relevant: the say-show distinction.

Wittgenstein regarded this distinction as the key to the book. He wrote to Russell in August 1919 (from a prisoner of war camp in Cassino, Italy), "Now I'm afraid you haven't really got hold of my main contention, to which the whole business of logical prop[osi-tion]s is only a corollary. The main point is the theory of what can be expressed (gesagt) by prop[osition]s—i.e. by language—(and, which comes to the same, what can be *thought*) and what can not be expressed by prop[osition]s, but only shown (gezeigt); which, I believe, is the cardinal problem of philosophy" (LT, p. 71).

For Wittgenstein logic has nothing to do with facts. Hence, logic cannot be described, for the language we have is a fact language; it represents facts. Logic is what makes that fact language possible. Logic is what propositions and the world referred to by propositions have in common, and this common scaffolding makes represen-tation possible. He writes, "The propositions of logic describe the scaffolding of the world or rather they represent it. They have no 'subject-matter'. . . . It is clear that something about the world must be indicated by the fact that certain combinations of symbols . . . are tautologies. This contains the decisive point . . . logic is not a field in which *we* express what we wish with the help of signs, but rather one in which the nature of the absolutely necessary signs speaks for itself" (T, 6.124).

Although the scaffolding cannot be represented or *said*, it can be *shown*. What appear to be propositions of logic, that is, attempts to say logic, are actually senseless (*sinnloss*). What are apparently propositions expressing logical truths do not express or refer to any-thing at all; they show or exhibit the logical form of the world. These are distinguished from attempts to express what transcends the world, which are nonsensical (*unsinnig*).

The picture Wittgenstein gives us is that of a world-whole whose boundary is logic. Everything within the world is the repre-sentation of facts and is structured by logic. The boundary has a spe-cial status, like Kant's bounds of reason; namely, that it is in one sense in the world and in another sense not in the world. Thus, propositions of logic are neither outside the boundary (nonsense) nor inside (sense); they are the boundary (hence senseless) and show, rather than say, the conditions for representation. Beyond the boundary is nonsense. Some of this nonsense, like ethics, is profound, indeed, is more important than anything inside the world (anything representable).[6] Some nonsense is the result of error, hence is "rubbish." Sometimes philosophy is profound nonsense, sometimes it is rubbish.

The legacy of Schopenhauer is apparent here. Wittgenstein had read *The World as Will and Representation* as a teenager.[7] Schopenhauer's influence on the *Tractatus* can be seen, especially in Wittgenstein's discussion of ethics and the mystical, to which we will turn shortly, and in his comments on the nature of the "subject" and solipsism. The first prominent expression of these themes had appeared in a June 1916 passage from Wittgenstein's notebooks in which he attempted to list "what I know about God and the purpose of life." He wrote,

> I know that the world exists.
> That I am placed in it like my eye in its visual field.
> That something about it is problematic, which we call its meaning.
> That this meaning does not lie in it but outside it.
> That life is the world.
> That my will penetrates the world.
> That my will is good or evil.
> Therefore that good and evil are somehow connected with the meaning of the world.
> The meaning of life, i.e. the meaning of the world, we can call God . . . (N, pp. 72–73)

The *I* makes its appearance in the world through the fact that the world is "my" world.[8] The "knowing subject" is not "in" the world (N, p. 86). Neither can it be inferred from the world (N, p. 80). "The subject does not belong to the world," Wittgenstein writes, "rather, it is a limit of the world" (T, 5.633). We can neither think nor say what is outside the limits of the world, for these limits are the same as the limits of language: "*The limits of my language* mean the limits of my world" (T, 5.6). So we cannot say or think what is not in the world, since that would require us to view the world's limits, Wittgenstein says, "from the other side."

This is the binary metaphysical picture of Schopenhauer, in which everything is either in or outside of the realm of facts, representation, knowledge. For Wittgenstein, to *value* the world of facts is to relate that world to something outside of it; namely, the will. Wittgenstein goes beyond Schopenhauer in his attention to the nature of the boundary, the conditions that make the factual world possible. For Wittgenstein, there must be an absolute distinction between facts and the conditions that make the representation of facts possible, that is, logic.

Wittgenstein makes an interesting remark about the relationship between idealism and realism. In the *Notebooks* he writes, "This is the way I have travelled: Idealism singles men out from the world as unique, solipsism singles me alone out, and at last I see that I too belong with the rest of the world, and so on the one side *nothing* is left over, and on the other side, as unique, *the world.* In this way idealism leads to realism if it is strictly thought out" (N, p. 85). In the *Tractatus*, he expressed this same thought by substituting 'solipsism' for 'idealism' in the last sentence. "The self of solipsism shrinks to a point without extension," he writes, "and there remains the reality co-ordinated with it" (T, 5.64).[9]

The distinction between what can and cannot be said is also the basis for understanding Wittgenstein's views on ethics and the mystical at the end of the *Tractatus*. These obscure remarks, which seem so out of place in a work on logic, are essential to Wittgenstein's project. He wrote in a revealing letter to Ludwig von Ficker in 1919 regarding the content of his yet unpublished *Tractatus*, "the point of the book is ethical. . . . my work consists of two parts: of the one which is here, and of everything which I have *not* written. And precisely this second part is the important one. For the Ethical is delimited from within, as it were, by my book; and I'm convinced that, *strictly* speaking, it can ONLY be delimited in this way. In brief, I think: All of that which *many* are *babbling* today, I have defined in my book by remaining silent about it."[10] Ethics, he remarks in the *Notebooks*, "does not treat of the world. Ethics must be a condition of the world, like logic" (N, p.77). That the world has meaning or value—which is the ethical concern for Wittgenstein—is due to the existence of the subject, or the mineness of the world, and the connection of the world to the will.

In the *Notebooks* he says that in art and in ethical valuation we see the world *sub specie aeternitatis*, under the aspect of eternity (N, p. 83). This is to see the world as "a limited whole," and to "feel" the world in this way, "it is this that is mystical" (T, 6.45). For Wittgenstein, "God does not reveal himself *in* the world" (T, 6.432). The "solution" to the "riddle" of life, to the problematic nature of existence as it appears to the will, lies "*outside* space and time." Here Wittgenstein is as firmly Kantian as he is Schopenhauerian.

Last, and a point to which we will return later, is Wittgenstein's notion of what a solution to the problem of life would involve, and its relation to philosophical inquiry. Obviously, whatever the solution is cannot be said. Such solutions are mystical, meaning that "*they make themselves manifest*," and cannot be put into words (T, 6.522). More than this, the solution consists merely "in the vanishing of the problem" (T, 6.521). Once we exhaust scientific knowledge, we have exhausted the realm of possible questions and answers: "there are then no questions left, and this itself is the answer" (T, 6.52). There are, however, two ways to read these passages. One is as the claim that *the cessation* of questioning is the answer to the problem of life. Another is that the valuation of the world as a whole is the answer, an answer in terms of feeling and not representation, and that *this feeling* is the answer. These are quite different, for cessation could be produced anyhow, such as by exhaustion or brain damage. The later interpretation implies that there really is an answer, albeit a nonpropositional one.

In this context, the sole aim of philosophy should be to point out the error presupposed by any "metaphysical" questions and answers. Wittgenstein claims that, "Most of the propositions and questions to be found in philosophical works are not false but non-sensical" (T, 4.003). The "deepest problems are not problems at all," but confusions due to misunderstanding the logic of language. The correct philosophical method, Wittgenstein famously remarks, would be, "to say nothing except what can be said, i.e. propositions of natural science—i.e. something that has nothing to do with philoso-phy—and then, whenever someone else wanted to say something metaphysical, to demonstrate to him that he had failed to give a meaning to certain signs in his propositions" (T, 6.53).

Wittgenstein is not afraid to apply this to his own work. Regarding his solution to problems in the theory of logic, he wrote in the Preface, "I therefore believe myself to have found, on all essen-tial points, the final solution of the problems. And if I am not mis-taken in this belief, then the second thing in which the value of this work consists is that it shows how little is achieved when these prob-lems are solved" (T, p.4). So the solution to these logical problems leaves us where we always were. Even more profoundly, Wittgenstein recognized the nonsensical nature of his own words, given the theory he has presented. Thus the famous concluding sec-tions of the *Tractatus*:

> My propositions serve as elucidations in the following way: anyone who understands me eventually recognizes them as nonsensical, when he has used them—as steps—to climb up beyond them. (He must, so to speak, throw away the ladder after he has climbed up

it.) He must transcend these propositions, and then he will see the world aright. (T, 6.54)

What we cannot speak about we must pass over in silence. (T, 7)

In connection with the remarks on ethics in the *Tractatus* it is instructive to consider Wittgenstein's "Lecture on Ethics," given a decade after the publication of the *Tractatus*.[11] There is much to explore in this lecture for the purpose of clarifying Wittgenstein's view of ethics.[12] But this is not our present interest. Our interest is in Wittgenstein's ethics as the primary case of profound nonsense.

In that lecture Wittgenstein continues the absolute distinction between matters of fact and judgments of value (what he calls "absolute value"). The consequence is that ethical judgments cannot be expressed: "Ethics, if it is anything, is supernatural and our words will only express facts" (LE, p. 7). Wittgenstein's reasoning is that only what is contingent or "accidental" can be represented. Ethical statements try to refer to what is necessary. It seems he could just as easily have said here that they try to refer to the *whole* of what is the case. Either due to necessity or universality, ethical 'statements' are nonsensical because their contrary is unimaginable or impossible. For example, the ethical remark, "I wonder at the existence of the world" is nonsense "because I cannot imagine [the world] not existing."

Ethical and religious language is based on "similes," apparent but misleading similarities between the absolute use of a term and its relative, instrumental, contingent use. Wittgenstein describes this special usage as based on "analogy" or "allegory." It is sensible to say that so-and-so is a "good football player," but through a simile we also believe that it is sensible to say that so-and-so is a "good human being." This is a mistake, because 'good' has changed its meaning drastically from something relative to something absolute.[13]

Yet, Wittgenstein continues, while ethical sayings in one sense refer to no facts and are nonsensical, in another sense they do refer to value-laden experiences that *are facts*, that arise at certain times and places. There is an apparent paradox here: "It is the paradox that an experience, a fact, should seem to have supernatural value" (LE, p. 10).[14] We have here two different perspectives that construe each other differently. From a worldly perspective, the ethical or religious valuation of things is a fact in the world; from the ethical or religious perspective the world is a limited whole that it is able to survey. Wittgenstein concludes,

I see now that these nonsensical [ethical-religious] expressions
were not nonsensical because I had not yet found the correct
expressions, but that their nonsensicality was their very essence.
For all I wanted to do with them was just *to go beyond* the world
and that is to say beyond significant language. My whole tendency
and I believe the tendency of all men who ever tried to write or talk
Ethics or Religion was to run against the boundaries of language.
This running against the walls of our cage is perfectly, absolutely
hopeless. Ethics . . . does not add to our knowledge in any sense.
But it is a document of a tendency in the human mind which I personally cannot help but respecting deeply . . . (LE, pp. 11–12)

This notion of ethics exhibits a significant continuity with Kant
and Schopenhauer. Wittgenstein's identification of knowledge with
objectivity and science, and the dichotomy of knowledge and ethics
or religion are Kantian. One could almost say that Wittgenstein is,
in effect, limiting knowledge to make room for faith, by limiting
what can be said to make room for what cannot be said. The most
important Schopenhauerian element is the depiction of the relationship of possible knowledge or representation and things in themselves as the relationship of two worlds or spheres that meet in the
human individual.

Wittgenstein's favorable view of Kierkegaard is relevant here.[15]
Kierkegaard shared Wittgenstein's separation of the religious
dimension from the objective and rational sphere.[16] In a conversation with Friedrich Waisman in December 1930 regarding the question of whether the Good is so because God wills it, or God wills it
because it is Good, Wittgenstein remarked, "I think that the first
interpretation is the profounder one: what God commands, that is
good. For it cuts off the way to any explanation 'why' it is good, while
the second interpretation is the shallow, rationalistic one, which
proceeds 'as if' you could give reasons for what is good" (VC, p. 115).
This is very like Kierkegaard. Whereas Kant wished to say that we
can reason regarding the boundaries of reason, if only hypothetically and so in a sense pragmatically, Kierkegaard and
Wittgenstein break with the rational and representable. The point
is pushed further when, in the same conversation, Wittgenstein
says, "If I were told anything that was a *theory* [of what value is], I
would say: No, no! That does not interest me. Even if this theory
were true, it would not interest me—it would not be the exact thing I
am looking for" (VC, p. 116).

The ethical looks at the world, imagines the world as a limited
whole. It is this spirit that seeks to transcend the "cage" of represen-

tation and thought. "The facts of the matter are of no importance for me. But what men mean when they say that '*the world is there*' is something I have at heart" (VC, p. 118). This attempt to see the world, to make the world an object of representation, is "hopeless." Hence the tragic spirit of Kant, that human being is fated to seek what it can never grasp, remains at the heart of Wittgenstein's thought.

Wittgenstein, Pragmatism and Peirce

Wittgenstein's most influential work, *Philosophical Investigations*, directly criticizes the theory of meaning he had developed in the *Tractatus*. Its aim is to reject a picture of meaning prominent in the history or philosophy, a theory Wittgenstein associates with Augustine in the first section of the book. It is the view that every word has a meaning, and that meanings are "objects" to which words refer. Connected with this is the belief that ostension, pointing, is by itself sufficient to acquire (learn) and to define the meanings of words. A corollary to the Augustinian picture that Wittgenstein will criticize later in the book is the notion that meanings are *mental* objects and hence private. Wittgenstein will make it clear that ostension is by itself insufficient to teach or define meaning, that context or stage setting is required for ostension to work; that we cannot make sense of the idea that meanings are mental, hence private, objects; and most fundamental, that the meanings of words and propositions obtain not through a relation between the signs and objects but through the role of signs in public contexts of activity, *practices*, which have a point or make a contribution to a *form of life*.

Wittgenstein's way of making these points is dialectical. He offers statements in one voice and then responds and questions in another. As with any dialogical format, this makes it difficult to ascribe positive positions to Wittgenstein; it is not always clear what he is *saying*. We must try to see what this method is *showing* about language and meaning.

Pragmatism is the claim that the meaning of a sign is its role in a context of purposeful activity. Under this reading, pragmatism is a kind of contextualism, that is, it claims that meaning obtains relative to context and, in particular, a certain kind of context, contexts of purposeful action. I will argue that, in this sense, the later Wittgenstein is at least an implicit pragmatist. His analyses of particular cases are consistent with the way a pragmatist would analyze their meaning, and he rejects other prominent approaches to meaning. In effect, we can explain and predict what Wittgenstein says about individual cases, as well as most of his occasional general remarks about language, by ascribing pragmatism to him. In the next section I will try to show the same thing regarding contextualism.

There is substantial prima facie evidence for ascribing pragmatism to Wittgenstein. The most famous expression of the pragmatic spirit occurs in *On Certainty*, where Wittgenstein quotes Goethe's Faust: "*Im Anfang war die Tat*," "In the beginning was the deed" (OC, 402). In the *Investigations* Wittgenstein tells us that, "For a large class of cases—though not for all—in which we employ the word 'meaning' it can be defined thus: the meaning of a word is its use in the language" (PI, 43). Words have diverse functions, like the tools in a tool box (PI, 11). Definition, fixing meaning by "drawing a boundary," is possible, but always serves some particular purpose (PI, 69). The meaning of a word is its role in a "language game," its rule-governed context of activity.[17] And the language game must have a point, must make a contribution to or play a role in a form of life, a customary way of living. He writes that, "To understand a sentence means to understand a language. To understand a language means to be master of a technique" (PI, 199). For Wittgenstein, "Words are also deeds" (PI, 546).

One may wonder about the possible historical connections between Wittgenstein and pragmatism. Wittgenstein had read William James early in his career and respected him throughout it; indeed, his interest in James was quite remarkable.[18] Although Wittgenstein's concern lay primarily in James's account of religion and psychology, he occasionally discusses pragmatism in connection with James. Certainly Wittgenstein could have discussed pragmatism with Russell, whose view of it was largely negative. Wittgenstein read books that prominently discussed pragmatism, and Peirce in particular, such as Ogden and Richards's *The Meaning of Meaning*.[19]

The most intriguing possibility is that Wittgenstein might have acquired an appreciation of pragmatism, and of Peirce in particular, through Frank Ramsey, the brilliant young philosopher of mathematics at Cambridge.[20] Ramsey explicitly identified himself with pragmatism. In an essay published in 1927, referring to his own view, he wrote, "This is a kind of pragmatism: we judge mental habits by whether they work, i.e. whether the opinions they lead to are for the most part true, or more often true than those which alter-

exciting place. You may find it depressing; I am sorry for you and you despise me. But I have reason and you have none; you would only have reason for despising me if your feeling corresponded to the fact in a way mine didn't. But neither can correspond to the fact. The fact is not in itself good or bad. It is just that it thrills me and depresses you. On the other hand, I pity you with reason, because it is pleasanter to be thrilled than to be depressed, and not merely pleasanter but better for all one's activities.[28]

We could easily see Wittgenstein's criticism of Ramsey as a criticism Wittgenstein might have made of pragmatism.[29] This would not be the only time pragmatism had been criticized as unphilosophical, scientistic, superficial, positive, and communitarian. It would be consistent with other attitudes of Wittgenstein's. Although Wittgenstein fancied himself an anti-elitist, hated academia, encouraged students into blue collar work, sympathized with Bolshevism and Tolstoyan altruism, these feelings shared his complex soul with Spenglerian cultural pessimism, the cult of the lonely genius he took from Otto Weininger, a Kantian ethical severity, and in general, contempt for what matters to most people in modern society.[30] It is safe to say that a certain anticommunal sentiment pervaded Wittgenstein's attitudes and that this sentiment may have determined his evaluation of Ramsey and of what he took to be pragmatism's *weltanschauung*.

The irony is that much of what Wittgenstein apparently disliked in the worldview he associated with pragmatism could be—and has been—said of his own late work: that it is based in convention, custom, that it avoids the difficult, technical issues that a real philosopher would address, that it is, in other words, superficial.[31] Wittgenstein says often enough that there is nothing hidden, nothing deep. If we, as we ought to, regard these charges as shortsighted then we must in effect say of Wittgenstein what Nietzsche said of the Greeks: "superficial—out of profundity" (GS, p. 38). Perhaps the same can be said of pragmatism.

Whatever Wittgenstein's attitude toward pragmatism, he exhibits a number of similarities with Peirce. Like Wittgenstein, Peirce's approach to meaning aimed to exclude definition of terms through reference to private feelings or other inexplicable phenomena or principles and explain meaning instead through public actions and consequences. Both deny that if a speaker uses a term in all respects like everyone else it could makes sense to say that he or she means something unique and unknowable. As we saw in Chapter Three, Peirce wrote that the pragmatic theory of meaning has "nothing to do with qualities of feeling. . . . Hence, could two qualities of feeling everywhere be interchanged, nothing but feelings could be affected" (CP, 5.467). Wittgenstein makes the same point in his famous remark about the possibility of a private language: "Here I should like to say: a wheel that can be turned though nothing else moves with it, is not part of the mechanism" (PI, 271).

For both thinkers, thoughts are signs. They both attacked skepticism and the very possibility of a universal doubt. Both denied that the derivation of laws of nature ended the process of inquiry. The laws of nature are not complete as explanations. Wittgenstein writes in the *Tractatus*, "The whole modern conception of the world is founded on the illusion that the so-called laws of nature are the explanations of natural phenomena. Thus people today stop at the laws of nature, treating them as something inviolable, just as God and Fate were treated in past ages . . . the modern system tries to make it look as if everything were explained" (T, 6.371–372). Peirce makes a similar criticism of the "Cartesian" spirit of modern philosophy, which generally "supposes some absolutely inexplicable, unanalyzable ultimate." But such a supposition, Peirce insists, can never be justified, because a supposition is justified only if it makes things more explicable, which the introduction of an *in*explicable cannot do (CP, 5.265). This applies to the laws of nature. He wrote in 1891, "To suppose universal laws of nature capable of being apprehended by the mind and yet having no reason for their special forms, but standing inexplicable and irrational, is hardly a justifiable position. Uniformities are precisely the sort of facts that need to be accounted for. . . . Law is *par excellence* the thing that wants a reason" (CP, 6.12).[32]

If Wittgenstein does accept, at least implicitly, a pragmatic account of meaning, does he also accept a pragmatic account of knowledge, validity, and truth? He may not *assert* such an account. But does he imply, show or effect it? Remember that it is not possible to keep the theory of meaning from having an impact on the theory of knowing. If meaning is in most cases use, then the meaning of 'truth' and 'knowledge' is likely to be their use.

In *Remarks on the Foundations of Mathematics* Wittgenstein addresses this question directly.

> For what we call "counting" is an important part of our life's activities. . . . Counting . . . is a technique that is employed daily. . . . And that is . . . why it is inexorably insisted that we shall all say "two" after "one", "three" after "two" and so on. —"But is this counting only a use, then; isn't there also some truth corresponding to this

[number] sequence?" The *truth* is that counting has proved to pay. "Then do you want to say that 'being true' means being usable (or useful)?"—No, not that; but that it can't be said of the series of natural numbers—any more than of our language—that it is true, but: that it is usable, and, above all, *it is used.* (RFM, I, 4)

Wittgenstein does not want to assert a philosophical claim about truth. But he seems to put us in the position that is equivalent to a pragmatic view of truth, in which we would treat truth as the pragmatist does. In *On Certainty* he writes, "Giving grounds, however, justifying the evidence, comes to an end;—but the end is not certain propositions' striking us immediately as true, i.e. it is not a kind of *seeing* on our part; it is our *acting*, which lies at the bottom of the language-game" (OC, 204). The foundation of judgment lies not in self-evident propositions or indubitable perceptions, not in *seeing*, but in *acting* in a context. Wittgenstein certainly appears to accept the extension of an implicit pragmatism to validity, truth, and knowledge.

Connected with his at least implicit pragmatism are Wittgensteinian comments that evoke a naturalistic spirit. They raise the issue of how *form of life* is to be understood. In *On Certainty*, he wrote, "Now I would like to regard this certainty [expressed by 'I know'], not as something akin to hastiness or superficiality, but as a form of life. (That is very badly expressed and probably badly thought as well)" (OC, 358). "But that means I want to conceive it as something that lies beyond being justified or unjustified; as it were, as something animal" (OC, 359). In the same work, he remarks that, "It is always by favor of Nature that one knows something" (OC, 505). And most blatantly, "I want to regard man here as an animal; as a primitive being to which one grants instinct but not ratiocination" (OC, 475).

Two differing points could be made here. First, Wittgenstein clearly believes that whenever language is used there is a background, context, or framework that is indispensable for meaning to obtain. That background is not constant, it shifts; but there must be *a* background. Further, the background includes within it human practices, aims, and ultimately a form of life. We can call this a kind of naturalism, if we do not presume too determinate a notion of naturalism. Wittgenstein's analysis necessarily puts semiosis in the context of physical events and actions; it establishes continuity between human representation and the activities of natural creatures. Or more simply, it presumes a *given* that is not psychic or phenomenological but public and natural. This is, to be sure, a fairly neutral naturalism, not a reductive naturalism, nor a naturalism "red in tooth and claw."

In the most abstract sense, Wittgenstein is certainly a naturalist, for he does not allow any discontinuous realms of being, he does not admit anything supernatural. The question is whether, on the basis of the preceding passages, one can ascribe a more concrete naturalism to Wittgenstein, a naturalism that understands human judgment in terms of biophysical categories? By evoking our animality and instinct Wittgenstein seems open to such a view, although he does not develop it further. We cannot, I believe, ascribe such a naturalism to Wittgenstein on the basis of these few passages. My point is only that, despite Wittgenstein's hostility to natural science, he is not hostile to a naturalistic perspective on human being.

This elementary naturalism in Wittgenstein does not signify that meanings and the validity of propositions *reflect* natural facts. That would be antithetical to the point of his late work. In *Remarks on the Foundation of Mathematics* he wrote, "The dangerous, deceptive thing about the idea: 'The real numbers cannot be arranged in a series', or again 'The set . . . is not denumerable' is that it makes the determination of a concept—concept formation—look like a fact of nature" (RFM, II, 19). The validity of these mathematical claims is not determined by a correspondence with facts of nature. Yet the language game of mathematics has a point that is its contribution to a form of life, and *this* is a fact of nature, albeit a social and cultural fact.

In conclusion, there are two possible reasons for denying that Wittgenstein is an at least implicit pragmatist, one bad reason and one possibly good reason. The bad reason is to ascribe other qualities to pragmatism that are not part of the definition I have been using. This is what Wittgenstein does with his comment on the difference in *weltanschauung*. There is a difference between the doctrine of pragmatism and the system of philosophy that one might draw from pragmatism. Still different are the cultural implications of pragmatism, its alleged *weltanschauung*. Wittgenstein objects to the cultural milieu and avoids the philosophical system; but this does not mean that his late work is inconsistent with the pragmatist account of meaning and validity.

The possibly good reason to deny that Wittgenstein accepts a pragmatic account of meaning is to deny that he accepts any account of meaning, that he accepts any theory at all. We will turn to this interpretation in the fourth section.

Wittgenstein's Conventionalism

What is Wittgenstein's commitment, explicit or implicit, regarding the validity of human judgment? Is he a realist or an antirealist or neither?

Wittgenstein attacks realism as a philosophical view. That is, he attacks the philosophical view that the validity of at least some judgments are determined by the judgments' relation to what is judged where the character of what is judged obtains independent of human judgment. But does he equally reject antirealism? I will offer a hypothesis: most of Wittgenstein's relevant remarks can be explained by attributing to him a relativist, and particularly a conventionalist, account of meaning. This would make Wittgenstein a relativist and a conventionalist in his account of validity, knowledge, and truth, as well, if only in an implicit sense. We will see how far this hypothesis will take us and what its limits are. First we will see whether Wittgenstein can be regarded as a relativist, then whether his form of relativism is conventionalism.

Wittgenstein's analysis of meaning must have implications for what we would normally call epistemology. Wittgenstein draws some of these in *On Certainty*, his most explicitly epistemological book. Here his contextualism is most beautifully and clearly expressed.

The circumstances of the book are poignant. It is largely a response to conversations with Norman Malcolm about G. E. Moore's refutation of skepticism in "A Defense of Common Sense"(1923) and "Proof of an External World"(1939). These conversations took place in Ithaca, New York, while Wittgenstein was visiting with Malcolm in the late summer and early fall of 1949. Back in England, Wittgenstein discovered in November that he had prostate cancer. He composed the 676 paragraphs of the book throughout 1950 and into the last stage of his illness, from February to April 1951. The final entry was made the day before he became comatose, and two days before his death on April 29.[33]

Moore had tried to argue against the skeptic—the one who doubts our usual knowledge of the existence of ourselves and the world—that our common sense knowledge was in fact certain. For example, if, when holding up a hand, you accept the truth of the statement, "Here is a hand," then from this the existence of the external world can be proved. Furthermore, we do know that the hand exists, although it cannot be proved.

Wittgenstein's point is not that Moore is wrong and the skeptic right, but that Moore is right about the skeptic's being wrong, but for the wrong reason. For Wittgenstein it makes no more sense to say "I know my body exists" than to say "I cannot know for sure that my body exists." Insofar as meaning is use, "I know my body exists" has meaning only in those circumstances in which the statement would have a use; and although imaginable, these would be very unusual circumstances indeed.[34]

To understand Wittgenstein's analysis we must see the power of his contextualism. Propositions operate against a background or framework. This central notion is described vividly in a series of paragraphs that deserves to be quoted at length.

> But I did not get my picture of the world by satisfying myself of its correctness. . . . No: it is the inherited background against which I distinguish between true and false. (OC, 94)

> The propositions describing this world-picture might be part of a kind of mythology. And their role is like that of rules of a game. . . . (OC, 95)

> It might be imagined that some propositions, of the form of empirical propositions, were hardened and functioned as channels for such empirical propositions as were not hardened but fluid; and that this relation altered with time, in that fluid propositions hardened, and hard ones became fluid. (OC, 96)

> The mythology may change back into a state of flux, the river-bed of thoughts may shift. But I distinguish between the movements of the waters on the river-bed and the shift of the bed itself. . . . (OC, 97)[35]

> But if someone were to say "So logic too is an empirical science" he would be wrong. Yet this is right: the same proposition may get treated at one time as something to test by experience, at another as a rule of testing. (OC, 98)

Propositions may be divided into the "grammatical" and the "material," or those that provide the structure of a context, like a riverbed, and those that can be affirmed or denied within the context, like the water that flows down the riverbed. But this means that validation of propositions is structured by the riverbed as well. Thus, "All testing, all confirmation and disconfirmation of a hypothesis takes place already within a system" (OC, 105).

What counts as certain, as indubitable, is not only what would usually be called logical or a priori propositions, but "countless general empirical propositions" (OC, 273). Speaking loosely, the effect of Wittgenstein's analysis is to make the a priori include empirical truths; any kind of proposition, and not only analytic propositions, can serve as the framework for meaning. For example, Wittgenstein tells us, "I want to say: my not having been on the moon is as sure a thing for me as any grounds I could give for it" (OC, 111). My not having been on the moon is as indubitable, and as much a part of the framework of most contexts in which I use language, as "two plus two is four."

Wittgenstein objects to Moore's, and philosophy's, use of the word *know*. He writes, "In its language-game it ['I know'] is not presumptuous. There, it has no higher position than, simply, the human language-game. For there it has its restricted application. But as soon as I say this sentence outside its context, it appears in a false light" (OC, 554). It remains true for Wittgenstein, as it has since the *Tractatus*, that a statement makes sense only if its denial also makes sense. Except that now making sense means having a possible use. In most contexts, "I know I have a body" and "I'm not really sure I have a body" are equally nonsensical.

It is worth noting that in questioning Moore's version of common sense philosophy, Wittgenstein is coming closer to Peirce's common-sensism. Wittgenstein rejects universal, explicit skepticism, the skepticism of Descartes, just as Peirce did. "A doubt that doubted everything," he writes, "would not be a doubt" (OC, 450). And, "A doubt without an end is not even a doubt" (OC, 625). And again, "Doubting and non-doubting behavior. There is the first only if there is the second" (OC, 354). He echoes the Peircean question: "Can I be in doubt at *will*?" (OC, 221). Wittgenstein endorses the notion that, although much is indubitable for us, we do not 'know' that these indubitables are true, which is exactly Peirce's view. That doubt presumes a framework does not mean that what composes the framework is known to be true. For, "At the foundation of well-founded belief lies belief that is not founded" (OC, 253). This is connected with pragmatism and naturalism. "You must bear in mind that the language-game is so to say something unpredictable. I mean: it is not based on grounds. It is not reasonable (or unreasonable). It is there—like our life" (OC, 559). Or as he says in the *Investigations*, "Explanations come to an end somewhere" (PI, 1).

Wittgenstein goes as far as to say, "I have a right to say 'I can't be making a mistake about this' even if I am in error" (OC, 663). How could he make such a claim? Because the framework is, within the language game, what is certain, even if, from a perspective outside the game, it is apparent that the framework is wrong. We must believe that the indubitables are true even if they are not.

Although Wittgenstein does not assert antirealism, he certainly undermines realism. The following passages make this clear.

> "But is there then no objective truth? Isn't it true, or false, that someone has been on the moon?" If we are thinking within our system, then it is certain that no one has ever been on the moon. (OC, 108)

> The difficulty is to realize the groundlessness of our believing. (OC, 166)

> Here we see that the idea of 'agreement with reality' does not have any clear application. (OC, 215)

> To say of man, in Moore's sense, that he knows something; that what he says is therefore unconditionally the truth, seems wrong to me.—It is the truth only inasmuch as it is an unmoving foundation of his language-games. (OC, 403)

Here we see that Wittgenstein is at least an implicit relativist. Indeed, if one had to select one notion underlying Wittgenstein's post-1936 work it would be an at least implicit contextualism. To take but one example from the *Investigations*, Wittgenstein remarks, "One thinks that one is tracing the outline of the thing's nature over and over again, and one is merely tracing round the frame through which we look at it" (PI, 114). Such remarks clearly imply that the framework determines judgmental meaning and validity, not some quality of what is judged that is independent of human judgment. But that is a denial of realism, and such a denial is just what antirealism is.

The most prominent form of relativism in Wittgenstein is conventionalism, or social relativism. For Wittgenstein, that to which he implicitly makes validity relative is the community. This is compatible with his pragmatism, for it is the community's practices, its shared form of life, to which validity is relative.

Now, some interpreters of Wittgenstein are at pains to deflect the charge of conventionalism. The attribution of conventionalism would mean, it is alleged, that Wittgenstein makes meaning and hence validity dependent on human agreement. The tenor of this suggestion is that under conventionalism there is no necessity in any of our utterances, because we might just change our agreements and make any linguistic result valid. We might just decide that two plus two is five. For a conventionalist, anything goes. Wittgenstein did not hold that absurd view, so, the arguement has it, he is no conventionalist.

For example, Oswald Hanfling argues that Wittgenstein cannot be a conventionalist.[36] He gives two reasons. First, he claims that conventionalism requires that grammar be a matter of "invention and choice," which implies the availability of "a perspective outside this invention or choice" and hence—he quotes a line from the *Tractatus* here—"outside logic" (T, 4.12). "But," he continues, "there is no standpoint from which we did or could invent or devise the original system" of our basic logic or grammar.[37] Second, there are matters in Wittgenstein that are not conventional at all. For example, the "logic of pain," unlike a political constitution, is not a matter of convention. "We could imagine a law being passed to prohibit the use of 'know' in regard to another person's pain; but this would not eliminate the concept or our need for it—the role it plays in our life."[38] Pain is part of "the given," claims Hanfling. Whereas, for example, "it is obvious that religion is not" because it is *not* true that "we could not understand what human life would be like without it."[39]

The first of Hanfling's points is especially odd, because it ascribes to conventionalism a notion that is typical of the realism conventionalism usually opposes; namely, the notion of an absolute standpoint. To describe conventionalism in this way is not only to make it impossible, but ridiculous. Conventionalism *surely* does not imply such a thing.

Regarding the second point, if we ignore the fact that there have been very long periods of human history during which most humans in fact could not understand human life without religion, Hanfling's reason for denying conventionalism in Wittgenstein makes sense. It is a straightforward turn to naturalism. There are natural facts about human existence, the recognition of which is not optional, hence not conventional.

This objection makes sense, but it is still problematic. First, conventionalism is *not* incompatible with naturalism, because under an adequate definition conventionalism need not deny the possibility of necessary or universal or unchangeable conventions. Second, it is not clear that Wittgenstein is a naturalist in the sense Hanfling implies.

The latter is, as I have already alluded, a difficult matter. Wittgenstein sometimes writes of forms of life in a naturalistic way. Yet one of his chief aims in his later work is to deny that natural facts determine meaning and validity. We cannot say that judgment is made true by a fact of nature as its *object*, but it is true that the form of life in which its meaning and validity obtains is itself a kind of fact of nature. It is not clear how far we ought to take this path, on which self-referential problems await us. For example, are our judgments *about* forms of life made true by 'natural facts'? For present purposes, it must suffice to say that the incipient naturalism in Wittgenstein does not seem sufficient either to save him from the frying pan of conventionalism or to plunge him into the self-referential fire of naturalism.

Hanfling also argues that Wittgenstein is as wary of realism as of conventionalism. This claim is consonant with the view that Wittgenstein held no position, and so failed to be a conventionalist in the same way that he failed to be a realist, a skeptic, or a historicist. Juliet Floyd makes the point this way.

> My reading . . . indicates at least the beginnings of an answer to the question whether Wittgenstein is ultimately offering a behaviorist or conventionalist account of logical inference and mathematical necessity. The answer he would give to such a question would be another question, viz., "Convention (or behavior) as opposed to what?" The opposed notion ("nature", "mind", "inner", "feeling", etc.) may be seen . . . to suffer from the same unclarity as the notions of "conventional" and "behavior" themselves.[40]

This response to an alleged Wittgensteinian conventionalism has less to do with conventionalism than with the character of Wittgenstein's philosophical project. We will return to it later.

Turning to Wittgenstein's texts, he does appear to criticize conventionalism in a number of passages. He certainly does not make *just anything* go. Nor does he make everything hang on human agreement. Two plus two can never be five, even if we all agree that it is.[41] A moment of actual universal agreement no more stands behind language use than—to use a non-Wittgensteinian example—an actual social contract lies behind human society.

But this does not end the story. The conventionalism thereby denied is a straw man. As I have claimed, conventionalism need not base norms on agreement or group decision. If conventionalism is defined less prejudicially, then an at least implicit conventionalism *is* applicable to Wittgenstein. For Wittgenstein is saying—insofar as he is saying anything—that meaning and validity are relative to contexts established by public, social constructions, which he occasionally calls "customs."

It is true that if someone moves a pawn backwards, even by agreement, then the game is no longer chess. Chess is not just whatever the participants agree it is. But it is also true that we could abandon chess for some game where something very *like* a pawn does move backwards. *Given* the context, it is not true that just anything goes. But the context itself is *given by* human practice in the sense of a collective social inheritance, and so can be changed or abandoned.

But what if some contexts apparently cannot be changed or abandoned? It might be said that two plus two can never be five because mathematics serves a purpose that no other system—such as one in which two and two makes five—would serve. Or it might be suggested that to add to the constitution of chess the rule that whoever arrives at the board wearing darker clothing wins is impossible, because it would no longer be a game of skill and so could not play the role in our form of life that chess currently plays. Agreed, but conventionalism says nothing about the modifiability or dispensability of contexts! There may indeed be necessary conventions, unchangeable conventions; they do not thereby cease to be human, social constructions.

Convention cannot mean *voting*; if it did, then conventionalism would indeed be ludicrous. If conventionalism is to avoid comedy, then convention must mean something like "a norm produced by human society." Given this, Wittgenstein is an implicit conventionalist. He writes in the *Investigations*, "'So you are saying that human agreement decides what is true and what is false?'—It is what human beings say that is true and false; and they agree in the language they use. That is not agreement in opinions but in form of life" (PI, 241). This is a sensible kind of conventionalism, one concerned not with "opinion," but with form of life or custom. When Wittgenstein asks himself whether the definition of *the same* would be "what all or most human beings with one voice take for the same," his answer is, "Of course not" (RFM, VII, 40). The basis of meaning is social practice, not voting; but to admit this *is* to admit conventionalism.

Look at the following passage in which Wittgenstein responds to his interlocutor's pique about the continuation of a number series.

> "Then according to you everybody could continue the series as he likes; and so infer *any*how!" In that case we shan't call it "continuing the series" and also presumably not "inference". And thinking and inferring (like counting) is of course bounded for us, not by an arbitrary definition, but by natural limits corresponding to the

body of what can be called the role of thinking and inferring in our life. . . . Nevertheless the laws of inference can be said to compel us; in the same sense, that is to say, as other laws in human society. . . . If you draw different conclusions you do indeed get into conflict, e.g. with society; and also with other practical consequences. (RFM, I, 116)

Conventions are not arbitrary. Nor is their existence incompatible with natural facts and "natural limits." And they can certainly be compulsory, like "other laws in human society. . . ."

A different kind of objection to conventionalism occurs in *On Certainty*. "To say: in the end we can only adduce such grounds as *we* hold to be grounds, is to say nothing at all. I believe that at the bottom of this is a mistake about the nature of our language-games" (OC, 599).

This I take to be an objection to any *explicit statement of* conventionalism. Wittgenstein is not a conventionalist in the sense of *espousing* conventionalism. But this is the problem of whether Wittgenstein holds any philosophical position, which we will take up in the next section.

Wittgenstein's Unspeakable Lesson

I have tried to show that Wittgenstein is an implicit antirealist, in that he is an at least implicit pragmatist and conventionalist. If he had a view, he had that view. Now we must deal with the question, did he hold any view at all in his later work? Is there a philosophical lesson to this work? Does it endorse or express a principle? Recall that philosophical judgments may be positive or negative and may assert or implicitly show or serve to effect a recognition on the part of their audience. Which does Wittgenstein do?

Well, in truth he does a number of things. Sometimes he makes positive general statements about language ("For a large class of cases . . . the meaning of a word is its use in the language"). Sometimes he makes negative statements about other philosophical approaches (the Augustinian picture, realism, his own early view). Sometimes he appears to assert that no positive philosophical statements can be made about language at all. Sometimes he appears to say that the falsity or inadequacy of other philosophical approaches cannot be asserted. The overall impression, however, is of a thinker whose aim is *to show* and *not to say* either what the nature of language is or what is wrong with other philosophical approaches. Yet he regards this project *as inquiry*, as a philosophical attempt to gain understanding.

The dominant strategy of his later work is to question the realist interpretation of each case that he brings up, without, by and large, *asserting* antirealism. He shows realism to be dubious or false. He does occasionally assert antirealism, both negative *and positive*. But the assertions of positive antirealism are less frequent than the assertions that realism is unjustifiable or false, and both are less frequent than the mere questioning of realism as applied to individual cases to *show* its untenability or to *provoke* uncertainty regarding it.

If it were true that Wittgenstein is no more an antirealist than a realist, then he ought to question the antirealist interpretation of cases with approximately the fervor and frequency with which he questions the realist interpretation. But he does not do so. Wittgenstein's target is realism. Even if we were to grant that he would not call himself a philosophical antirealist, that does not mean that what Wittgenstein's dialectic leads us to the *equality* of realism and antirealism as regards their validity.

The question is, Why does Wittgenstein fail to assert antirealism? I interpret Wittgenstein's reticence to assert relativist antirealism as evidence of his awareness of the inconsistency that would be involved in asserting it.[42] That is how I read Wittgenstein's two remarks: "Naturally, my aim must be to say what the statements one would like to make here, but cannot make significantly" (OC, 76); and "Here I am inclined to fight windmills, because I cannot yet say the thing I really want to say" (OC, 400).[43]

If the assertive judgment "the validity of any assertive judgment is determined by its relation to a context of judgment" is true, then the validity of that very judgment is also contextually determined. Consequently, the judgment is true only in relation to some context (whatever it may be), implying that there may be other contexts in which it is not true, that is, in which judgmental validity is not contextual. The judgment does not imply that there *are* such contexts, but only that there *may* be. It implies that there would be *no contradiction* if there were contexts in which judgments inconsistent with it were true. By limiting its own validity, the assertion ceases to be incompatible with the claim that there is, in some context, a valid noncontextual judgment, despite the fact that, on its face, that is what the judgment appears to deny. This is not a self-contradiction, but it is certainly self-compromising.

Any assertion of contextualism generates this problem. Consequently, if the norms of valid assertion and inquiry bar us from inconsistency, *contextualism must be shown and not said.* "Am I not getting closer and closer to saying that in the end logic cannot be described? You must look at the practice of language, then you will see it" (OC, 501). This was the *Tractatus* view, except that in Wittgenstein's later work what counts as the logic of language has been greatly expanded. Logic is grammar and grammar is contextual—except that this cannot be said. The hypothesis that Wittgenstein is a subtle contextualist, that is, a contextualist who recognized the performative inconsistency of any assertion of contextualism, is sufficient to explain both his analysis of language and his refusal to assert a philosophical position.

One last point. It might be said that the later Wittgenstein's dominant or most characteristic method is to question individual cases without making general claims, except for his occasional metaremarks. One might say: "Just look at what he *does*! That is the point. Any attempt to characterize Wittgenstein's practice with a general assertion about language or philosophy is a mistake."

I suggest that this purely "performative" interpretation is not an adequate philosophical characterization of what Wittgenstein does. For a set of at least unspoken principles must guide his use of examples and his analysis of cases, the divination of which allows readers to say that they "understand" what Wittgenstein is getting at. If there are no such principles, then we are wrong to say that he is getting at anything at all, wrong to invent new examples and call our analyses of them "Wittgensteinian." Without principle, Wittgenstein's late work would be a catalogue of several hundred linguistic analyses, from which no lesson could be drawn and attributed to him. If the lesson of Wittgenstein cannot be expressed in any sense, then on what evidence can we believe there is one?

Wittgenstein's Nonsense

We cannot separate the foregoing from our assessment of how Wittgenstein stands with respect to philosophy. Realism, antirealism, and contextualism are philosophical views about knowledge. Philosophy itself is a kind of knowing, or at least an attempt to know. In particular, Wittgenstein's last work, *On Certainty*, is about knowing. We will consequently find that text especially revealing. After reviewing Wittgenstein's various remarks about philosophy we will return to the argument of *On Certainty*.

Wittgenstein was certainly a radical critic of philosophy. But we must keep in mind that he referred to himself as a philosopher and felt compelled to devote his life to philosophical research. What is especially remarkable is that after leaving philosophy for almost a decade on the belief that the *Tractatus* had solved or dissolved all important philosophical problems, and despite his continuing hatred for the academic world, Wittgenstein returned to philosophy at the age of forty. In this century of antiphilosophy, no one sought to put an end to philosophy more determinedly than Wittgenstein. Yet it is equally true that he pursued a rarified ideal of philosophical inquiry with virtually religious fervor to the last days of his life.

In the *Tractatus* Wittgenstein's pronouncement on philosophy was that, "Most of the propositions and questions to be found in philosophical works are not false but nonsensical. . . . Most of the propositions and questions of philosophers arise from our failure to understand the logic of our language. . . . And it is not surprising that the deepest problems are in fact *not* problems at all" (T, 4.003). Consequently, as we saw earlier, the correct philosophical method would be purely negative or therapeutic.

In the *Investigations* Wittgenstein's remarks about philosophy are virtually all positive. He represents his own inquiry as philosophy. Philosophy is a descriptive inquiry whose aim is to clear up misunderstandings. So,

> Philosophy is a battle against the bewitchment of our intelligence by means of language. (PI, 109)

> The results of philosophy are the uncovering of one or another piece of plain nonsense and of bumps that the understanding has got by running its head up against the limits of language. (PI, 119)

> Philosophy may in no way interfere with the actual use of language; it can in the end only describe it. For it cannot give it any foundation either. It leaves everything as it is. (PI,124)

Wittgenstein seems explicitly to deny philosophy any normative function. He wrote in the *Remarks on the Foundation of Mathematics*, "What I am doing is, not to shew that calculations are wrong, but to subject the *interest* of calculations to a test. . . . Thus I must say, not: 'We must not express ourselves like this', or 'That is absurd', or 'That is uninteresting', but: 'Test the justification of this expression in this way'. You cannot survey the justification of an expression unless you survey its employment . . . (RFM, II, 62).

Descriptive philosophy's task is to remove the misunderstandings on which normative philosophy was based and point to the phenomenon now clearly in view, which can be simply *seen*. "Philosophy simply puts everything before us, and neither explains nor deduces anything.—Since everything lies open to view there is nothing to explain. For what is hidden, for example, is of no interest to us" (PI, 126). As was noted earlier, the similarity to Nietzsche is striking. For both, depth is misleading.

Understood as therapist the philosopher is a very good thing for Wittgenstein, being both a healer and a liberator. "The philosopher's treatment of a question is like the treatment of an illness" (PI, 255). "What is your aim in philosophy?—To show the fly the way out of the fly bottle" (PI, 309).

So, in most of his remarks on philosophy in the *Investigations*, Wittgenstein describes philosophy as having an important and beneficial, if largely negative, task. On the other hand, there are remarks like this: "When we do philosophy we are like savages, primitive people, who hear the expressions of civilized men, put a false interpretation on them, and then draw the queerest conclusions from it" (PI, 194). This statement identifies philosophy, not with the cure, but with the illness. In a personally revealing passage Wittgenstein wrote, "For the clarity we are aiming at is indeed *complete* clarity. But this simply means that the philosophical problems should *completely* disappear. The real discovery is the one that makes me capable of stopping doing philosophy when I want to.— The one that gives philosophy peace, so that it is no longer tormented by questions which bring *itself* in question" (PI, 133). Philosophy may be good, but philosophical *problems* are not. They are an illness to be cured. But if we were to take this metaphor seriously then whether the absence of philosophical problems were to be obtained by solving them or by never proposing them in the first place ought to be a matter of indifference. Who would prefer being sick and subsequently cured to never having been sick at all?

In one of the *Zettel* remarks, Wittgenstein muses, "Some philosophers (or whatever you like to call them) suffer from what may be called 'loss of problems'. Then everything seems quite simple to them, no deep problems seem to exist any more, the world becomes broad and flat and loses all depth, and what they write becomes immeasurably shallow and trivial. Russell and H. G. Wells suffer from this" (Z, 456).

Did the diagnostician suffer from the same disease? Evidently not in the same way. Yet Wittgenstein's devotion to philosophy was no less, but more fanatical than Russell's. For Russell could live with what he regarded as unsolved and, for himself anyway, unsolvable problems, a situation Wittgenstein found intolerable. It may be true that Wittgenstein had no fear of the flat, depthless plains of analysis. But why did he so fear any outcroppings of problems that he spent the rest of his life bulldozing the philosophical earth to keep it flat?

What causes our philosophical misunderstandings? What is the source of mystification and what exactly is its relation to philosophy? Wittgenstein writes, "A *picture* held us captive. And we could not get outside of it, for it lay in our language . . ." (PI, 115); "The confusions which occupy us arise when language is like an engine idling, not when it is doing work" (PI, 132); "For philosophical problems arise when language *goes on holiday*" (PI, 38).[44]

Wittgenstein is not questioning the use of an expression outside its normal context, even by philosophy. He is not enforcing "ordinary" language, not demanding the we avoid abnormal uses of our expressions. He is rather criticizing our *forgetfulness*. We habitually forget the extraordinary nature of our abnormal usages; we drag old grammatical expectations into a new situation, then ask perplexing questions based on that old, misapplied grammar. We forget that it is *we who did this*, who bent language to a new use, and act as if the odd grammatical situation were a puzzle determined by the nature of things. This mistake is canonized by realism, which ascribes the determination of puzzling expressions to nonhuman reality.

Yet, the issue seems to be more than a matter of habitual forgetting. Wittgenstein implies that there is a *drive* to forget and misunderstand. Otherwise, we would not be disappointed or argue against the charge of misunderstanding when it is pointed out; it would not matter to us. But it does seem to matter. To bend or push language out of shape, to "run against the walls of our cage," seems to be a need, not a lapse. This is a reappearance of the Kantian theme: we *must* attempt to push language and thought too far, despite the confusion thereby generated.

Wittgenstein's fascinating debate with himself over the sense of Moore's position in *On Certainty* is relevant here. For his discussion of whether it makes sense to say "I know my body exists" is really a dialogue on the *sense of philosophical assertion*. Philosophy is an attempt to know, including the attempt to know what we can and do know. This is one of the reasons that Wittgenstein's response to Moore is so interesting and so unlike the other polemics Wittgenstein carried on, like that versus the Augustinian picture or versus realism in the interpretation of mathematics. In those polemics he opposed various philosophical theories about certain topics (e.g., language, mathematics, mental objects). But in *On Certainty* he is arguing with Moore over the use of "I know" by a philosopher, that is, by Moore. In effect, he is examining *philosophical assertion* per se.

Wittgenstein's basic point against Moore is that "Moore does not *know* what he asserts he knows," but rather, "it stands fast for him, as also for me" (OC, 151). Later he reconsiders, and his self-doubt about whether Moore is right runs throughout the second half of the book. He writes, "Haven't I gone wrong and isn't Moore perfectly right? . . . I do not think to myself 'The earth already existed for some time before my birth', but do I *know* it any the less? Don't I show that I know it by always drawing its consequences?" (OC, 397). Later, Wittgenstein continues, "What I am aiming at is also found in the difference between the casual observation 'I know that that's a . . .', as it might be used in ordinary life, and the same utterance when a philosopher makes it" (OC, 406).

The philosopher's use of 'I know' and the ordinary use are different, and the difference is such that Wittgenstein wants to deny that the former is a proper use at all ("I want to reply [to Moore] "you don't *know* anything!" OC, 407). The problem is one of context. 'I know' is "meaningful *in particular circumstances.* . . . But when I utter [it] outside those circumstances, as an example to shew that I can know truths of this kind with certainty, then it at once strikes me as fishy" (OC, 423). It appears as if the philosophical use is an attempt to supervene all context and purpose, to push the intrinsically contextual phenomenon of language into a super-contextual role. But even here Wittgenstein wonders about its striking him as fishy, "Ought it to?" (OC, 423).

There is a problem bothering Wittgenstein in these passages. He is in the rather odd position of saying that, although the skeptic is talking nonsense—it is senseless to say that I can, while in England, doubt whether I am in England—it is *also* nonsense to say against the skeptic that *I know* those very things he doubts, such as that I know I am in England. "The queer thing is that even though I find it quite correct for someone to say 'Rubbish!' and so brush aside the attempt to confuse him with doubts at bedrock,—nevertheless, I hold it to be incorrect if he seeks to defend himself (using, e.g., the words 'I know')" (OC, 498).

Wittgenstein is torn by two contrary impulses. One impulse is to say that the response to the skeptic, "I know I am in England," is as senseless as the skeptic's doubts. For if the doubt is unreal to begin with—and the temptation is to say that it would only arise among philosophers—then Wittgenstein wants to say that it cannot provide a context in which the response—"Oh yes I *do* know . . ."— could have a role. However, once someone does utter such a doubt, Wittgenstein's impulse is to say that there can be a meaningful denial of its sense. "Rubbish!" ought to make sense. But in terms of their roles in the context, "Rubbish!" and "Yes, I do know I am in England" mean the same thing. Given that their point, their function, is virtually the same, if "Rubbish!" makes sense, then why does not "Of course I know I am in England!" make sense? By Wittgenstein's own criteria, it should.

One way to reconcile these impulses is to justify the distinction of "Rubbish!" and "Of course I know . . ." even though they seem to play the same role. We might say that "Rubbish!" is a logical remark that merely denies sense, while "Of course I know . . ." is not logical but material, it is a move in a game, and that is why the latter is incorrect. But all this depends on context. We can imagine circumstances that would make me doubt whether I am in England. Then 'I know' would make sense. Wittgenstein remarks, "But now it is also correct to use 'I know' in the contexts which Moore mentioned, at least *in particular circumstances*. (Indeed, I do not know what 'I know that I am a human being' means. But even that might be given a sense.) For each one of these sentences I can imagine circumstances that turn it into a move in one of our language-games, and by that it loses everything that is philosophically astonishing" (OC, 622). So he admits that virtually any case of the expression "I know" can have meaning because some context in which it would have a role can be imagined. But Moore's *philosophical* use of "I know" does *not* have meaning, because philosophy is not a context, not a practice, philosophy is the attempted negation of context and practice. Doubting that I am in England (in Moore's sense) does not occur in a meaning-setting context, because it is philosophical.

But why can we not say that philosophy is a context, a practice, making a contribution to a form of life? Well, we could, but then the meaning and validity of philosophical inquiry would be contextual. Where Wittgenstein criticizes or undermines philosophy he presumes it to be a use of language that *imagines itself to be* non- or supercontextual, hence as determining meaning and validity for all contexts.

Wittgenstein faces another problem. He has analyzed 'I know' as indicating the impossibility of error. That is one of the differences between 'I know' and 'I believe'; the latter admits the possibility of error, the former means to rule it out. But we know people *can* be mistaken. Hence, although people in perfectly ordinary contexts say "I know," they are, in a sense, *wrong*. And yet those who use 'I know' seem to recognize the fact that error is possible, at least at other moments. So what does 'I know' mean after all? Wittgenstein admits the odd position he has led us to. "'I can't be making a mistake" is an ordinary sentence, which serves to give the certainty-value of a statement. And only in its everyday use is it justified" (OC, 638). "But what the devil use is it if—as everyone admits—I may be wrong about it, and therefore about the proposition it was supposed to support too?" (OC, 639).

Trying to make sense of this fact, he suggests that, "There is a difference between a mistake for which, as it were, a place is prepared in the game, and a complete irregularity that happens as an exception" (OC, 647). In other words, the notion of mistake is as contextual as anything else, and what would count as a mistake that *I know* excludes must have its "place" prepared by the context, as opposed to a *nonsensical* mistake, which has no place in the language game. To be wrong about certain things is not a mistake, but something else—a dream, a delusion, madness, being under a magical spell.

Wittgenstein continues to go back and forth on this issue. In a paragraph that he begins by insisting that I cannot be mistaken about whether I have just had lunch, he then corrects himself, "But that isn't true. I might, for example, have dropped off immediately after the meal without knowing it and have slept for an hour, and now believe I had just eaten" (OC, 659). Note that Wittgenstein is being forced by the nature of the issue to imitate the kind of philosophy he elsewhere rejects. He is asking himself, what can I not be mistaken about, what if I were dreaming, are there imaginable conditions under which I could be wrong, as if he were Descartes writing the *Meditations*! Having admitted the possibility of error about whether he has eaten, he concludes the paragraph: "But still, I distinguish here between different kinds of mistake."

Wittgenstein then suggests, "The sentence 'I can't be making a mistake' is certainly used in practise. But we may question whether it is then to be taken in a perfectly rigorous sense, or is rather a kind of exaggeration which perhaps is used only with a view to persuasion" (OC, 669).

This raises a fundamental question. What criterion is Wittgenstein using when he in effect says that although people use

"I know" to mean "I can't be mistaken," *they are mistaken about that* (that is, they can in fact be mistaken), hence their claim that they cannot be mistaken may not be meant in a "perfectly rigorous" sense? How can he know that people who say they know in fact do not know in the sense that they mean? Only if Wittgenstein knows better than they do. What does this tell us about the context and the grammar of Wittgenstein's *own* 'I know,' his knowledge that they (the ordinary users of *I know*) are mistaken? The answer is as simple as it is paradoxical: *Wittgenstein is using the philosophical 'know,'* Moore's 'know,' a 'know' that, he has told us, makes no sense.

Philosophy, even as Wittgenstein practices it, is all about coming to know things. Even to know the limits of knowing, the inadequacy of philosophic theories of meaning, or the circumstances for the sensible use of a word, is still to know something. In *On Certainty* he has focused his desire to know on the meaning of 'to know.' But in doing so, Wittgenstein has run up against the inescapable grammar of his own practice, namely, the kind of knowing called philosophical inquiry.

We have now to push the question of the sense of philosophy to a new level. If philosophical *assertions* make no sense because they are, or aspire to be, noncontextual, why should philosophical *questions* make sense either? Philosophical questioning is *as* guilty of acting *as if* it were noncontextual as is philosophical asserting.

What sense can it make to write a book that asks, "Does it make sense to say, 'I know I have a body'?" In what imaginable circumstances would it make sense? Does it make any more sense than to write an essay that asks, "Do I have a body?" No, by Wittgenstein's own criteria it should not. The inquiry embodied in *On Certainty*, and for that matter Wittgenstein's late work as a whole, makes sense only if there is a context in which philosophical questions make sense. But if there is no such context for metaphysical statements, or for Moore's "I know I have a body," then neither is there one for "*Does* 'I know I have a body' *make sense?*" Wittgensteins' inquiry must be as nonsensical as Moore's or as any other work of philosophy.

What is the framework of philosophical discourse? Presumably it cannot be described. Is Wittgenstein showing it to us? Are we still on the last page of the *Tractatus*, where Wittgenstein tells us that his own inquiry is nonsense? Is Wittgenstein deconstructing the realm of philosophical nonsense from within? This is a deeper problem than we have hitherto allowed, for it implies that Wittgenstein's dialectical questioning is just as senseless under his criteria as his assertion of a philosophical position would have been. If logic cannot be described or *said*, then it cannot be questioned either, not given Wittgenstein's contextualist analysis of meaning. The rather startling conclusion is that not only is Wittgenstein making an inquiry whose point is to get us to recognize something that cannot be sensibly asserted, the inquiry itself, the very question he asks, does not make assertive sense either. Wittgenstein can show us the walls of our cage only by running against them himself.

Running Against the Walls

Can philosophy make valid ultimate judgments for Wittgenstein? Wittgenstein's later work points out the unjustifiable nature of realism and the nonsensical nature of philosophy. These are two different issues. We push language and bend it and drag old grammar to the new use, where it does not belong. That is *nonsense*. But then we ascribe the determination of this situation to things in themselves. That is realism, and it is the *worst* kind of nonsense.

Certainly philosophy cannot make valid judgments in a realist sense, for there are no valid judgments in a realist sense at all. Philosophical judgment can be valid only in the sense that it can *show* or *do* something that is valid. Wittgenstein evidently believes that his philosophical inquiry is valid in this sense. It shows the valid way of understanding language use, shows the valid way of handling philosophical problems, and last, shows the nonsensical nature of philosophical assertion, including Wittgenstein's.

Yet the body of Wittgenstein's query is certainly inquiry. He is engaged in a systematic or methodical interrogative process of judgment, judgment that aspires to being true. Hence it is inquiry. He makes both negative and positive philosophical assertions. His inquiry operates at the philosophical level of generality or comprehensiveness. It examines philosophies, judges them. It points out their inadequacy. It is, in other words, ultimate inquiry.

How does all this affect our view of nonphilosophical language games? Wittgenstein does not restrict his criticism to philosophy. He describes how meaning obtains, how we are driven to push meaning out of shape, then forget that we have done so and ascribe its grammatical anomalies to things in themselves. This can occur anywhere, not only in the literary tradition labeled *philosophy*. Wherever it occurs, Wittgenstein's analysis ought to exhibit and criticize the misunderstanding. We may, if we want, call this a critique of philosophy alone, but only if we allow that philosophy can pop up anywhere.

Is Wittgenstein, like Kant, showing both the inevitability as well as the hopelessness of philosophical questions? Yes, and philosophy is inevitable in two ways. First, we are driven to push language out of shape. Then those of us who are *even more driven* must keep doing philosophy to undo the "hold" the misshapen language has on us, to point out the source of its deformity. Not all philosophers are equal. Realists, who believe that the determination of grammatical puzzles is in things independent of human judgment, are wrong. Antirealists are not wrong as much as they are inconsistent if they assert their position. But if they merely exhibit it and act on it, they are merely nonsensical, as is Wittgenstein's own work. What is shown most implacably by Wittgenstein's late work is the impossibility of ceasing philosophical inquiry, of ceasing to push against the bounds of human judgment.

7

BUCHLER'S
OBJECTIVE
RELATIVISM

> The flight from perspective is a dream.
> —*Toward a General Theory of Human Judgment*

We have examined Justus Buchler's theory of judgment, but we must now turn to his thought as a whole to trace the appearance of antirealism, and particularly relativism, in his work.[1] We will see that Buchler presents us with two unique challenges. First, Buchler is an explicit, objective, metaphysical relativist. That is, he posits a relativist or contextualist interpretation not only of judgment but of the objects of judgment. He pushes contextualism so far that our notions of realism and antirealism will be stretched to their limits in the attempt to interpret his system. Second, Buchler regards philosophy as intrinsically exhibitive. Although he is not alone in this, as we have seen, his view allows a particularly clear and straightforward characterization of this exhibitive dimension. Reading Buchler shows that there is nothing apocalyptic or antiphilosophical in recognizing this dimension or function of philosophical discourse.

I will argue that Buchler's philosophy, despite his intentions, is antirealist. Linked by a common naturalism to Nietzsche and by a shared contextualism to Wittgenstein and, as we will see, Derrida, Buchler presents a unique variation on these themes. His, in some respects, nonfoundationalist defense of philosophical knowledge and systematic philosophy remains, like Peirce's attempt at a nonfoundationalist realism, unsupportable on its own terms.

Buchler's philosophy bears an ambivalent relationship with the classic American philosophical tradition, of which he is a legatee who refused much of his inheritance. He professes no allegiance to

229

pragmatism. Although the pragmatists had correctly tried to connect judgment and action, by understanding the former in terms of the latter, they failed, in Buchler's view, to recognize that "action as such was judicative." Buchler lacks the concern with science that is dominant in both Peirce and Dewey. He remarked on his own development,

> My feeling in general was that sign-theory (Peirce, Royce, Mead, Cassirer) had to be superseded metaphysically by a theory of human production—the basis of our ubiquitous discriminativeness being the way we produce; or conversely, each of our products being our way of discrimination or selecting (judging). . . . I was preparing (it was around 1950) a category that would or could, if necessary, replace the notion of "experience"; that would take Dewey's great broadening and reconstruction of the latter notion for granted, while showing why Dewey could not avoid often lapsing into the views he thought he was abandoning.[2]

One way of reading Buchler's central preoccupation is as an attempt, like that of the pragmatists, to demote discursive cognition from the lofty authoritarian role among the various powers of the human process granted it by much of the philosophical tradition. But unlike the pragmatists, he tried to do so without subsuming propositional thought under a newly established hegemony of action (or rationalized action). The principle of *parity* that Buchler formulated in metaphysics runs throughout his system. Nothing is more real or actual than anything else; assertion, action, and exhibition are equal as forms of judgment; and the poles of the classic philosophical oppositions (active-passive, actual-potential, independence-dependence, etc.) are metaphysically equal. To take one example, Buchler differs from Dewey and Whitehead in denying that the world exhibits more continuity than discontinuity. Discontinuity, irrelevance, and indifference are no less characteristic of things than relatedness and continuity.

This theory of judgment, and its important extension into a theory of query or methodical judgment, was then remarkably framed by a general theory of what is, a metaphysics of "natural complexes." Although we are already familiar with the former, an acquaintance with Buchler's metaphysics is essential to understanding his philosophy.

Natural complex is the fundamental term of Buchler's metaphysics. Whatever is, in whatever sense, whatever can be discriminated, is a natural complex, or *complex*, for short. Actual things, possibilities, fantasied objects, my cat, the essence of my cat, actions, God, past, present, and future, and the term 'natural complex' are all natural complexes. There are two implications of the term. First, nothing is nonnatural. Being nonnatural would mean being "discontinuous with any of the possibilities or actualities of the world . . ." (ML, p. 104). 'Natural complex' embodies a denial of any supernatural realm or any order of things wholly discontinuous with all other orders of things.[3] Second, there are no simples. Everything is susceptible of further analysis or discrimination. "The simple, the seamless, the absolutely pure and non-complex, is in effect the traitless," and something without traits just is not (ML, p. 104).

Every complex is located in an indefinite number of *orders*, sets of related complexes, and is itself an order in which other complexes are located. Complexes "prevail" or "alesce," are "actual" or "possible," and have whatever traits and relations they do have, always in some order. The traits of a complex are themselves complexes for which the original complex is an order. Every order is a natural complex. A complex has a character or *integrity* in each order in which it is located. The integrity is the relational character of the complex, what the complex is in an order. The continuity or constellation or direction manifested in all of a complex's integrities is its gross integrity or *contour*.[4] The contour is the most pervasive of a complex's integrities. Buchler uses the notion of countour to interpret identity. The identity of the complex, "is the continuous relation that obtains between the contour of a complex and any of its integrities" (MNC, p. 22).

"Whatever is," Buchler writes, "is in some relation," although what is is "not only relational" (MNC, p. 24). Nothing is entirely unrelated to other things. There are two kinds of relatedness or relevance. If A is *strongly* relevant to B then A affects or conditions B's integrity, what B is, in some order. If A is *weakly* relevant to B then A affects or conditions only B's scope, or comprehensiveness or pervasiveness, in some order. When I move to a new city I affect its scope (its population), but not its integrity, and so am weakly relevant to the city.

Buchler's metaphysical categories characterize their objects distributively, not collectively. His system attempts to provide, not a perspectiveless "view from *nowhere*"[5] nor a totalizing view from *everywhere*, but a distributive view from *anywhere*, a description of what must obtain for each complex, from each location. It is a *local* metaphysics, a characterization of what every locale must contain, hence, in effect, a *contextualist* metaphysics.[6]

Buchler introduces a principle of metaphysical thinking that he calls *ontological parity*. He writes, "Let us contrast a principle of ontological priority—which has flourished from Parmenides to Whitehead and Heidegger . . . with a principle of ontological parity. In terms of the latter, whatever is discriminated in any way . . . is a natural complex, and no complex is more 'real,' more 'natural,' more 'genuine,' or more 'ultimate' than any other" (MNC, p. 31). The difference between my idea of $100 and $100 in my pocket is not the difference between unreal and real money, but between a real order of imagination and an equally real order of spatial-physical relations. Parity is a powerful cleansing weapon, refreshing to the philosophical traveler weary of the problems of reconciling talk of reality with talk of appearance and the parade of philosophies differing in which kind of complexes they wish to flatter with priority. We will speak of it again.

The notions of ordinality and natural complex supply the basis for Buchler's account of the "human process." *Proception* occupies a place in Buchler's account analogous to that occupied by 'experience' in other systems (e.g., Dewey's). For Buchler, "Proception is the natural historicity of the individual . . ." (NJ, p. 114). It is propulsive, cumulative, and directed. It is a "natural process, distinguishable in specific terms from other natural processes" (NJ, p. 111). For each human individual there is a dominant *proceptive direction*, a cross section of which yields a *proceptive domain*. That domain includes all *procepts* (Buchler's substitute for "experiences"), which are "whatever relates to or affects the individual *as* an individual" (NJ, p. 121).

A *perspective* is an order of procepts. "Perspective, then, is a property of proception, a natural and inevitable fact of a natural process" (TGT, p. 125). In every judgment a perspective is embodied or put into action. Perspectives are not "in" the mind, they are facts of nature, conditions holding for a natural creature and its relations with the world. It is more correct, Buchler writes, to say that individuals are "in" perspectives than that perspectives are in the minds of individuals. Alternately, a perspective is "that kind of order in which a given set of natural complexes function as procepts for a given proceiver or (distributively) for a community of proceivers" (TGT, p. 124). A perspective is a "sphere of relevance" in the proceptive domain; it is the context that makes relevance possible within proception. Perspective is essential to meaning; perspectives are what judgments function to enact and what gets articulated in procepts that mean.

We ought to note that Buchler's metaphysics already rules out certain epistemological strategies. For Buchler nothing is simple, unanalyzable, pure, or immediate. Nothing is free of relations, nothing is more or less related than anything else. Nothing is wholly indeterminate or entirely determinate. Nothing is more real or genuine than anything else. Nothing is absolutely unique or absolutely particular. These denials hold for judgments as for any other natural complex. The Peircean tone of much of this is evident. But so is the non-Peircean element of ontological parity.

Five sections follow. The first presents Buchler's account of judgmental validation and the second places it in the context of his naturalism. The third section will examine whether there is a hidden pragmatism in Buchler, and a whether this is symptomatic of a problem connected with his concept of active judgment. The fourth section will explore the question of relativism and hence antirealism in Buchler. The final section is a discussion of his notion of philosophy and its application to Buchler's own work.

Validation

In *Nature and Judgment*, Buchler distinguished three "concentrically" related "worlds" or contexts in which judgment must be placed with respect to what it judges. The most inclusive is the proceivable world of complexes that are or could be related to an individual. Then there is the individual's world, the world "without which the individual would not be," which includes all complexes related to the individual *as* a natural complex. Last, there is the world that includes only those complexes related to the individual uniquely, *as* that individual, the world "without which he would not be what he is" (NJ, p. 120). This is the individual's *proceptive domain*, the totality of what is strongly relevant to the individual, what stabilizes or modifies the individual's proceptive direction.

Buchler's theory of judgment embodies a conception of human being. Human being is, first of all, natural. Its unique nature is to be a process, and in particular a propulsive, urgent, incomplete, and cumulative process. A human being is a *history*. What is proceived is whatever affects the intrinsic "historicity" of the individual.[7] Each judgment becomes part of the cumulative history of the individual and is subject to interpretation and validation by subsequent judgment. Validation is therefore a process that is never complete. It is also perspectival. A judgment can be validated only relative to a given perspective. Indeed, Buchler goes so far as to say that "for *any* judgment, *some* validating perspective can be found" (TGT, p. 159).

Buchler's most sustained discussion of validation occurs in *Toward a General Theory of Human Judgment*. As we will see, validation is connected to two other topics, query and compulsion. Buchler asserts that, "As events in nature the products of men are complete and inexpugnable. But as potential vehicles of communication they stand in need of a certain kind of actualization which, we shall suggest, can never be wholly achieved: they require to be validated. In the last analysis validation is justification" (TGT, p. 140). For Buchler all judgments need to be validated. This is because every judgment, act, assertion or exhibition is incomplete. It implicitly makes a demand on future judgment, a claim that needs to be ratified, a commitment that needs to be secured. All acts, assertions, and exhibitions naturally and inevitably seek the security, continuance, or completion, that is validation. Buchler writes, "Every judgment implicitly seeks justification, because of the commitment incurred by the proceiver in judging. The primordial claim latent in human existence itself is the claim of valid continuance. Inventiveness implies satisfaction of a methodic intent or demand . . . this demand is the very core of the validation process. Validation aims to secure, not necessarily to resolve . . ." (TGT, pp. 141–142).

Each judgment seeks to be effective, which is to say, compulsive (TGT, p. 76). When an individual's proceptive direction makes a judgment inevitable in a given situation, it is compulsive. Gross or simple compulsion is "the efficacy of accumulated life" (TGT, p. 62). Query, or systematic interrogative judging, especially seeks compulsion, that is, the development of a sequence of judgments to determine future judgments. Query aims to result in products whose assimilation is characterized by some kind of assent or acceptance (TGT, pp. 76–79).[8] Let us look more deeply into the conditions that make validation possible.

First, validation is made inevitable by human inventiveness, which for Buchler primarily means query. Invention is precarious and so demands ratification, agreement, validation, although this ratification is never completed. Acknowledging a debt to Peirce's claim that all explanation is a matter of hypothesis, Buchler describes validation as "a process of guessing and applying—good and bad guessing, good and bad applying" (TGT, p. 144).

Second, validation is required by communication. Communication is the manipulation and assimilation of signs in response to

some procept. In *reflexive* communication one proceiver communicates with himself or herself. In *social* communication, multiple proceivers share a dominant procept and jointly manipulate and
assimilate signs in response. Each participant must simultaneously
be engaged in reflexive communication. Like others influenced by
the tradition of Peirce and Mead, Buchler holds that both kinds of
communication presuppose the existence of community (or more
precisely, communities).[9] "The individual, then, is not 'entitled' to
whatever he utters. He must substantiate; he must validate or render secure the products that emanate from his own perspectives. He
must . . . accept as data of validation the critical query of others who
may share some part of the same perspective" (TGT, p. 160).
Consequently, validation is largely a communal process.[10]

The third factor is the propulsive character of proception.
Proception is a process that is driven forward. It is, in this sense,
future oriented—a notion central to Peirce. But a further connota-
tion is evident in Buchler's description of proception and the place of
validation in it; namely, expansiveness. Judgments and the perspectives they embody do not, so to speak, merely rest in their own
moment of being rendered, but seek to be applied as extensively as
they can. They are progressively appropriative. Their validation,
Buchler says (echoing Dewey), "leads to a consummation," but presumably never a complete consummation, because validation is,
again, never complete. In this sense, validation is the name for an
impulse implicit in proception, and hence in all components of proception (procepts, perspectives, judgments, query), toward expansion and greater efficacy.

There is a vitalistic flavor to this idea. Judgments are events in
the living, human process. They share in the "primordial" claim,
inherent in human existence itself, to "valid continuance" (TGT, p.
141). This vitalistic, propulsive, dynamic context is most important
for understanding validation. Buchler's naturalism is applied to
validation through the notions of continuance, survival, and security—terms consonant with the idea of self-preservation. The
point here is not that Buchler puts the validity of judgments in the
service of the survival of the judge; that may be, but it is not the
point here. It is rather that judgments are seen as propelled toward
their own security and survival due to their inclusion in self-secur-
ing life. The naturalistic theme of survival provides the background.

Buchler spends little time delineating his notion of knowledge.
What is clear is that knowledge for Buchler can indifferently characterize action and exhibition as well as assertion. He writes,

"What does it mean to attribute 'cognitive' significance to a judgment? Presumably, that the judgment is a vehicle whereby we can acquire or transmit knowledge. Are all three modes of judgment cognitive in this sense? Unquestionably. . . . In the most fundamental sense, knowing is that process by which an organism gains from its own continuing living or from the world available to it the capacity to produce or to experience in different, unprecedented ways" (NJ, p. 33).

Buchler's most sustained discussion of knowledge occurs in the final chapter of his last book, *The Main of Light* (1974). He explains, "To get to know is to make a certain kind of gain. To know . . . is to have acquired a certain kind of power. . . . This is not all. To be cognitive, a specific power of judging, along with its actualizations, must be one that is required for the augmentation of the order in which it functions. The actualizations must be depended upon. They must be needed. . . . They must have a compulsive character. . . . The compulsiveness is the validity or 'objectivity' or efficacy that belongs to knowledge" (ML, p. 149–150). He adds that "efficacy consists in the difference that a complex makes by being that complex" (ML, p. 158).

Later Buchler indicates, in a discussion of what the admonition to "write well" might mean, that, "Writing 'well' is not prescribed but discovered on the basis of writing that takes place. The writing is what provides the means to determine the 'well,' to ascertain its possibilities" (ML, p. 153). Norms are discovered in the process of query and cannot be understood except in relation to the history of the phenomenon of which they are claimed to be the exemplar. This will be instructive for our understanding of truth as norm for assertive judgments.[11]

We will examine in the following sections whether this description of validation exhibits any of the kinds of antirealism we have been pursuing.

Sheer Geniture

Buchler is clearly a naturalist. His basic metaphysical category characterizes everything as natural. "Whatever is, in whatever way," he begins his *Metaphysics of Natural Complexes*, "is a natural complex" (MNC, p. 1). Importantly, although anything discriminated is a natural complex, it is not true for Buchler that all natural complexes are discriminated, nor do we know whether all can be discriminated by human beings. Indeed, "it is hard to avoid the conviction that . . . innumerable complexes of nature elude the range of finite creatures" (MNC, p. 2).

At the metaphysical level Buchler does not wish to endorse any particular conception of nature; he attempts to keep the role of nature in his system bare and abstract. In 1966 he defined nature "in the barest sense . . . [as] the presence and availability of complexes" (MNC, p. 3). Buchler's metaphysical naturalism has been fairly characterized as "a commitment to the view that there is no being or reality which is wholly different from and discontinuous with any other being."[12] This is an austere *ordinal naturalism*, equivalent to no more than a denial that anything is nonnatural.[13]

One reason for the abstractness of this characterization is that Buchler denies that the world, or the totality of things, is a natural complex, a discriminable something. Thus "everything" cannot be characterized as something. It would be misleading to say that everything is 'in' nature. If 'nature' or 'natural' somehow characterizes everything, or whatever can be discriminated, then for Buchler it is not clear what that characterization could mean.

Buchler's most sustained examination of nature and naturalism appears in his 1978 essay, "Probing the Idea of Nature." In that essay Buchler contrasts two "orientations" in the history of the philosophical interpretation of the meaning of nature, and the frequently met opposition of the natural and the nonnatural. For the *domain* orientation nature is a domain or sphere. In this view, the nonnatural is what is outside nature, an alternative realm, the *super*natural. For the *trait* orientation, nature is a principle of traits or characteristics. Hence it is said that each thing has *a* nature. Here, the nonnatural is the *un*natural, a principle (not a realm) alternative to the natural; that is, the *artificial*.

Either of these orientations may conceive of nature as *restricted* or *unrestricted*. If nature is restricted or limited, then there is something nonnatural (either supernatural or artificial); if it is unlimited or unrestricted, then there is nothing nonnatural. A naturalistic philosophy would obviously assert the latter. But here Buchler raises an objection: "There is no order without delimitation, trait-delimitation. If nature [as unrestricted] were an order, it would be an order of all orders. But if it is unlimited, not delimited, it cannot be an order at all. . . . The conclusion, then, must be that if nature is an order it is limited in scope and that if it is unlimited it is not an order" (PN, p. 162). Buchler states the principle more generally, "An order differentiated only by the all-inclusiveness ascribed to it, and itself without a principle of integrity, is as self-contradictory as an infinitely extended enclosure, a territory without boundaries, a habitation without environment, a definition without limits" (PN, p. 163).

This has some wide-ranging consequences for usual philosophical talk. For Buchler the terms "the order of nature," "the unity of nature," "the system of the universe," "the rationality of nature," which are meant to refer to a principle characterizing the domain of all complexes, actually refer to nothing at all. For Buchler, nothing is either "contrary to nature" or especially "in accordance with nature." What we normally associate with nature and naturalism is some restricted domain or some particular principle. Science is concerned "not with nature in an unqualified sense but with a given world . . . the physical world, the social world, the psychological world" (PN, pp. 163–164).

Buchler develops his own interpretation of the unrestricted concept of nature. The most basic meaning must be "orders, of whatever variety and number." But this meaning can be given more delimitation by distinguishing the correlative ideas of 'world' and 'nature'. The former (which will be discussed in more detail in the following section) expresses the "human sense of encompassment," while the latter "may be thought of . . . as express[ing] the human sense of characterization and traithood."

Consequently *world*, in Buchler's gloss, must mean "innumerable complexes," and *natural* must mean the ordinality of any complex and the complexity of any order. The idea of world expresses the collectivity, the "crop" of complexes, *natura naturata*, but not the "seeding" or "productive principle" of complexes, which is indicated by 'nature.' He writes,

> Some years ago I defined nature as providingness, the provision of traits. The intent was to abstract from the partly eulogistic common suggestion of purposive or planned accumulation, as well as of agency, and to amplify the suggestion of sheer putting forth or bringing forth, sheer geniture, for better and for worse. The conceptions of nature as providingness and as ordinality are continuous with one another and with the conception of nature as "orders". . . . Nature as ordinality is *natura naturans*; it is the providing, the engendering condition. Nature as "orders" is *natura naturata*; it is the provided, the ordinal manifestation, the World's complexes" (PN, p. 165).

There is a remarkable similarity between Buchler's interpretation of nature and Nietzsche's "Dionysian world" devoid of goal or unifying principle, which is to say, the world conceived as the will to power (WP, 1067). Buchler eschews the "eulogistic" and "purposive" concepts of nature in favor of "sheer geniture," providingness, and the complexity or multiplicity of what is provided, "for better and for worse."[14] This is an amoral and non-teleological conception of nature. "Sheer geniture" is not very far from the will to power, once the later is purged of misinterpretation in terms of one of its species, the will to domination.

When applied to human beings, Buchler's naturalism assumes a more familiar shape. "Man is born in a natural state of debt," Buchler opens *Nature and Judgment*, "being antecedently committed to the furtherance or continuation of acts that will largely determine his individual existence" (NJ, p. 3). Moral obligation is a species of "animal obligation." This indebtedness impels the process of judging, for, "Debts, obligations, are met by producing" (NJ, p. 4). "Human nature," he writes, "is characterized by perspective . . . as other phases of nature are characterized by binary fission, by oxidation, by tidal ebb and flow, by hibernation, by mineral deposits" (NJ, p. 197). Buchler strips validation of its usual mentalistic and non-natural properties. "The experiential relation, " he insists, "is an 'object-object' relation, rather than a 'subject-object' relation" (NJ, p. 144). He obliquely refers to his view as a "critical naturalism" (TGT, p. 112). Human judgments are "facts of nature in the very same sense that the falling of snow flakes and the orbits of the planets are" (TGT, p. 111). Human facts are natural facts, and the particular character of some human facts is that they occur in a process called proception, which is driven by obligation or need. Here Buchler's naturalism assumes the more familiar shape characteristic of a *vitalistic* or *biotic* naturalism that locates proception and judgment within the context of a life whose needs compel it actively to adapt and respond to circumstance.

There is a question as to whether the austere ordinal naturalism of Buchler's metaphysics of natural complexes (and "Probing the Idea of Nature") is compatible with the more familiar vitalistic or biotic naturalism of his account of human judgment. At the very least, they represent two different senses of naturalism. A simple example of this is provided by the dramatic opening passage of *Nature and Judgment*, that, "Man is born in a state of natural debt . . ." This is naturalism in the traditional, biotic sense. For, what is the meaning of the phrase *state of natural debt*? What does *natural* mean here? It seems not to be the sheer geniture of complexes, for what "debt" could obtain for "sheer geniture"? Buchler is here locating human being in a particular order, the order of needs, physical compulsion, and reaction.

Whence the necessity of regarding human being as intrinsically incomplete, indebted, and hence propulsive? It is possible to regard human being otherwise; there are metaphysical and religious perspectives that interpret this incompleteness and indebtedness as illusory. In the opposite philosophical direction, a physicalist perspective that locates human beings in the order of material objects might regard humans as no more indebted and propulsive than stones. Buchler seems to recognize this difference when he writes, as we have seen, that, "As events in nature the products of men are complete and inexpugnable. But as potential vehicles of communication they stand in need of a certain kind of actualization . . . (TGT, p. 140).

The conflict lies between a notion of naturalism that can abide the contextualism or ordinalism of Buchler's metaphysics, and the kind of antisubjectivist account Buchler wants to give of the human process. At the very least there is a problem of justification. For ordinality and parity must imply that, in the preceding example, the indebtedness of human being is an *ordinal* fact, no more real or primary than the trait of completeness (nonindebtedness) that human beings might have in other orders (e.g., a religious order or the order of "events in nature"). That would mean that Buchler's theory of the human process is itself a contextual description, a theory of the human in an order. Yet Buchler asserts indebtedness as if it were a universal trait, as if the orders in which indebtedness obtains are more primary than those in which it does not.

We will return to this question later; for the moment the issue is how Buchler's naturalism affects his account of judgmental validation. Buchler's sometimes vitalistic naturalism has some controversial implications. For, what is *validity* in the context of the human process, naturalistically considered? Can it be distinguished from natural *efficacy*? We have already seen that for Buchler the validity of a judgment lies in what that judgment enables the judge subsequently to judge. The norms of validity are aspects of power, of capacity for future discrimination. Buchler's discussion of knowledge in *The Main of Light* explicitly makes knowledge a power. Of course, this means the power to judge further, not power in a solely active sense. Nevertheless, nothing binds or determines or limits these norms of judgment but the propulsive process of cumulative modification, and the complexes it encounters.

Remember that what primarily distinguishes assertive validity is evidential compulsion. Evidence, Buchler writes, "compels by defining the adjustive limits of human action. It compels because it is a necessary condition of adaptation, exploration and control. Nothing is so requisite to sanity as the estimate of reasonable control. . . . We cannot 'disagree' with scientific inquiry; it is a formalization of our own proceptive demand for guidance among the complexes of fact" (TGT, p. 73). This statement makes assertive validity a function of the need to limit action for the sake of survival and prosperity. Judgments governed by truth recognize the compulsion of evidence out of a need for controlled survival.

Simply put, Buchler appears to make validity a kind of efficacy, understood as a contribution to survival, continuance, security, power, growth, or future effectiveness. To be sure, validity is often communal, so that it cannot be the arbitrary will of an individual, or at least can rarely be that. But the issue at the moment is not conventionalism versus solipsism or egocentrism, it is whether assertive validity is independent of what it governs, that is, is separate from power, efficacy, impact, and so forth. The answer in Buchler's system appears to be, no.

The whole character of Buchler's naturalistic account of the human process gives us reason to attribute to him the claim that truth is to be understood in terms of power or efficacy. Buchler makes the validity of a judgment, the difference between a valid and invalid judgment, a product or characteristic of *the process of judgment itself*. His analysis makes it inevitable that the norm governing the process of judgment be *a product of* that process. Hence validity cannot be separate from efficacy or power. The norms governing the human process cannot be imported from the supernatural. If the human process has its own immanent aims, and if it invents the norms that serve to evaluate it, then it is hard to see how those norms could be independent of the aims they are supposed to evaluate. If the criterion of being a good or true or valid result of some process, is itself a product of the process, then the criterion presumably expresses and serves the intrinsic aims of the process.

Now, this does not mean that the human process or human judgment has but one intrinsic aim, for example, pleasure or domination or power, which the norms of validity must then serve. The aims may be plural; or there may be a single aim of great generality, like continuance. But however this is decided, there clearly can be no discontinuity between efficacy and validity, between judgment's power and its norm conformity, between continuance and *valid* continuance, or between efficacious assertion and *true* assertion.

To draw this apparently Nietzschean implication from Buchler is not as odd as it may first appear. Both are naturalists. Both make the human process continuous with nonhuman nature. The particular slant that Nietzsche sometimes gives to power by interpreting it as domination or mastery is, of course, not characteristic of Buchler. The spirit of Buchler may seem far from the spirit of Nietzsche. But the underlying principle, shorn of dramatic poetizing and political rhetoric, is the same. The meaning of the will to power in Nietzsche is the will to energy, to efficacy, the capacity to do and experience, the will to creativity, of which the will to domination is merely one case (albeit one needing emphasis, in Nietzsche's view, as a counterweight to the historical dominance of morality). For both Buchler and Nietzsche, judgments of good and evil (and truth and beauty) spring from a source "beyond good and evil." They are expressions of *sheer geniture*.

The Question of Pragmatism

There is a related question regarding Buchler's account of judgment. By way of introduction we might recall Buchler's description of evidence as "defining the adjustive limits of human action," as a "necessary condition of adaptation, exploration and control" (TGT, p. 73). To explain evidential compulsion in these terms is to explain assertive validation in terms of active judgment. Where Buchler tries to explain on a deeper level the nature of assertive validity, his explanations often utilize active categories and, implicitly, the norm of success. This is problematic, for it would seem to violate the parity among the three functions of judgment that Buchler's philosophy aims to maintain.

Note that Buchler's explication of assertion in terms of action cannot be defended by saying that, in certain contexts, assertion serves an active function. For assertion is itself only a function. According to Buchler the primary distinctive trait of the validation of judgments insofar as they serve an assertive function—which is to say, their validation as true or false—is reliance on evidential compulsion. Yet his most explicit account of the nature of this compulsion is to refer it to the active function of judgment. Buchler appears to make action and its traits conditions for assertive validation. Ironically, this is exactly what Buchler criticized the pragmatists for doing.

To be sure, he has done it in a more subtle way, that is, he has resorted to pragmatism at a deeper level of analysis. It was pragmatism's aim systematically to interpret assertion through the category of action. Buchler has rejected that project. But at a deeper level, in the process of trying to find a way to articulate what are the determining factors of evidential compulsion, he confronts a real problem. To explain the basic terms of a mode of judgment means to derive them from some condition, to show what determines them, to put them in a context of which they are instances. What can this condition or context be like?

There seem to be three explanatory options in trying to go beyond his initial characterizations of assertion. Either Buchler could discover a single condition that determines and is distinct from all three modes of judgment; or he could explain action and exhibition in terms of assertion; or he could explain assertion in terms of either action or exhibition. The first would effectively eliminate the plural theory of judgment by making the three modes manifestations of an underlying monistic principle. The second would deny that a further explanation of assertion is possible. The third is reductive. Buchler gives no indication that he believes the first strategy is possible. Instead, he walks a tightrope between the second and third, between redundancy and reduction. In the present case he seems to have lost his characteristic balance and fallen into the latter. In other words, in the deeper levels of his account where he tries to explicate the meaning of assertive validity, Buchler appears to fall into pragmatism.

This fall is a natural one; it is directly connected to Buchler's naturalism. Buchler is, I have suggested, a naturalist in two senses, an austere, careful, *ordinal naturalist*, and a not so austere *biotic naturalist* in his account of the human process. It is this latter Buchler who says that moral obligation is a special case of "animal obligation." Thus he can assert that human existence contains an implicit demand or impulse for valid continuance and can use the language of survival, preservation, and so on. In this kind of biotic naturalism, as it has been incorporated into the philosophical tradition since the late nineteenth century, it would be entirely "natural" to regard assertive judgment as serving the organism's survival. This kind of naturalism is implicit in some versions of pragmatism. Thus, the explanation for the concept of truth is that we need those judgments that are true to survive; false views can get us killed. Buchler does not, of course, make this kind of claim, but he seems to be using the same principle.

This apparent reduction of assertion to action may be symptomatic of a basic weakness in Buchler's theory of judgment. It may be that Buchler, who emphasized that philosophy was a combination of assertive and exhibitive judgment and who had a special interest in interpreting the latter and promoting its rational equivalence with the former, had an inadequate notion of action all along.[15] In *Nature and Judgment* he admitted that action is "the most difficult mode of judgment to regard intelligibly" (NJ, p. 27). In *Toward a General Theory of Human Judgment* the closest he gets to a definition is to say that active judgments "comprise all instances of conduct to which the terms 'act' or 'action' are ordinarily applied" (TGT, p. 48). Whereas Buchler is able to articulate a number of defining traits of assertion and exhibition, he is less successful with action. In passages where he tries to explicate active judgment or some category as it relates to active judgment he usually resorts to negative characterizations, saying what action is not, not what it is.

Buchler offers only one clear criterion for active judgment: "An active judgment may be identified by the fact that it is subject to the application of moral predicates" (NJ, p. 28). This is difficult to interpret, especially because of the phrase *subject to*. If Buchler means that only those judgments that actually are given moral predicates are actions, then he would exclude most of what we normally call actions. If, on the other hand, he means to refer to any judgments that *could* be given moral predicates, then the statement is quite vague. For what we would normally call assertions and exhibitions can be morally evaluated as well as what we would otherwise call actions. To try to define action in terms of morality seems convoluted, if not circular. In the sentence immediately preceding the quote, Buchler offers what could be read as a wider criterion. He distinguishes the three modes of judgment in terms of their norms of validity: "true or false (assertive), good or bad (exhibitive), right or wrong (active)." This could be interpreted more broadly than the moral criterion, because nonmoral actions can be considered right or wrong in the sense of efficacy or success.

I believe that yet another concept of active judgment is far broader and more vague and serves an entirely different role in Buchler's writing. It is this concept that causes the trouble, although it may have emerged because Buchler had difficulty giving a more adequate definition of action along other lines. It is, roughly, anything that may be called a "doing." The problem with this usage is that the other two modes of judgment can themselves be regarded as something we *do*. The result is that Buchler sometimes uses active judgment in such a way that it is a synonym for judgment in toto.

Thus it appears that the category of action serves two inconsistent functions in Buchler's theory. Narrowly defined (in terms of morality) it is analogous to the other two modes of judgment. But in its most general or vague version it is really not a mode of judgment at all, but a synonym for judgment or judging. For the latter tendency, doing is not to be classed alongside saying and making; rather, saying and making are things we *do*. The earlier concept of action as governed by success may contribute to this problem. For assertion and exhibition *as such* could be described as seeking their own success or efficacy, thus making the norm of action ubiquitous.

If this more vague and ubiquitous sense of action as doing is present in Buchler, then it would explain the ambivalent and ambiguous place action has in his system. On the one hand, Buchler often seems least interested in this mode of judgment. After all, his main interests were in poetry, which is primarily exhibitive, and in philosophy, which, as we will see, was for Buchler primarily assertive and exhibitive. On the other hand, by virtue of its vagueness, this notion of active judgment gains a kind of priority over the other functions of judgment in the sense that its predicates—success, survival, efficacy—come to be applied to all judgment at a deeper level.

To summarize, in Buchler's account of validity the impulse of his biotic naturalism pushes him into a kind of pragmatism at the deeper levels of his theory of judgment, a pragmatism not consistent with the stated aims of his theory. This hidden pragmatism in Buchler returns us to our earlier question, Can Buchler's ordinal naturalism give an adequate realist account of validation? Or is it, in the final analysis, antirealist?

Objective Relativism

Three different elements of Buchler's system bear on relativism. Each of these must be examined before we can ask whether Buchler is a realist or an antirealist. First, the validity of every judgment is relative to some perspective. Buchler is at least as great a "perspectivist" as Nietzsche. Second, every natural complex is ordinal, that is, its identity and integrity are relative to context or order. This makes him an *objective relativist*, to use his own term, a relativist regarding the objects of judgment. Third, because the whole, the collection of all complexes, cannot be related to anything outside itself, it is not a complex and so cannot be judged. We will explore these three elements in order.

Every judgment is a "situational recognition" of the individual's world. It is necessarily perspectival, that is, it obtains in an order of procepts, as does its validation. Consequently, the "flight from perspective is a dream" (TGT, p. 127). No judgment can be valid or more valid than another *in every respect*. For Buchler, "the expression 'superior in all respects' is nonsense. The type of qualification required is one of evaluative choice or perspective" (TGT, p. 167).

If this appears to lead to relativism, then not all appearances are deceiving. But it is not a subjective or egocentric or mentalistic relativism. Procepts, judgments, and perspectives are facts of nature, like their objects; they are not private or incommunicable. Buchler announces that, "Thus 'naive realism,' 'representationalism,' and similar approaches grounded in a dubious metaphysics have no meaning here. On the other hand, the general approach sometimes called 'objective relativism' is given support" (NJ, p. 128). Buchler is a *metaphysical* relativist in the sense of regarding things themselves as relational. Buchler writes, "The metaphysics of natural complexes denies the discriminability of anything without ramification and constitution—of anything unrelated and not located in an order, of anything free of traits affecting and affected by other traits" (MNC, p. 20). Things are not solely relations; relations are only one kind of thing that is. Nor is everything related to everything else. But there is no thing that fails to be dependent on some relations to some things. This means that everything is *plural*, everything has a series of integrities dependent on the orders in which it stands.

Although Buchler is no idealist in the sense of making reality mental, he has adopted a strategy analogous to that of idealism. For he has changed the notion of the object of judgment in such a way that his relativist account of judgmental validity appears to be rendered realist nevertheless. Remember that this was true of Peirce. Peirce defined truth in a relativist manner, but his idealist notion of reality made reality and judgment conform. Buchler performs the same trick, but without mentalism or panpsychism. His ordinal metaphysics makes every object of judgment plural *in itself*. What the object is in a given order is determined in part by the nature of the order; likewise the judgment is relative to that order.

So, in a sense, ordinality plays the constitutive role in Buchler that imagination does in Kant. The thing in itself is perfectly knowable, but indeterminate and plural. It is never completely known

(Buchler) or infallibly known (Peirce); whereas for Kant it was never *really*, but only *apparently*, known. Contrasting his view with Kant's claim that "nature or the world as a whole cannot be . . . objects of possible experience," Buchler writes that, "*nothing* as a whole can be an object of possible experience or be given, since we must take into account the indefinite spread of its relations and its potentialities. . . . nothing at all is present as a "whole" in experience . . ." (PN, p. 162). This powerful claim echoes Peirce: not only can we not know everything, we cannot know everything about anything. For everything is related to an indefinite number of other things, and each of those relations adds to what the thing in question is.

Buchler would never admit that this scheme violates realism. For, "Any complex is determinate, whether it is related or unrelated to mind. . . . It is determined by and determines other complexes" (MNC, p. 87). He writes,

> A procept is not "in the mind" . . . nor is it "external" to the mind. . . . A procept is the *existence itself*, the existing fact, state, situation, or other natural complex *in so far* as it is relevant to an individual as individual. Likewise, proception *is* the continuing interrelation of the individual with other existences of whatever kind. . . . The complexes of nature are not "presented' to experience. They occur, and when their occurrence involves an individual they *constitute* experience. (NJ, pp. 122–123)

What is proceived and judged *is* the natural complex, not a phenomenon problematically related to the natural complex. Yet it is always a complex in an order. The thing itself, so to speak, is constituted by its various orders. Consequently, the relativity of judgmental validity is matched by the relativity of the object, and the realist relation between judgment and object is maintained—so far, at least.

As mentioned earlier, in Buchler's 1978 essay, "On the Concept of 'The World'," he argues that the term 'world' does not refer to any natural complex. Every complex must be ordinally located, must be related to things outside itself, must "make a difference *for* other complexes," and any such interaction presumes an order in which the affecting and affected can be located. But the referent of *world* cannot be such a thing: "The world cannot be a complex, because there could not be anything besides the World to which it could be related" (OCW, p. 573). 'World' can mean, for Buchler, only "innumerable complexes," *not* all complexes. Buchler concludes:

> Since the Innumerable Complexes do not constitute an Order, and
> since in consequence no order has an "ultimate" location, if follows
> that no order has absolute priority over any other. . . . Priorities of
> all kinds there certainly are . . . but all are conditional. Being con-
> ditional means being ordinally determined. . . . Among
> Innumerable Complexes there are innumerable differences and
> innumerable similarities, but there is no final hierarchy of com-
> plexes. The World has no form, no boundaries, no constitution. It is
> not mappable. . . . Innumerable Complexes, the World, has no
> beginning and no ending. (OCW, pp. 577–578)

Two important points are being made here. The first is the obvious one that Buchler eschews the meaningfulness of any supposed
reference to natural complexes taken collectively. The collection of
all things is not a thing. This is Buchler's concept of the limit of
human judgment, and it bears comparison with Kant's and
Wittgenstein's. It is a straightforward implication of Buchler's
contextualist theory of judgment. What is not located in a context
cannot be judged.

But there is a second implication. Not only can there be no ultimate perspective *collectively*, no ultimate perspective on everything
taken together, there also can be no ultimate perspective *distributively* or locally, that is, no ultimate perspective on *any* thing. For
Buchler, nothing is first, nothing is unconditionally prior to anything else. This means that nothing is unconditionally first *in toto*,
with regard to everything, *and* that nothing is unconditionally first
in regard to anything in particular. The priority of something or
some judgment or some perspective over others is established only
in relation to an order. Buchler's denial of completion and priority
must be distributive as well as collective.

Now, the absence of an order of orders does not mean that anything goes. In response to the claim that it is physically impossible
for insects to talk, but logically possible (because, allegedly, "no contradiction is involved"), Buchler writes, "But a contradiction certainly is involved, a contradiction of the concept of 'insect,' an area of
knowledge, and the conditions of linguistic meaning" (OCW, p. 576).
This is reminiscent of Wittgenstein's expanded notion of logical possibility and impossibility in *On Certainty*. Buchler is using 'order' in
much the same way as 'circumstances' and 'language game' function
in Wittgenstein. Of course, Buchler's 'order' means context not only
for judgments but for any complex. Nevertheless, in application to
judgment, they are close. Buchler and Wittgenstein are both contextualists.[16]

Buchler continues, "the so-called logical . . . possibility turns out not to be about insects at all. The alleged pure possibility free from all ordinal limitations is . . . determined in and by an order of complexes, but an order covertly introduced—in this case, an order of envisioned images" (OCW, p. 576). That we can indeed imagine insects talking is evidence that we have introduced "an order of reverie." The insectlike talking creatures in that order of reverie cannot be the same creatures we encounter in the visible world called "insects," because one of the inescapable traits of the latter is dearth of speech. The two are not reconcilable. This does not mean, though, that the physical order has priority over the imaginative order. For, "The dynamical order in which railroad tracks actually never converge has no intrinsic priority over the visual order in which they actually sometimes converge" (OCW, p. 577). They are simply different orders, any ranking of which must be, again, relative to an order.

Let us now try to determine what effect Buchler's relativism has on the possibility of realism. Does his brand of relativism deny a realist account of the determination of judgmental validity?

Buchler has not hesitated before the implications of his relativism. He admits that for every (at least, every non-self-contradictory) judgment some perspective can be found in which it is valid. For, "however misdirected a judgment may be . . . its proper purview may be defined" (TGT, p. 161). The choice of perspectives is itself perspectival. There is no escape, he has told us, from perspective. The validity of judgment, including the validity of science, is always relative to perspective.

Despite this apparent relativism, if we ask whether judgmental validity is determined by what is judged, where what is judged is independent of the judgment, Buchler's answer is, yes. Buchler's conception of the object of judgment is as relative and plural as his notion of judgment; the relativities, so to speak, match up. Buchler can say that the validity of judgment is determined by its relation to what is judged, even given the requirement that what is judged obtains independent of the judgment. It cannot obtain—hence validity cannot obtain—independent of the order, but the order need not be given by judgment (by mind, so to speak).

However, this apparent realism is not unqualified. To determine its nature more clearly we need to determine more precisely what the object of judgment is for Buchler.

The role played in Kant by the distinction between the apparent and the real object or thing in itself is played in Buchler by the distinction between the object in the given order and the object in all orders; that is, between the various integrities of the complex. The whole of the object, the totality of its possible ordinal integrities, cannot be proceived or judged. Indeed, I do not see how the totality of its *actual* or present ordinal integrities could be proceived or judged—not to mention past and future integrities—because they are indefinitely many. One might say that this pluralism merely indicates the inescapable incompleteness of judgment and the complexity of its objects, that no complex is ever completely judged, and that what matters is the contour of the complex, the continuity of its ordinal integrities.

But what limits, if any, govern the possible relations among the integrities of any complex? Can they be inconsistent or contradictory? Buchler tries to deny this. Consistency, whose manifestation in the assertive sphere is logic, is inescapable. "Logical compulsion . . . is an elemental framework within which proception and communication occur. Consistency is a condition of survival in utterance, exhibitive and active as well as assertive" (TGT, p. 69). Elsewhere he makes the community the condition of "boundaries for latitude of decision" (TGT, p. 104). Regarding the example of insects that talk, he insists that the integrities of a complex must be "reconcilable . . . otherwise we are thinking only of animals |e.g., talkative 'insects' and silent ones| arbitrarily given the same name."

It would seem, however, that consistency can be a condition for judgments of a complex only *within* an order. Buchler claims that every judgment is valid in some perspective. A valid judgment of a complex characterizes the complex's integrity in some order; Buchler says that it "actualizes" the complex's traits in an order. We plainly make judgments that are inconsistent some of the time. Each of the inconsistent judgments must be valid in some order, and so the complex *must have* the traits it is judged to have in its respective orders. But then the complex could have contradictory traits in different orders.

We make such judgments commonly and in nontrivial cases. The scientific analysis of the human person has no place for an immortal soul and Divine justice, but the Christian analysis requires them. It is one of the prime motivations of Buchler's system, one feels, to deny that there is a single scale of judgmental validity according to which only one of these judgments can be valid. Rather, each is valid *in its order*. But this fact implicitly ascribes contrary traits—such as mortality and immortality—to the same complex—human being. It would seem that the prevalence of contrary traits in different orders, hence the validity of contrary judgments in those orders, cannot be avoided in Buchler. This contrariness is allowed by Buchler at a price: the abandonment of an essential condition of realism.

It might be objected that my analysis has taken the wrong approach. It may be that Buchlerian validity ought to be conceived as a diachronic, dynamic, and relational notion, that validity in Buchler cannot be analyzed as a state or condition. Perhaps the epistemological question—"Is this judgment true?"—ought to be translated into Buchler's language as, "Which judgment is more true?" If all judgments are valid in some order, then the issue may be, not truth versus falsity, but greater, more complete, more important truth, versus narrow, idiosyncratic, limited truth. Truth and falsity may mean the *relative weight and scope* of the validity of an assertion compared with other, say past, assertions. If this is right, then when inconsistent judgments compete for validation, Buchler could say that greater validation means greater breadth, recognition in a wider collection of perspectives, or more dominant perspectives. So the problem of inconsistent valid judgments would disappear.

This reading of Buchler is Peircean in spirit, in that it emphasizes the relative and collective weight of judgments and their place in a process of inquiry. It echoes the future orientation of validity (that is, truth) in Peirce. But Buchler does not have Peirce's belief in convergence, fate, and the eventual unity of belief, and these elements made Peirce's otherwise relativistic and processural notion of validation at least nominally realist. Without them, the process of validation can be interpreted only in terms of relative contextual efficacy, such that, the judgment relatively more powerful or effective in relatively more important contexts must be the most valid.

If we read Buchler in this way, then we can see that he gives us an essentially *third person* account of judgmental validity. Buchler tells us neither how to decide what is true or valid nor what it means to be true or valid (that is, other than efficacy). He tells us that whatever comes to be considered more true or more valid than alternative judgments is more synthetic, more comprehensive, more compelling in perspectival application and importance. He tells us what traits judgments we in fact judge to be true or valid do have and will have; he does not tell us the traits they *ought* to have. This is characteristic of Buchler's system as a whole: his aim is primarily to describe, not prescribe. Indeed, he criticizes philosophers who import moral norms into their description of the world (e.g., Dewey).

In an interesting passage in *Toward a General Theory of Human Judgment*, Buchler attempts to stave off the seemingly relativistic implications of his account of assertive validity by trying to show in what respects blind faith is not the equal of science. The discussion is couched in terms of whether we can say that one method of query is superior to another, a project reminiscent of Peirce's "The Fixation of Belief."

Buchler claims, as we have seen, that the notion of some method being superior in all respects is "nonsense," that superiority is always relative to a perspective and an end. "If the end is control and prediction," he says, "then faith through critical selection of evidence is superior" (TGT, p. 166). If the end is different, then blind faith or any other method may be superior. In fact, in a given community, wherein a "moral similarity" is likely to obtain, the ends generally desired will be "best promoted" by one method. This method will probably be "validated in practice" through experience of its results. Buchler concludes, "Far from proving ultimate circularity, this would reinforce the concept of the (reciprocally describable) connection of judgments or sub-perspectives within a perspective. The moral and scientific perspectives within a larger human perspective would presuppose or imply . . . each other . . ." (TGT, p. 167).

No doubt this is true. It is also no normative help. It is a description of fact, not a rationale for a prescription. Now there is nothing wrong with this. But it is striking the degree to which Buchler's account avoids normative talk.[17] Certainly Buchler can describe normative commitments; they are complexes and judgments like any other. But his system seeks to avoid making normative commitments (with imperfect success, we will see) and even appears to undercut the possibility of our making and justifying normative commitments.

This absence of prescription in Buchler is symptomatic of a more general condition of his philosophy. This condition makes Buchler an antirealist in a subtle and deep sense. It constitutes a denial of the last of the constituting elements of realism I listed in Chapter Two. Buchler passes all the tests of realism but the last one. What makes Buchler an antirealist is his *radical pluralism*.

The reason that he provides us no help in making normative decisions is that he asserts the existence of indefinitely many contexts in which norms and decisions can be valid. There is no dominant context or set of relations either for the objects of judgment or for judgment itself, no Peircean community or convergence. There is no 'us,' no single community of inquirers that would provide a privileged context whose norms would have priority over other possible norms. Norms are as contextual, and so as plural, as anything else.

As I argued in Chapter Two, realism must be able to say that, with regard to some characteristics of what is being judged, there must in principle be at most a single valid decision that can be made as to whether the object does or does not possess those characteristics. Realism cannot allow contrary judgments to be valid. But this is precisely what Buchler's pluralism allows. For him many different *but valid* decisions can be made regarding the same complex.

Buchler's notion of identity—that the manifold integrities of the thing judged have a relation—cannot salvage realism here. For we may want to know which integrity is the true one, the real one, *the right one?* We may want to know of the religious understanding of the human spirit and the naturalistic and scientific understanding, which is right? This is undecidable in Buchler; or more precisely, multiple, contrary, equally valid decisions are possible. It is in this sense that Buchler is an antirealist.

As I argued with respect to Nietzsche's perspectivism, we ought not become sanguine about the implications of a robust or thoroughgoing contextualism combined with pluralism. The implications are very radical. Relativism means more than mere cognitive incompleteness or lack of "absolutes"; it means that the validity of every judgment is relational, is "validity with respect to" some perspective. This includes the judgment that inquiry itself, or reason, or community, or respect, or tolerance, or the will to create, or freedom is better than its alternative.

Now some philosophers seem to want to respond by saying, "So what? As long as we occupy a context, meaning and validity *can* be determined. When we do science, theological explanations are invalid. When we worship, they are valid. A supercontextual, metaphysical unity is indeed denied by this contextualism, but inquiry and life can go on nicely without it."

Certainly contextualism does not imply that anything goes. Contexts limit, structure, and dictate. We always operate in some given context. But the problem is, What delimits or constitutes the given context? What is the nature, what are the limits, of any context? For contextualism every answer to this question *must itself be contextual*. To say that "Now I am doing science, so the question of the soul cannot arise" is only the stimulus to more questions. For, what is science? Every attempt to decide *that* question is, for contextualism, contextual. So, against those who want to include the soul in science—to take a contemporary example, to call "creationism" science—all objections will be valid only contextually. There may then be different notions of science (e.g., creationist science and Darwinian science), each contextually valid *as science*. Furthermore, why *ought* we occupy one context rather than another? Why is one right, better, more cogent, more fruitful? All the answers given to these questions are susceptible of only a contextual validity. The *interpretations of* those answers are again contextual—and so on, and so on.

Those who accept relativism without blinking an eye seem to be avoiding its radically antirealist consequences for inquiry and human living, through tacitly making some subset of the following assumptions. First, that relatively few alternative contexts (e.g., "religion," "science," "modern liberalism") are legitimate contenders for belief. Second, that there is some dominant, stable, virtually unquestionable macro-context—provided by science or civilized social practice or nature or liberal polity or rational inquiry—whose validity is not open to question. Third, that judgments about the limits, the nature, and the interpretation of contexts are somehow super- or noncontextual, hence their validity is immune to relativity. The first and second assumptions are unjustifiable on relativist grounds; they are additional assumptions that must receive their justification from elsewhere, although such justification must be contextual. The third is a prima facie inconsistent recourse to a meta-context in which all other contexts are weighed and measured.

The key factor that can either limit relativism or allow it to develop its most radical implications is whether another doctrine is asserted that effectively limits the plurality and variability of contexts, or gives some context or small set of contexts priority over all others. Normally, such a judgment of priority is offered as if it were valid super- or noncontextually, which is an inconsistency. Nevertheless, if we are contextualists who assert, however unjustifiably, that there is only one context for judgment, or there is one necessary or unavoidable context, or that one context has some nonepistemic priority over all others, then our contextualism can look very much like realism.

Here it is useful to contrast Buchler with Peirce, Nietzsche and Wittgenstein. Peirce is a relativist and a conventionalist in the very significant sense that he defines reality in terms of the opinions of the community. But he limits his relativism by granting one community priority—the community of inquirers, who all accept the same method of fixing belief—and by asserting the convergence, or growing unity of belief, of that community's opinions. Nietzsche espouses perspectivism, a kind of relativism. But he is also a naturalist, which causes him to regard certain perspectives or contexts as having priority, for example, those rooted in instinct, especially the instinct for the expression of power. This kind of biotic naturalism and incipient pragmatism tend to curb relativism. So although Nietzsche does not endorse realism, he does effectively limit his relativism. Last, Wittgenstein is, as I have argued, a conventionalist in his account of meaning and validity. But he is also a pragmatist who regards the role of a sign in community sanctioned practice as determinative of meaning. The variability and plurality of contexts is limited by this pragmatism and by the notion of "form of life."

In principle if not always in practice, Buchler accepts none of these limitations. That is, he is less of a pragmatist than Peirce, Nietzsche, or Wittgenstein. With the exceptions of the occasions when his biotic naturalism comes forward (and another exception which we will presently examine), Buchler insists on the parity and unlimited plurality of contexts. There is no barrier in his system to diversity, contradiction, and revision. Simply put, there is less unity in Buchler.

The Priority of Parity

Philosophy, Buchler writes, "is not sacrosanct, and not by itself morally better than any other form of query. It is simply a different mode of encompassment" (NJ, p. 8). But its method and scope are unique. Philosophy "effects a distinctive realization: that the categorial struggle to encompass structures of indefinitely greater breadth is both inevitable and valid" (TGT, p. 81).

Buchler's most extensive and interesting discussion of philosophy appears at the end of *The Concept of Method*. "Philosophy," he insists, "is kin with art as much as with science" (CM, p. 164). He continues,

> An exhibitive dimension . . . is implicitly expected in a philosophic structure. . . . The philosopher perforce exhibits a structure of concepts, as the artist exhibits an auditory, narrative, or visual product. . . . The character and force of the function always depend in part upon the types of dramatic interplay that are to be found among the concepts. . . . The view that an exhibitive dimension is basic to philosophy must not be confounded with the stylish allega-

tion that philosophy is to a large extent "non-cognitive." The exhibitive aspect of the discipline may be no less cognitive than the
assertive. Any methodic deployment of natural complexes which
stimulates further methodic activity of whatever kind may contribute knowledge . . . (CM, pp. 165–169)[18]

Whereas the products of art are self-sufficient, philosophy "is
required by its assertive dimension to defend as well as to contrive
and show" (CM, p. 172). Philosophy can also function actively for
Buchler; but the assertive and exhibitive modes are most prominent.

"Probing the Idea of Nature" contains a similarly interesting
account of philosophy's task.

metaphysical judgment is not always best articulated . . . in the
form of assertions. Not less fundamental is the force of mutually enhancing ideas which recur in different contexts. These form a conceptual array . . . [which] communicates metaphysical query. . . . In
the exhibitive mode of metaphysical judgment we discriminate
traits that are not only comprehensive . . . but meant to be satisfying in virtue of that comprehensiveness as *portrayed*. The degree of
satisfactoriness . . . will reflect itself in continuing query compelled
by the original portrayal, by the conceptual array. (PN, p. 164)

Buchler is pushing the limits of our understanding of philosophy.
The array of conceptual discriminations exhibits, and the exhibition
is meant to be satisfying as such. The measure of exhibitive validity
is the power of the array to compel further query. The exhibitive
dimension is essential to philosophy in a way that it is not for other
forms of inquiry.

Related to the exhibitive nature of philosophy is the inevitability and legitimacy of vagueness and metaphor in philosophic language. In a marvelous passage, Buchler lists metaphors used by
philosophers who championed literalness and clarity, a list including Hobbes' "Leviathan" and the "command" of the law of nature,
Locke's "empty cabinet" of mind on which ideas are "stamped" or
"conveyed" by the senses, and Hume's "bundle" of the self, the "testi-
mony" of the senses, and the "authority" of experience (NJ, pp.
187–189). Philosophy has always and must always employ
metaphor.

Philosophy seeks a unique comprehensiveness or breadth and
must do so in a way that is both assertive and exhibitive. For these
reasons, it cannot achieve the determinateness attainable by sci-

ence (CM, p. 172). The philosopher "is unable to adjust means to ends with any semblance of the definitiveness attained in other forms of discipline" (CM, p. 173). In this sense, it is true that "philosophic problems are never solved." Inevitably, "Philosophic methods . . . are transcended by philosophic aims." Thus is philosophy ever "lame."

This is a sensitive and subtle statement of the predicament of philosophic query. Philosophy, like all query, is never-ending. Query shares this unfinished character with human life in general. Buchler writes, "At least for man, absolute determination—perfect boundaries, incorrigible knowledge, total freedom from indecision (which is freedom from decision)—would be death" (MNC, p. 8).[19] But more than other forms of query, philosophy is blessed by or condemned to two further indeterminacies, the "indefinitely greater breadth" of its constructions, and its jointly assertive and exhibitive nature. It is often claimed that there is an exhibitive dimension in other forms of inquiry, for example, mathematics and the sciences. No doubt this is true.[20] Any statement or theory may function exhibitively. The question is whether the exhibitive function is indispensable or inescapable in the type of query as such, whether, for example, the beauty of mathematical or physical theory is intrinsic to its argumentation. Buchler means to say that this involvement is closer in philosophy, more inextricable.

Buchler's position has powerful implications. The exhibitive dimension is a source of deep indeterminacy for philosophy. Makings that show—versus sayings—cannot be contradicted by other makings, and evidence cannot compel or prevent assent to them. There is, in other words, a dimension of philosophic activity, a phase of any philosophy, that is exhibitive and so *not subject to assertive validation, evidential compulsion, and the norm of truth*. There is a dimension of the philosophical product whose power cannot be adequately evaluated assertively.

We may wonder how Buchler can account for the validity of his own perspective and judgments. We may wonder how the most basic elements of his perspective can be validated. As we saw earlier, even his initial characterization of human being as "born in a state of natural debt," which Buchler presents as if it were a universal and necessary characterization of the human process, must be, on the basis of his ordinalism, a contextual trait that may not hold for all integrities of the complex, human being. All traces of familiar biotic naturalism in his theory of the human process must face this relativity as well.

But the implications of contextualism seep even more deeply into Buchler's methodology. What of the principle of parity itself? Earlier we suggested that Buchler's system not only avoids prescription, but appears to undercut the possibility of normative philosophical decisions. The reason for this is simple and deep: normative decisions impose absolute priority among orders. They put something first absolutely. "Thou shalt love God above all" imposes an absolute restriction on all orders; it orders all orders. This imposition may be silly, or mistaken, or unobserved; nevertheless, it has been meant and understood as absolute, as nonordinal. Belief in unconditionality is a fact. Buchler's principle of parity makes it impossible for his system to understand such commitments as they are understood by those making them. We, the Buchlerian philosophers, must say that, although people do make such absolute judgments, the judgments in fact are only ordinally valid. The result is, I suggest, that the ordinal description of the world *leaves something out*, something it cannot comprehend, namely, absolute priority.[21]

Indeed, what is the justification of the principle of parity? *Why ought parity have priority?* This is the heart of Buchler's commitment, the key to his system, to its strength and its weakness. At the risk of sounding mystical, nothing is missing from Buchler's system, and that is its limitation. What is missing is the possibility of self-limitation that accompanies every ranking, the possibility of ruling things out. What is missing is the possibility of absolutism. Of course, this privation is in many respects a virtue. But, if normative commitments are absolute and if parity rules them out, then a philosophy that cannot make normative judgments is missing something. A Buchlerian philosopher can certainly describe priorities and absolutism, just as he or she can describe any other complex. But the Buchlerian philosopher cannot *have* priorities, cannot assert a priority, for the system is ruled by parity.

Now, what I have just written is only half-right. For Buchler does make normative decisions and commitments: indeed, parity is one of them! Buchler makes *parity a priority*. Inquiry, like all human activities, presumes an absolute priority, a search for normative compulsion, for a place to stand not merely equivalent to others but better, more right, more true. For Buchler, the validity of parity lies in the advantage it gives over the traditional philosophical forms of priority.

Buchler admits to a commitment that we could regard as absolute. It is inscribed in his definition of reason. For Buchler, reason is "a form of love . . . love of inventive communication . . . devotion to query" (TGT, p. 168). Rationality is a "willingness to discover other perspectives, to attain community of perspective, and to reconcile community with conviction" (TGT, p. 116). Buchler's most basic commitment is to query. What validates his system for him is its encouragement of endless, cumulative query, or if you will, the further creation and interpretation of culture. For query is simply the life of human culture. Just as his great teacher, Peirce, was above all committed to the growth of *inquiry*, Buchler is above all committed to the growth of *query*. He combines the Peircean interpretation of reason as community with his own concern for diversity and plurality, his abhorrence of the stultification caused by an insistence on unity and harmony, and his multifunctional approach to judgment that avoids Peirce's scientism.

So, Buchler makes normative judgments and commitments, as do all persons and all inquirers. He inscribes these in a system that makes any other commitments and normative decisions impossible for the philosopher. This is just as self-compromising as the claim that the validity of all judgments is relative, for it leads us to ask, as I have already, why ought parity have priority? How can Buchler validate his system?

Although Buchler provides interesting and subtle arguments against competing philosophical positions, he almost never provides argument or evidence to support the claim that his system is valid, beyond showing how it avoids problems he sees in others. Buchler asserts contextualism or relativism. But what he does not assert is that this contextualism holds for all perspectives in all respects. He merely presents the contextualist system and offers negative arguments against alternatives. Having said that all saying is contextual, he cannot say that *that saying* ("all is contextual") holds for all contexts. This is precisely the problem of the last page of Wittgenstein's *Tractatus*, the impossibility of consistently or sensibly asserting limitations on the scope and validity of all asserting.

Consequently, the validity of Buchler's system, on his own criteria, cannot be entirely evidential. It must also be exhibitive. We must regard Buchler as offering his system up for exhibitive and active validation. His conceptual array promotes a certain spirit, a position or stance with respect to things, a habitual mode of appreciating whatever is to be encountered. Buchler would say that this conceptual array has its intrinsic satisfactions as such; and in this he would certainly be right. But he could not, and would not, attempt to give a positive justification of his system beyond pointing out these benefits and satisfactions.

For Buchler, I believe that was enough. And it was the path of wisdom to recognize that it was enough, for the philosopher, to take one's place in the endlessly various process, devoid of decisive, absolute points of reference, that is human culture.

8

DERRIDA'S
SEMIOTIC
RELATIVISM

... there is nothing outside context.
                    —*Toward an Ethic of Discussion*

Jacques Derrida's impact on American philosophy has been a complex affair.[1] In what may be called the mainstream of American philosophy he has had very little influence, except perhaps to be taken as a model for the way that philosophy ought *not* to be done. To many philosophers his work is irrelevant; to others, it is dangerous. But among those concerned with recent European philosophy Derrida has been a most significant figure. Whether Derrida's work is to be interpreted as philosophical or not hangs on how narrowly philosophy is defined. For my purposes, it is enough to say that his work is relevant to philosophy, and in particular, relevant to the philosophy we are doing in this book.

My reading of Derrida will show that he is engaged, at least part of the time, in philosophical inquiry, that he exploits a version of relativism, namely a semiotic contextualism, in ways that are particularly radical.[2] Derrida is an antirealist who is keenly aware of the self-contradiction that would result from asserting antirealism. The result of his analysis is to show the impossibility of philosophical knowledge, in the sense of the impossibility of the attainment of any decisive validation of philosophical judgments. But this result undermines itself, and the truth of the contextualism on which it is based. In other words, Derrida's work is subject to his own criticism. Derrida knows this; he is consciously exploring the boundaries of inquiry. Indeed, his unusual critical strategies largely flow from this aim and this recognition. These remarks do not mean that Derrida is "wrong," but that we cannot regard his work as con-

261

stituting a form of judgment that escapes the problematic it diagnoses.

One task will be to determine the precise object of Derrida's critique. Otherwise careful commentators often run together a number of possible candidates for the object of Derrida's criticism. To take one example, in his very interesting book on Wittgenstein and Derrida, Henry Staten paints the following portrait of the kind of philosophy that both philosophers seek to undermine. "I want to appropriate the term transcendental . . . as a synonym for . . . that dimension of heightened power and generality that philosophy tries to gain for its language. Wherever philosophy speaks of necessity, whether essential or logical, or of universality or the *a priori* or the *in principle* . . . that is what in this study will be called the 'superhard' or the 'transcendental'."[3] The various traits applied to philosophy, or to metaphysics, in this passage need to be distinguished and clarified. Generality, necessity, essentiality, the notion of the a priori, the search for "heightened" linguistic power, and the "metaphysics of entity" that Staten mentions later are all quite different targets of criticism. Which of them is Derrida unmasking or criticizing? The answer cannot be *all* of them. For, as Staten recognizes, Derrida himself uses the terms *a priori* and *in principle*, and Staten describes Derrida as establishing the "conditions of the possibility" of semiosis, a phrase that captures Kant's original use of the term 'transcendental.' To give an account of the conditions or traits of all signs or all linguistic units or all philosophical concepts is to make a *universal* claim. If the phenomena in question must have these traits or meet these conditions then a claim of *necessity* is being made. If whatever has these traits or meets these conditions must therefore be a sign and whatever does not must not be a sign, then a claim about the *essence* of signs is being made. To say that a kind of discourse uses the concepts of "a priori," "universality," and "necessity" is quite a separate matter from ascribing to it a metaphysics of "entity" or "presence." Nothing is necessarily metaphysical about universality, necessity, or essentiality, unless claims like "All baseball games must include pitching" are metaphysical.

It will be helpful to mention at the outset two interpretive issues. First, does Derrida have a philosophical view at all, in particular with respect to realism? This is the same question we faced with Wittgenstein, and it is not easy to answer, for Derrida has explicitly denied most of the forms of antirealism we might be tempted to ascribe to him. The very idea of taking a philosophical or epistemological position may seem out of place in Derrida's work. I will nevertheless argue that Derrida is an antirealist in two senses: he gives us an account of semiosis, an account he offers as true, and this account is a contextualist one, with relativist implications for epistemology; and he consequently adopts a negative and implicit relativism regarding philosophical knowledge. Derrida is, in my terms, a negative antirealist.

The second issue has to do with the more basic question of what fundamental principle determines Derrida's critical work. Derrida's work is so complex and so variously understood and misunderstood that precisely what his critical targets and intentions are remains controversial. One way to account for Derrida's work is to see in it a pluralist contextualism, with radically relativist and polysemic implications for the interpretation of all semiotic phenomena. Another is to see Derrida as primarily a critic of the philosophical or metaphysical habit of positing certain fundamental distinctions (e.g., the transcendental versus the empirical), a critique that shows these distinctions to be self-undermining. Each of these alternatives has, of course, much more to be said about it. My question will be whether the latter, which is associated with a variety of conceptual phenomena that Derrida analyzes as dissemination, repression, transgression, absence, rupture, and so forth, can be adequately understood as determined or generated by the former. I will argue that, if contextualism is properly understood, they can be.[4]

Five sections follow. The first sketches the philosophical background of Derrida's work in phenomenology, as developed by Husserl and Heidegger. In the second I will give a brief rendition of Derrida's account of signs and his claims about philosophy, relying mostly on his early work, that is, material published by 1972. In the third section I will suggest a heretofore largely neglected comparison between Peirce and Derrida. My aim is not a complete or definitive comparison, but only an indication of the most fruitful points of contact. The fourth section will explore Derrida's relation to the various forms of antirealism, especially relativism. The final section will pursue the implications for Derrida's view of philosophy in general, and of his own work in particular.

Husserl, Heidegger, Derrida

Derrida's work exhibits a varied inheritance of European influences, including that of Hegel, Nietzsche, Marx, Freud, and Ferdinand De Saussure. Hegel's negative or dialectical method of internal criticism, Nietzsche's critique of truth, Marx's analysis of oppression, Freud's notion of repression, and De Saussure's structural linguistics all play a role. But an especially relevant line of development reaches from Edmund Husserl to Martin Heidegger to Derrida. Husserl is the most prominent subject of Derrida's early work; Derrida's first published essay (1959), his first book (1962), and a second early book (1967) all principally concern Husserl. Although Derrida did not devote such sustained attention to Heidegger until more recently,[5] Heidegger appears frequently in Derrida's essays throughout his career. It is clear that Heidegger has always been in the background of Derrida's thought, and that certain Heideggerian themes have been formative for Derrida's early work; these themes, and not a general comparison of Heidegger and Derrida, concern me here. The connection with phenomenology is then a natural starting point. It affords a straightforward characterization of Derrida's achievement: an *Aufhebung*, a dialectical dissolution, of phenomenology. To pursue this connection we must first make a few remarks about phenomenology in Husserl and Heidegger. This will be the most cursory of sketches.

After his initial attempt to clarify the *Philosophy of Arithmetic*, Edmund Husserl embarked on a four-decades-long project of establishing a nonnaturalistic, nonempirical theory of meaning as arising out of immediate, preconceptual experience. His "phenomenology," which bears contrast to the phenomenologies of Hegel and Peirce and the phenomenalism of Hume, sought to exhibit the "things themselves," meaning the phenomena themselves as they arise in experience, prior to and independent of the assumptions of the "naturalistic standpoint," the conclusions of modern science, or any other interpretive stance. The attempt to work out this approach as a new "a priori science," beginning with *Logical Investigations* (published 1900–1901), and passing through major revisions in *Ideas*, volume one (1913), *Cartesian Meditations* (1931), and *The Crisis of the European Sciences and Transcendental Phenomenology* (written 1934–1937), led Husserl to formulate a "transcendental phenomenology" for which the pure, nonempirical life of meaning is constituted by transcendental subjectivity.

There are many ways to appreciate and to criticize Husserlian phenomenology. It can be appreciated for its devotion to philosophical knowledge as sheer "seeing,"[6] or for opening up a new science of the correlation of conscious acts and intentional objects,[7] or for initiating European philosophy's greatest counter-attack against the worship of modern science and technology. It can be criticized as an antinaturalist, idealistic metaphysics, or for its tran-

scendental notion of the self or ego, or as a new form of Cartesianism.

Derrida takes a different, albeit a related, approach. He focuses
on certain problematic distinctions that Husserl's project forces him
to make or, one might say, on one problematic distinction that
Husserl is forced to make again and again in different ways and on
different levels of analysis. This is the distinction between the ideal
and the historical, or the transcendental and the empirical, or most
simply, the interior and the exterior, which for Husserl inevitably
means the distinction between the (egoistic) source of meaningful
lived experience and the manifold concrete vehicles (signs) and concrete contents (empirical objects) of those meaningful acts.

This line of criticism is best laid out in *Speech and Phenomena*.[8]
Derrida begins by drawing attention to the distinction Husserl
makes in his *Logical Investigations* between "expression" and "indication."[9] Although all signs "stand for" something, not all "express" a
"meaning"; for example, notes or marks. Those that do not are mere
indications, as opposed to expressions. The value of this distinction
for Husserl will be that expressions "function meaningfully even in
isolated mental life, where they no longer serve to indicate anything."
Derrida will show that this seemingly harmless prefatory distinction is only the earliest and most mundane representative of a series
of distinctions that are crucial to Husserl's project of giving a fully
idealized account of meaning, an account of meanings as independent of all "indications," or as Derrida will say, independent of
the essential "exteriority" of all signs. He will further show that this
account of meaning, despite its putative ideality, is connected with
the metaphor of talking to oneself, hence with a notion of speech as
the event in which the human self is most fully present to itself, and
ultimately with the metaphysics of *presence* to which Heidegger
calls our attention. He will show that the series of distinctions
(expression/indication, meaning/sign, interior/exterior, ideal/empir-
ical) cannot be maintained by Husserl; they undermine themselves.
The ideal/empirical distinction is inherently unstable; the attempt
to clarify it shows that the ideal cannot be distinguished from the
empirical, or rather, that it can be distinguished only by involving
the notion of "presence"—and its opposition to "nonpresence"—
which cannot be maintained (SP, p. 37).

This discussion is more than an internal criticism of Husserl.
For Husserl's project is not idiosyncratic, it is a particularly stubborn and acute attempt at nothing less than determining what is
the *source of meaning*, a project that is virtually contiguous with the

enterprise of Western philosophy itself. Derrida will argue that the metaphysics of presence, the notion of full self-presence, the "phonocentric" connection of self-presence to voice, and the consequent devaluation of writing, are to be found throughout the Western philosophical tradition.

Derrida's relationship with Heidegger is more complex. For Heidegger is aware of many of those elements in Husserl and in the Western philosophical tradition that Derrida will criticize. Heidegger reformulates phenomenology in light of them. He adopts a subtle critical position that is neither acceptance nor rejection—which is true, in some ways, of Derrida as well. Yet, despite their affinity, Derrida will conclude that Heidegger remains identified with the tradition, indeed that he intensifies it, rather than gaining freedom in relation to it.[10]

Heidegger's single greatest work remains *Being and Time* (1927), in which he reformulated the phenomenological method through both a return to ancient Greek thought and an infusion of existentialism, all in service of his lifelong project: to think the meaning of Being (*Sein*). In the ensuing decade a continued meditation on the Greek notion of truth as *aletheia* or unconcealment, along with sustained attention to Nietzsche, led to a "turn" in Heidegger's thinking that remains evident in the rest of his work. The attempt to think the meaning of Being is linked to the attempt to think other topics in the light of the meaning of Being, especially the meaning of the modern industrial, scientific, technological age.

Beginning with *Being and Time* Heidegger seeks to "destroy" the history of metaphysics, which means, to give an account of that history in order to reveal our forgotten presuppositions regarding the meaning of Being.[11] He finds that the most fundamental characterization of Being in the Western philosophical tradition is the most ancient one, presence, the determination of Being as both what is present in the sense of what is immediately before a subject in experience, and in the sense of what belongs to the particular mode of time we call the *present*.

Being and Time is an existentialist work. Later on Heidegger will distance himself from existentialism, because of its apparent humanism and subjectivism.[12] But existentialism is undeniably one of the elements that most clearly differentiates Heidegger from Husserl, and if conceived minimally enough it can be seen to remain with him. Strictly, existentialism is the view that existence logically precedes essence, that the nature of or truth about a thing (its essence) cannot *be*, and cannot be known, prior to or independent of the actual manner of existence characteristic of that thing. In *Being and Time* Heidegger applies this doctrine to Dasein or human being, so that, "The 'essence' of Dasein lies in its existence."[13]

Sometimes existentialists have formulated their doctrine so that the priority of existence over essence applied only to human beings. This restriction often constituted of a kind of humanism for which the priority of existence was equivalent to an ascription of absolute freedom, most famously in the work of Jean-Paul Sartre.[14] However, the priority of existence can certainly have a wider application, absent the imputation of freedom. If there is no God, no transcendental legislator, then the essence of physical nature cannot precede its existence either. Understood in this way, existentialism is a rejection of dualism, a denial of the transcendental character of the necessary features of things. In this sense Heidegger's existentialism is a permanent character of his thought by which he denies the transcendental nature of the most fundamental traits of whatever is under his consideration: human being, truth, technology, freedom, ethics, or philosophy. Thus, from the beginning Heidegger denies many (though not all) of the classical oppositions that are at the center of Husserl's thought: ideal versus historical, transcendental versus empirical. This is a reason for kinship with Derrida.[15]

What Derrida finds most fruitful in Heidegger are those moments when Heidegger makes recourse to ways of writing that belie the ability of philosophical language to encompass the issues he is trying to address. For example, in the 1938 lecture, "The Age of the World Picture," Heidegger makes use of the notion of the "between." Reflection on Being, and on the contemporary situation of human living in relation to Being, "transports the man of the future into that 'between' in which he belongs to Being and yet remains a stranger amid that which is," a between that is the "openness-for-Being [Da-sein] . . . the ecstatic realm of the revealing and concealing of Being."[16]

Heidegger had early on attempted to think of Being in terms of "Nothing," in reaction against our tendency always to try to think of Being in terms of beings or things. Being is not a thing, hence its affinity with "no-thing."[17] Following this recognition of the inadequacy of our subjectivist modes of representation, in the 1955 essay "On the Question of Being," Heidegger writes Being as "~~Being~~."[18]

Heidegger's attempt to think beyond what can be captured by "representational thinking" takes on a particularly Derridean cast in "The Onto-Theo-Logical Constitution of Metaphysics" (1957). We fail to think the ontological difference, the difference between Being and beings, as fundamentally as we can if we think of it as a secondary relation between the relata, Being and beings. Rather than thinking of the difference "in respect of *what* differs in the difference . . . without heeding the difference as difference"(my emphasis),[19] we should recognize that, "Being and beings are always found to be already there by virtue of and within the difference."[20] The "difference as such" is behind all sameness, behind every phenomenon. Heidegger writes, "That differentiation alone grants and holds apart the 'between,' in which the overwhelming [Being] and the arrival [of beings] are held toward one another. . . . In our attempt to think of the difference as such, we do not make it disappear; rather, we follow it to its essential origin. . . . This is the matter of thinking, thought closer to rigorous thinking—closer by the distance of one step back: Being thought in terms of the difference."[21]

Heidegger's reading of the history of philosophy occasionally resembles Derrida's. The most striking example is Heidegger's "The Anaximander Fragment" (1946), in which he discusses the "self-veiling essence of Being," which causes the inevitable "oblivion of the distinction between Being and beings" at the very outset of the Western tradition.[22] It is possible that this distinction can be remembered. However, "the distinction between Being and beings, as something forgotten, can invade our experience only if it has already unveiled itself with the presencing of what is present; only if it has left a *trace* which remains preserved in the language to which Being comes"[23] (my emphasis). Derrida will discuss this very passage in his essay "*Différance*," and the notion of trace will be central to his work.

Derrida concludes that Heidegger's thought, in some respects so subtle and so open to what Derrida will call nonpresence, nevertheless remains within what it criticizes, within the circle of presence and the myth of return to the lost origin. This is what Derrida calls the "ambiguity of the Heideggerian situation with respect to the metaphysics of presence and logocentrism" (OG, p. 22). Heidegger's work, even his allegedly antisubjectivist later work, is peppered with phonocentric metaphors reflecting the belief in the priority of speech over writing because of the alleged self-presence of meaning in speech. Heidegger is still seeking the "ground" or "origin" of the human relation to Being. For Heidegger we come "near" to Being when we hear the "call" of the "Voice of Being." Derrida writes, "The ontico-ontological difference and its ground (*Grund*) in the 'transcendence of Dasein' . . . are not absolutely originary. Differance by itself would be more 'originary,' but one would no

longer be able to call it 'origin' or 'ground,' those notions belonging
essentially to the history of onto-theology" (OG, p. 23).

The sense in which Heidegger remains identified with the tradition is made most clear in Derrida's 1969 essay "The Ends of
Man." There Derrida shows that Heidegger thinks of Being and
human being as related, as proximal. This was clear in *Being and
Time*, where, "The value of proximity, that is, of presence in general,
therefore decides the essential orientation of this analytic of Dasein"
(M, p. 127). But it is no less true of Heidegger's later work, even of
the "Letter on Humanism" (1947), which aims at destroying humanism. Certainly the classical "subjectivist" (e.g., Husserlian) humanism is missing in Heidegger. Heidegger criticizes that humanism as
an expression of subjectivity's attempted domination of Being, characteristic of modernity. But what has replaced active domination in
Heidegger, according to Derrida, is a passive proximity of *Dasein* to
Being. Derrida writes, "Whence, in Heidegger's discourse, the dominance of an entire metaphorics of proximity, of simple and immediate presence, a metaphorics associating the proximity of Being with
the values of neighboring, shelter, house, service, guard, voice, and
listening. As goes without saying, this is not an insignificant
rhetoric . . ." (M, p. 130). Heidegger has exchanged domination for
proximity, but in doing so has retained the valuation, even more
fundamental to the tradition, of presence: "if Heidegger has radically deconstructed the domination of metaphysics by the *present*,
he has done so in order to lead us to think the presence of the present. But the thinking of this presence can only metaphorize, by
means of a profound necessity from which one cannot simply decide
to escape, the language it deconstructs" (M, p. 131). Hence, in
Heidegger, "Man is the proper of Being, which right near to him
whispers in his ear . . ."(M, p. 133). It is this "security of the near,"
the "co-belonging and co-propriety" of Being and human being, that
Derrida is questioning.

Semiosis and Deconstruction

A description of Derrida's early work must be given to orient
our examination. It is possible to divide the relevant portions of
Derrida's work into four thematic parts: his account of semiosis, his
critique of the inadequate accounts of semiosis (phonocentrism and
logocentrism), his critical reading of logocentric texts (deconstruction), and his view of the status of the foregoing in light of
itself. We will discuss these in order.

First, Derrida gives an account of semiosis and the place of semiosis—rightly understood—in relation to experience, judgment, and philosophy. By semiosis I mean signification or the phenomena of signs, which at least include language, speech, and writing. It may be disputed whether Derrida presents a "theory" or "philosophy" of these phenomena; but such a dispute invariably revolves around the meaning of *theory* and *philosophy*, not the meaning of Derrida. He certainly gives an account of some kind. He makes statements that he means to be true about these phenomena. True, his account is often negative; that is, it often functions as a denial of the adequacy of other accounts or a denial that certain traits characterize the phenomena in question. But negativity cannot efface his work's discursive status; to deny that signs are ever complete, for example, is to assert something informative about signs. And his account is not solely negative; he makes positive assertions about, for example, the essential "iterability" or repeatability of signs.[24]

In *Of Grammatology* Derrida characterizes his semiotic account as an account of writing. But this is Derrida's expanded notion of writing as *arche-writing*, the condition of the possibility of all language, speech and "vulgar" writing, writing in the usual sense. Arche-writing is

> all that gives rise to an inscription in general, whether it is literal or not and even if what it distributes in space is alien to the order of the voice: cinematography, choreography, of course, but also pictorial, musical, sculptural 'writing.' One might also speak of athletic writing. . . . All this to describe not only the system of notation secondarily connected with these activities but the essence and the content of these activities themselves. It is also in this sense that the contemporary biologist speaks of writing and *pro-gram* in relation to the most elementary processes of information within the living cell. And . . . the entire field covered by the cybernetic *program* will be the field of writing. (OG, p. 9)

This is a broad field. *Writing* in this sense signifies "inscription and especially the durable institution of the sign . . . "(OG, p. 44). Arche-writing is graphic and nongraphic, it constitutes "the movement of the *sign-function* linking a content to an expression" (OG, p. 60). This writing leaves a mark or trace, which is the inscribed sign. The field of arche-writing is all of semiosis.

Among the characteristics of signs for Derrida are the following. First, they are arbitrary, which is to say, they are instituted or conventional. This does not mean that signs are the product of decision or that meanings are not subject to rule; it means only that these rules are not "natural" in the sense of being caused by the phonic, graphic, physical features of the sign or the biophysical setting in which the sign arose. (This rules out accounts of the origin of all language in "natural cries.") Signs cannot be derived from, fixed or explained by nonsemiotic processes. Second, they are exterior or material, which is to say, they are not solely mental or intentional. Signs are primarily physical configurations, sounds, or visible marks. Third, a sign is general, repeatable and open to substitution: general in the sense that a sign's identity cannot be reduced to an "irreplaceable and irreversible empirical particular";[25] repeatable or iterable in that it must be able to be repeated as the same sign; and hence open to substitution in that each occurrence must be able to count as a substitution for the sign itself (SP, p. 50). This is quite crucial. A sign can function, can mean, only if it is capable of being repeated in different contexts and relationships with other signs and yet remains identifiable as the same sign.

But the trait from which the most important implications flow is that signs are never fully *present*, to use the term Derrida borrows from the philosophical tradition. A sign is what it is by virtue of its membership in a system of different but related signs *and* its membership in a temporal chain of signs, so that the elicitation of or reference to preceding and succeeding signs is essential to its meaning. This dual spatial and temporal difference, if you will, this "differing" and "deferring," is a condition of the sign's meaning, and meaning is a condition of its being, or at least functioning as, a sign. Hence a sign and its meaning can never be complete, simple, univocal, fully determinate, or immediate. Signs and their meanings are incomplete, complex, polysemic, indeterminate and mediated.

One of the aspects of this nonpresence is the endlessness of semiosis, that is, the fact that each sign is incomplete without its predecessors and successors, and so can *never* be complete. Derrida opened *Speech and Phenomena* with a passage from Husserl's *Ideas*: "A name on being mentioned reminds us of the Dresden gallery and of our last visit there: we wander through the rooms and stop in front of a painting by Teniers which represents a gallery of paintings. Let us further suppose that the paintings of this gallery would represent in their turn paintings, which, on their part, exhibited readable inscriptions and so forth."[26] Derrida remarked later that his early books *Speech and Phenomena*, *Of Grammatology*, and *Edmund Husserl's Origin of Geometry: An Introduction* were all "only the commentary" on that passage, on the structural possibility embedded in every sign, that it can generate a sign of itself, that the generated sign can generate a sign of itself, and so on (P, p. 5). Every sign is the sign of a sign, and every sign is signified by another sign. The identity of any sign includes its difference from and relation to these other signs. Hence the signified is never fully present, its identity is never complete. Derrida can define writing in terms of this endlessness, as "the impossibility of a chain arresting itself on a signified that would not relaunch this signified, in that the signified is already in the position of the signifying substitution"(P, p. 82).

The term Derrida proposes to signify the nonpresence and the becoming of signs is *differance*. The trace or mark of the sign is the "pure movement which produces difference"(OG, p. 62) and thereby "the absolute origin of sense in general. . . . The trace is the différance which opens appearance and signification" (OG, p. 65). The term *differance* was the subject of a 1968 lecture of the same name.[27] Derrida began the lecture by noting that the verb *différer* means both to differ and to defer (hence *différer* "seems to differ from itself"). The first indicates nonidentity, the second delay. Suggesting that there must be a "common root" that unites these two meanings, Derrida proposes a new name for that root by changing the spelling of *différence* in a way that is not audible, hence only appears in writing and not in speech. "We provisionally give the name *differance* to this *sameness* which is not *identical*: by the silent writing of its *a*, it has the desired advantage of referring to differing both as spacing/temporalizing and as the movement that structures every dissociation" (D, pp. 129–130).

This new term indicates "the irreducibility of temporalizing," and the "origin or production of differences . . . the *play* of differences . . ."(D, p. 130). Derrida wastes no time in asserting the unique status of this term, as well as its historical importance.

> Differance is neither a word nor a concept. In it, however, we shall see the juncture . . . of what has been most decisively inscribed in the thought of what is conveniently called our "epoch": the difference of forces in Nietzsche, Saussure's principle of semiological difference, differing as the possibility of [neurone] facilitation, impression and delayed effect in Freud, difference as the irreducibility of the trace of the other in Levinas, and the ontic-ontological difference in Heidegger. (D, p. 130)[28]

Later in the lecture, Derrida explains *differance* as "the nonfull, nonsimple 'origin'; it is the structured and differing origin of differences," and the "movement by which language, or any code, any system of reference in general, becomes 'historically' constituted as a fabric of differences" (D, p. 141).

We have just seen that the nonpresence and nonfinality of signs is described by Derrida as "play." Derrida writes that the impossibility of "totalizing" or completing any sign and its meaning,

> can also be determined . . . no longer from the standpoint of a concept of finitude as relegation to the empirical, but from the standpoint of the concept of *play*. . . . This field [of language] is in effect that of *play*, that is to say, a field of infinite substitutions only because it is finite, that is to say, because . . . there is something missing from it: a center which arrests and grounds the play of substitutions. One could say . . . that this movement of play...is the movement of *supplementarity*. (WD, p. 289)

Or more simply, "Play is the disruption of presence" (WD, p. 292).

The immediate implications of Derrida's analysis can be summarized in five points.

First, the signified, either in the Saussurian sense of the concept meant by the signifier, or a thing in the world, is non-present or *absent*. That is, the relation of sign to referent is always mediated by other signs, so the referent is never directly accessible independent of signs. Second, signs are *polysemic*, they have indefinitely many meanings. The reason is the *relativity* of the sign, the fact that the meaning of a sign is constituted by its relatedness to other past, present, and future signs.

Here there is already some controversy. In "Signature Event Context" Derrida insists that writing is "a *dissemination* which cannot be reduced to a polysemia" (M, p. 329). In "The Double Session" he denies that the "undecidability" of semiosis can be interpreted "by some enigmatic equivocality, some inexhaustible ambivalence" of words (D, p. 220).[29] In *Positions* he gives a fuller statement.

> The attention brought to bear on polysemia . . . doubtless represents progress in relationship to the linearity of the monothematic writing or reading that is always anxious to anchor itself to the . . . *principal* signified of a text. . . . Nevertheless, polysemia . . . is organized within the implicit horizon of a unitary resumption of meaning, that is, within the horizon of a dialectics . . . a teleological and totalizing dialectics that at a given moment, however far off, must permit the reassemblage of the totality of a text into the truth of its meaning. . . . Dissemination, on the contrary . . . marks an irreducible and *generative* multiplicity. (P, p. 45)

Derrida denies, not the fact of polysemia, but only that his notion of dissemination can be reduced to it. Derrida understands polysemia to be compatible with the view that a stable, complete, totality of meaning is logically achievable, that it could be reached if there were "world enough and time."[30] This view would indeed be foreign to Derrida, for whom dissemination means a multiplicity that is "irreducible and generative," that leads to *ambivalence*, to irreconcilable meanings. But it is not necessary to understand polysemia in the objectionable way.

Third, every occurrence of a sign is nonidentical with the sign's other occurrences and with all other signs. Every instance or "token" of a sign necessarily is located in a new context, with a new set of relations. This means that there can be no synonymy, no identity of meaning, in a strict sense. Fourth, our judgments about the meaning of a sign necessarily alter the meaning of the sign by inscribing it in a new context. Interpretation and translation *re-write* the sign. The act of judging a sign is not transcendent to the sign's identity, it is part of the sign's identity. Last, every judgment of meaning must *repress* polysemia and nonidentity. When I read a sign I must circumscribe its meaning; there is no meaning without circumscription, without the selection of some contexts as normative and the suppression of others as aberrant. Combined with the earlier points, this leads to a paradoxical conclusion: The meaning of signs is dependent on both the existence of unlimited possibilities and the limitation of those possibilities. This is the nub of what is most exciting and disturbing in Derrida, as we will see.

Derrida's account of semiosis is really a meditation on its first point, the nonpresence of all semiotic activities and events, which is to say, a meditation on what is implied by the word *representation*. Representation cannot be identical to presentation, for there is always a difference, a deferral, a modification of what is present in its being re-presented. Derrida asserts that experience, meaning, judgment, the concepts of philosophy, the "totality of what one can call experience," all intentionality, whether "conscious or not, human or not" (L, p. 129), and even reality itself, as dependent on semiosis are infected with this nonpresence.

> What I call "text" implies all the structures called "real," "economic," "historical," socio-institutional, in short: all possible referents. Another way of recalling once again that "there is nothing outside the text." That does not mean that all referents are . . . enclosed in a book. . . . But it does mean that every referent, all reality has the structure of a differential trace, and that one cannot

refer to this "real" except in an interpretive experience. The latter neither yields meaning nor assumes it except in a movement of differential referring. (L, p. 148).

Semiosis is the condition of the possibility of any sense or meaning, and hence of anything we can experience or judge, of anything that obtains in, appears in, experience or judgment. From the beginning of his work Derrida questioned without collapsing the distinction between signified and signifier, a distinction on which the concept of representation is based: "every signified is also in the position of a signifier" (P, p. 20), the signified is "originally and essentially . . . trace" (OG, p. 73). Being, reality, entity, the ontic-ontological difference, all are already constituted by the trace (OG, p. 47). For Derrida, "Nothing . . . precedes *différance* and spacing" (P, p. 28). Nevertheless, although Derrida defines writing in the broadest possible way, the kind of semiosis he actually investigates is more restricted. Derrida is concerned with linguistic texts, not with the meaning of thunder and red tides.

The second relevant component of Derrida's work is his analysis of inadequate accounts of semiosis that have dominated the history of Western philosophy. These inadequate accounts are *phonocentrism* and *logocentrism*, the former being an interpretation of signs, the latter being a metaphysics associated with the former.

Phonocentrism is the dominant Western tradition that interprets graphic signs, and all semiosis, as derivative of phonic signs or spoken language. Derrida's analysis of phonocentrism constitutes some of his most fascinating work. Speech is that form of semiosis which above all entails the presence of human subjectivity, indeed, which is powered by the breath of life itself. Phonocentrism conceives the "voice" as the form of semiosis that most nearly matches the ideality of thought, which semiosis is believed to signify. The ideal realm of thought is then conceived as an interior monologue, as "hearing oneself speak" (SP, p. 76). Phonocentrism views vulgar writing, and non-phonic semiosis in general, as connected with the absence of the subject, the distance between signifier and signified, the endlessness of interpretation, and ultimately, with death.

Logocentrism is the "metaphysics of phonetic writing" (OG, p. 3).[31] It interprets being, or the "transcendental signified," meaning and truth in terms of the presence to consciousness of some content. According to it, the implicit goal of all semiosis is to achieve presence in semiosis, which can occur only in literal assertive speech (and derivatively in literal assertive writing).

Logocentrism and phonocentrism are motivated. Presence and absence in semiosis have, in the broadest sense, moral significance, value with respect to human aspiration. Logocentrism serves to maintain presence throughout the repression or control—if only within the realm of semiosis or imagination—of difference, distance, and death, which is to say, of absence. Phonocentrism serves this program by repressing writing. As such, the field of logocentrism is vast. Derrida says often enough that it is the dominant Western philosophical tradition and is embedded in Western nonphilosophical culture as well.

Is logocentrism false for Derrida? This is a deep problem, which can be adequately addressed only later. For the moment, I would suggest that, for Derrida, logocentrism makes assumptions that it neither recognizes or is able to validate, assumptions that limit and determine its account of semiosis and everything related to semiosis. Thus logocentrism is inadequate as an account of semiosis. *If* inadequacy is a sufficient condition for falsity in inquiry, then logocentrism is false.

On the other hand, phonocentrism and logocentrism are not as simple as I have portrayed them. They are, like all systems of signs, complex and carry with them reference to what is not present. This fact brings us to the third element of Derrida's work.

What would, in the hands of most philosophers or theoreticians, be the object of 'critique' in the sense of an inquiry culminating in assertions of the truth or falsity of phonocentrism and logocentrism, must in Derrida's hands, because of the account of signs he presupposes, be somewhat different. Derrida is required by the implications of his account to develop a special form or strategy of critical reading, a strategy called *deconstruction*. Many readers of Derrida have focused their attention on this method of intervention while neglecting what Derrida asserts about the phenomena that both he and his historical interlocutors investigate. It seems to me, however, that deconstruction can be understood only in the context of Derrida's account of semiosis and logocentrism, as the kind of work one would be forced into if one accepted the essential nonpresence of semiosis as a ubiquitous condition.

Before describing deconstruction, it is important to note Derrida's statements about what deconstruction is *not*. In 1983 Derrida insisted that deconstruction is not a method, a form of analysis, a critique, an act, or an operation. It is not destructive; it is not a "negative operation." It can be applied to itself: "It can be deconstructed" (NO, p. 68). Literally, deconstruction cannot be defined or described. Derrida insists that, "All sentences of the type 'deconstruction is X' or 'deconstruction is not X' a priori miss the point, which is to say that they are at least false" (NO, p. 68).

Two things are happening here. On the one hand, Derrida is simply applying to the sign 'deconstruction' what he says about all signs. "Like all words," Derrida says, 'deconstruction' acquires meaning only in a "chain of possible substitutions." Such chains are interminable. On the other hand, this term (and its possible substitutions) exhibits a special indefinability.

The special problem in trying to understand deconstruction is explained by the fact that, as Derrida claims, we cannot escape logocentrism. In the 1966 lecture, "Structure, Sign and Play in the Discourse of the Human Sciences," he insists, "There is no sense in doing without the concepts of metaphysics in order to shake metaphysics. We have no language—no syntax and no lexicon—which is foreign to this history; we can pronounce not a single destructive proposition which has not already had to slip into the form, the logic, and the implicit postulations of precisely what it seeks to contest" (WD, pp. 280–281). It is important to recognize that this is true not only of philosophical or theoretical discourse, for even "everyday language . . . is the language of Western metaphysics" (P, p. 19).[32] Thus we are put in the position of having somehow to recognize and criticize certain conditions (i.e., logocentrism), while also recognizing that our recognition presumes the same conditions. The problem is how to grasp and represent the insight into the ubiquity and inadequacy of logocentrism in such a way that we derive benefit, we learn or gain understanding, from doing so.

One of the fullest discussions of deconstruction is in the interviews contained in *Positions*. There Derrida felt free to refer to "a kind of *general strategy of deconstruction*" (P, p. 41). The aim of this "strategy" is "to avoid both simply *neutralizing* the binary oppositions of metaphysics and simply *residing* within the closed field of these oppositions, thereby confirming it" (P, p. 41).

This requires a "double gesture." First one must "overturn" the philosophical hierarchy in question. This overturning prevents our deconstruction from being a mere "neutralization," an attempt simply to deny the dichotomy at work ("*neither* this *nor* that"). It is a never-ending project because the hierarchy "always reestablishes itself." This first phase remains within the conceptual array of the text to be deconstructed: It only reverses its polarization. The second "gesture" is to "mark" the dichotomy, or the "interval between" the dichotomous concepts with a "new 'concept'" that cannot be included in the deconstructed conceptual array. This is where Derrida's strange new technical terms come in: play, writing, hymen, mark, spacing, dissemination, differance, and so on. Each of these terms, as Derrida remarks of *dissemination*, "In the last analysis . . . means nothing" (P, p. 44). They are "undecidables"; "that is, unities of simulacrum, 'false' verbal properties (nominal or semantic) that can no longer be included within philosophical (binary) opposition, but which, however, inhabit philosophical opposition, resisting and disorganizing it, *without ever* constituting a third term, without ever leaving room for a solution in the form of speculative dialectics . . ." (P, p. 43).

This undecidable mark can only be made in a "*grouped* textual field"; it is impossible for a single author or a "unilinear text" to "*point* it out" (P, p. 42). That is, it cannot be simply asserted but must be exhibited in the interval of the deconstructed text. Deconstruction can be only a kind of commentary; by itself it says nothing. It judges by *doing* something to or *exhibiting* something in an object-text. The object-text is the medium for its judgment.

Before continuing, the notion of 'undecidable' needs to be clarified. In 1988, Derrida took care to distinguish undecidability from indeterminacy, remarking that, "I do not believe I have ever spoken of 'indeterminacy,' whether in regard to 'meaning' or anything else" (L, p. 148). Undecidability, on the other hand, is "always a determinate oscillation between possibilities. These possibilities are themselves highly determined in strictly defined situations. They are pragmatically determined" (L, p. 148). Derrida makes it clear that he associates indeterminacy with vagueness and even relativism. Undecidability refers to the condition of juxtaposed determinate signs, or systems of signs. It is undecidability that Derrida wants to exhibit, not indeterminacy.[33]

To return to *Positions*, Derrida describes his method as follows.

> I try to respect as rigorously as possible the internal, regulated play of philosophemes . . . by making them slide . . . to the point of their nonpertinence, their exhaustion, their closure. To "deconstruct" philosophy, thus, would be to think—in the most faithful, interior way—the structured genealogy of philosophy's concepts, but at the same time to determine—from a certain exterior that is unqualifiable or unnameable by philosophy—what this history has been able to dissimulate or forbid. . . . By means of this simultaneously faithful and violent circulation between the inside and the outside of philosophy—that is of the West—there is produced a certain textual work that gives great pleasure. (P, pp. 6-7)

The problem Derrida is trying to handle is how to represent and critically examine our judgments about intellectual conditions that are so basic and ubiquitous that we cannot cease to embody and employ them. Derrida's response is, I suggest, that *there is no consistent assertive way to do this*. His way—which, if he is right, is a particularly fruitful, educational, productive way—is to make two judgments, to do two things, that are not consistent. First, he inquires into the array of concepts of the text in question to show that it is not what it appears, that the term it posits as that in relation to which all other terms are to be defined is itself defined through those other terms. This phase of deconstruction generates a kind of *aporia* within the system. It is an internal, assertive inquiry that is negative in that it makes no positive philosophical claims, except about the text (about which it certainly does make positive assertions). The second judgment is a positive proposal, a positing, of a term that is outside the system, or more precisely, that appears in the system but does not conform to the system's rules. We posit something *in* the system that nevertheless escapes it. But proposing this novelty presupposes a standpoint outside, independent of the rules of the system.

This is the sticking point. In respect to the system that he is interested in deconstructing—logocentrism—Derrida refuses to grant that any outside, any independent standpoint, can be represented. The independent term cannot be the object of an assertion, because all our assertions must conform to the system and a judgment that does not conform ceases to make sense as an assertion. Here Derrida must say that *we cannot say* what this novel term means; it cannot be asserted. But it can be *judged*. We can speak or write it or about it, but in doing so our words function actively or exhibitively, not assertively. The terms differance, arche-writing, mark, trace, supplement, hymen, pharmakon, spacing, and so forth, are really one term, or members of one chain of terms, a chain that cannot be adequately interpreted by the concepts of logocentrism. They judge exhibitively. Of course, for Derrida, nothing is adequately interpreted by logocentrism. But these terms are constructed to exhibit this fact.

The fourth and last thematic element is something we will spend much of this chapter exploring. It is the self-reflexive implications of Derrida's account of signs and his account of logocentrism for his own inquiry.[34] This is the deepest and most difficult phase of Derrida's work for the reader to assimilate. Derrida presents his work already within a recognition of these self-reflexive implications. Indeed, one of the most interesting aspects of his work is his attempt to deal with this self-reflexivity, whose occurrence in the work of philosophers is itself one of his objects of study. The point is that in one sense or in one context Derrida's key terms—*dissemination, spacing, trace,* and so on—must be words that mean, whereas in another sense or another context they must not mean at all, for they are outside of meaning.[35] Derrida's writing strives to be simultaneously inside and outside the realm of assertive meaning, which means it cannot be consistent, as we will see.

Derrida and Peirce

There are many points of comparison between Derrida and Peirce, only a few of which can be noted here. Most relate to the idea of the sign, but I will begin my comparison elsewhere. Perhaps more explicitly than any other philosophers, Derrida and Peirce deny the doctrine of *privilege* in experience.

We have seen that Peirce denies the existence of intuitions, cognitions determined solely or immediately by a relation to non-semiotic things. Echoing Peirce, Derrida flatly states that there are no "perceptions." In a remarkable note in *Speech and Phenomena,* he writes,

> In affirming that *perception does not exist* or that what is called perception is not primordial, that somehow everything "begins" by "re-presentation" (a proposition which can only be maintained by the elimination of these last two concepts: it means that there is no "beginning" and that the "representation" we were talking about is not the modification of a "re-" that has *befallen* a primordial presentation) and by reintroducing the difference involved in "signs" at the core of what is "primordial" . . . we are here indicating the prime intention—and the ultimate scope—of the present essay. (SP, pp. 45–46, n. 4)[36]

For both Derrida and Peirce, this denial of immediacy is a consequence of the analysis of signs. It is in the field of semiotics that most of the textual material for a comparison of the two philosophers lies. It will be helpful first to recall Derrida's discussion of Peirce in *Of Grammatology.*[37] This occurs in the context of an examination of what Saussure had called the arbitrary or conventional nature of signs. Derrida notes that in Peirce's semiotics, conventional (e.g., linguistic) signs are "symbols." Derrida quotes Peirce's remark that "symbols grow" out of other symbols. This is important for Derrida, for he is trying to expose and question the dominant view of conventional signs as rooted in and derivative from "natural signs," which would compromise the essential non-presence of signs.

Derrida admits a further approval of Peirce's subordination of logic to semiotics. For Peirce, logic in the general sense is "only another name for semiotics . . . the quasi-necessary, or formal, doctrine of signs," while logic in the narrow sense of the science of valid inference is a part of semiotics. Derrida refers to Peirce's appropriation of the Scotist doctrine that semiotics consists of three parts, pure grammar, logic proper, and pure rhetoric. The first studies the conditions of meaning, or what what must be true of a sign if it is to have meaning for a "scientific intelligence"; the second studies what must be true of the signs of "any scientific intelligence in order that they may hold good of any object, that is, may be true"; and the third studies how in any scientific intelligence "one sign gives birth to another," or what Peirce elsewhere calls the *power* of the sign (CP, 2.229). To Derrida this indicates that Peirce makes the sign and its manifold phenomena more fundamental than truth, truth being only one of the characters a sign may have (namely, the character of the sign in relation to its object).

Derrida makes a remarkable statement about the extent to which Peirce has anticipated his own work.

> Peirce goes very far in the direction that I have called the de-construction of the transcendental signified, which, at one time or another, would place a reassuring end to the reference from sign to sign. I have identified logocentrism and the metaphysics of presence as the exigent, powerful, systematic, and irrepressible desire for such a signified. Now Peirce considers the indefiniteness of reference as the criterion that allows us to recognize that we are indeed dealing with a system of signs. *What broaches the movement of signification is what makes its interruption impossible. The thing itself is a sign.* (OG, p. 49)

Derrida uses Peirce's term for sign, "representamen," to say that the "represented is always a representamen," the signified is a signifier. He refers to Peirce's remark about each sign's determination of another sign as its interpretant, that, "If the series of successive interpretants comes to an end, the sign is thereby rendered imperfect, at least" (CP 1.303).[38] Derrida concludes, "From the moment there is meaning there are nothing but signs. We *think only in signs.* Which amounts to ruining the notion of the sign at the very moment when, as in Nietzsche, its exigency is recognized in the absoluteness of its right. One could call *play* the absence of the transcendental signified as limitlessness of play, that is to say as the destruction of onto-theology and the metaphysics of presence" (OG, p. 50).

Therefore Derrida credits Peirce with a rudimentary critique of the *metaphysics of presence*, of *logocentrism*, of the rigid dichotomy of the order of signs and the order of being, of *onto-theology* and the *transcendental signified*, and with anticipating the idea of the *play* of signifiers and even *deconstruction* itself. This sense of complicity is not at all farfetched.[39]

First, both insist on a characteristic of signs that Derrida refers to with the terms "exteriority" or "materiality" and Peirce refers to as the "public" nature of signs.[40] Signs in their primary mode of being cannot be purely ideal; they must have a nonideal component. They must be actual marks on paper, or sounds, or visible movements, or physical configurations. Thought-signs (whose materiality is neurological) are derived from these public, "exterior" signs.

Second, both make the meaning of any sign dependent on the meaning of other signs. Signs are constituted both by a system or context of signs and by a temporal chain of signs. Peirce's vehicle for this is his inclusion of a sign's interpretant in its very identity. For the conventional linguistic signs with which we are most concerned, this interpretant is itself a sign. For Derrida as well, the meaning of a sign is never fully or completely grasped; it is deferred, put off, partly absent. Every sign is a member of a chain that does not end. As we saw, Derrida had noted Peirce's remark that, "Symbols grow" (CP, 2.302). Commenting on the chain of translations in which any sign is embedded, Derrida writes that, "the translator must assure the survival, *which is to say the growth*, of the original. Translation augments and modifies the original, which, insofar as it is living on, never ceases to be transformed and to grow" (E, p. 122).

Coupled with this is the fact that both thinkers make semiosis fundamental not only to thought, but experience, and even reality. Semiosis is ubiquitous. For Peirce, thoughts are signs, perceptions are a kind of sign, and reality is defined in terms of signs; that is, as the object of community opinion in the long run. He writes, in a remarkable passage that is worth repeating in relation to Derrida, "What distinguishes a man from a word? . . . men and words reciprocally educate each other. . . . the word or sign which man uses *is* the man himself. For, as the fact that every thought is a sign, taken in conjunction with the fact that life is a train of thought, proves that *man is a sign*. . . . Thus my language is the sum total of myself

. . ." (CP, 5.313–314; second emphasis mine). "Man is a sign"—a remarkable statement for one whose thought is supposed to be utterly foreign from the spirit of structuralism and post-structuralism! For Derrida, what we call reality is dependent on arche-writing or semiosis, and even nature itself is continuous with a kind of semiosis, for example, in "genetic inscription" (OG, p. 84). Thus human nature itself can be understood as a form of writing.[41]

But if it is true that the fundamental idea that drives Derrida to his seemingly radical approach to philosophy is largely present in Peirce, what accounts for their differences? Certainly these differences are many and cannot be comprehensively engaged here, but a few suggestions can be made. One way to ask the question is, What restrains the effects of the incompleteness, play, or absence of semiosis in Peirce?

There is what may seem to be an obvious factor, that Peirce defines signs not only in terms of their ground or quality and their interpretant or succeeding sign, but also in terms of their objects. Signs stand for something to someone. Derrida, however, does not include in his account of signs their relation to objects in themselves, that is, things as they obtain independent of representation, except to refer to the concept of the thing in itself as the *transcendental signified.* Derrida's inquiry is aimed at the realm of representations, not the represent*ed.* His point is that there is no presentation of objectivity outside or independent of representation; *for us* there is no objectivity without representation. Derrida confines his discourse to this realm; the world as it obtains independent of all representation does not enter into his account of signs.

Now, this ubiquity of semiosis causes some to see in Derrida an unprecedented and absurd denial of the existence of non-semiotic phenomena. This is a mistake; Derrida does not make this denial, and his approach in this matter is neither unprecedented nor absurd. It is characteristic of the empiricist tradition going back to Hume, Berkeley, and Locke,[42] of the German idealist and phenomenological tradition from Kant to Heidegger, and of Saussurian linguistics, not to mention other philosophies of experience, like that of John Dewey. Kant confined his attention in the first *Critique* to appearances (although he added an indeterminable relation to the thing in itself), Hegel in his *Phenomenology* to the phenomena of consciousness, Husserl in *Ideas* to intentional phenomena, Saussure in his *Course in General Linguistics* defined the signified as a concept, not a thing, and Dewey in *Experience and Nature* described his project as the exploration of experienc*ing.* Derrida, like the tradition on which he draws, is an anti- or nonnaturalist in the sense that he refuses to regard the natural, physical world, conceived as prior to human experience and representation, as a determinant of what human experience and representation mean.[43] Peirce, on the other hand, endorses naturalism and insists on the irreducibility of Secondness or otherness to Thirdness or relation. Peirce criticized Hegel for making just that reduction, and we must imagine that he would regard phenomenology and Derrida similarly (on this score).

This apparent difference with Peirce is a symptom of a more complex relationship. For Peirce's notion of objectivity is a semiotic one. Peirce does not make the object a sign, but he asserts that it can be defined only in terms of a sign. What supports Peirce's notion of objectivity is his notion of convergence, a teleological notion foreign to Derrida, which rests on the unity and singularity of the community of inquirers. Peirce does not accept privileged cognitions, but he does accept a privileged *context*, the context of the community of rational inquirers.

Unlike Peirce, Derrida is a *radical pluralist*. Derrida accepts no privileged perspective or community.[44] The context of inquiry has no exclusive claim on the essence of writing, on the fulfillment of semiosis. Derrida is a pluralist who marks his own context (inquiry) as a limited particular that cannot exhaust the possibilities of semiosis, that cannot be ultimately contextualized by pragmatism's normative end of "concrete reasonableness."

One may be tempted to say that what distinguishes Derrida from Peirce is the Nietzschean questioning of truth. Certainly Peirce does not question truth in the sense that Nietzsche does. But Derrida animates this questioning from the same point as Peirce; namely, the incompleteness, supplementarity, and ubiquity of semiosis. The relationship of Peirce, Nietzsche, and Derrida is triangular; each pair exhibits a commonality and difference from the third. The factor that separates Peirce from Derrida unites him with Nietzsche; namely, a straightforward naturalism. Peirce and Nietzsche interpret semiosis, or certain kinds of semiosis, in terms of the survival and practical needs of a creature in an environment. Derrida does not accept biophysical naturalism, and this distances him from Nietzsche as from Peirce.

Semiotic Relativity in Derrida

Is Derrida an antirealist? Just asking the question raises a host of difficulties. It may be argued that Derrida asserts no view, no "ism," and so neither realism nor antirealism. This may be so, but it is not obviously so. Derrida does make assertions, some philosophical. He deconstructs some "isms" but not others. As we will see, it cannot be claimed that Derrida's relation to realism and to antirealism is symmetrical. The issue of Derrida's relation to antirealism is a real one.

There are two obvious senses in which Derrida may appear to be an antirealist. Realism believes that a relation exists between assertive judgments and independent objects that is determinative for the validity of those judgments. Although Derrida does not deny this relation, he does deny that it can be determinative for our judgments of meaning and validity. The second factor is the critique of privilege. Derrida is an antirealist at least in this limited and purely negative sense, that his account of semiosis undermines one of the central pillars of many forms of realism. No one has pushed the critique of immediacy further than Derrida.

Before examining the core of Derrida's antirealism, we must clarify his relation to naturalism and pragmatism. As already mentioned, in a sense Derrida is an anti-naturalist. He excludes from the discussion of the validity of judgment reference to any biotic or physical determinants. This distinguishes him from Peirce, Nietzsche, and Buchler. However, two caveats must be added to this characterization. There is a single intriguing hint of a more concrete naturalism in *Of Grammatology*, which was mentioned earlier. In a fascinating passage Derrida identifies differance with life and extends the notion of arch-writing to include *genetic encoding*.[45] This implies that writing extends beyond the realm of what is instituted by human beings. Genetic encoding, if we accept the word of science—and to speak of genetic encoding at all is to accept science's word—is a fact that predates the existence of humanity and so all human semiosis. It indicates that nature writes, microbiology writes, the elements write.[46] Second, by refusing to accept transcendentalism or dualism, to grant meaning a status that transcends the material sign, Derrida is making a characteristically naturalist gesture. Although this has little to do with biotic or physicalistic naturalism, a suggestive relationship remains here, to which I will return later.

Turning to pragmatism, our story becomes a bit more subtle. If pragmatism can be not a doctrine but a matter of interest—that is, if any attention paid to the pragmatic or active contexts of meaning, to pragmatics, can be called *pragmatism*—then one could speak of pragmatism in Derrida without any problem. Derrida has explicitly discussed the pragmatic or performative dimension of semiosis. In "Signature Event Context" and in the 1976 lecture "Declarations of Independence," for example, Derrida explores the relation of the constative or assertive content of certain written utterances to the instituting performance of uttering them. The presence of a signature, like Thomas Jefferson's signature of the American Declaration of Independence, embodies that performative and introduces certain undecidable elements into the text.[47] But even in other writings, where the performative is not the topic of discussion, the pragmatic context of writing enters into Derrida's analysis of a text. He makes his openness to this kind of pragmatism clear in a note to "Toward an Ethic of Discussion," a note in which he quotes another passage of his own: "I propose calling 'programmatological' the space of an indispensable analysis 'at the intersection of a pragmatics and a grammatology.' . . . Grammatology has always been a sort of pragmatics, but the discipline which bears this name today involve too many presuppositions requiring deconstruction . . . (L, p. 159, n. 16).[48]

If, on the other hand, pragmatism means the claim that assertion is action or that the meaning of assertive judgment is to be defined in relation to action, and so may be evaluated with the norms of action, then Derrida is *not* a pragmatist. Indeed, it could be argued that pragmatism in this sense is Derrida's true *opponent*. For he repeatedly seeks to deny the authority of the norms of active judgment (success, instrumental value in achieving goals, and especially moral rightness) over *his own* meaning, writing, or inquiry. He denies that his inquiry may legitimately be judged in terms of its contribution to *decision making*. He says in a parenthetic remark in *Positions*, "When I try to decipher a text I do not constantly ask myself if I will finish by answering *yes* or *no*, as happens in France at determined periods of history, and generally on Sunday" (P, p. 52). This refusal to make the purpose of his inquiry the achievement of a decision makes Derrida difficult and frustrating for many philosophers. This fundamental point deserves comment.

There is nothing wrong with requesting decisions from inquiry; neither is their anything wrong with refusing to subordinate inquiry to the demand for decisions. To demand decisiveness is to place inquiry in a context of decision, which is sometimes evidence that inquiry is being placed in a larger context of action or even social concern. Nothing in Derrida's work, I believe, denies the possibility or legitimacy of this, but his work is refractory to such demands. What he denies is that inquiry *must* lead to such decisions, so a query that does not do so is disqualified from the realm of inquiry altogether. This leaves Derrida in the position of declaring that deconstruction is a kind of inquiry that, generally speaking, cannot serve certain purposes. The "decisive" inquirer tries to serve those purposes. The deconstructionist is not wrong, but different. Any argument between the two—at this level—is usually a matter of talking past one another.

We now turn to the most promising candidate for antirealism in Derrida, contextualism. We have already seen that for Derrida meaning is relational, that privilege or immediacy is under "erasure," that he accepts no unitary community or context of contexts. In the 1972 essay "Signature Event Context" Derrida tries to clarify both the importance of context and the reasons that he is *not* a contextualist. He denies contextualism for three reasons. First, context itself is "indeterminable." I take this to mean that every attempt to delineate the context that supposedly determines the meaning of a sign will be inadequate. Every context is, after all, a sign like any other, and hence characterized by differance. Second, signs are structurally, essentially capable of breaking out of any "given" context, or being taken out of context, while continuing to mean or function as signs. The most extreme example of this is "citation." I can take any sign in any context, put it in quotes, such as 'x', and cite or mention it. This capacity to move outside any given context is important for Derrida; it is part of the "very structure of the written" (M, p. 317). Third, the contextualist account of speech acts or of signs exhibits a self-reflexive problem. It cannot apply its characterization of signs or speech acts to itself and, especially, to its norms, the criteria that govern its own inquiry. This is not a problem in the natural sciences, but it is inescapable in the human sciences (L, p. 72). We will return to this self-reflexive difficulty, to which Derrida is very sensitive, later.[49]

The first two points are, however, no objections to a *subtle* contextualism that does not assume the limitation and determinability of contexts. Contextualism need not assert "context" as a metaphysical first principle, a successor to God, substance, form, natural law, and so forth. A consistent contextualism must regard even context, and every determination of a context, as contextual and hence, in Derrida's sense, undecidable. The third point is a version of the same self-reflexive problem we have been confronting all along in Derrida. It is true that contextualism cannot be consistently asserted. Derrida's objections do not hold for an implicit and subtle contextualism.

In the 1988 written interview "Toward an Ethic of Discussion," Derrida comes very close to endorsing contextualism. He defines deconstruction in terms of context. He writes,

> One of the definitions of what is called deconstruction would be the effort to take this limitless context [the "real-history-of-the-world"] into account, to pay the sharpest and broadest attention possible to context, and thus to an incessant movement of recontextualization. The phrase which for some has become a sort of slogan, in general so badly understood, of deconstruction ("there is nothing outside the text"), means nothing else: there is nothing outside context. In this form, which says exactly the same thing, the formula would doubtless have been less shocking. (L, p. 136)

Derrida ridicules the notion that the deconstructionist "is supposed not to believe in truth, stability, or the unity of meaning, in intention or 'meaning-to-say' . . ." (L, p. 146).[50] This understanding of the deconstructionist is "*false* (that's right false, not true) . . ." Derrida insists that, once this is comprehended, "Then perhaps it will be understood that the value of truth (and all those values associated with it) is never contested or destroyed in my writings, but only reinscribed in more powerful, larger, more stratified contexts. And that within interpretive contexts . . . that are relatively stable . . . it should be possible to invoke rules of competence, criteria of discussion and of consensus . . ." (L, p. 146). Indeed, Derrida claims that deconstruction presumes a stable context of consensus, without which interpretation cannot even get started: "But I believe that no research is possible in a community (for example, academic) without the prior search for this minimal consensus and without discussion around this minimal consensus" (L, p. 146). Derrida claims that this does not entail relativism because relativism is philosophical whereas his work questions philosophy and because deconstruction never claims "any absolute overview." Yet, deconstruction does not and cannot "renounce" the values dominant in the historical, social, institutional, linguistic context in which it takes place, for example, the value of truth (L, p. 137).

Given Derrida's account of signs as contextually determined, with the resultant polysemia, Derrida's account of semiosis is a *positive contextualism*, which is to say, a positive relativist account. Relativism in the most general sense is the claim that what is under examination is relational. Derrida asserts that meaning is constituted by a system of differences among signs. The meaning of each instance of a sign is constituted by its difference from and relation to previous and succeeding occurrences of "itself" (in quotes because this implies a judgment of sameness), to other contemporary signs, and to other preceding and successive signs. This is a contextualist and a relativist account. But this semiotic relativism does not necessarily imply a relativistic account of knowledge (not yet, anyway).

Is the undecidability of signs in Derrida, their nonpresence, a product of the contextual nature of semiosis, or is it due to the contextual nature of inquiry, the fact that when *we try to say* what signs are we cannot include in our account the conditions or limits or context of our own statement? Is contextualism sufficient to account for the semiotic phenomena that Derrida describes? Or is the hypothesis of contextualism a domestication of Derrida, an inadequate amalgamation of dissemination to a humdrum pluralism?

I suggest that, given certain facts about signs that Derrida describes (e.g., their exteriority), contextualism is adequate to account for the semiotic phenomena Derrida describes, as long as we understand contextualism *radically* enough. Derrida deconstructs any account of semiosis or of what depends on semiosis that denies the relativity of its objects. This does not mean that Derrida takes the position that everything is a relation, that nonrelations do not exist, or that relatedness and continuity are more primary than particularity and discontinuity. Rather, his view is that the identity and hence the meaning of every sign is constituted by difference and relation, and that consequently, the meaning of any sign can never be exhausted or completely determined. My hypothesis in attempting to account for Derrida's work is that relativity or the ubiquity of context is sufficient to account for this conclusion and for the further complexities of deconstruction that we are investigating. This does not mean that Derrida *asserts* relativism, or that he could. Relativism cannot be asserted with consistency. Every doctrine, including relativism, comes under deconstruction. But, so does deconstruction itself, so that is no disqualification. Let us briefly try to reconstruct deconstruction on a contextualist basis.

One basic element of Derrida's account must be presupposed; namely, the exteriority and hence iterability of signs. It must be the case that a sign retains an element of sameness from one context to another. If not, then signs would be neither polysemic nor changeable: every token or occurrence or sign-in-this-context would be a unique and separate individual. For a sign to change, grow, and multiply its meanings from one context or relation to the next it must be the same sign from one context or relation to the next. This sameness or iterability is provided by the exteriority of the sign, the fact that the sign is a physical mark or sound or artifact that endures and can be repeated as the same sign across contexts.

Derrida's assertion of the absent or mediated nature of the sign's relation to referent and intended meaning has an interesting twofold effect. On the one hand, it removes a barrier to the proliferation of signs, to the claim that the meaning of signs is constituted by yet other signs. For the relation of a sign to things and intentions is always mediated by another sign. Yet, on the other hand, Derrida's point makes semiotic phenomena remarkably *objective*! For we are now obligated to discover the meaning of a sign in other actual or possible signs and not in a privileged relation to the author's intent. If someone can point to a context in which a sign functions, then we must include that context in our account of the sign's meaning; we are not permitted to privilege the author's intent and discount the actual functioning of the sign. Derrida understands the meaning of every sign to be constituted by relativity, by indefinitely many relations to other signs and to other instances of itself.

Relativity implies that every judgment of a sign's meaning—all interpretation and translation—is the establishment of an order of inclusion and exclusion. Some relations must be selected and others excluded. This selection represses relativity and alters meaning. And every interpretive judgment is itself constituted by a system of relations. Meaning requires that we institute signs whose meaning is relational hence multiple and fluctuating, and yet at the same time, it requires that we deny polysemia and flux. This is the dialectical heart of Derrida's work: We *must repress relativity* in order to mean, yet *relativity is the condition of the possibility of meaning*. This fact indicates how radical the implications of contextualism can be. All writing, all inscription, all signifying violates itself. Hence dissemination, semiotic fecundity, textual repression, the self-undermining distinctions that structure the history of philosophy for Derrida can all be understood as the consequences of *contextualism*.

There is one last element of our reconstruction of Derrida, which requires untangling yet another Derridean circularity. Logocentrism is the philosophical ideology of univocal and nonrelative meaning. Derrida asserts that it is false; that is, inadequate as an account of meaning. Although every semiotic act represses, and must if it is to mean, Derrida objects to the *philosophical justification of* repression. Derrida commits himself to inquiry, hence to the responsibility to exhibit multiplicity and relativity. At the same time he recognizes that, first, logocentrism cannot be renounced but only deconstructed, and second, the deconstructionist exhibition of relativity must restrict itself, must presume the ultimate value of truth and even "consensus" among inquirers. It is to Derrida's understanding of the status of his own work and its relation to philosophy that we must now turn.

The Derridean Difference

Most of Derrida's statements about deconstruction and philosophy make it clear that deconstruction is not a philosophy or a part of philosophy. It may also be that deconstruction is not "nonphilosophy" either (E, p. 120).

As we have seen, Derrida insists that his work is not beyond truth, not outside of query governed by truth. Deconstruction seeks to give accounts, to be precise, to avoid self-contradiction and inconsistency, to be clear, to improve our understanding of what is at hand. Deconstruction does not subordinate logic or assertion to rhetoric or exhibition.[51] In short, Derrida portrays deconstruction as a kind of inquiry.

There are, however, passages in the Derridean texts where it might appear that truth, hence inquiry, is being put out of action altogether. For example, in *Dissemination*, Derrida insists, "Nontruth is the truth. Nonpresence is presence. Differance, the disappearance of any originary presence, is *at once* the condition of possibility *and* the condition of impossibility of truth" (DS, p. 168). In *Spurs*, he writes, "Truth in the guise of production, the unveiling/dissimulation of the present product, is dismantled. The veil no more raised than it is lowered" (S, p. 107). In *Of Grammatology*, he remarks, "This experience of the effacement of the signifier in the voice is not merely one illusion among many—since it is the condition of the very idea of truth. . . . This illusion is the history of truth . . ." (OG, p. 20). And in *Speech and Phenomena*: "But as the classical idea of truth . . . has itself issued from such a concealment of the relationship with death, this 'falsity' is the very truth of truth" (SP, p. 54, n. 4).

Like Nietzsche, Derrida is seeking to question truth, but that does not mean that he thinks he can *abandon* it. This leaves him, again like Nietzsche, in a position that cannot be consistently asserted or said, a position that seeks to question the conditions of the possibility of inquiry, and hence truth. What he writes in *Of Grammatology* about presence holds also for truth, "To make enigmatic what one thinks one understands by the words 'proximity,' 'immediacy,' 'presence' . . . is my final intention in this book" (OG, p. 70).

In this connection it is instructive to note a passage in the discussion *The Ear of the Other* (1988), in which Derrida interprets philosophy as based on a thesis regarding translation. He writes,

> the philosophical operation . . . defines itself as a project of translation. . . . Meaning has the commanding role, and consequently one must be able to fix its univocality or, in any case, to master its plurivocality. If this plurivocality can be mastered, then translation, understood as the transport of a semantic content into another signifying form, is possible. There is no philosophy unless translation in this latter sense is possible. Therefore the thesis of philosophy is translatability in this common sense, that is, as the transfer of a meaning or a truth from one language to another without any essential harm being done. . . . without an essential loss. (E, p. 120)

Derrida does not accept this thesis of translatability, that is, he does not believe it is true. But neither does he renounce it as false, because it is part of the necessary structure not only of philosophy but of inquiry in general, and so cannot be given up. It is part of the metaphysics that, Derrida elsewhere claimed, cannot be rejected because we have no other language, we have no other culture (P, pp. 19–20).

In the same work, regarding his relation to philosophy, Derrida suggests, "Likewise, I wouldn't say that I am not at all a philosopher, but the utterances I proliferate around this problem are put forward from a position other than that of philosophy. This other position is not necessarily that of poetry either. . . . I ask questions of philosophy, and naturally this supposes a certain identification, a certain translation of myself into the body of a philosopher. But I don't feel that that's where I'm situated" (E, p. 140).

So, what is the status of philosophical judgments in Derrida? One way to understand Derrida as philosopher is to compare him with the foregoing philosophers, especially with Wittgenstein and Nietzsche.

Wittgenstein is closer to commonsensism than Derrida. Wittgenstein can say at a certain point in explanation, "I have reached bedrock, and my spade is turned. Then I am inclined to say, 'This is simply what I do'" (PI, 217). The desideratum of meaning and validity is fixed by social practice (which does not mean it is unchangeable). But Derrida does not take this pragmatic, commonsensist recourse; he is closer to Hume whereas Wittgenstein is closer to Reid.[52] For Hume and Derrida there is a discontinuity between inquiry and practical human life, or more precisely, between inquiry and the needs and purposes embedded in social living. To govern inquiry with criteria and demands drawn from social life—for example, needs for decisive answers to guide action, for stability, for social benefit—is to *violate inquiry*. In Reid and Wittgenstein, there is a point at which *inquiry must stop*; namely, the point at which inquiry ceases to be rooted in living practice.

Derrida avoids rooting semiosis or writing or inscription in biotic nature or anything presemiotic because to do so would allow inquiry to be decided by, say, practical considerations. This eliminates a source of stability for meaning. But Derridean instability ought not be overstated. For Derrida, context and meaning are *unstable*, but so, as we know, are human practices, speciation, and the geography of the earth. To read Derrida as denying that there is any stability at all is to misread him as making semiosis, hence human existence, impossible.[53] Derrida never denies the existence of stability, determinacy, reliability, and constancy in semiosis. He denies that this stability is ever *complete*. There is stability, but only relative, incomplete, limited, in other words, contextual stability.

We ought not misunderstand Derrida on a related score. Derrida speaks of the need for ethical and political reflection; he has been involved in both political work and in educational reform. He wishes to read his own work as questioning but not disconnecting, not putting out of action, the practices and contexts of meaning. To deconstruct ethical and legal contexts, he stressed in "Toward an Ethic of Discussion," does not and ought not mean to destroy them, but to understand their deep relativity, their human institution, their undecidability and indeterminacy (in the sense of incompleteness). Derrida sees this as opening possibilities, as making us free to reinterpret, reread, and hence rewrite our reality.

I have no wish to repeat in these pages what I believe to be the fruitless "is the glass half empty or half full?" argument between German and American social philosophers, who usually emphasize the need for a positive, normative foundation for social freedom, and the French, who stress the negative need to clear away normative obstacles, to open possibilities for social freedom. The question here is not, What are the socio-political implications of deconstruction, if any, but rather, Can we learn more about deconstruction and its difference from other approaches by recognizing in it a unique divorce from "common sense" and social practice? Derrida must admit that deconstruction loosens ethical and legal obligation in much the same way as the loss of mythical and religious guarantees of punishment and reward loosens the sense of spiritual and ethical obligation. But if the latter is no argument against the Enlightenment, then the former is no argument against deconstruction, or against what Derrida wants to call, a "new, very new *Aufklärung*" (L, p. 141).

The point that most separates Derrida from the likes of Peirce, Wittgenstein, and Buchler is his view that every judgment of the meaning of a sign is, in a sense, *a lie*. That every judgment of meaning is inadequate is a straightforward implication of contextualism, with which Wittgenstein and Buchler might agree. But Derrida pushes contextualism further. Not only are judgments of meaning inadequate to the polysemia of the sign, they also alter that meaning by their mere utterance, by inscribing the sign in a new context, and repress polysemia. Meaning institutes and is based on relativity and yet must deny and limit it. This is Derrida's Nietzschean inheritance.

In Nietzsche, the critique of truth is naturalistic. The will to life is capable of evolving cultural forms that deny life. Inquiry and knowledge, at one level, oppose life. Truth is a lie, assertion and inquiry dissimulate, as life requires. In Derrida, the repression of differance, a motivated failure to recognize relativity, is a lie that is required if we are to speak any kind of truth—indeed, if we are to mean at all. Every assertive judgment, operating in a sea of differences, is a decision or a commitment to accept signs as univocal and potentially synonymous, a commitment belied by the sea that keeps semiosis afloat. Or to use a biotic metaphor, every sign and every judgment is like an organism in nature, which must separate and protect itself from the natural environment to remain an individuated living thing, while at the same time being utterly dependent on continued exchange with that environment. It is here that we may ascribe to Derrida a *metaphorical naturalism*, for which nothing transcends the flow of semiosis, including the attempt to know semiosis, and the condition of the possibility of the existence of every semiotic individual (every meaning) is its location in a process that ultimately breaks it down, destroying its identity.

We can now see that Derrida's deconstruction is the exhibition, via analytic, assertive inquiry, of the deferred elements and the system of differences that, via distinction and relation, make any meaningful utterance or inscription possible. This exhibition, being itself an inscription, is an intervention in the context intended to provoke us to recognize both what structures the meaningful utterance or inscription and what its limits are. Deconstruction's aim cannot be to provoke us to change those conditions. All we can do is exhibit this context and its networks of relations. And there is no consistent way to assert this fact. So, if we must use the tempting spatial metaphor, the aim of inquiry is to reach a kind of border or boundary at which this context can be glimpsed in some manner, although in another sense it cannot be glimpsed or judged at all, because it constitutes all our judging. We are at Kant's bounds of reason, a boundary that he could judge only through the mechanism of the "as if." Except that—and here is where the spatial metaphor is inadequate—Derrida would show how *all* of Kant's writing is invaded by that boundary, that there is no distinction between center and periphery, no inland safe from the indeterminacies of a dangerous shoreline. Every point is on the border.

Derrida's work shows the necessarily contextual and hence dissimulative nature of semiosis. This dissimulation is unavoidable. What is avoidable is to regard our semiosis as non-problematic, that is, to affirm logocentrism. Philosophy cannot *abandon* logocentrism, which is merely the theoretical expression of that dissimulation, but it can cease to regard it as non-problematic.

Derrida's approach might seem to be antirealist in the sense that it denies knowledge altogether, but that is not so. It is antirealist in that it makes our knowledge contextual. It does not make impossible decisiveness in general, the answering of a question with truth's binary "yes" or "no." It is not, in other words, a Pyrrhonist skepticism, an abstention from philosophical claims or from claims about reality. It makes the validity of all such decisions contextual, hence dissimulative, hence problematic. Derrida's account makes the achievement of an *ultimate* truth, a "yes" or "no" in ultimate inquiry, impossible. For decisiveness presumes the neglect of differance. The philosophical doctrine whose aim is to reinforce this dissimulation, to justify it as free of problems, is inadequate or false. Yet we cannot abandon it. All we can do is cultivate the double consciousness of its inadequacy through a critical, deconstructionist analysis whenever it occurs.

Derrida's account is self-compromising, because it is a set of assertions—indeed, philosophical assertions—governed by truth. Derrida's inquiry does not escape the criticism it aims at others, it only tries to admit that vulnerability. Deconstruction, as he has said, can be deconstructed. This admission entails that there be an essentially exhibitive and active component to Derrida's work. This does not mean that he is not an inquirer, but that the non-assertive moment is essential to his meaning. Consequently, Rorty is wrong, as I will suggest in the following chapter, to read Derrida as transcending philosophy. Derrida is engaged in ultimate inquiry; what else could we call the work I have reviewed in this chapter? It is primarily inquiry, and it is certainly ultimate, because it accepts no limitations. The fact that its results are often negative and are not purely assertive does not disqualify it from philosophy. It is philosophy, even as it puts all of philosophy in question. More than anyone else, Derrida has made it clear that the critique of philosophy is no escape from the philosophical *kirkos*.

9

RORTY'S ANTIPHILOSOPHICAL PRAGMATISM

The various strains of the debate over the possibility of philosophical knowledge have been admirably collected by Richard Rorty.[1] He has forged a synthesis of the pragmatic response to philosophy's traditional aims with the sophisticated critical strategies of Nietzsche, Wittgenstein, Heidegger and Derrida. Rorty has expressed his view in straightforward language; he is secure enough to allow himself to be attacked as simplifying complex scholarly matters, rather than blunt his impact through cautious overqualification. In the contemporary philosophical scene, this is no small virtue.

Rorty's own negative metaphilosophical attempt to refuse both realism and antirealism, to avoid answering certain philosophical questions is, it has been rightly noted by David Hiley, akin to the rhetoric of Sextus Empiricus, the expositor of Pyrrhonist skepticism.[2] It will be illuminating briefly to discuss Sextus in this connection, for the classical skeptic's position would seem to provide Rorty an avenue of escape from philosophy. Rorty shares with Sextus the conviction that the valid response of philosophical inquiry to an important range of philosophical questions is *abstention* from assertive judgment. Rorty, who is familiar with Peirce, James, and Dewey, uses pragmatism as a rationale for this abstention. I will try to show that this abstention is problematic, that it does not constitute a valid escape route from the problems of philosophy.

Of the following seven sections, the first presents a criticism of Sextus Empiricus. The next five sections present my analysis of Rorty's view, the fifth of which discusses Arthur Fine's notion of the "Natural Ontological Attitude" in relation to Rorty's position. The last section is a brief conclusion.

The Pyrrhonist Abstention

During the second century A.D., in his *Outlines of Pyrrohnism*, Sextus Empiricus presented the most clear and complete rendition of the skepticism of the Greek philosopher Pyrrho of Elis (360–270 B.C.). According to Sextus, when confronted by a philosophical claim, which is to say, any claim regarding what is "nonevident" or beyond appearances, the Pyrrhonist juxtaposes to it an antithetical claim and, through a process of reasoning, concludes regarding the opposing claims that each is "No more" (*ouden mallon*) true than the other. The Pyrrhonist then suspends judgment regarding each claim's truth. The aim of this procedure is to achieve peace of mind or *ataraxia*. Philosophical opinions make peace impossible: "For the man who opines that anything is by nature good or bad is for ever being disquieted . . ." (PH, I.27).³ For the Pyrrhonists, on the other hand, "Our life . . . is unprejudiced by opinions." (PH, I.231).⁴

With this approach the Pyrrhonist avoids the self-refuting traps into which skeptical assertions, like "Nothing is true," would fall. The Pyrrhonist merely *abstains* from assertion, thereby practicing *epoche* (abstention). Sextus admits that the skeptic uses certain assertions or "formulae" in reasoning (e.g., "all things are nonapprehensible"), but insists that, "we do not fight about phrases nor do we inquire whether the phrases indicate realities, but we adopt them, as I said, in a loose sense. Still it is evident, as I think, that these expressions are indicative of nonassertion" (PH, I.195). Skeptics mean their own formulae as stating how things "appear to us," not how they are absolutely (PH, I.191). This is enough, because the skeptic offers assertions not for their truth but for their *effect*. In a famous figure, Sextus writes, "For, in regard to all the Skeptic expressions, we must grasp first the fact that we make no positive assertion respecting their absolute truth, since we say that they may possibly be confuted by themselves, seeing that they themselves are included in the things to which their doubt applies, just as aperient drugs do not merely eliminate the humours from the body, but also expel themselves along with the humours." (PH, I.206).

Regarding the guidance of life, which always presumes belief, the skeptic "gives assent to the feelings which are the necessary results of sense-impressions" (PH, I.13) and follows custom and law, as well as the "instruction of the arts." The sense appearance, as "involuntary" and "not open to question," constitutes the "criterion" of skepticism in the sense of being "the standard of action . . . in the conduct of life" (PH, I.21). Sextus relates, "Adhering, then, to appearances we live in accordance with the normal rules of life, undogmatically, seeing that we cannot remain wholly inactive" (PH, I.22–23).

To the Pyrrhonist, even Protagoras's famous relativistic claim that "Man is the measure of all things" is a dogmatism. Likewise dogmatic are the skeptics of the New Academy who positively declared that all things are inapprehensible,[5] and the Empiric school, which dogmatically claims that the nonevident is inapprehensible. He sympathizes only with the Methodic school, "for it alone of the Medical systems appears to avoid rash treatment of things non-evident by arbitrary assertions as to their apprehensibility or non-apprehensibility, and following appearances derives from them what seem beneficial, in accordance with the practice of the Skeptics . . ." (PH, I.237).

The reasoning used by Pyrrhonists to achieve the skeptical conclusion "No more" involves the use of "modes," a set of considerations meant to undermine any dogmatism. The most inclusive list of modes enumerates ten: differences among animals, human beings, sense organs, and circumstances; compoundings and institutions; positions, admixtures, relativity, and frequency of occurrence. These ten can be grouped respectively under three headings: differences referring to the subject judging, the object judged, or both. These three in turn, "are also referred to that of relation, so that the Mode of relation stands as as the highest *genus*, and the three as *species*, and the ten as subordinate *sub-species*" (PH, I.39). Thus Pyrrhonism accepts the relativity of all appearances and all truth regarding appearances. Sextus explains, "we conclude that, since all things are relative, we shall suspend judgement as to what things are absolutely and really existent. But here we must notice—that here as elsewhere we use the term 'are' for the term 'appear,' and what we virtually mean is 'all things appear relative'" (PH, I.135).

We may note in passing that Sextus's skepticism exhibits a surprising coincidence with the commonsense philosophy of Thomas Reid. Both accept the basic principle of commonsensism, that the validity of commonly held beliefs or principles embodied in everyday practice is not open to philosophical question. Both Reid and Sextus interpret the kind of everyday judgments that are exempt from philosophical question as natural and pragmatic; natural in that they are caused in us by nature, pragmatic because they are tied to necessary and normal human activities. Both accept a *discontinuity* between philosophy, or a type of philosophy, and commonsense judgment and knowledge. They utterly disagree on one point. For

Reid skepticism is an expression of philosophy's absurdity, whereas for Sextus all philosophical assertion, including Reid's, is the culprit. Consequently, Reid does not abstain from philosophy, but merely from the kind of philosophical questioning that presumes to go too far. Sextus, on the other hand, puts all philosophical assertions in conflict with the tranquility of the person without "opinions." To lead a good human life literally requires the abandonment of philosophical decisions about what is true.

One way of reading Sextus is as making a clear division between the kind of judgments that are natural or commonsensible and philosophical judgments. This division allows him to abstain from the latter while accepting the former. Without it, Sextus's abstention from assertion would have to extend to non-philosophical judgments. If this reading is accurate—and we will shortly turn to an alternative interpretation—then Sextus's analysis hangs on the plausibility of his distinction between philosophical and nonphilosophical judgments.

Sextus tries to mark the division of commonsense and philosophical ("dogmatic") judgments by characterizing the kind of judgment involved, the object of judgment, the cause, and finally the function of judgment.[6] Absolute judgments are to be avoided, relative judgments accepted; judgments of the nonevident or what is "by nature" are to be avoided, judgments of the evident or apparent are accepted; judgments caused by sense impressions or nature, law, or custom are to be accepted, others avoided; judgments that are "expedient" or have an effect in the practical conduct of life are acceptable, those that do not are not.

Each of these distinctions fails either because it implies too little or too much. Rather than examine all of them, I will consider only the most prominent, the one Sextus uses most consistently, the distinction between the evident and the nonevident.

An immediate objection against Sextus might be that this distinction implies too little. The claim that that all things appear to be relative, hence that appearances are relative, still seems to be a universal philosophical claim. One can philosophize without speaking of "things in themselves." However, Sextus's principle of relativity makes it clear that by the *evident* he must mean what is evident to a particular individual at a particular time in particular circumstances. The opposite of the evident is the absolute, what is "by nature" or nonrelative. This means that the principle of relativity not only serves as the *rationale* for abstaining from dogmatic judgment, it is also the *criterion* for demarcating what is dogmatic.

The question that arises is whether sense impressions, naturally caused feelings and beliefs, custom, law, and the "instruction
of the arts" can be understood in accordance with relativity and
without naturaly stimulating philosophical inquiry. I suggest that
the answer is no. Common sense, to which Sextus wants to return
us, does not accept his principle of relativity. Furthermore, nonrela-
tivistic inquiry—that is, systematic questioning and answering to
achieve the nonrelative truth—seems naturally and occasionally to
arise in nonphilosophical common sense, for example, in science,
law, and the interpretation of culture. If philosophy is continuous
with that kind of inquiry, then philosophical questions and answers
(dogmatism) are a part of ordinary social living. My point is not
merely that philosophical disturbances inevitably break out in the
peaceable kingdom of common sense, but that, if one could draw up
a list of what nature, custom, law, and the arts lead one to believe,
that list will inevitably include philosophical, dogmatic, nonrela-
tivist beliefs.

It is possible, however, to interpret Sextus more radically as
abstaining not merely from philosophical assertions, but from *any*
assertions. It has been argued by Michael Frede that Sextus literally asserts nothing; he makes no truth-claims at all.[7] His is a negative procedure meant to show that, on the basis of dogmatic claims
and the "canon" or method of philosophical reasoning, hence on
grounds internal to his opponents' position, assent should be with-
held. Therefore, any attempt to ascribe to Sextus the self-referential
problems consequent upon asserting the dubiousness of all assertions fails to understand the nature of his task. Sextus is motivated
by an "impression" or a "view," not a "position," on the impossibility
of justifying beliefs, an impression he does not claim, or even think,
to be true. I cannot give a complete response to Frede's interesting
proposal here, but a brief clarification will be helpful to the ensuing
discussion of Rorty.

First, Frede claims that Sextus judges appearances and not
things in themselves or "by nature." To repeat a point, that Sextus's
utterances concern appearances does not by itself disqualify them
from being truth-claims or assertions, because we make truth-
claims about appearances all the time.

Second, Frede regards Sextus as offering a "view" or an
"impression" rather than a position or claim. Frede writes that the
skeptic, "naturally is left with the impression that, given these standards, nothing will pass the test [of inquiry] and hence that nothing
is, or even can be, known."[8] This is quite an "impression." It is cer-

tainly not a sense impression. The examples of impressions and views Frede refers to are propositional in form. Because they appear to have the same form as any proposition, claim, or assertion, something other than failure to appear in the form of a truth-claim must disqualify them from being truth-claims.

Third, Sextus's apparent claims, Frede suggests, are actually "autobiographical reports" to the effect that Sextus has such and such an impression (e.g., "I am warmed"). As reports, however, such utterances can still be truth-claims, such as if I report in a civil court that I have suffered great anguish. Such remarks are representations of personal matters that might not be subject to public validation, but they are truth-claims nonetheless. Furthermore, this interpretation of Frede's causes problems for our reading of Sextus's general expressions of the skeptical position; for example, "all things appear to be relative." If they are autobiographical reports, what is the point of uttering them? If his statements truly function as autobiographical reports, then "all appears to be relative" and "one should withhold assent" must play a role in inquiry similar to that of the report, "I am in a good mood today" being made by a party to a philosophical discussion. In other words, if they are meant as autobiographical, then they would be irrelevant.

Fourth, even if Sextus is reporting on impressions that he recognizes to be incapable of validation through the rules of public validation or inquiry, this does *not* mean that Sextus fails to regard them as true! It is common to make assertive judgments that we feel unable to validate publicly; that we cannot imagine the validation procedures does not mean that we do not believe in the truth of our judgments. Such is the nature of all *tentative* judgments. When one says of another, "My gut feeling is that he is a phony," the judgment is being offered without hope of sufficient evidence, but that does not mean the speaker fails to accept it as true. The burden of truth is not necessarily lifted by failure to offer a view as capable of validation.

Last, Frede suggests that Sextus's aim is a purely internal critique of the philosopher's discourse, which judges the philosopher unable to justify assertions on the basis of the philosopher's own canon of inquiry. Now, even if this is true, Sextus does make positive statements (e.g., "all things appear to be relative") that he uses in the negative critique. Furthermore, we may ask whether Sextus believes that *it is true that* the philosopher is inconsistent. If Sextus does believe it is true, then he accepts a truth-governed assertion. If he abstains from this, then the question arises as to what is the point of his discourse? If Sextus really does not accept the truth of *any* of his utterances, including that "It is true that one ought to abstain from assertion" or "It is true that the dogmatist is inconsistent," then in what sense are we to understand their intended contribution to the discussion we, his readers, are having with Sextus?

My point is that if Sextus had—as, I believe, he has not—consistently avoided making utterances that he meant as true, the point of his discourse would then be entirely unclear. It would be like thrusting a painting into the midst of a philosophical or scientific discussion and silently expecting the question under discussion to be decided by the sheer presence of the art work. But even if the painting were to contribute to the discussion in some way, the discussants would have to interpret its meaning, which they would do by making truth-claims. Otherwise the exhibitive judgment of the painting could have no influence on the inquiry taking place.[9]

Sextus cannot offer judgments without them being subject to validation. If his utterances are relevant to inquiry, then they are subject to validation by inquiry. Even if they are not truth-claims, they are *claims nonetheless*, to our attention, consideration, appreciation, and evaluation. Does that make them false or uninformative or worthy of dismissal? I believe not. But it does mean that they provide no magical way to be *in* inquiry but not *of* it. If utterances are offered as free of inquiry's grasp, hence free of its obligations, then this can only mean that they are irrelevant to inquiry.

We will now see that this combination of skepticism regarding philosophy and a metaphilosophical pragmatism justifying abstention from philosophical claims, even from skeptical claims, has been revived by Richard Rorty.

Beyond Philosophy

Rorty's impact on contemporary American philosophy has been great. In his recent program, initiated by *Philosophy and the Mirror of Nature* (1979)[10] and continued and modified in a series of books and collections, Rorty has articulated in plain terms the most unavoidable issue of contemporary philosophy: the issue of its own meaning and validity.

Rorty's view is well-known. Philosophy has traditionally understood its task as transcendent to all other cultural activities and forms of inquiry, because it seeks to explain why and how human knowledge is possible. Its explanation has generally been based on the notion of truth as correspondence to fact. The claim that our assertions or beliefs are true of the world in the sense of correspondence presumes a comparison of belief with parts of the world. This comparison must itself employ beliefs or a language in which beliefs are embedded. Thus the outcome of the determination of the validity of the original beliefs depends on the validity of the beliefs implicit in this comparison. Still presuming truth as correspondence, the latter beliefs must now be compared to the world, a comparison that must either presume the beliefs to be tested, hence be circular, or presume yet other beliefs that must subsequently be tested, that would require another comparison, and so on. Reminiscent of Hans Albert's Münchhausen Trilemma, the attempt to validate our beliefs is either circular or leads to an infinite or indefinite regress. The reason is simple: The comparison of belief and world must itself presume belief. In the most telling metaphor, philosophy has sought to know how all language "hooks onto" the world. But this task is impossible, because there is no way to escape language in toto to judge its objective adequacy, so to speak, from the outside.[11]

Rorty has distinguished between this kind of foundationalist, transcendence-seeking philosophy and a chastened philosophy that has renounced transcendence, at one time referring to the former with the upper case, *Philosophy*.[12] Rorty has described the chastened philosophy as (quoting Wilfred Sellars) "seeing how things, in the largest sense of the term, hang together, in the largest sense of the term" (COP, p. 226); a "study of the comparative advantages and disadvantages of the various ways of talking which our race has invented" (COP, p. xl); as a contributor to the "redescription" and, hence, remaking of our society; as not fundamentally different from literary criticism; as practiced by "ironists" who recognize that their views cannot be validated as true (CIS, p. 73); and by "all-purpose intellectuals who [are] ready to offer a view on pretty much anything, in the hope of making it hang together with everything else" (COP, p. xxxix).

Rorty accepts a kind of Pyrrhonist skepticism with regard to philosophical judgments. That is, he doubts their veracity, and refuses to assert such judgments or their contraries. Aware of the looming self-referential problems of claims about the dubiety of all philosophical claims, he tries to adopt an approach reminiscent of Pyrrhonist nonassertion, replacing such talk with assertions about their usefulness or uselessness. He calls this negative approach *pragmatism*. Like Thomas Reid, Rorty aims to return us to common sense and nonphilosophical intellectual discourse, the "conversation of culture."[13] This seems not far from Pyrrhonian *ataraxia*, perhaps the kind of peace that Wittgenstein wrote would ensue when we lost the *compulsion* to do philosophy: "The real discovery is the one that makes me capable of stopping doing philosophy when I want to—the one that gives philosophy peace, so that it is no longer tormented by questions which bring *itself* in question."[14]

Rorty makes three suppositions that I will argue against. First, he believes that philosophy and common sense are discontinuous. This crucially allows him to claim that the latter are not subject to his critique, that they are immune to the disease Rorty finds in philosophy and hence will be unaffected by its cure. Second, he believes that his own inquiry is *not* philosophical in the objectionable sense and so is not subject to self-referential problems. Third, he believes we can *stop* doing philosophy in the objectionable sense. I will argue that those three beliefs are false.

Rorty's Relativism

My first aim is to show that Rorty, despite his disclaimers, has often asserted a positive relativism. He has been at least a part-time antirealist. Second, even if we restrict our attention to his more careful formulations, where he believes he has transcended the realism versus antirealism debate through recourse to pragmatism, here too he has failed to transcend epistemology. He is still doing the kind of Philosophy he claims to avoid. Third, there are serious problems with his pragmatic approach to knowledge and philosophy. We will see that the recourse to pragmatism does not magically put an end the problem of philosophical validity. The point of this discussion is to deny that Rorty has successfully *dissolved* the problem of philosophical knowledge.

In 1989 Rorty suggested the term *final vocabulary* for the set of beliefs or judgments ultimately presupposed by any assertion (CIS, p. 73). The justification of any assertion must ultimately depend on the validity of its final vocabulary. But final vocabularies are incapable of any noncircular justification in terms of correspondence to the world. Consequently, the proposed philosophical justification of synthetic judgments that they "correspond" to what they judge cannot itself be justified. Philosophy, at least traditionally, depends on the claim that correspondence determines the acceptability of belief. But philosophy can neither explain nor justify this notion of correspondence. Rorty says that to explain acceptability by correspondence "is no more enlightening than 'opium puts people to sleep because of its dormitive power'" (ORT, p. 6).

Notice first of all that Rorty is claiming that realism is false or unsupportable, not merely unuseful or disadvantageous to believe. He rejects its claim to *truth*. Realism is a false belief in the possibility of a certain kind of appeal in justifying our beliefs.

It is worth mentioning that in his discussion of final vocabularies Rorty introduces the notion of *irony*. In 1989 he offered irony as the proper intellectual response to our inability to justify our vocabularies. Rorty proposes three conditions for being an "ironist." An ironist is someone who (a) "has radical and continuing doubts about the final vocabulary she uses"; (b) "realizes that argument phrased in her present vocabulary can neither underwrite nor dissolve these doubts"; and, (c) "does not think that her vocabulary is closer to reality than others," because "anything may be made to look good or bad by being redescribed," and so sees the choice between vocabularies as one of "simply playing the new off against the old" (CIS, p. 73).

If, for the sake of the argument, we assume the cogency of Rorty's notion of final vocabulary,[15] my critique of Rorty can be focused simply by saying that I accept the first and second conditions but deny the third. It may be true that we maintain radical doubts about our ultimate beliefs and hold out no hope of a noncircular validation of them; but that does not imply that we can abandon realism and truth as a norm, as the third condition intends. I will argue that the third step not only cannot be justified, it cannot be consistently made at all.

Rorty has identified final vocabularies with cultural traditions and consequently has urged us to be "frankly ethnocentric" (EHO, p. 168). He has claimed that "solidarity" is the only ground of our beliefs and defined pragmatism in terms of the "reduction" of objectivity to solidarity (CIS, p. 22). According to this view, "there is nothing to be said about either truth or rationality apart from descriptions of the familiar procedures of justification which a given society—*ours*—uses in one or another area of inquiry." (ORT, p. 23). In one his recent volumes, "contexts" play the role of that to which validity is relative.

> For us [pragmatists], all objects are always already contextualized. They all come with contexts attached. . . . So there is no question of taking an object out of its old context and examining it, all by itself, to see what new context might suit it. . . . Once one drops the traditional opposition between context and thing contextualized, there is no way to divide things up into those which are what they are independent of context and those which are context-dependent. . . . there are no candidates for self-subsistent, independent entities

save individual beliefs. . . . But these are very bad candidates indeed. For a belief is what it is only by virtue of its position in a web [of belief]. (ORT, pp. 97–98)

Rorty is arguing against the truth of the correspondence theory on the basis of his own truth-claims about the context of belief and justification. He has given an account of how we know. This is positive antirealism, in particular, *conventionalism*. It is an account of truth and knowledge that makes validity relative to vocabulary, context, solidarity, community, and culture.

Rorty has occasionally tried to fend off the charge of relativism. In a 1979 address he defined relativism as the view that "every belief on a certain topic . . . is as good as every other," thereby denying that he, or anyone, is a relativist (COP, p. 166). This is a hopelessly narrow conception of relativism. One page later he emended it to say that pragmatists are in fact relativists regarding philosophical theories, but not regarding "real" theories. So, although no one is or has ever been a real-theory relativist, pragmatists are those who think that one philosophical theory is just as good as any other.

In a later essay Rorty gives a more complex account in which he admits to a kind of relativism.

> Three different views are commonly referred to by . . . ["relativism"]. The first is the view that every belief is as good as every other. The second is the view that "true" is an equivocal term, having as many meanings as there are procedures of justification. The third is the view that there is nothing to be said about either truth or rationality apart from descriptions of the familiar procedures of justification which a given society—*ours*—uses in one or another area of inquiry. The pragmatist holds the ethnocentric third view. But he does not hold the self-refuting first view, nor the eccentric second view. (ORT, p. 23)

Here Rorty admits that his pragmatism is a form of relativism, albeit a cautious, negative form: it denies any sense of truth other than what survives our culture's justification procedures.

Rorty wants to avoid the appearance of a positive view. In the Introduction to the 1982 volume, he made clear that the pragmatism he endorsed was less a philosophic theory of knowledge than an avoidance of any such theory. As he later wrote, "To say that we should drop the idea of truth as out there waiting to be discovered is not to say that we have discovered that, out there, there is no truth. It is to say that our purposes would be served best by ceasing to see truth as a deep matter, as a topic of philosophical interest . . ." (CIS, p. 8). Rorty explains that pragmatists do not have an alternative theory of truth, "They would simply like to change the subject" (COP, p. xiv).

There is a reason for insistence on this point. Rorty correctly saw that his criticism of philosophical or epistemological theories was so global that if it were to issue in a positive philosophic generalization, a self-contradiction would result. He would be open to the charge of "self-referential inconsistency" leveled at philosophers "claiming to know what they themselves claim cannot be known" (CIS, p. 8, n. 2). If the pragmatist's language "is too philosophical it will embody Platonic assumptions which will make it impossible for the pragmatist to state the conclusion he wants to reach" (COP, p. xiv). So the pragmatist's strategy is not to deny the truth of non-pragmatist approaches, but to deny their fruitfulness, interest, or value, and so stand outside of the debate between realism and antirealism.

Rorty's Pragmatism

Let us, for the time being, ignore the positive statements of antirealism cited earlier and attend to Rorty's more consistently "pragmatic" formulations. In the 1991 Introduction to *Objectivity, Relativism, and Truth* Rorty suggests a new name for his position. *Representationalism* is the view that language represents reality, that something "makes" beliefs true (or false). Realism and antirealism are two opposed versions of representationalism offering different claims as to what it is that "makes" our beliefs true, correspondence to reality (realism) or coherence of belief (antirealism). Rorty espouses "antirepresentationalism," which abstains on a principled basis from any account of what makes beliefs true. In Rorty's words, antirepresentationalism is, "the attempt to eschew discussion of realism by denying that the notion of 'representation,' or that of 'fact of the matter,' has any useful role in philosophy" (ORT, p. 2). In the process of objecting to the view that "'mind' or 'language' or 'social practice' . . . constructs reality out of something not yet determinate enough to count as real," Rorty urges that, "Antirepresentationalists need to insist that 'determinacy' [e.g., of the objects of knowledge] is not what is in question—that neither does thought determine reality nor, in the sense intended by the realist, does reality determine thought. More precisely, it is no truer that 'atoms are what they are because we use "atom" as we do' than that 'we use "atom" as we do because atoms are as they are.' *Both* of these claims . . . are entirely empty. Both are pseudo-explanations" (ORT, p. 5).

This is Rorty's most sophisticated attempt to transcend the realism versus antirealism debate. He is especially trying to avoid falling into some version of idealism or the coherence theory of truth, something he was less careful about in his earlier work.[16] Despite the new terminology, however, the basis for Rorty's position remains that there is "no way of formulating an independent test of accuracy of representation—of reference or correspondence to an 'antecedently determinate' reality—no test distinct from the success which is supposedly explained by this accuracy. Representationalists offer us no way of deciding whether a certain linguistic item is usefully deployed because it stands in these relations, or whether its utility is due to some factors which have nothing to do with . . . 'representing' or 'corresponding' . . ." (ORT, p. 6). The utility or success of belief is a prephilosophical fact for all to see. Philosophical realism is offered as an *explanation* of that fact. But truth has no legitimate "explanatory" use.[17] Rorty suggests that realism (like antirealism) fails to fulfill this explanatory role; it is a pointless pseudo-explanation (like the "dormitive power" of opium). No explanation of the success of belief is necessary, beneficial, or reasonable.

Rorty wanted to be silent on the matter of truth and thereby escape epistemology. This neutral approach is perhaps what John Rawls has called the *method of avoidance*.[18] But this silence on the role of correspondence in effect asserts that *success* is the norm of assertive judgment and inquiry. Rorty does not hear this assertion as breaking his vow of silence. He believes success is a cultural, pragmatic, prephilosophical fact, a "narrative" and not a "metanarrative" fact, to use Lyotard's distinction. Correspondence, on the other hand, is a philosophical *explanation of* that fact, a philosophical metanarrative. Thus, "it is one thing to say that a prehensile thumb, or an ability to use the word 'atom' as physicists do, is useful for coping with the environment. It is another thing to attempt to explain this utility by reference to representationalist notions . . . (ORT, p. 5).

This is a positive application of pragmatism. Rorty's pragmatism is not only constituted by his *avoidance* of realism and definitions of truth, but by his description of the acceptability of assertions in terms of their success or utility. Rorty recognizes this as an at least implicit version of Jamesian pragmatism, without

James' mistaken and unnecessary attempts to explain success further (ORT, pp.127–128).

This raises a very difficult question: *What is success or utility for beliefs?* 'Success' implies that beliefs serve aims. What are they? We know that they cannot include the aim to know what is true in the sense of correspondence, but what else can we say about them? Presumably beliefs may serve whatever aims people may have. What are the criteria for success with respect to these aims? Given the variety and density of human aims—the fact that the same act might serve several different aims simultaneously—it would seem that we have to leave the criteria of success up to the people with the aims. In other words, context and community will decide what is success, hence what is true. This is a return to relativism. Rorty's term "success" presumably means "success with respect to what are the aims of the relevant community at the time." Rorty is not asserting relativism at this point, but he is asserting something (success) that is inevitably relativistic.

Presumably, even if people were implicitly to accept success as the criterion of acceptability for beliefs, they would disagree about what it means for a belief to succeed. People would deny that beliefs which work for others work for themselves or deny that the fact that a belief works for other people makes the belief true. Worse yet, there would probably be people—"real" people, not philosophers—who will *deny* that their truth is "what works" at all! They will say, "*Your* truth may be whatever works for you, but *our* truth is determined by the nature of reality or by the dictates of an omniscient God." How can the antiphilosopher even *validate* the claim that success is the norm of belief in the face of such disagreement, not to mention answer the relativism it generates when accepted?

Perhaps Rorty has a different answer to what success means and how to deal with the problems it entails. Even so, to address these questions he would have to engage in the kind of philosophical discussion he faults in William James as a lapse into epistemology (ORT, p. 127). Even if he were not to regard the discussion as an attempt to define truth, even if *truth* were never mentioned, Rorty would still be attempting to define his de facto norm of assertive acceptability—*success*, which either determines or replaces *true*. If Rorty demurs, if he will not join the argument about the meaning of *success*, then his position entails silence not only about truth, but also about success. The curtain of silence would thereby advance through his argument, threatening to prohibit questions about whatever term functions as the norm of belief acceptance. If we cannot investigate the meaning of the norm for belief acceptance, what sense does it make to continue to maintain that success is that norm? Why not simply say that we accept the beliefs we accept, and reject those we reject, in other words, why not refuse to enter into any discussion of norms with respect to belief? But, of course, Rorty has not opted out of this discussion. He could not, for that would mean a de facto acceptance of whatever criteria are currently employed for belief-acceptance, which currently would *include* correspondence. In short, Rorty has failed to escape epistemology.

Rorty's Metaphilosophical Pragmatism

Suppose we once again restrict our critical sights and grant Rorty his pragmatic antiepistemology, forgetting about the unclarity of "success." Even this does not end the epistemic story. Rorty wants to criticize foundationalist philosophies on the grounds that they are unprofitable. In other words, he rejects interpretations of 'true' as something more than 'successful' on the grounds that such interpretations have not been successful. He writes, "Conforming to my own precepts, I am not going to offer arguments against the vocabulary I want to replace. Instead, I am going to try to make the vocabulary I favor look attractive by showing how it may be used to describe a variety of topics" (CIS, p. 9).

This suggests that Rorty at least occasionally adopts a *metaphilosophical* pragmatism. That is, he sometimes presents his own putatively philosophical judgments as actions, as judgments intended to be valid in terms of their effect, not their truth.

There is a potential confusion here. Consider two different critical strategies. One is to say that, "Foundational philosophy is false, or dubious, or unsupportable as true." The other is to say that, "Foundational philosophy is useless or disadvantageous." If Rorty asserts the former, then he is saying that *it is true that* foundationalism is false. He wants to avoid this (although as I have suggested, he cannot). So he asserts that foundationalism is useless or disadvantageous. But this certainly is another truth-claim. To assert it is to say that *it is true that* "Foundationalism is useless." "Foundationalism is useless" is a claim about practical benefit, not truth, but it is still a truth-claim.

So, even if the norm being used to evaluate the tradition is benefit or success and not truth, that does not end the work of truth-seeking inquiry in this matter; on the contrary, our work is only beginning. For if Rorty is claiming that foundationalist philosophy is or was useless, that is something he is obligated to justify with reasons. A very long argument would then ensue about the political, economic, psychological, and cultural effects of foundationalist philosophy. This argument would not be new. As we have seen, since Socrates philosophers have offered the practical effect of philosophical inquiry as philosophy's justification. The absence of such a systematic discussion in Rorty's work makes the depth of his conviction on this matter dubious, unless we read him as making only a practical suggestion; that is, "Let us try getting along without truth and see what happens." This would be an entirely plausible suggestion. But if it is meant seriously as a competitor to other suggestions (e.g., "No, we are better off with correspondence, we just need to tinker with it a bit") in determining our future, we will still need pragmatic reasons for accepting his suggestion over others, and again, these are not provided.

But what if Rorty is attempting a more radical move? What if his apparent claims are not meant as truth-claims at all? What if Rorty means to offer the statement that "Foundationalism is useless" *not* on the basis that it is true, but on the basis that it would be practically beneficial or aesthetically satisfying to believe it. Or, to put it differently (because to believe a statement presumably means to believe *it is true*), what if he regards the statement "Foundationalism is useless" as practically beneficial or aesthetically satisfying in some way other than as belief—in the way that, for example, an imperative can be useful or a poem satisfying. Then the norm of his statement or judgment would be practical goodness or aesthetic quality, not truth.

Even if this were true, even if, in effect, Rorty were not making truth-claims at all, *we* would still debate the aesthetic quality or practical goodness of his work with our own truth-claims. We would have to decide whether *it is true that* Rorty's work, or the vision it portrays, or the effect it has, is good or aesthetically satisfying, like any social or literary critic. Even if we were to grant Rorty a visa to move his discourse from the territory of truth into a region governed by goodness or beauty, he would not thereby escape questions about the value or validity of his work, questions whose norm will be truth.

My point is that in this duel Rorty may have his choice of weapons—truth, goodness, or beauty—*but he must defend himself in any case.* Even philosophical silence, the abstention from the call to answer philosophical questions, if it is offered as valid, as a response that judges the validity of the conversation from which it abstains, is open to the demand for justification. We may ask, is such silence good, is what it shows aesthetically satisfying, are its effects on us beneficial? In other words, silence has no privilege. If offered as a move in the game, it remains open to the need for validation in the argument over what is best.

Doing Fine Without Philosophy

We have seen that Rorty cannot escape the philosophical discussion of the norms of belief acceptance. There is a related problem with his basic distinction between philosophical discourse and the rest of culture. A useful way to explore this distinction is to examine two papers by Arthur Fine, "The Natural Ontological Attitude" and "And Not Anti-Realism Either," of which Rorty has written that they contain "the best recent account of why we ought to get beyond the [realism-antirealism] struggle" (ORT, p. 150, n. 61). On the relevant distinction, Rorty and Fine are in agreement.

In "The Natural Ontological Attitude," Fine attempts to capture what he regards as the intuitive, prephilosophical conviction that seeks expression in scientific and philosophical forms of realism.[19] This common sense realism accepts the "confirmed results of science" and the "evidence of one's senses," "in the same way."[20] Fine claims that everyone (including nonscientists) implicitly believes in the "homely" realism of the "core position," according to which the results of science are true in the same sense as everyday or "homely" truths.

Realists and antirealists differ in what they add to this position. The former adds a correspondence notion of truth "to explain what makes the truth true," whereas the latter adds a pragmatic or instrumentalist notion of truth. To affirm the core position by itself is to adopt the Natural Ontological Attitude, or NOA. The NOA is committed to the existence of the referents of terms in true scientific theories, but not to scientific progress, the stability of reference across paradigm shifts, or commensurability. It accepts a minimal "Davidsonian-Tarskian" notion of truth, and is distinctive by its "stubborn refusal to amplify the concept of truth, by providing a theory or analysis or even a metaphorical picture."[21] This is in contrast to the realist, who, "tries to stand outside the arena [of the game of science] watching the ongoing game and then tries to judge (from this external point of view) what the point is. It is, he says, *about* some area external to the game. The realist, I think, is fooling himself. For he cannot (really!) stand outside the arena, nor can he survey some area off the playing field and mark it out as what the game is about."[22]

Taking the standpoint of the NOA reveals the excesses of realism and antirealism. Each makes an unwanted addition to the core position. Fine writes that,

> realism adds an outer direction to NOA, that is, the external world and the correspondence relation of approximate truth; antirealisms (typically) add an inner direction, that is, human-oriented reductions of truth, or concepts, or explanations. . . . NOA suggests that the legitimate features of these additions are already contained in the presumed equal status of everyday truths with scientific ones, and in our accepting them both as *truths*. No other additions are legitimate, and none are required.[23]

In the sequel paper, "And Not Anti-Realism Either," Fine insists that antirealism is as much of a supervention of the NOA as realism. The antirealist interprets the truth of a theory P as "amounting to the fact that a certain class of subjects would accept P under a certain set of circumstances."[24] In response, Fine cautions, "But it would be a mistake to think that we will find truth there. For the anti-realism expressed in the idea of truth-as-acceptance is just as metaphysical and idle as the realism expressed by a correspondence theory."[25]

Given that Rorty cited these essays approvingly, Fine's thesis can, I believe, be used to clarify Rorty's position. The NOA is part of the prephilosophical common sense world to which Rorty wishes to return us. Both global skepticism and realism transcend the NOA. For Rorty, the proper philosophical task is the negative one of undermining that transcendence, rather than the positive one of asserting the "truth" of the NOA from some position outside it. There is no position outside it.

A single project ties together Sextus, Fine, and Rorty. Just as Fine seeks to distinguish the NOA from realism and antirealism, and Sextus segregates philosophy or dogmatism from custom, Rorty tries to exclude philosophical questions and answers from the field of acceptable discourse, which includes "real" theories and the "narratives which hold our culture together" (EHO, p. 167). Rorty endorses the parallel distinction, made by Jean-François Lyotard in his influential *The Postmodern Condition: A Report on Knowledge*, between "narratives" and philosophical "metanarratives" and accepts the "postmodernist" claim that not only are metanarratives incredible, our culture no longer needs them.[26]

Can these distinctions—which are at heart one distinction, that between the kind of philosophy that is objectionable and everything else—bear the burden laid on them? Fine implies that scientific practice does not include within itself an interpretation of the value, meaning, and validity of science. Scientists do not properly go beyond the NOA in their views of their own activity. If and when they do, they have overstepped their proper epistemic bounds. This puts Fine (like Rorty) in the rather artificial posture of correcting the practitioners of science about their own ideas by drawing what would seem to the practitioner to be an arbitrary line between the permissible, "Now I see a scientific truth," and the impermissible, "Now I see a truth that holds both inside and outside of scientific practice." I do not see how any such line can be drawn nonarbitrarily.

Like Rorty, Fine's project turns on calling our attention to whatever "goes beyond practice." I do not believe Fine can adequately describe this pristine, prephilosophical, "natural," preinterpretive "practice."[27] Science does not, he suggests, "need" an interpretation, does not need to be placed "in a context." I do not know what science "needs," but it seems clear that science (a) is often given an interpretation, both by those who practice it and by others and (b) is already in a context, or rather a number of nested contexts, such as the context of self-controlled human activity, the context of human social institutions, and the context of the natural world. The NOA allegedly takes science "on its own terms" and does not "read things into science."[28] But the question is, *What are science's "own terms"?* Instead of answering that fundamental question, Fine has simply thrown us back to it. The attempt to say what the terms of science are is a philosophical task on which people, including scientists, differ. Baldly put, my objection to Fine is that the NOA is an abstraction that cannot be reasonably be said to characterize scientific practice; not to mention that it is difficult to see what is "natural" about it.[29]

A second objection follows closely on the first. Fine's account is *relativist*, in particular, contextualist. Fine claims that the validity of a result within the "game" of science cannot be claimed to hold outside that game. Fine does not tell us what he thinks of truths outside science, but he presumably must accept one of two unappealing alternatives. Either there is no truth outside of science—that is, 'truth' obtains only within the game of science—or other extrascientific games have their own truths, which then may very well contradict the scientific truths.[30] Regarding questions like "what is the aim of science?" he writes, "As we grow up I think we learn that such questions really do not require an answer, but rather they call for an empathetic analysis to get at the cognitive (and temperamental) sources of the question, and then a program of therapy to help change all that."[31]

If so, then we cannot interpret science's contribution to culture. Suppose that a parent, who is a scientist, upon returning home from the lab discovers her spouse about to treat her infant son's high fever and diarrhea with magical incantations based on ancient mythic narratives, in lieu of a visit to the hospital. Will the scientist fail to object to this form of treatment because she is no longer in the laboratory, the validity of the scientific work to which she has devoted her life being purely internal to the practice of science? Does anyone really doubt that at some point in the ensuing argument, as her husband dances and chants, the scientist would shout, "But modern science, hence modern medical theory, is more true than magic," or "Things are more like the way science says they are than the way magic says they are," or in abbreviated form, "I'm taking him to the damned hospital!"

The "natural" fact is that we can and do make choices between contexts, and the desire to find the most valid or most widely effective context is a "natural" response to the responsibilities of choice. This does not mean that we can *escape* context. It is perfectly sensible for someone to try to "stand outside" the game of science to say what it is about, because science is only one of our "games" or, better, science does not exhaust human judgment. We must choose which "games" to play and when.[32] Common sense must judge the whole of science, because our prescientific stance incorporates various modes of judgment and possible methods of query—science being the mature expression of one of these. Hence, the possibility of competition and contradiction between modes and methods of judgment is built into our commonsense dealings with the world. To push my claim to its natural conclusion, the realism-antirealism debate has its roots in *prephilosophic judgment*, both in and out of scientific inquiry.

Returning to Rorty, it is clear that in the normal course of social practices people *do* make metanarrative or Philosophical claims. They make them with a frequency and in ways that imply that the claimants regard them not as accidental to the context, but as essential. Further, people must often make choices between social practices, narratives, even cultures, and to do so implies the application of norms external to the contexts being judged. If they make these choices reflectively, if they try to reason about what they ought to do, they will find themselves asking questions and giving answers that are indistinguishable from philosophical questions and answers. The professional philosopher addresses these questions more systematically and expertly, perhaps, just as a professional plumber deals with a leaky pipe more systematically and expertly than the average do-it-youselfer. But this difference *in degree* cannot hold the burden that Rorty would need it to bear.

Rorty attempts the same point in his reading of Jacques Derrida. Rorty objects to those, like Christopher Norris and Rodolphe Gasché, who interpret Derrida as doing philosophy, because, in their interpretation, Derrida regards "logocentrism," or what Rorty would call *metaphysics*, as ubiquitous.[33] For Rorty, Derrida is "circumventing" philosophy, and this is possible because philosophy, like logocentrism, is not "pervasive" in culture (EHO, pp. 85–106).[34]

Rorty nowhere gives a full explication of what he means by philosophy, or Philosophy, or metaphysics. His failure to draw clear boundaries to philosophy allows him to describe the project of Derrida, Wittgenstein, himself, and doctrines like nominalism and pragmatism, as somehow outside of philosophy. Rorty states, without argument, that notions like "self-evident" and "intuitive" are "not commonsensical, but obviously philosophical" (EHO, p. 109). Does it really make sense to say, when persons in everyday discourse point to an experiential fact or to what they consider an obvious and undeniable truth, that their meaning is unrelated to what philosophers call *self-evidence*? Is it reasonable to draw an absolute distinction between the use of a term—'rights,' 'God,' 'real' etc.—by philosophers and its use by laypersons? If the everyday use is philosophical, then philosophy is part of everyday culture, something Rorty cannot admit without having to apply his critique to culture in general.

Rorty casts the question of the relation of philosophy to culture in terms of philosophy's alleged "pervasiveness," thereby creating a straw person. Philosophy is not "pervasive" in everyday life, but it is *continuous with* everyday life. To claim continuity means to deny that the distinction between *some* of the questions, claims, and arguments of cultural actors, on the one hand, and the questions, claims, and arguments of philosophers, on the other, is anything more than a distinction in *degree* of systematicity, sophistication, and precision. The distinction is the same kind of distinction we would draw between the way my wife works on our plumbing and the way a professional plumber does, or the way I play basketball and the way Charles Barkley does. In each case people—the plumber and my wife, Barkley and I, the professional philosopher and the citizen—are doing the same kind of thing, just doing it better or worse, more systematically or spectacularly or less. Faced with the prospect of playing a basketball game against me, Barkley's response would presumably be not, "What game is this fellow playing? I don't recognize it as basketball. Could someone please tell me the rules and the point of this new game?" but rather, "Must I play this chump?"

The only way to deny the continuity of philosophy and everyday inquiry, it seems, would be to claim that philosophical questions, claims, and arguments have a status in everyday life like, in Wittgenstein's simile, a "wheel |that| . . . is not part of the mechanism" (PI, 271). That is, they constitute a bit of decoration that has no real—pragmatic—function in the everyday context. But it seems that everyday persons do not recognize this alleged fact, that a portion of their discourse is irrelevant to their pragmatic doings. If we philosophers say that the apparently philosophical portion of their discussions is irrelevant, then we are claiming *to know better than* they, to know what is "essential" to the everyday context better than the cultural actors themselves. The justification for *that* kind of claim, I suggest, would look rather tortured. It would be at least as artificial, non-commonsensible, and elitist as Rorty has accused Philosophy of being.

Ironically, the attempt to distinguish what Rorty has called *real*, meaningful, reliable nonphilosophical judgments, for example, scientific judgments, from unreal, pointless, unjustifiable Philosophical judgments is an epistemological project of the most straightforward kind. It is a direct descendent of that tradition, active from Kant to Carnap, concerned to identify "pseudoproblems" in philosophy.[35] To draw a distinction between philosophy and all other cognitive acts is a time-honored philosophical task. In short, Rorty cannot help but do the kind of philosophy he criticizes.[36]

The Consolation of Antiphilosophy

Rorty has tried to use philosophy to escape from philosophy. This cannot work. The means of escape from philosophy must themselves be nonphilosophical. The nonphilosophical way out is to abstain from philosophical inquiry on an *un*principled basis; that is, to abstain from philosophy without holding up that abstention as having a validity, as revealing something, that philosophy ought to recognize. It judges philosophy externally, not internally. Unprincipled abstention terminates or avoids philosophy out of boredom or exhaustion or disinterest or to do something else. But unprincipled abstention neither says nor shows anything about philosophy that philosophy must recognize and so cannot serve Rorty's purposes.

Principled abstention offers itself as the right response to what Sextus called the "continually disturbed" life of the philosopher and demands that philosophy recognize that rightness. It purports to reveal something important about philosophy (and about life) that philosophy is obligated to take into account. But to offer something as valid is to open oneself to the demand for validation, regardless of whether that validation is in terms of truth, goodness, or beauty. Rorty is trying to make a valid point. To expect philosophy—whose norm is truth, whose method is inquiry—to recognize that valid point is to claim the status of philosophical validity. This is inevitably self-compromising. The only escape that is not self-compromising is to stop making judgments *about* philosophy: to *simply stop*.

Again, if we interpret Rorty as making only practical and aesthetic suggestions, with no claim to truth, so that my complaints about self-referential inconsistency become irrelevant, then this makes for only a change of venue, it does not end the trial. For then the question becomes, Is the form of discourse and "post-Philosophical culture" to which Rorty invites us preferable to the culture that is continuous with foundationalism or traditional philosophy? This is, I believe, a tactical error on the part of antiphilosophy, for practical benefits are foundationalism's strong suit. Antiphilosophy would be better advised to keep the battle on the grounds of evidential justification, where, although it may be unable to justify its own truth, it can point out foundational philosophy's inability to do the same. Whatever the apparent vices of foundational philosophy (e.g. Eurocentrism, phallocentrism, logocentrism), it has arguably assisted the development of science, liberal democracy, and public morals, not to mention the careers of foundationalist philosophers, and has created a fascinating literary genre. Minimally put, it has a record of achievement, something antiphilosophy lacks.

None of this is sufficient to demonstrate foundational philosophy's *truth*; but if truth is not the issue, that insufficiency is irrelevant. If the real measure of a vocabulary is its practical value, it is going to be very hard to show that antiphilosophy could serve us better than the final vocabulary of the claim, "We hold these truths to be self-evident, that all men are created equal; that they are endowed by their Creator with certain inalienable rights . . ." There is no more foundationalist statement than that.

From my perspective, the problem with Rorty's view is not its pessimism, but its optimism. Rorty frees common people and postmodern intellectuals to believe without having to face the apparently unanswerable questions generated by these beliefs. I am less optimistic. Philosophic questions, perhaps insurmountable, emerge in the extension of inquiry to ultimate questions that arise in reflective living. The only ways to avoid philosophy are to place arbitrary limits on inquiry or to avoid inquiry altogether. Both options are ever present, and I do not suggest that choosing either of them is ignoble, immoral, or wrong. We have not established that there is any moral, practical, or aesthetic value to philosophical inquiry. The argument I have offered thus far only denies that antiphilosophy is valid, it does not show that philosophy is or can be valid. If antiphilosophy wishes merely to *be*, or to *be valid* in some way that philosophy need not recognize, I have no objection whatsoever. It would then truly be, or be part of, a distinct, nonphilosophical literary genre, which no more denies the validity of philosophy than poetry denies the validity of the novel. But it evidently intends more than this, otherwise it would not issue in long books and essays aimed at convincing philosophers of something.

Desite his criticism of the urge to transcendence, Rorty's antiphilosophical commonsensism offers its own soteriology, a prospective paradise where we are somehow not moved to ask ourselves unanswerable questions. David Hiley suggests that Rorty is a moralist who sees philosophy as an obstacle to the good life—or given his pluralism, to good lives. It seems to me that Rorty's moralism is more utopian than that. He wants to lead us to a prephilosophical Eden, a place of Pyrrhonian *ataraxia* undisturbed by philosophical worries. But, for better or worse, that is impossible. Once we have eaten of the fruit of the tree of knowledge, there can be no such place for us.

10

THE ENDS
OF
PHILOSOPHY

Can characteristically philosophical judgments be validated? To ask this question is to attempt to judge the "ends" of philosophical inquiry, to use that ambiguous word. Has philosophy reached an end in the sense of a *termination* of its progress, an abandonment of its hopes? Have we entered or ought we enter a "post-Philosophical culture" in Rorty's phrase? To speak of a possible termination of philosophy is to impute limits to philosophy. But here we should distinguish limits and bounds.[1] By *limits* I mean parameters that stop philosophical inquiry, that halt it in its pursuit of an aim. By *bounds* I mean constitutive borders that distinguish philosophy from other forms of endeavor. Bounds and limits are conceptually independent; I can imagine a river that is endless, without source or mouth, but not one without banks. Have we finally come to the limits of philosophy, or have we rather come up against its constitutive bounds?

On the basis of my analysis of attempts to resolve and dissolve the problem of philosophical validity in Chapters Three through Nine, I will draw four conclusions. The first section that follows will briefly summarize the results of our explorations of Peirce, Nietzsche, Wittgenstein, Buchler, Derrida, and Rorty and present two conclusions, the first of which was prepared by Chapter Four, the second by Chapter Nine. The second section will discuss my third and principal conclusion regarding the possibility of characteristically philosophical knowledge. The third section will explore the role of exhibitive and active judgment in philosophy, hence, the divergent ends philosophy may be claimed to have, and present a fourth conclusion. A final section will apply these conclusions to the present work.

The Philosophical *Kirkos*

I have tried to show that all the accounts of knowledge and philosophy posed by our "circle" of philosophers are problematic, either by virtue of begging the question or self-referential inconsistency or both.

Peirce, our house realist, gives a justification of knowledge in general, and philosophical knowledge in particular, that is dependent on the validity of his convergence theory. Convergence is likewise dependent on his notion of the unity of the community of inquirers. The existence and definition of this community is dependent on the validity of inquiry and hence the convergence theory. The only independent justification of all of this is the necessity of Peirce's hope, his insistence that we *must* believe in the validity of inquiry. Even if this claim were not dubious—and it is dubious—it would not, by Peirce's own reasoning on other occasions, justify the *truth* of what is thereby hoped.

Nietzsche, Wittgenstein, Buchler, Derrida, and Rorty present us with four sophisticated forms of antirealism. They employ, respectively, naturalism, conventionalist, objective, and semiotic relativism, and pragmatism, with negative and implicit metaphilosophical strategies aimed at avoiding the self-referential problems of an explicit antirealism. Nietzsche and Buchler, adopting a positive naturalism, leave us with a circular justification. Nietzsche asserts a naturalism that denies truth and accepts the vicious circle into which this leads him. Buchler's naturalistic perspectivism applies to his own system. The analyses of Wittgenstein and Derrida, which are more strictly negative in their antirealism, similarly apply to themselves, as both philosophers admitted. Rorty's antiphilosophy remains philosophical, hence self-compromising. In other words, these approaches cannot avoid the problems they diagnose as intrinsic to the philosophical project.

On this basis I draw two conclusions. The first is that the nonfoundationalist attempt to save philosophy by limiting it, which we can see in contemporary pragmatic realism and, in particular, Peirce and Buchler, cannot succeed if philosophy is ultimate inquiry. Nonfoundationalism cannot answer the radical, ultimate criticisms brought by antiphilosophy. Its strategy is to deny the validity of such criticisms, but it has no ultimate, that is, philosophically adequate justification for the lowered, less radical standard of validity it employs to validate itself. It must remain circular, and ultimately, pragmatic in its self-justification. Hence, this attempt to *resolve* the problem of philosophical knowledge fails.

My second conclusion is that the attempt by Nietzsche, Wittgenstein, Derrida, and Rorty to *dissolve* or undercut the possibility of philosophical knowledge also fails. For despite their often sophisticated reliance on negative, implicit, and nonassertive strategies, they nevertheless make ultimate judgments that are open to a demand for validation that is not, and cannot be, satisfied. To put the matter controversially, the views of our antifoundationalists are no less problematic than the philosophical foundationalism they criticize. This does not mean that they fail to teach us anything, that they are less than brilliant in conception and execution, or that they can be dismissed. It means that the metaphilosophical strategies of Nietzsche, Wittgenstein, Derrida, as well as Rorty, are themselves philosophical decisions, if only negative or implicit ones, with farreaching implications. As decisions they lack philosophically adequate justification, and their implications are problematic, just like the positions they undermine. Despite the distance they have pushed thought beyond earlier positions, they leave us with the same deep problem we have always had: the questionable legitimacy and validity of philosophic inquiry. What they have done is to exhibit for us, with unsurpassed sophistication, what philosophy is and what its inherent problems are. But they have not given us a valid, nonproblematic judgment of philosophy. Their work is shot through with the very problems they seek to address.

As we have seen, negative and implicit metaphilosophical approaches provide no immunity from the need for validation. The method of avoidance, which is in effect the method of silence, is a judgment like any other, requiring validation like any other. It is always possible to ask the practitioner of silence: "Why ought one be silent? Why do you believe that silence is the superior response for the inquirer? What is the justification of your silence?" A deliberate abstention from assertion, if offered as a significant philosophical move, needs justification no less than any positive assertion. Such justification may make recourse to truth or to active or exhibitive norms like goodness, benefit, success, or aesthetic satisfaction, but in any case it is open to validation.

Of course, the practitioner of silence may, in response to requests for validation, remain silent or make responses that cannot be incorporated into inquiry (e.g., respond with an art object, some act, or irony). Here inquiry's answer must be clear: "I am one thing and not another. Not everything that happens in the world is relevant to inquiry. Your response is such a thing. Your judgment may have a validity I cannot see; inquiry does not exhaust human judgment. But unless you play by my rules you cannot expect me to regard you as relevant. And one more thing: publicly justifiable truth is *my* affair. To it you may make no claim, unless you play *my* game."

This is to say that no principled abstention from philosophy can be philosophically valid. Antiphilosophy cannot validate itself philosophically. Consequently, in a principled or valid sense, *there is no escape* from the philosophical *kirkos*. As was said in the preceding chapter, this does not rule out an unprincipled abstention from philosophical inquiry, one which makes no explicit or implicit claim to validity. I may stop philosophizing because I am sick and tired of philosophy or because I have something else to do, or I may never begin to philosophize for reasons of taste, motivation, and so forth. In these cases, however, I do not claim that my abstention has a kind of validity that inquiry ought to recognize. *I just do it.* This is different from a philosophical silence that is intended to *judge* philosophy with its silence.

Now, the advocates of the philosophers I have examined might respond that their philosophers know all of this. That is, they know that their positions are problematic, indeed, that was their point all along: to exhibit the intrinsically problematic nature of philosophizing, which their own work must share with the philosophies they criticize. After all, Nietzsche admits his philosophy is a circle, Wittgenstein calls his own work nonsense, Derrida says that deconstruction can be deconstructed, and Buchler claims no superperspectival justification of his perspectivism. What they sought, it may be argued, was not to propose a new doctrine or a new philosophy. It was not to escape the tradition, but merely to generate a new relation to, a new attitude toward, a few degrees of freedom within, that tradition. Hence, although it is correct in one sense to say that they share the tradition's problems, they are not guilty of certain fundamental philosophical gestures endemic to that tradition—for example, logocentrism (Derrida), the ascetic will to truth (Nietzsche), ontological priority (Buchler), metaphysics (Wittgenstein), or for that matter, representational thinking (Heidegger), Philosophy (Rorty), or dogmatism (Sextus)—and so there is another sense in which they do *not* share the tradition's problems.

This objection is partly right, but we should take it at its word. One cannot have it both ways. One cannot utilize a perspective, swear allegiance to it, protect it from all attacks, yet deny that it makes unique judgments from its own novel perspective that could be subjected to criticism, in other words, pretend that it has no content and so escapes the demand for validation. Either the work of each of our antifoundationalists constitutes a set of judgments whose meaning (whether assertive, exhibitive, or active) transcends the tradition, or it does not, or in some sense it does both. To the extent that it does *not* transcend the tradition, it shares the tradition's problems in the deepest and most complete sense. We cannot then say that it is more right or valid (in any sense) than the tradition. To the extent that it does transcend the tradition it is a judgment with positive content, with a meaning, that needs validation. It says or shows or does something of its own, something not found in the tradition, something whose validity is open to debate, however subtle and nontraditional that debate needs to be.

The Bounds of Philosophy

Philosophy, by opening itself to unlimited inquiry, to inquiring into the truth of every belief, opens itself to the demand for ultimate validation, validation that leaves no stone unturned, no presupposition unexamined, no belief untested. My third and principal conclusion is that *no belief can receive ultimate validation as true.* Thus philosophy cannot ultimately validate its judgments. But philosophy by its very nature demands such validation. Hence, philosophy, as unlimited inquiry, cannot issue in judgments that are assertively valid for it, judgments that ultimate inquiry can validate as true. Differently put, the validity of philosophical judgments is in principle *undecidable* by philosophy. In this sense, there is no philosophical knowledge at all.

This conclusion may seem absurd. Philosophers appear to know many things, for example, that Hobbes proposed a social contract, that Plato was Aristotle's teacher, that one plus one is two, that the daytime sky is blue. But from the outset I have inquired about characteristically or uniquely philosophical knowledge, about philosophy's ability to answer the kind of fundamental questions posed in the first chapter. Philosophers' knowledge of authors, texts, ideas, history and many other things is not at issue here.

The justification of my conclusion is based on nothing other than the nature of philosophy as ultimate inquiry. Insofar as it is philosophy's task to question every relevant belief, to ask for an ultimate validation of judgment, its cannot validate its judgments to its own satisfaction. All it can do is trace the presuppositions, the network of interconnected judgments, that form the validation of any belief in question. At some point further validation is unavailable. This is true of philosophy as a whole; the belief in the validity of philosophical judgments cannot be adequately validated as true. Inquiry cannot give an ultimate validation of itself. To use the language of contextualism, for ultimate or unlimited inquiry the context within which any analysis, interpretation, and justification is to be carried out must forever be in question. Whether a phenomenon, of whatever kind, is to be understood naturalistically, materialistically, mentalistically, scientifically, artistically, and so on, must itself be a nonnegligible issue within the task of inquiring into the phenomenon. I cannot imagine, then, how the task of inquiry could be completed with regard to any phenomenon, unless limits are placed on inquiry. But for ultimate inquiry such limits must always be in question.

That philosophical assertions cannot be adequately validated does not mean that we should abandon philosophy or even that we could abandon it. That philosophical inquiry is intrinsically indecisive would justify its abandonment only if making decisions were a criterion that philosophy must satisfy. But that is a *pragmatic* criterion whose validity is, for philosophy, a philosophical question on which decision is elusive.

My conclusion may seem half-right to those who agree that philosophy can never sufficiently validate any philosophical claim if ultimate validation is required, but who *deny* that it is required. The very fact that indecisiveness or inconclusiveness results from the demand for ultimate validation is, they suggest, reason to deny the validity of that demand. But I have argued against the alternative of limiting validation in Chapter Four that such limitation is satisfactory only if we do not subject its validity to serious question.

My conclusion may seem half-wrong to others, who see it as a admirably critical but unnecessarily tied to the traditional notion of philosophy as a search for publicly justifiable assertive validity. We will discuss this objection, which proposes some end for philosophy other than assertive truth, in the following section. To the extent that we disagree about the ends of philosophy, agreement on any issue within philosophy is elusive. I will ask only that those who employ a different notion of philosophy's aim ponder the implications of their views and be faithful to them.

My conclusion is consistent with at least part of our philosophical practice, even the practice of those who disagree with it. Part of the time we act as if philosophy necessarily implied a demand for ultimate validation. If this were not the case, then any philosophical discussion could legitimately be ended with the statement, "I have shown my claims to be valid in an incomplete sense, and because such validation is sufficient for truth-claims in philosophy, no further questioning of my claims is philosophically required." But we philosophers do ask more questions, questions for which we may have no answers. Why do we do this? We do it because as philosophers our search for validation is open-ended, meaning that we strive for a *completion*. I am claiming that this completion cannot be achieved, that ultimate inquiry is in principle indecisive.

The issue here is not the subjective experience of doubt. It is that the demand for validating assertions, a demand that is at the heart of inquiry, if allowed to roam without restriction across the landscape of belief, cannot be satisfied. A structural indecisiveness is built into inquiry itself and is normally masked by limitations. As ultimate inquiry, philosophy subjects every assertive judgment to an open-ended demand for inferential-evidential validation. Philosophy, understood as inquiry pushed to the extreme, as inquiry shorn of its normal constraints, can thus never be decisive. If utter indecisiveness is madness, then it is not misleading to say that philosophy is a kind of madness.

Now, justified or not, philosophers do reach conclusions all the time. They do so in four ways. The simplest way is to stop philosophizing, which means either to stop inquiring before one begins to ask ultimate questions and seek unlimited validation or, having reached some philosophical conclusion, to avoid questioning it. This, as I called it earlier, *unprincipled* abstention from philosophy must not attempt to justify itself, for that is the game it is refusing to play. This nonphilosophical option avoids responding without attempting to justify its avoidance in terms of the inquiry under way. The simple refusal to philosophize is always an option, and there is no philosophically adequate denial of its legitimacy.[2] That is, the philosophical justification of the obligation to philosophize or to continue philosophizing is as indecisive as any other philosophical justification.

We philosophers regularly take this option in the sense of ceasing inquiry for nonphilosophical reasons. We get tired, the book is long overdue, we must be published or we will perish, and so forth. Every research project must, after all, stop sometime. The philosophical significance of this unprincipled cessation is that it often protects the conclusions reached from further questioning—only temporarily, of course.

Philosophical inquiry is a grueling and unyielding path. As Peirce said of scientific inquiry, so it is true of philosophic inquiry that it requires the inquirer not primarily to establish true beliefs, but unceasingly to disconfirm all his or her current beliefs and hypotheses. Understood in this way, the philosopher must daily put the match to yesterday's conclusions. But unlike the scientist, the philosopher may take nothing for granted, at least not indefinitely. The philosopher is responsible to bring to bear on any phenomenon philosophical perspectives that are utterly foreign, because in philosophy there is no complete agreement on fundamental issues. Regarding almost all fundamental philosophical questions there are respectable, well-subscribed philosophical schools whose views on those questions are so different as to appear incomparable. But the philosopher is responsible eventually to consider all those views and thereby to question his or her most basic presuppositions about the problem under consideration and even about the nature and aims of his or her activity as a philosopher. This is a heavy load, this infinite and indefinite task. So to claim, "I have done enough, I need not consider any more alternatives, I affirm my conclusion and will question it no more" is a permanent temptation.

The three other ways for attaining conclusiveness are alternative interpretations of either the *degree* of validation required in philosophy, or the *meaning* of assertive validity, or the *kind* of validation required.

The first of these is recourse to the idea of limited or comparative validity I discussed in Chapter Four, which may inevitably refer to pragmatism. There I argued that, if philosophy is ultimate inquiry, this idea cannot be supported adequately.

Now, an important qualification must be made here. My conclusion does not disbar us from philosophical inquiry that accepts limits in any particular case; it prevents us from denying only the provisional nature—*provisional* being understood in a strong sense—of such limits by forgetting the ultimate obligations of philosophy. Here, the notion of philosophy as hypothesis has its place. It is entirely legitimate to argue that, given certain assumptions or certain limits placed on the scope of inquiry, a conclusion follows as true. The conclusion is accepted as true provisionally, in the sense that its truth is dependent on the validity of other beliefs that we have not validated. Provisional truth in this sense does not merely mean a partial or incomplete truth, or a truth that lacks certainty, which later inquiry might conceivably achieve. For the point is that later inquiry may just as well overturn this alleged 'truth.' Provisional truth is hypothetical, it is a truth *if* something else is true, where we do not know if the latter is true.

The second way is simply to turn to antirealism. Antirealism appears to make complete validation attainable by making validity relative to the inquirer's perspective, community, purposes, or needs. I say 'appears' because antirealism is, like any doctrine, open to unending question, as would be any philosophical view that was claimed to be true in a realist sense. Nevertheless, antirealism is sometimes used to conclude philosophical inquiry, on the assumption that a validity relative to ourselves (our judgments, communities, etc.) would be completely achievable. So, for example, if truth is relative to convention, we may be able to fix convention and so cease to question the validity of our knowledge.

But, as mentioned earlier, the discussions of Nietzsche, Wittgenstein, Buchler, Derrida, and Rorty have shown that antirealism faces intractable problems. The first is that any positive statement of any powerful form of antirealism risks undermining its own truth value. Second, although self-contradiction can be circumvented by various metaphilosophical strategies, especially in the hands of masters like Nietzsche, Wittgenstein, and Derrida, these strategies do nothing to *validate* antirealism. Negative and implicit forms of antirealism remain philosophical choices or decisions whose only justification is that they avoid some of the problems of realism. But given that antirealism has its own problems, this is not much of a justification. The subtle antirealisms of the thinkers we have studied leave us in just as much trouble as realism.

The final option is to introduce into inquiry, or more precisely, to fail to isolate one's inquiry from, nonassertive modes of validation; that is, pragmatic and aesthetic modes. This means having recourse to the idea that, for example, a view must be true because we find that we must act as if it were true, or because it is most consistent with our practical purposes, or because it is most satisfying or novel, or because when combined with other beliefs it makes of our lives a beautiful whole. In this way, inquiry is not strictly distinguished from other forms of query; it is, so to speak, *embedded in query*. We will discuss this option in the following section.

My conclusion leaves me with a kind of skepticism or *fallibilism*, one shorn of Peircean convergence. This kind of fallibilism is not, however, part of the scientist's view of his or her work, as Peirce claimed; rather it is part of the *philosopher's* view of that work. A radical or extreme fallibilism is incumbent upon those who inquire ultimately, not upon those who accept certain limitations on either the scope of inquiry (e.g., given by a scientific subject matter or method that rules some things out of the scope of inquiry) or the extent of the validation required. Of course, Peirce emphasized the continuity of science with philosophy. Philosophy is an extension of inquiry that includes the questioning of the possibility of knowledge, the meaning and value of truth, the validity of the laws of thought—all of which fall outside the bounds of the natural sciences as normally understood. Philosophy does more or less follow what Peirce described as the method of science, but this method is quite broad. It would be more correct to say that what Peirce calls "science" is inquiry itself, of which natural science and philosophy are kinds. At any rate, philosophy, even in Peirce's view, although it must conform to the experimental results of current science, need not accept the metaphysics or cosmology associated with that science.

It is striking that Peirce, the inventor of pragmatism, could also insist on the absolutely unlimited nature of inquiry, which ought never be "blocked" by certainty, and on the utter impracticality of this enterprise. He made it clear (particularly in his "Detached Ideas on Vitally Important Topics") that the search for truth has no practical value. Science inhibits the practical spirit, because its primary aim is to disconfirm beliefs, never to establish them. In a sense, my conclusion constitutes an endorsement of Peirce's fallibilism and his view of inquiry's impracticality or indecisiveness, coupled with a criticism of his belief that these views are compatible with his doubt-belief theory, his pragmatism, his convergence realism, and his cosmology. They are not compatible; the latter restrict the former. Fallibilism unchained admits such incompatibility and hence is uncertain about philosophical judgments, the best current science, and even the meaning, value, and truth of inquiry. It is not sure that we "must" believe in the truth of the products of inquiry.

One may wonder whether this unchained fallibilism is in effect a modified Pyrrhonist skepticism. There is a difference: the Pyrrhonist-Rortyan position rests on a problematic, ultimate, philosophical judgment. For any attempt, like Sextus's and Rorty's, to make a distinction between the meaningful and the meaningless, the "real" judgments and the "unreal," the apparent ("evident") and the superapparent ("dogmatic" or Philosophical) is an epistemological project of an entirely traditional kind. It must fall under its own knife. In other words, Pyrrho is a dogmatist and Rorty is a Philosopher, in the same sense that Wittgenstein's work is nonsensical by his own criteria, in the same sense that Derrida admits that deconstruction can be deconstructed. For a radical fallibilism, any proposed distinction between the philosophical and the nonphilosophical must be subjected to the same demand for validation as any other philosophical claim.

The issue here is not to what extent our everyday and scientific assertive judgments are true in a realist sense; it is to what extent philosophy can *know* they are true. Here I can only agree with the nonfoundationalists that the validation of all knowledge must be limited, not ultimate. In other words, if we subject the assertive knowledge of everyday life and science to unlimited inquiry, to philosophical questioning, we cannot find complete or ultimate validation. This of course may not bother us in everyday life or in scientific practice. Here an argument about the standards and criteria of sufficient validation would naturally ensue. But that very argument would be an unlimited or ultimate philosophic argument.

Let us take as an example a reasonable description of our epistemic predicament. Joseph Margolis opens his book, *Pragmatism Without Foundations*, with the statement that "We cannot seriously believe that science utterly misrepresents the way the world is; and we cannot accurately determine the fit between the two."[3] The first phrase describes what we think we know, the second indicates our philosophical incapacity. This formulation is admirable, but Margolis admits that these two "intuitions" are not "altogether irresistible." And he is right, for philosophically, this very reasonable statement is utterly questionable. It is probably true that most living human beings think that modern science, insofar as it belies their traditional and religious beliefs, *mis*represents the world and does so utterly, if "utterly" can mean "fundamentally." It is probably true that most of "us," that is, most recipients of modern education, cannot seriously believe that science utterly misrepresents the world, but then, the vast majority of that "us" probably fail to understand most of what modern science claims about the world.

Take as a simple example the belief that *I will die*. What could be more obvious and less dubious? Only a fool would doubt it, I am tempted to say. But, although the belief in one's own impending death appears to be absolutely certain to secularized individuals, hundreds of millions, perhaps billions of people believe that it is absolutely certain that *I will not die*, that my spiritual being, which is my true being, will survive my physical death. Now, truth not being a matter of majority rule, the fact that so many people reject mortality does not make it false. However, it ought to temper our confidence in the indubitability of our judgment. It ought to make us wonder whether an issue of cultural and philosophical differences, an issue that is not decidable by science and common observation, lies behind this apparently noncontroversial bit of inductive knowledge. This does not mean we know nothing, but rather, that *once we think philosophically we cannot be sure* that we do. For philosophy as ultimate inquiry is precisely a liberation of inquiry from its usual constraints, a liberation that necessarily entails a demand for open-ended or ultimate validation.

The combined force of my two conclusions, then, is this: There is no philosophically valid escape from philosophy *and* no answer to philosophical questions that is valid from the point of view of philosophy. In other words, to accept the task of philosophy is to accept an obligation that cannot be fulfilled.

Episteme, Praxis, Poiesis

I have throughout this book understood philosophy as inquiry, hence as assertive query whose norm is truth. It might be objected against this study that truth is not a property of assertions or propositions, or that philosophy is not ultimately or solely concerned with assertive truth, or that truth is to be understood in a very different way than it has been here. These objections open a complex field of considerations. Before pursuing them we must begin at a more general level to survey the various ways that philosophy and truth can be interpreted.[4]

What, after all, is 'philosophical'? What is the subject of the term *philosophy*? 'Philosophy' and 'philosophical' have referred to all of the following: a way of experiencing the world (e.g., the sense of wonder); the state of being a certain kind of person (e.g., contemplative or wise or mystical or one who honors the better argument); the condition of having a certain role in society (e.g., the gadfly or the educator); or a kind of query or search for something. Philosophy can be all these things. Most familiar to us, it can be a search for wisdom, what Aristotle called *phronesis*, an attempt at being a wise human being, an aim distinct from the search for knowledge that can be said and publicly justified as true. Philosophy as query can be viewed as having various aims: as improving society via knowledge; as satisfying needs for redemption; as conceptual clarification useful in other forms of research; as creating novel possibilities for living; as returning us to lived experience; or as gaining truth for its own sake.

Even if we restrict ourselves to the definition of *philosophy* in terms of the pursuit of truth, the situation remains complex, because 'true' and 'truth' can be predicated of many things. 'Truth' has been understood as a characterization of things themselves, phenomena, experience, judgments, propositions, or persons. One might argue that any one of these meanings is primary. For example, Heidegger's *aletheia* makes truth primarily a condition of things or phenomena, as opposed to propositions. Nietzsche's analysis of truth makes it dependent on "truthfulness" or honesty; that is, a trait of persons. In nonphilosophic usage, in various languages the word for 'true' is often applied to persons, things, and experiences to mean "genuine," "real," "actual," "loyal," "honest," and so on. Whatever the primary locus of truth is, we are presently limiting ourselves to the question whether philosophy can be true in the sense of making true judgments.

Even if philosophy is primarily inquiry, the attempt to say what is true and why it is true, it is almost never solely inquiry. Philosophers frequently make recourse to exhibitive and active judgment in their work; nonassertive validation typically enters into the stream of assertive argument. This is a stronger claim than saying that all works of inquiry function exhibitively or actively. Any assertion can be taken in an exhibitive or active way; hence a mathematical proof may strike us as "elegant." It is a more significant matter if the elegance becomes a stated reason offered for accepting the proof. It is this kind of case I mean, where exhibitive and active validation make a difference to the philosophical reasoning in question.

Like other inquirers, philosophers seek to maintain the separation of inquiry from the other modes of query. Entirely to fail to do so would be to allow the beauty or the goodness of any judgment to determine its acceptance; it would be to merge inquiry with art or morality. Some degree of abstraction or insulation is necessary for inquiry to be inquiry. At times philosophers achieve a more or less strict insulation of their work as inquiry and appear to denude it of any exhibitive and active elements, or better, to prevent such elements from affecting the direction and progress of their inquiry. But this insulation is never complete for long. Inevitably, the thinker enters a phase of his or her work where a dedifferentiation, or a failure to differentiate, takes place. At such times the nonassertive meaning of the philosopher's propositions affect the point, the validation, the direction of the work. The philosopher's propositions then have a meaning that is due not only to what they assert, but also to their active or exhibitive functioning, and this multiple functioning endows the judgments with a validity, for the author or audience, that the proposition could not have as a pure assertion on solely inferential-evidential grounds. Thus decisiveness is achieved.

This raises a host of problems. Is the attempt to isolate inquiry from the other modes a hopeless mistake? If separation is problematic, what then is the status of truth? Apparently, modern Western thought has been concerned to effect and perfect this isolation. Theories of modern Western "rationalization," the most famous of which belongs to Max Weber, have made the differentiation of the spheres of science, art, and morality a defining characteristic of modernity and an necessary condition for rationality.[5] One could argue that inquiry ceases to be rational to the extent that assertions are evaluated in terms of their moral rightness, practical expediency, or aesthetic satisfaction, despite the fact that we all recognize some role for pragmatic and aesthetic factors in inquiry, even in science, and certainly in philosophy. Differentiation of some kind seems indispensable.

The role of the nonassertive may be more subtle and far-reaching than is usually supposed. Certainly, few philosophers assert that "The following conclusion is true because it is beautiful. . . . ," or that "Moral obligation requires that I believe that the following is true. . . ." Nevertheless, it would be difficult to deny that any particular conclusion in a particular research effort is made more convincing and appealing to the researcher by its neatness, its symmetry with respect to related ideas, its harmonious place in an overall structure, or its representation of the subject matter as having those properties. Philosophical language is filled with metaphors that appeal to us aesthetically, even, as Buchler pointed out, in the work of philosophers who explicitly set out to denude philosophy of metaphor.[6] Likewise, few philosophers fail to imagine the practical consequences of their assertions for themselves, their profession, the community of inquirers, or human beings in general. It is sometimes possible to distinguish philosophies and philosophical movements according to whether they *explicitly* give a prominent role to nonassertive judgment in philosophic inquiry. Some thinkers have explicitly reformulated the search for truth in ways that interpret truth, knowledge, or the philosophical project as exhibitive or active in an important sense.

We could understand philosophy's ultimate *aim*, its *norm* of validity, and the *criteria* or condition for satisfying that norm, *each* in at least three different ways relative to the modes of judgment.[7] Simplifying the resulting wealth of combinations, it is possible to regard the function and validity of philosophical judgments as consisting of three types. The validity may be provided by the sheer quality of what is exhibited or expressed in an experienced something, where philosophy's task is a construction of something that exhibits this quality. It may be constituted by the judgment's adequate representation of the real, that is, of what obtains independent of judgment, as in the classically realist notion of science. It may, last, be found in the judgment's relation to human action, hence purpose and need, which are always social. These three perspectives can be applied at various levels in an overlapping fashion, so their use does not imply that only three possible interpretations of philosophy exist.

Thus, we may understand the ideal of a purely assertive inquiry as making the aim of philosophy the assertion of the most comprehensive or complete knowledge, truth being the norm of validity for philosophical assertions (i.e., they are valid or acceptable if true), with the condition of a sentence's truth being some kind of correspondence to what is judged. Any departure from this tripartite standard would entail a partial introduction of exhibitive and active modes into philosophy; there are many degrees and levels of exhibitive or active involvement. It would be one thing to make the aim of philosophy the achievement of an aesthetic quality, another to make the norm of valid philosophical judgments an aesthetic quality (i.e., they are valid if beautiful), another to make truth their norm but to conceive of truth in aesthetic terms, for example, to see truth as the achievement of an exhibitive relation to the objects of judgment (i.e., aesthetic quality is the criterion of truth). Likewise, it would be one thing to make social improvement the aim of philosophy, another to make goodness or utility the norm of valid philosophical judgments (i.e., they are valid if useful or good), another to make truth their norm but to conceive of truth in pragmatic terms, or to see truth as the actualization of possibilities in the objects of judgment (i.e., goodness or utility is the criterion of truth). Further, one might try to combine the modes and norms of judgment, to understand philosophical validity as *omnivalent*, as indifferently or equally a matter of truth, goodness, and aesthetic quality, as valid in an undifferentiated sense. For example, if wisdom were to be conceived not as primarily practical, but as somehow equally assertive and active, this would be an attempt to transcend the differentiation of assertive truth and practical goodness.

Some of the most important distinctions between modes of philosophic thought in the twentieth century can be interpreted in terms of these three perspectives. Heidegger's description of phenomenological method in *Being and Time*, his account of truth as *aletheia* or unconcealment, and his later notion of the task of thinking, present the goal of thought as attending to and appreciating a nonrepresentational experiential "truth," a task more akin to poetry than to science.[8] Dewey regards philosophic inquiry as a way of reconstructing experience and social life, hence as inherently active (which is not to imply that he ignores the aesthetic or "consummatory"). Most philosophers continue to endorse, at least explicitly, the assertion of what is true about the world as the aim of philosophy. But even given this endorsement, how is truth, or the criterion that indicates when we have found the truth, to be interpreted? Is truth to be interpreted as a property of a judgment that adequately represents the real, or as something given in preinferential experience, or as related to socialized human purpose? One may claim that the aim of philosophy is to say what is true in a realist sense, as did Peirce, but also claim that the truth of such sayings is established pragmatically or actively. The question is, then, What is the final context, the last horizon, in which the philosopher locates the philosophic search for truth?

I am suggesting that at least three such horizons or contexts are dominant in twentieth century philosophy. Each construes knowledge, or the goal of philosophy, differently. Of course, there are disparate views within each of these horizons and disparate versions of the horizons themselves. Each horizon can be applied within and to the other, so that the three overlap at different levels of argument. Nevertheless, regarding most recent Western philosophers, I believe it is usually possible at any point in their arguments to identify, lying behind their judgments, one of these three perspectives informing their most basic descriptions or images of the philosophic task and the knowledge it seeks. Certainly my account of them can be only general and stereotypical.

One perspective can be called *phenomenological* or *phenomenal* or *exhibitive*. It understands the aim of philosophy as *poiesis* and *aisthesis*, as a making (*poiesis*) that expresses the pre-inferential immediate qualities for experience (*aisthesis*).[9] This phenomenological perspective can be formulated in either "subjective" or "objective" terms; that is, in terms of experience and intentionality, on the one hand, or in terms of the unconcealment or showing of things or phenomena, on the other.[10] A second perspective can be called *assertive* or *representationalist*. For it the aim of philosophy is *episteme*, science, to utter important true propositions about things, 'true' meaning something like adequate representation or correspondence. A third perspective can be called *social* or *pragmatic*. It understands the aim of philosophy as a refinement of *praxis*, as reconstructing or re-creating the relation of human beings to each other and the world. The object of knowledge is related to human being and not merely by the act of knowledge; hence this perspective is intrinsically anthropocentric and, like all human action, social. It can be interpreted in a "subjective" or "objective" way; that is, truth may be understood in terms of purposes or as the actualization of the possibilities of the things known in and by the process of knowing.

One way of describing these horizons is through the character of the fundamental distinctions they make. For the representationalist, there is always the binary distinction between the real and what is not real, the idiosyncratic, the relativistic, the illusory. The values of realist judgments are determined by the binary opposition, true/false. The pragmatic perspective is similarly binary in its norms: good or bad, right or wrong, successful or unsuccessful, fecund or barren, leading to the future or leading to nothing. The phenomenological perspective, by contrast, is unconcerned with purpose or with reality as something independent. When the theorists of the real erect a construct and declare it to be the cause of all experience or phenomena, the phenomenologist does not dispute the claim. Rather, he or she regards the realist's efforts as more phenomena to be exhibited. In this sense, the phenomenological task is descriptive and nonnormative, except insofar as aesthetic phenomena themselves are always value laden and hence compelling. Philosophical statements are meant not primarily to represent but to express or evoke, to call up something that is not an "object" in the representationalist or scientific sense. Phenomenology is not about saying or doing, it is about seeing, making, and showing.[11]

Because I obviously connect the phenomenological and pragmatic perspectives to the contemporary philosophic movements of the same names, I might be expected to identify the assertive-representationalist horizon with analytic, post-Fregean, or Anglo-American philosophy.[12] But this is not quite right. *Episteme* is, I suggest, the dominant perspective in philosophy *generally*. Most philosophers regard most of their linguistic judgments as attempts to say the truth in something like a representationalist sense; this includes most phenomenologists and pragmatists, at least part of the time. The latter wish to augment or contextualize their assertions within a larger horizon that is not representationalist or epistemic. What is usually called *analytic* philosophy, stemming from Frege, Moore, and Russell, is that form of contemporary philosophy that seeks *most completely* to separate the assertive, representationalist function from the others. What distinguishes it from pragmatism and phenomenology, within this scheme, is not that it is assertive but that it has often sought to be exclusively and purely so (although this is certainly not the sole difference among these "schools" of thought).

These are massive generalizations about idealized stereotypes, to be sure. I insist only that there is at least some truth to them, and that amount of truth is significant. One often finds that, in a philosophic discussion among so-called analytic, pragmatic, and phenomenological philosophers, at a certain point in the conversation the very aims of the philosophers diverge and, necessarily connected with these aims, their views of what counts as knowledge. During a discussion of some particular view, when the analyst insists that no assertive validation of the view in question is available, and so the view cannot legitimately be asserted, the pragmatist will imagine what effect it would have on the human future if that view were accepted and may accept the view on that basis. The phenomenologist may object to the same view on the basis of the qualitative immediacies that are occluded by that view. At a certain point in the discussion of a judgment, the analyst's focus is on the assertion and its representation of what is judged, the pragmatist's is on the future world in which human action will be guided by the judgment, the phenomenologist's is on the qualitative integrity of the given as expressed by the judgment.

It is possible to tell a story about the development of recent Western philosophy consonant with this tripartite characterization. It is only one among many possible stories; I suggest it as one thread of a more complex truth.

One can see the second half of the nineteenth century as a critical period in which an older tradition of philosophy came into question. The older tradition was systematic, it understood philosophy as aspiring to comprehend the intellectual aims of humankind in a complete system. This tradition had most recently been epitomized by Hegel. Younger philosophers (Feuerbach, Marx, Kierkegaard, Comte, J. S. Mill, Nietzsche, Frege, Husserl, and others) attacked this older tradition in different ways, and important schools of twentieth century philosophy followed the lead, seeing their own work as a revolutionary departure from the older tradition (the latter being construed differently in each case). For Russell the anachronistic tradition was idealism; for Husserl, naturalism (hence psychologism); for Dewey, dualism or transcendentalism.[13]

So far this story is not unfamiliar. I will add a novel sub-plot. The older tradition made recourse to exhibitive and active judgments and norms within a primarily assertive inquiry. At crucial moments assertive inquiry was augmented by exhibitive or active validation. Thus it was possible in the older philosophical tradition to say that science must be limited for the sake of morality, or to assert that an idealist cosmology must be true for the same reason, or to use aesthetic criteria of harmony and perfection to justify a conclusion, or to ascribe moral and aesthetic qualities to being itself (e.g., to call reality a "perfection"). Of course the theocentric nature of traditional philosophical thought was a crucial factor here. From the early Middle Ages at least through Hegel the Ground of Being was understood as providing not only existence, but the possibility of knowledge, the basis for morality, and the aesthetic completeness of things. The very idea of God showed that, at some level, the modes of judgment and the ideals of thought—truth, goodness, beauty— must be or have been unified. I am suggesting, in other words, that a certain amount of unashamed omnivalence, or fusion of the modes of validity, a conviction that goodness and beauty were connected with truth, was a longstanding component of traditional, pre-1870s philosophy. To be sure, this omnivalence was not explicit. Truth reigned as the end of philosophy. But it was a truth that was interpreted in harmony with beauty and goodness.

What happened in the second half of the nineteenth century, so this story goes, was a double rebellion. There was a rebellion against the traditional omnivalence by those who wanted a fully differentiated inquiry purified of exhibitive and active validation, hence more like science and mathematics. The second rebelled against the traditional philosophy for a different reason: It raised doubts about realistic, representational truth and sought to put inquiry more completely in the service of exhibition or action. Hence it also rejected the other rebels, the pure, quasi-scientific philosophers. The first rebellion, inspired by the success of science, mathematics, and the new logic, eventually became idealized in Anglo-Saxon or analytic philosophy, the philosophy inspired by Frege, Moore, and Russell. The second rebellion was actually a number of more or less simultaneous insurrections that eventually became two camps, the phenomenological or existentialist camp and pragmatist and/or process philosophy camp.[14]

The two branches of the second rebellion developed in stages. Regarding the phenomenological tradition, the initial move was to conceive of philosophy's aim as the true description of uninterpreted experience (as for Husserl).[15] For this phase, the mistake of traditional philosophy was its importation of questions of reality, ontological status, and causal explanation into an arena that ought to be merely descriptive. In this view the new analytic philosophy, aping science, made the same mistake, albeit in nontranscendental terms. The aim of philosophy is to return us to experience, to the phenomena themselves.

In time, however, a chasm appeared to open in this tradition between the desire to *return* to the phenomena and the means of *describing* the phenomena. Can true linguistic descriptions of prelinguistic experience be provided? Or does the language of inquiry inevitably modify the phenomena? Is the real truth of experience captured by our descriptions of it? The result was the emergence of the view that philosophy ought to be a nonrepresentational evocation or exhibition of experience. Here, with great simplification, our story puts the later Heidegger. If the proper form of philosophic thinking is akin to poetry, then philosophy does not seek to mirror experience but to *be* a kind of experience.[16]

In the other branch of the second rebellion, philosophy and inquiry in general were interpreted as activity. Hence the criteria of 'truth,' the putative end of inquiry, must be active and related to purpose (said James). One can then interpret inquiry as either serving needs, as actualizing or completing its objects, or as fulfilling human existence.[17]

In short, this story attributes to the last hundred years or so a radical new differentiation of the functions and norms of judgment between philosophical schools. Of course, the awareness of the distinctness of the modes of judgment is not recent. The ability to distinguish experimental, inferential, evidential reasoning from artistic and moral-practical validation is very old. What has changed is the role that inquiry has been given in human culture, the degree of independence accorded it. As far as we know, in the Western tradition the Greeks expanded inquiry's role beyond engineering and other practical matters to determine the ultimate conditions of existence, a task previously entrusted to art and religion. Since that time, and especially in the modern era, the right of inquiry to determine judgment about ultimate matters has been accepted, albeit within certain limits; namely, that it be augmented by religious, moral, and aesthetic considerations. What happened in the late nineteenth century was, among other things, a growing dissatisfaction with the traditional balance of the modes of query within philosophy. Some demanded the purification of inquiry: Let inquiry stand on its own, they demanded, 'though the heavens fall. Others, driven by a different view of the role of philosophy in culture and life, sought another balance of the three modes.[18]

Whatever the merits of my story, I propose as my fourth conclusion that the three horizons for philosophical activity are *irreducible and inescapable*, that we cannot transcend or integrate them without presuming and giving priority to one of them. I am suggesting that the division of twentieth century Western philosophy into divergent "traditions," "cultures" or "styles" reflects a deep, unbridgeable, and undecidable difference. This does not mean that the partial rapprochement now apparently taking place among the three is impossible or undesirable. It means that any such meeting must take place either on the basis of an assumption of one of the three perspectives or at a level not sufficiently deep to engage the fundamental disagreement among them.

The choice between the three is undecidable because it is a choice about what philosophy is, what one expects to get from philosophy, what philosophy is supposed to contribute to culture. Either one understands the aim of philosophy as the assertion of the representational truth, or the actualization or reconstruction of the world or experience, or the exhibition or embodiment of the immediate qualities of experience. Philosophy is *episteme*, or *praxis*, or *poiesis*; it is most like *science*, or *practice*, or *art*; it tries to *represent* experience, or to *reshape* experience, or to *be* an experience; its valid products are either *true*, or *good*, or *qualitatively satisfying*; truth is either *irreducible* or describable in *practical* or *aesthetic* terms; the criterion of truth is either *evidential*, or *consequential*, or *consummatory*.

The three perspectives can be combined; we combine them all the time. But they cannot be reconciled or synthesized. Any apparent synthesis could only be a dedifferentiation of the functions of judgment. The goal of philosophical query would then be explicitly omnivalent validity. The omnivalence that we usually find in contemporary philosophies is catch as catch can; it appears when an inquiry turns to aesthetic or pragmatic validation at key points. It is not explicit or consistent. An explicit and consistent omnivalence would mean nothing less than ceasing to prize either the true, the good or the beautiful more primarily than the others as values to be used in evaluating philosophical utterance. This would not make philosophy into art, for art is not omnivalent. It would make philosophy simultaneously and equally into art, science, and action.

The fact of the three horizons raises a new question about the present study; namely, in what horizon does *it* function, and does this mean that its validity is necessarily limited? Clearly, my study has aspired to *episteme*. I have defined knowledge in terms of representational truth and have sought evidential-inferential validation for my own philosophical claims. I have treated my own task as a search for assertive knowledge of what obtains independent of my judgments. I have written as if the ultimate aim of philosophy were to avoid false beliefs, to accept only those beliefs that are inferentially-evidentially validated. I have tried to engage philosophy as pure inquiry.

It is in this context that I can finally address certain objections that have been looming since the outset. For, by assuming that philosophy is primarily inquiry aimed at a publicly justifiable truth, I have opened this study to the charge of irrelevance by those who reject that assumption in the first place. This rejection presumably comes in two forms, as denying either that philosophy is the search for true representations, as opposed to goodness or aesthetic quality, or that truth is to be interpreted a norm of publicly available assertion, as opposed to, say, success or aesthetic quality.

For the pragmatist, philosophy inevitably and legitimately serves the aims of social reconstruction. The hypothesis of a unity of ultimate perspectives would presumably aid action, whereas a belief in their ultimate irreconcilability would likely inhibit it.[19] Philosophy is a doing; it is absurd to put philosophy in service of skepticism or the inhibition of belief (as James argued against Clifford).[20] The aim of philosophy is not the assertion of truths that have no practical relevance but a wisdom that is not reducible to a list of assertions. Conclusions that make such wisdom impossible fall short of philosophy. A plausible harmonization of the three perspectives would be more valid than the pessimistic claim of irreconcilability. The burden is on the critic (that is, on me) to show how the proposal of irreducible irreconcilable horizons is consonant with his own actions in the real world, which actions imply at least a hypothetical unity of belief.

The phenomenologist would presumably find my inquiry irrelevant. For philosophic wisdom in phenomenological perspective is

sensitivity to that which is prior to either the abstractions of inference or the *techne* of social manipulation. The philosopher seeks
knowledge in the sense of seeing and tries to share this seeing by
crafting language that shows, lights up, the phenomena for others to
see. The function of philosophy is to enhance a kind of knowledge
that cannot successfully be captured by assertions that purport to
"correctly represent" what is as "objects." My talk of inhibiting belief
in the unity of the ultimate perspectives is inadequate on two levels:
as a way of showing the phenomena it obscures more than it reveals,
and it fails to understand itself as *poiesis* enhancing *aisthesis*.

My response to these objections and their implied alternative
understandings of the end or aim of philosophy is twofold. I question
whether the denial of the primary obligation and concern of the
philosopher as inquirer—to say what is true and why it is true—is
entirely genuine or consistent. Does the pragmatist believe that *it is
true that* the aim of philosophy is or ought to be the reconstruction of
experience? Does the phenomenologist believe that the judgment
that truth is *aletheia* is a true assertion? Presumably the utterances
of those who seek an alternative to philosophy as primarily
assertive inquiry have multiple functions. Some of their talk is
meant as assertive, presumably, and must be interpreted as truth-
claims, whereas some is meant as exhibitive and active and ought
not be interpreted as truth-claims. Obviously, this raises the problem of the relationship between the two kinds of judgments within
the context of their discourse as a whole, especially if that discourse
is claimed primarily to be nonassertive or to be justified nonas-
sertively. Mixing functions of judgment is by no means illegitimate,
but it does raise the question of whether assertive truth is really,
that is, consistently, being subordinated to some other norm. If it *is*,
if representation, proposition, assertion, and truth are displaced
from their determining, guiding role in the query of philosophy,
then this decision must be consistent. One cannot attack these
notions while implicitly offering one's attack *as true* in the senses
thereby rejected. To repeat: One cannot claim to win a baseball
game with a touchdown.

To a *consistent* avoidance of philosophy as inquiry I can make
only one response: that we differ on a matter that in principle cannot be decided, because resolution would require that we regard inquiry and the kind of validation appropriate to it in the same way,
but that is just the issue between us. I must add, however, that I
regard these critics not as wrong, but as different, as engaged in a
project whose purpose and standard of adequacy are different from

mine. Here I tread on the proper subject of my final section, the application of my conclusions to my own work.

Closing My Circle

We began this book by asking philosophical or ultimate questions. This led us to ask about the possibility of giving answers to those questions that we could know to be true, to question the possibility of philosophical knowledge.

The first part of this chapter's answer to that question was that doubt has been cast both on the attempt to justify philosophy by limiting the demands of philosophical validation and on the claim that we cannot make true philosophical judgments about what is real; that is, both nonfoundationalism and antiphilosophy have been shown to be problematic. The second part of our answer was that, although we *may* have true realist philosophical judgments, we do not and cannot *know* that we have them. Principled attempts to dissolve, resolve, or solve philosophical questions cannot be successful; that is, they remain philosophical, hence problematic.

In the preceding section we added another element; namely, that we cannot philosophically decide what is the right criterion for a philosophical answer, there being at least three different notions of what the *end* of philosophy might be. These different notions are determined by the status of inquiry and its norm, truth, within the broader category of query. If we do not accept the strict independence of truth and inquiry from goodness and activity, or from quality and exhibition, then philosophical judgment *can* be validated, albeit not simply or strictly as true.

So we are left with something like this. Whether our philosophical assertions are true or false, we cannot know that they are. No philosophical decision about validity—that is, a decision that a philosophical claim is ultimately true or valid—is philosophically justifiable if philosophy is ultimate inquiry. This includes the philosophical decision to cease philosophizing. Philosophical questions, of the kind I asked in the opening chapter, are in principle undecidable by philosophical inquiry. We remain within the philosophical *kirkos* even when we argue against it.

Having come to a conclusion, I must hold myself to the same standard I have applied to others. I must ask how my inquiry judges itself. What is the result of applying the conclusions I have reached in this chapter to themselves?

My conclusion is the apparently decisive philosophical claim that philosophical claims cannot be validated as true, at least in a sense acceptable to philosophy. This is not a self-contradiction, for its truth does not imply its falsity. But it is *self-compromising*, because if it is true, then it cannot achieve ultimate validation. The validation I have given my conclusion, and could give it, will always be incomplete. And this incompleteness is not innocuous: it means that assent to my conclusion is *not* philosophically justified insofar as philosophy is ultimate inquiry. It means that my conclusion cannot count as philosophical knowledge, because it declares philosophical knowledge unavailable. For inquiry, then, my conclusion ought strictly to have no weight, no convincing power.

It may be possible however to validate my conclusion in a non-assertive sense. To put it strategically, in uttering my conclusion I have in effect marked the bounds of philosophy, as others have done, albeit in my own way. This conclusion achieves, in my judgment, a construction that is both aesthetically satisfying and pragmatically useful. The picture it presents is that inquiry has its own distinct nature, which we ought not confuse with active and exhibitive considerations, that is, we ought not mix the three without recognizing that we are mixing them. Inquiry, even without limits, has its bounds. It is bounded by the nature of assertive validation, by the rules of inquiring and publicly validating judgments as true in a minimally realist sense.

It may be that the various powers of human judging cannot achieve satisfaction independently. Inquiry is unable to complete its own project, because ultimately it is but one of the powers of judgment, methodically expanded. If it is true that the comprehensive expression and achievement of human query, which is to say *culture*, presumes the continuity of the three modes of judgment, then it would seem that those modes cannot achieve their own completions independently. They cannot be, so to speak, internally complete, complete independent of the other two. Consequently, the method of inquiry could not complete its task, the achievement of ultimate or philosophical truth, independent of active and exhibitive judgment.

This is perhaps jointly a Nietzschean, a Deweyan, and a Weberian consideration. For just as Nietzsche claimed that the sole justification of the world is aesthetic, Dewey argued that in the aesthetic dimension human experience and even nature itself are completed. This view expresses the conviction that the aspiration to knowledge embodied in philosophical inquiry must ultimately be coordinated with a heightening and a unification of the totality of the powers of human being. At the same time, as Max Weber argued regarding modernity, the differentiation of those powers required by progress in any cultural medium entails a permanent tension.

Certainly my employment of this view can no more be justified than can Nietzsche's or Dewey's. That the conclusion of my inquiry coheres with this picture does not make my conclusion *true*. Nor can I justify my truth-claim to practical or aesthetic validity here. Any such justification would be indecisive with respect to its truth. My aim, at this point, is solely to make the values operative in my judgment explicit, to recognize the pragmatic and aesthetic values that are at work at the edge of my inquiry as it shades into query.

At the same time, although any achievement of decisiveness through the incorporation of nonassertive elements is a kind of completion, it is not a completion of *philosophy's* task, as long as philosophy is primarily inquiry. For the query taking place would, to the degree that it is nonassertive, no longer be inquiry aimed at truth. It is presumably essential to the function of philosophy, like any cultural medium (e.g., art, science, religion), that it select and restrict the modes of judgment abroad in human life. Query, culture, in short, *human life is omnivalent*. That is, all the modes of judgment and validity are proper to culture and human life. Inquiry is not life's sole method, truth is not life's only goal. Nor can we point to a single function that life or culture must serve to determine its one proper or primary modality and norm. Each cultural medium, as a part, a manifestation, a servant of life or culture, must restrict judgmental validity. Otherwise it would presumably cease to perform any special function for life, cease to fulfill its raison d'être, and would merely reproduce the multifarious interests, methods, and norms found in life or culture as a whole.

Here we are faced with the final undecidability, the deepest source of philosophy's frustration. Presumably inquiry, and philosophy as one of its species, must pursue a goal that is only one of life's aims or values; that is, truth. But philosophy occasionally decides that inquiry, assertion, truth, representation, and public validation are not enough, not sufficient to its ultimate task. It periodically feels that some dimension of life or experience—the aesthetic, the soteriological, the expressive, the constructive, the practical—has been left out, not as object, but as method, as interest, as mode of judgment.[21] It seeks to incorporate other cultural methods, to express a larger share of the totality of human interests and energies, perhaps to embody all of them. Philosophy then seeks to *encompass and epitomize life.* This is not a universal and necessary concern; there are philosophical schools and methods that eschew this open-ended, omnivalent demand.[22] Nevertheless, its recurrence and insistence shows that philosophy is always open or subject to the demand, even when it is not heeded.

Since Kant, we are familiar with the claim that philosophy cannot grasp the whole because the totality of things is not a thing, not a possible object of inquiry. This claim is echoed in the contextualism of Wittgenstein and Buchler. My current point is that there is an additional problem in philosophy's attempt to grasp everything, a problem of aim or method, not object. A philosophy that attempts to grasp the whole must attempt to embody the whole range of human judgment. It must recognize that truth is only one aim of judgment and somehow register in its thinking the force of active and exhibitive concerns.

Unfortunately, to the extent philosophy would succeed in such a grandiose aim, it would simultaneously fail. To the extent that philosophy accepts methodic variety, incorporates omnivalence, it loses its ability to achieve a definite result. For in this incorporation philosophy becomes *too much like life.* If all of life's interests and energies have a legitimate place in philosophical method, then philosophy ceases to be different from the whole of which it is but a part, thereby losing its raison d'être. If, for example, philosophy incorporates aesthetic evaluations into its method, it may then capture more of the values operative in human life, but it will to that extent abandon the possibility of validating judgments publicly and evidentially as true. If philosophy becomes more personal, more expressive, then its conclusions become that much less able to command impersonal acceptance.

For example, what would happen if mathematicians tired of the abstractness and methodological severity of their discipline and called for a mathematics "more like life"? What if they incorporated sensual metaphors and practical interests into their arguments? Not only would mathematics cease to be true to its tradition, it presumably would cease to perform the function it has traditionally served for human society. Evidently human life needs mathematics to be unlike life, to be the expression of a limited human interest, to be specialized, an abstraction.[23] And what about art? Should art be more like human life, or was art invented as an escape from and a commentary upon life? What happens to art, or any cultural medium, when it ceases to be insulated from the interests and energies of the rest of social life, when, for example, it explicitly serves political or economic purposes?

Whether such deinsulation is felt to be advantageous presumably depends on historical circumstances. For the consequences of fusion or incorporation and, at the other extreme, abstraction or insulation may each be evaluated positively or negatively. The former may eliminate the differential contribution of the cultural medium in question, whereas the latter may denude it of significance and relevance. At one point in time a cultural medium may be felt to be too abstract and removed from life, and its prospective deinsulation seen as an enriching, broadening realism. A generation later, at the other end of the pendulum's arc, the medium may be experienced as fragmented, sordid, and politicized, as having abandoned the ideal and the form that had earlier made it satisfying.

This indeterminacy holds for philosophy as for any other cultural form. Philosophy must therefore be permanently incomplete, either by virtue of failing to embody all the modes of human judgment, or by failing to perform the special function that alone justifies its existence. I do not believe that either extreme insulation or utter omnivalence, or any mixture in between, can be justified as true or valid. In each case philosophy may be frustrated and lacking. A philosophy that accepts severe methodological limitations gains clarity and can be assured of making a limited contribution to life, but that contribution may be minimal and irrelevant. On the other hand, a philosophy that sought or even achieved the impossible aim of expressing all of life would have, for that very reason, exchanged the prospect of *serving* human life for the role of *reproducing* or *embodying* that life. Philosophy cannot escape its incompleteness, even by becoming complete.

CONCLUSION

What is the point of the foregoing, or of any philosophizing? Has anything been gained in this long detour, this circle back to myself? Have we obtained any knowledge in answer to the first-order philosophical questions we asked at the outset? Has there been any gain in understanding? Where may we go from here?

My conclusions have been, first, that the attempt to save philosophy by limiting it, in response to the attack by skepticism and postmodernism, is circular, hence inadequate if philosophy is ultimate inquiry. Second, the postmodernist project of providing a nonarbitrary or principled end to philosophy likewise fails. Third, no philosophical judgments can achieve philosophical, which is to say ultimate, validation. Last, philosophy's intended comprehensiveness makes it subject to a deep source of indeterminacy; namely, the location of inquiry and truth in the greater, omnivalent context of human judgment, culture, and life. The tension among the ends of philosophy is irremediable.

With respect to the philosophical questions with which I began, the questions not about our idea of life but about life itself, I seem no closer to any answers—unless I have gained knowledge about myself in the attempt. Is learning about our ideas, tracing the contours of inquiry, charting its pitfalls, a gain of self-knowledge? No doubt it is self-knowledge of a kind. But this knowledge of self, like improved knowledge of the world, of our modes of inquiry, or even of philosophical texts, must be fallible too. So there may well have been a gain, but to be clear about the real nature of this gain would itself be a philosophical matter about which we could not gain philosophically adequate knowledge. Not to mention that to speak of "gain" at all is to evaluate the foregoing study in comparative terms, as an improvement on some state of personal or collective contemporary understanding, the limitations of which we explored earlier.

Whatever the gain and however important it is, philosophy is in principle unable to achieve what it ultimately seeks. To say this is to admit that as long as we philosophize *we are lost*. Philosophy is the setting adrift of one's judgments on the endless sea of the demand for public, assertive validation, the sea of inquiry without limits. One might ask, Is philosophy the cause of being lost or is it only the recognition of being lost, the articulation of a pre- and nonphilosophical, a human incompleteness? I believe it is the latter. Philosophy is only an extension of a universal human activity, and its indecisiveness shows something universal. Philosophy is the human community's response to ultimacy through inquiry, and its incompleteness indicates that ultimate concerns cannot be resolved solely through inquiry and truth. So, in this sense, everyone is lost. But this is to say, everyone is lost *from the perspective of the philosopher*; that is, from the perspective of one who allows his or her inquiry to float toward ultimacy. Only the mind open to the call of ultimacy can feel that it, and all, are lost in this sense. The mind that does not hear the call does not know what it is to be lost, and the mind that has heard but answered the call with limited inquiry or another mode of query, experiences itself as *found*.

Yet, in another sense, philosophy is the response to the state of being lost only if philosophy is understood as a search. To describe philosophy as lost is already to understand it in terms of inquiry. My conclusion, that philosophical questions are in principle undecidable and hence that the philosopher is lost, was foreordained by my starting point, generated by the set of ultimate questions to which I wanted inquiry to grant answers. Every work of philosophy must similarly be guided by some notion of philosophy's end, hence by an acceptance of bounds. The most fundamental determinant of any philosopher's conclusion is his or her understanding of the end of philosophy, the obligations and commitments the philosopher implicitly accepts in the act of philosophizing. Differently put, if I am a philosopher, then there is no escape from the philosophical circus because there is no escape from myself.

Here at the close of our search, the final looming question is, Where to, now? To ask this is to step out of our commitment to philosophy as inquiry, so as to judge it from the outside (because truth is unconcerned with where I may go). Three possible avenues for thought come into view.

The philosopher might simply declare that certain presuppositions or limits on inquiry are necessary or valid. This is to accept that the absence of a noncircular justification of philosophical claims is no problem. The justification of this acceptance would presumably be pragmatic; that is, the justification of the limitation on the demand for validation, a limitation that makes philosophical decisiveness possible, is presumably pragmatic. So this option is in effect a decision that philosophic inquiry, even if aimed at truth, gains its confidence from serving practical ends.

One might continue to pursue the ever unfulfilled task of philosophy as ultimate inquiry, while recognizing it as such. This does not preclude using philosophical inquiry for practical ends or suggesting tentative conclusions in limited contexts. It bars us only from endorsing any of our conclusions fully, hence, philosophically. This is, so to speak, a tragic or Kantian response, an acceptance of both the necessity and the radically unfulfilled nature of ultimate inquiry. It is a recognition that one ceases to judge *qua philosopher* when one endorses a philosophical judgment as valid and when one abandons the search for such judgments.

Last, one may seek to modify philosophy's single-minded pursuit of representational truth, to incorporate the active and exhibitive into philosophy's aims and methods. This can be done in numerous ways. One may try, within philosophy aimed at truth, to interpret truth as something utterly unlike assertive representation, an option whose consistency I have questioned from the outset. Taking a step further, one may simply replace truth as the end of philosophy with goodness or aesthetic satisfaction, or with an undifferentiated, omnivalent notion of validity. But as I have tried to show, at least a portion of any philosopher's discourse must be inquiry governed by representational truth, so it does not seem that a consistently non-truth-functional philosophy is possible.

Somewhat more ambiguously, one might accept philosophy as fundamentally fissured, as obligated not only to assertive truth but to goodness and beauty as well. To accept this is to adopt a dialectical attitude toward truth, which seeks a balance among the norms of judgment. It is to accept a permanent tension in philosophy between its obligation to truth and its aspiration to encompass the whole panoply of human values. One might argue that this is in fact our approach. We always combine in our thought the various ends of philosophy, because we combine in our hearts the various ends of life. Life is omnivalent, and the philosopher, unlike other inquirers, is driven by an urge to comprehensiveness that is dissatisfied with limits. Yet truth must be philosophy's primary task and public, evidential validation its primary method. Hence philosophical method is fissured by the question of the place of inquiry, truth, and philosophy itself in life. For this reason philosophy can neither avoid nor answer the question, What character ought the ultimate determinants of human judgment be?

If this third path were chosen, a path of self-conscious and measured omnivalence, the next metaphilosophical step would be to speculate on the relations among the three functions of judgment. If I were to take this step, I would suggest, following Peirce, that aesthetic value is simply the value any quality has in itself. Hence all value or validity is, in itself, ultimately aesthetic. Goodness and truth are types of aesthetic values. This is not to aestheticize truth or morality in the sense of making truth and goodness resemble other aesthetic qualities, like beauty; nor does it collapse the other functions of judgment into the exhibitive. Beauty is one among many different aesthetic values, and its vicissitudes are not those of truth or moral goodness. The distinction between truth and all other values is not diminished by the recognition that aesthetic valuing is the valuing of something in and for itself.

The point would then be that the validation of inquiry, hence of philosophy, must ultimately be aesthetic. To pursue truth for its own sake, without regard to its pragmatic value, is to value truth aesthetically. What can it possibly mean, to value truth in itself and without reference to any other thing, other than to value its sheer quality, and what can this mean other than to value it aesthetically? Likewise, to pursue truth for its practical benefit or moral value is to pursue goodness for its own sake, thereby valuing goodness aesthetically. This echoes Nietzsche's early claim, in *The Birth of Tragedy*, that the world can be justified only aesthetically. The validation of truth governed inquiry can go only so far. It must stop in what is valuable in itself. Although we *can* make assertive judgments about the omnivalent whole of life and the place of truth and inquiry in it, the validation of the truth of these judgments cannot be ultimate.

The recognition of inquiry's place in query, hence of the bounds of a philosophy committed to inquiry, does not suggest an abandonment of that commitment. Everything has its bounds: if philosophy were understood primarily as exhibitive, active, or omnivalent it would have different bounds, not be *un*bounded. In any case, whether one accepts pragmatic limitations in service of a philosophy that improves the world, or stoically endures the tragic life of a philosophical Sisyphus, or ambiguously locates truth within a greater omnivalent context while tolerating its implicit indeterminacy, philosophy remains both inescapable and undecidable. The ever expansive nature of human query, that is, the propulsive character of our appropriation of the world, is not satisfied with the frugality of arbitrary limits. At the same time, the complexity of human judgment, that is, the multiform nature of our appropriation, makes finality, hence decisiveness, impossible. Thus does our nature deny us the luxury of simplicity. And thus does it ensure that philosophy has not reached its terminus. For as we can now see, philosophy cannot be at an *end* because it can never succeed in simplifying its *ends*.

NOTES

Introduction

1. From "Me and Bobby McGee," written by Kris Kristofferson, most famously recorded by Janis Joplin (Columbia Records, 1973).

2. Peirce was fired from his instructorship at Johns Hopkins University in 1883, at age 44, because of his evident relationship, while legally married but separated, with an unmarried woman. He never again held a regular academic post. The greatest philosophical mind America has produced was eventually reduced to abject poverty, to stealing food, to wandering homeless in the streets of New York City. For the circumstances of Peirce's dismissal, and the rest of his tragic life, see Joseph Brent's *Charles Sanders Peirce: A Life* (Bloomington: Indiana, 1993).

3. Although Rorty had once associated himself with 'postmodernism' (see his 1984 essay on Lyotard and Habermas, reprinted in EHO, pp. 164–176), he has more recently recanted (see the 1991 Introduction to EHO, p. 1). However, his reason for recanting is his skepticism about the cultural-historical implications of the term, in particular, its ascription of a cross-disciplinary, culturewide unity to a historical period. Hence Rorty ought to be equally as skeptical of 'modernism.' This skepticism is wise, I believe, but it does nothing to distance Rorty from the modes of criticism we usually refer to with the term *postmodernist*.

4. It is instructive to return to Paul Crosser's vituperative *The Nihilism of John Dewey* (New York: Philosophical Library, 1955) to see the mild-mannered supporter of the Enlightenment tradition of science, democracy, and freedom vilified in terms similar to those hurled at Derrida today. Dewey's attempt to "destroy all philosophy" with his "extreme relativism" and "sophism" has, we are told, "greatly weakened the intellectual potential of American leadership at home and abroad." See Crosser, pp. ix–xi.

5. The phrase belongs to John Rawls. See his "Justice as Fairness: Political not Metaphysical," *Philosophy and Public Affairs* 14: 223–251, (Summer 1985), pp. 231 and 240, n. 22. Although it is true that not all ques-

355

tions ought to be answered as asked, because some are misleading, this strategy of avoidance is very dangerous and ought to be used sparingly. Otherwise one might just as well avoid engaging in inquiry at all.

6. I am taking liberties with Erazim Kohák, *The Embers and the Stars: A Philosophical Inquiry into the Moral Sense of Nature* (Chicago: University of Chicago Press, 1984), p. 62: "A man alone is a waste of good firewood . . ." The passage in which this line appears is the most remarkable philosophical description of the experience of nothingness of which I am aware.

7. In what follows, *antifoundationalism* refers to the radical response to foundationalism, which seeks to root out any kind of foundationalism. This entails undermining philosophy itself. *Nonfoundationalism* understands foundationalism more narrowly, e.g., as the Cartesian search for an indubitably true first principle. Nonfoundationalism rejects only that narrow foundationalism. Consequently, nonfoundationalist philosophy remains continuous with much of the philosophical tradition. This distinction will be amplified in Chapter One and Chapter Four.

8. This is not to say that other antiphilosophers exhibit no trace of pragmatism, only that Rorty is uniquely explicit in his synthesis. As we will see, there are affinities between Peircean pragmatism and the work of Nietzsche, Wittgenstein, and Derrida. Disentangling the threads of pragmatism and what is called *postmodernism* is one of secondary aims of this study.

9. See Jacques Derrida, "The Ends of Man," in *Margins*. Christopher Norris uses the same ambiguous term in his title, *What's Wrong with Postmodernism: Critical Theory and the Ends of Philosophy* (Baltimore: Johns Hopkins University Press, 1990). Heidegger's similar title, "The End of Philosophy and the Task of Thinking," does not employ the ambiguity of *end*.

10. Rorty's work is itself a "cross-cultural" comparative effort.

11. This was Moses Mendelssohn's description of Kant. John Herman Randall, *The Career of Philosophy* (New York: Columbia, 1965), vol. 2, p. 105.

12. I am not even addressing the far greater cultural divisions between what we conveniently but misleadingly call 'Western' and non-Western philosophy.

13. Max Weber, "Religious Rejections of the World and Their Directions," in *From Max Weber*, trans. H. H. Gerth and C. Wright Mills (New York: Oxford university Press, 1946), pp. 323–359, reference on p. 356.

14. *The Bhagavad Gita* 2.19, trans. Juan Mascaró (Baltimore: Penguin Books, 1962).

Chapter One. The Question of Philosophy

1. Plato, *Theaetetus*, 147A, translation in G. S. Kirk and J. E. Raven, *The Presocratic Philosophers* (Cambridge: Cambridge University Press, 1957), p. 78.

2. Justus Buchler's theory of judgment is presented in two books: *Toward a General Theory of Human Judgment* (1951) and *Nature and Judgment* (1955).

3. This does not mean that assertion is always linguistic or language always assertive. I have coupled the terms (linguistic and assertive) to highlight what is most provocative in Buchler's theory; namely that a nonlinguistic nonassertion, e.g., walking to the store, can be a judgment.

4. I would suggest that, more precisely, the three modes are *relative functions*. That is, the description of a judgment as an instance of one of the three means that, in a particular context, that function of the judgment is the dominant or decisive or most efficacious one. Buchler implies as much (NJ, p. 21). So, a judgment may function assertively, exhibitively, and actively at the same time, but in relation to different contexts or perspectives, with one function being dominant in each.

5. There is a problem here that will be discussed in Chapter Seven.

6. See also ML, p. 148.

7. Buchler does not say whether or not active judgments have this trait.

8. Justus Buchler, "Reply to Ross," *Southern Journal of Philosophy* 14, no. 1 (Spring 1976): 108. The emphasis is Buchler's. Throughout this book I will make no indication when the emphasis in a quotation is the author's, only when the emphasis is mine.

9. I will use 'governed' to indicate the norm in terms of which a judgment is meant to be evaluated. So, as we will see, assertions are "truth governed," meaning that when a judgment functions assertively, the appropriate norm of validity for it is truth.

10. I do not wish to enter into the controversy over this idea, suggested by Frank Ramsey (see his *Foundations of Mathematics and Other Logical Essays*, [London: Kegan Paul, 1931], p. 44). Suffice to say that in inquiry we normally assume that "It is true that . . ." is implied by assertion, with the proviso that the meaning of this implication needs to be explained. See Joseph Margolis's objection to the so-called redundancy of truth,

Pragmatism Without Foundations (New York: Basil Blackwell, 1986), p. 109.

11. This reference is to Sextus's *Outlines of Pyrrhonism*, in standard form. See my Chapter Nine, note 3.

12. See David Hiley, *Philosophy In Question: Essays on a Pyrrhonian Theme* (Chicago: University of Chicago Press, 1988).

13. John Herman Randall, *The Career of Philosophy* (New York: Columbia University Press, 1965), vol. 1, p. 3.

14. I do not offer this as an adequate, which is to say 'complete,' definition of philosophy, partly for the reason already given, that philosophy includes more than ultimate matters. Nevertheless I think 'ultimacy' and 'inquiry' are necessary components of any adequate definition, and that is enough for my purposes.

15. As I have said, I will assume that philosophy is primarily, although not exclusively, assertive.

16. Plato, *Meno*, in *Great Dialogues of Plato*, trans. W. H. D. Rouse (New York: Mentor Books, 1956), 86C.

Chapter Two. Realism and Philosophical Knowledge

1. Hao Wong suggests the importance of the distinction among these questions in his *Beyond Analytic Philosophy: Doing Justice to What We Know* (Cambridge, Mass.: MIT Press, 1986).

2. I will accept that truth, however else it is to be characterized, is the indispensable norm for assertions. Whether it is possible to eliminate the term 'truth' seems to me irrelevant for the discussion that follows. Insofar as 'truth' is disquotational, to say that a proposition is true is just to say that things are as the proposition says they are. Whether or not we use the term 'true,' it remains the case that we do and must have a notion of what assertions or propositions aim to do (e.g., to say how things are) and a notion of what it means for that to be accomplished.

3. The antiphilosophical, or as he puts it, *antirepresentational*, view of Richard Rorty also rejects this approach. But as I will address Rorty and other radical critics of philosophy later, I do not include such views here.

4. The phrase is Abner Shimony's. See "Reality, Causality, and Closing the Circle," in his *Search for a Naturalistic World View*, vol. 1 (Cambridge: Cambridge University Press, 1993).

5. I do not mean to imply that this family of positions accepts a metaphysical monism for which everything is part of one substance. Members of

this family may be metaphysically pluralistic in the sense of asserting the existence of many things, but they do not assert the existence of kinds of things so different as to be discontinuous. They are antidualists and, to use Quine's phrase, "methodological monists" (although not Quinean behaviorists).

6. See Alfred North Whitehead's 1929 *Process and Reality: An Essay in Cosmology* (New York: The Free Press, 1978); Robert Neville, *Recovery of the Measure: Interpretation and Nature* (Albany: State University of New York Press, 1989); and Abner Shimony, "Reality, Causality, and Closing the Circle," and his "Integral Epistemology," and "Introduction" in *Naturalistic Epistemology: A Symposium of Two Decades*, ed. Abner Shimony and Debra Nails (Dordrecht: Reidel, 1987), pp. 299–318 and 1–13, respectively.

7. Michael Dummett, *Truth and Other Enigmas* (Cambridge: Harvard University Press, 1978), p. 146.

8. Ibid., p. 155.

9. Jarrett Leplin, *Scientific Realism* (Berkeley: University of California Press, 1984), p. 1.

10. Ibid., p. 42.

11. There certainly are other relevant characterizations. One is, as stated by Boyd, that, "The historical progress of mature sciences is largely a matter of successively more accurate approximations to the truth . . ." A related notion is the definition of realism in terms of the *aim* of scientific inquiry. For Bas Van Frassen, scientific realism holds that, "The aim of science is to give us a literally true story of what the world is like; and the proper form of acceptance of a theory is to believe that it is true." See Leplin, ibid.

12. This does not mean that we cannot, further down the road, decide that assertive judgments are subject to exhibitive and active considerations. It merely restricts our question as to what determines the validity of assertive, versus active and exhibitive judgments. Also, from now on, unless otherwise indicated, I will use the term 'judgment' to mean only assertive judgment.

13. Howard Stein, "Yes, But . . .: Some Thoughts on Realism," *Dialectica* 43, no. 1–2 (1989): 47–65, reference on pp. 57–58.

14. For example, Arthur Fine claims that realism must presume a "definite" world. I agree that realism does presume the independence of the real and the partial definiteness or determinateness of the real, but not its *complete* definiteness or determinateness. See his "And Not Anti-Realism Either," *Nous* 18, no. 1 (March 1984): 51–65.

15. W. V. O. Quine, "What Price Bivalence?" *The Journal of Philosophy* 98 (1981): 90–95, quote on p. 91.

16. Alfred Tarski, "The Concept of Truth in Formalized Languages," in *Logic, Semantics, Metamathematics*, trans. F. H. Woodger (Oxford: Clarendon Press, 1969), pp. 187–188. I do not mean to imply that Tarski's is what is *usually* understood by a correspondence theory of the truth relation, although I do think that it is possible to formulate a correspondence characterization of the truth relation sufficiently minimal that it is compatible with Tarski. That is, a minimal and cautious version of correspondence is not far from Tarski, even if he did not intend to offer such a view.

17. If, however, unconcealment or actualization or causation cannot be made compatible with correspondence, then I am allowing that they are not possibilities for a realist view of truth.

18. Hilary Putnam, *The Many Faces of Realism* (LaSalle, Ill.: Open Court Press, 1987).

19. Donald Davidson, "On the Very Idea of a Conceptual Scheme," in *Inquiries into Truth and Interpretation* (Oxford: Clarendon Press, 1984), pp. 183–198.

20. It is true that some philosophers have claimed some judgments are self-validating. I will deal with the kind of judgments referred to shortly. However, even regarding such judgments it is not clear that a nonrelational, "self-validation" is an apt description. For example, if one claims that a judgment is validated by virtue of an intuition, the "light of nature," a set of definitions, grammatical rules, or its inclusion in a linguistic system, then we could still reasonably say that its validity is dependent on the judgment's relation to something other than, or more than, itself.

21. What I call *immediacy* is included in what Joseph Margolis calls "privilege." Margolis means by privilege the status of a judgment that is claimed to be unquestionable because it is immediately related to its object. I will separate the two terms, using 'privilege' to mean the judgment's unquestionable and superior status and 'immediate' to mean the fact that grants this status, namely, an immediate relation to what is judged. I do so because 'privilege' is sometimes used by postmodernists to mean the valuation of some concept or phenomenon as superior to another, and I will occasionally use 'privilege' in this way, where it need not imply immediacy. See Joseph Margolis, *Pragmatism Without Foundations* (New York: Basil Blackwell, 1986).

22. Again, see Joseph Margolis's interesting discussion of privilege and realism in ibid.

23. Antirealists (and realists) are certainly free to accept immediate knowledge of objects whose character is not independent of judgment: e.g., appearances or phenomena or sense data.

24. An attack in which the present author has participated. See my *The Dilemma of Modernity: Philosophy, Culture, and Anticulture* (Albany: State University of New York Press, 1988).

25. This is my modification of Sidney Gelber and Kathleen Wallace's definition of *naturalism* in "Nature, Power and Prospect: Justus Buchler's System of Philosophy," in Armen Marsoobian et al., *Nature's Perspectives: Prospects for Ordinal Metaphysics* (Albany: State University of New York Press, 1991), p. 51. As stated, their definition better suits monism than naturalism, although it serves their aim well, which is to distinguish Buchler's ordinal version of naturalism from common biophysical versions.

26. Whether the distributive use of such a term escapes this problem is not clear. The issue is relevant to my inquiry in that Buchler has tried to exploit the difference between collective and distributive metaphysical terms in his metaphysics of natural complexes. For Buchler there is no name for *everything*, but there is a name for *anything* ("natural complex").

27. Gelber and Wallace, "Nature, Power, and Prospect," p. 51.

28. W. V. O. Quine, "Natural Kinds," in *Ontological Relativity and Other Essays* (New York: Columbia University Press, 1968), pp. 126–127. I should add here, because Quine and I use the same language, that we see the "continuity" of science and philosophy differently. For me, the continuity does not mean that all knowledge is scientific knowledge—unless by *science* we simply mean rational inquiry. Also, although I agree with Quine that no first philosophy that claimed to study inquiry, so to speak, from the outside, is possible, I do not take 'first philosophy' to have that absurd meaning, and so do not regard the continuity of science and philosophy as excluding the possibility of first philosophy.

29. As we will see in Chapter Four.

30. This is Gerhard Vollmer's position. He claims that an evolutionary account applies "*to perception and everyday experience, but not to theoretical knowledge.*" See his "On Supposed Circularities in an Empirically Oriented Epistemology," in Gerrard Radnitzky and W. W. Bartley III, *Evolutionary Epistemology, Rationality, and the Sociology of Knowledge* (LaSalle, Ill.: Open Court Press, 1987), p. 191.

31. The most obvious, and most frequently recognized, version of this problem arises if a strict determinism is ascribed to nature, hence human freedom is denied. For it becomes difficult to account for the human ability to alter beliefs on the basis of new evidence or a rethinking of old evidence if belief acceptance is strictly determined by factors outside of cognition. See, for example, Anthony Flew, "Must Naturalism Discredit Naturalism?" in ibid., pp. 401–421.

32. See Shimony's "Introduction" and "Integral Epistemology" in Shimony and Nails, *Naturalistic Epistemology*, pp. 1–13 and 299–318.

33. See, for example, Michel Foucault, *Power/Knowledge*, trans. Colin Gordon, Leo Marshall, Hohn Mepham, and Kate Soper (New York: Pantheon Books, 1980), p. 133: "'Truth' is to be understood as a system of ordered procedures for the production, regulation, distribution, circulation and operation of statements. 'Truth' is linked in a circular relation with systems of power which produce and sustain it, and to effects of power which it induces and which extend it." See also Jean-François Lyotard, *The Postmodern Condition: A Report on Knowledge*, trans. Geoff Bennington and Brian Massumi (Minneapolis: University of Minnesota Press, 1984), pp. 46–47.

34. That Nietzsche is a naturalist can be denied on only two grounds. First, one can presume a narrow, materialistic or scientific concept of nature. Second, one can try to claim that Nietzsche held no philosophical views in the conventional sense. The former strategy reflects a provincialism that, regretably, remains all too common among continental philosophers. They appear to have retained the pre-twentieth century notion of a mechanistic nature, thereby adopting the oppositional role played earlier by idealistic humanism. This retention is odd, given that continental philosophy since Heidegger has abandoned idealistic humanism, presumably rendering the fight against naturalism anachronistic. But there are many more ideas of the natural than are dreamt of in such philosophies. In my opinion, this anachronistic anti-naturalism, whose effect is to make everything a product of mind or intentionality or semiosis or human activity, is a stultifying force in the otherwise rich and creative continental tradition. The latter objection, that Nietzsche held no philosophical views in a conventional sense, is another matter. It raises a deeper question that I will try to answer in Chapter Five.

35. William James, *Pragmatism* (Indianapolis: Hackett, 1981), pp. 32–33.

36. Ibid. p. 37.

37. Ibid. p. 96.

38. Ibid. p. 100.

39. John Dewey, *Logic: The Theory of Inquiry*, vol. 12 of *The Later Works, 1925–1953*, ed. Jo Ann Boydston (Carbondale: Southern Illinois University Press, 1991), p. 15.

40. John Dewey, *Experience and Nature* (New York: Dover Press, 1958), p. 358.

41. There is no intention to ridicule Dewey here. He is trying to solve a problem I believe is not solvable; if I were to choose a solution, his is among the most appealing. That problem is, How can there be a continuity between human values and the natural world? I imagine there are two possible answers. One is that human values and nature share a common origin in

God. The other is Dewey's, which ascribes emergent moral and aesthetic values to nature itself. I remain skeptical of any such continuity, but I fully sympathize with the urge to believe in it. That is, I admit that the world remains recalcitrant to human aspiration absent such an answer.

42. Hans Albert, *Treatise on Critical Reason*, trans. Mary Varney Rorty (Princeton, N.J.: Princeton University Press, 1985), p. 18.

43. This is not to say that Albert is a relativist.

44. See Karl Otto Apel, "The Problem of Philosophical Foundations in Light of a Transcendental Pragmatics of Language," in Kenneth Baynes et al., *After Philosophy: End or Transformation* (Cambridge, Mass.: MIT Press, 1987), pp. 250–290; Apel's *Towards a Transformation of Philosophy*, trans. Glyn Adey and David Frisby (London: Routledge, 1980), Chapters Five and Seven; and Jürgen Habermas, "Discourse Ethics: Notes on a Program of Philosophical Justification," in *Moral Consciousness and Communicative Action*, trans. Christian Lenhardt and S. W. Nicholsen (Cambridge, Mass.: MIT Press, 1990), pp. 43–115.

45. Habermas, "Discourse Ethics."

46. Donald Davidson, "On the Very Idea of a Conceptual Scheme," *Inquiries into Truth and Interpretation* (Oxford: Clarendon Press, 1984), pp. 183–198, reference on p. 197.

47. Donald Davidson, "The Method of Truth in Metaphysics," in ibid., pp. 199–214, reference on p. 201.

48. Donald Davidson, "A Coherence Theory of Truth and Knowledge," in Ernest LePore, *Truth and Interpretation: Perspectives on the Philosophy of Donald Davidson* (Oxford: Basil Blackwell, 1986), pp. 307–319, reference on p. 314.

49. Ibid., p. 309.

50. Ibid., p. 307

51. Ibid., p. 309. The term "non-internal" is a reference to Hilary Putnam.

52. There are other possible objections to Davidson's argument, in particular, to the idea of the omniscient interpreter, which, if it fails, would eliminate the justification for claiming that the beliefs we share with the speaker actually are true.

53. Certainly not only Kant; I am simplifying greatly. Peirce was also influenced by the Medieval logicians, especially Duns Scotus, and by Thomas Reid. Wittgenstein's career began as an attempt to solve the philosophical problems of Frege and Russell, hence of the founders of "analytic" philosophy, and this approach to philosophy owes much to Leibniz. Yet Frege also mentions the importance of Kant. Derrida's thought must be

understood in relation to a range of predecessors: Hegel, Husserl, Heidegger, Nietzsche, De Saussure, Levi-Strauss, not to mention Freud and Marx. My point is only that, if we were to do a background check on each of our philosophers, the most prominent recent name that would show up in each check would be Kant.

54. David Hume, *An Inquiry Concerning Human Understanding* (New York: Liberal Arts Press, 1955). This book was published in 1748 under the title, *Philosophical Essays Concerning Human Understanding*. Hume changed the title to its present "Inquiry" in 1758.

55. Ibid., p. 57.

56. David Hume, *A Treatise of Human Nature* (Oxford: Oxford University Press, 1975), Book One, Part IV, section VI, pp. 263–274. Books One and Two originally appeared in 1739 and Book Three in 1740.

57. Ibid., p. 266.

58. Ibid., p. 179.

59. Ibid., p. 179.

60. Ibid., p. 268. Hume regards philosophy and science as continuous, both part of the "refin'd reasoning" that leads to skepticism. Therefore the critique of philosophy is also a critique of science.

61. Ibid., p. 269.

62. Ibid., p. 269.

63. Hume, *Inquiry*, p. 167.

64. Ibid., p. 168.

65. Hume, *Treatise*, p. 269.

66. Ibid., p. 270, Hume's emphasis.

67. Ibid., p .271.

68. Ibid., p. 271.

69. Hume, *Inquiry*, pp. 168–169.

70. Ibid., p. 173.

71. Thomas Reid, *Inquiry and Essays*, ed. Ronald Beanblossom and Keith Lehrer (Indianapolis: Hackett, 1983). See Ronald Beanblossom's Introduction, p. xii.

72. Ibid., p. 5.

73. Ibid., p. 7.

74. Ibid.

75. Ibid., p. 19.

76. Ibid., p. 109.

77. Ibid., p. 53.

78. Ibid., pp. 98–102.

79. Ibid., p. 58. Peirce makes the same claim in his "critical common-sensism" (CP, 508). Peirce's emendation is to insist that the "acritically indubitable is invariably vague" (CP, 446).

80. Ibid., p. 36.

81. Ibid., p. 119.

82. Ibid., p. 54.

83. Immanuel Kant, *Critique of Pure Reason*, trans. Norman Kemp Smith (New York: St. Martin's Press, 1965), BXXX, p. 29. All references will be made to the pages of Kant's second or "B" edition of 1787, by the usual convention of, e.g., B5 standing for page five of that edition.

84. As we will see, Kant describes our legitimate presuppositions regarding the relation of God to creation as a "symbolic anthropomorphism."

85. Kant, *Critique of Pure Reason*, B434.

86. Ibid., B436.

87. "This *unconditioned* is always contained in the *absolute totality of the series* as represented in imagination" (B444).

88. There is another way to think the unconditioned totality of conditions, namely, as simply the whole of the series. That is, one may think of the series as a whole as unconditioned, but of every member of the series as conditioned, thus not invoking the idea of an unconditioned first member of the series. But here we cannot imagine a completed regressive synthesis of the actual conditions, because that would go on infinitely. Kant calls this idea of the unconditioned only "potentially" infinite (B445).

89. Immanuel Kant, *Prolegomena to Any Future Metaphysics*, trans. James W. Ellington (Indianapolis: Hackett, 1977) sec. 57–59, German pp. 350–365, English pp. 91–104.

90. Ibid., German 353, English p. 93.

91. Ibid., German 360, English p. 100.

92. Ibid., German 357, English p. 97. This text is very suggestive for a Derridean approach.

93. Ibid., German 354, English p. 94.

94. Kant means the anthropomorphic notion of God—as opposed to God's relation to the world—which Hume famously criticized in his 1779 work, *Dialogues Concerning Natural Religion* (New York: Hafner, 1948).

95. Ibid., German 354, English p. 94.

96. Ibid., German 353, English p. 94.

97. This has been discussed more thoroughly in my *The Dilemma of Modernity: Philosophy, Culture, and Anti-Culture* (Albany: State University of New York Press, 1988), Chapter Three.

98. Kant, *Prolegomena*, German p. 353, English p. 94.

99. Ibid., German p. 362, English p. 102.

100. Arthur Schopenhauer, *The World as Will and Representation*, trans. E. F. J. Payne (New York: Dover Books, 1969). The book first appeared in 1818. The 1844 edition was expanded into two volumes, the second of which consists of commentary on and an expansion of the first volume. All of my references are to vol. 1 of the Dover edition.

101. Heidegger used the German of this term to a related but different purpose.

102. Schopenhauer, *The World as Will and Representation*, p. 281.

103. Ibid., pp. 333, 360–362.

104. Ibid., p. 152.

105. Ibid., p. 292.

106. Ibid., p. 502.

107. Friedrich Nietzsche, *Untimely Meditations*, trans. R. J. Hollingdale (Cambridge: Cambridge University Press, 1983), pp. 127–194, reference on pp. 140–141.

108. This touches on the problem of whether Nietzsche is a metaphysician, which I do not want to address. Suffice to say that if one regards the will to power in Nietzsche as being outside of or nonidentical with appearances, this need not mean that the will to power is a thing, an existent, or a ground. Heidegger dwells on this problem in his *Nietzsche*, trans. Joan Stambaugh, David Krell, and Frank Capuzzi (New York: Harper Books, 1987), vol. 3.

109. It should be noted that the school within which Wittgenstein was then working, the Frege-Russell logicist project, had itself been influenced by Kant, even though logicism was a direct attack on some Kantian doctrines (e.g., the synthetic nature of arithmetic). In his *Grundlagen*, Frege writes of Kant, "I have no wish to incur the reproach of picking petty quarrels with a genius to whom we must all look up with grateful awe; I feel

bound, therefore, to call attention also to the extent of my agreement with him, which far exceeds any disagreement. . . . In calling the truths of geometry synthetic and a priori, he revealed their true nature" (pp. 101–102). Kant's error was to define analyticity too narrowly, but otherwise his approach was sound. Frege subsequently explains the mission of his own work by remarking, in very Kantian terms, "We might say, indeed, almost in the well-known words: the reason's proper study is itself" (p. 115). See Gottlob Frege, *The Foundations of Arithmetic*, trans. J. L. Austin (Evanston, Ill.: Northwestern University Press, 1980). I thank Steven Gerrard for pointing out this connection to me.

110. The very complex story of Peirce's relation to many of the central epistemological and logical concepts of the post-Humean tradition cannot be told here. One interesting part of that story is the ambiguity introduced into the analytic-synthetic dichotomy by Peirce's distinction between "corollarial" and "theorematic" reasoning, pointed out by Jaakko Hintikka in his essay, "C. S. Peirce's 'First Real Discovery' and Its Contemporary Relevance," *The Monist*, 63, no. 3 (July 1980): 304–315.

111. Certainly there are other great Kantians of the past century— Ernst Cassirer being the most prominent. But Cassirer's Neo-Kantianism, whatever its virtues, has been tangential to the dominant schools of twentieth century philosophy. And of course, one could include Frege's critical response to Kant as one of the most formative influences on this century's philosophy. Also, I am obviously restricting myself to epistemology, metaphysics, and methodology in these comments.

112. This important difference connects with several components of Peirce's thought. First, it is part of his account of the validity of induction, as he points out in a very interesting footnote to the 1868 essay, "Questions Concerning Certain Faculties Claimed for Man," concerning the difference between Kant and himself (see CP, 223, n. 2). Second, Peirce's "synechist" metaphysics, which asserts the reality of continua, ascribes generality to things (this is Peirce's late version of his long-time commitment to Scotistic realism). Last, it is obviously in accord with his idealism.

113. A simplification of Kant not unlike Schopenhauer's.

114. These are two of Kant's three great questions that summarize the interests of reason, the third being, "What ought I to do?" (*Critique of Pure Reason*, B833)

Chapter Three. Peirce's (Anti)Realism

1. The epigram is from Peirce, CP, 2.654. All references to Peirce in the text unless otherwise noted will be to *Collected Papers of Charles Sanders Peirce*, ed. Charles Hartshorne and Paul Weiss, 8 vols.

(Cambridge, Mass.: Harvard University Press, 1931–1958); the final two volumes were edited by Arthur Burks. Following standard practice, references to this collection will give the volume number to the left of the decimal point, and the paragraph number (not the page number) to the right. Hence "CP, 2.654" indicates paragraph number 654 of vol. 2 of the *Collected Papers*.

2. In addition to 12,000 pages of Peirce's work that were published are some 80,000 handwritten pages of unpublished manuscripts. See *The Writings of Charles S. Peirce: A Chronological Edition* (Bloomington: Indiana University Press, 1982), vol. 1, p. xi.

3. See Joseph Brent, *Charles Sanders Peirce: A Life* (Bloomington: Indiana University Press, 1993).

4. Justus Buchler, "The Accidents of Peirce's System," *Journal of Philosophy* 37, no. 10 (May 9, 1940): 266. This response to a 1939 paper by Paul Weiss ("The Essence of Peirce's System") is an interesting document, in what it reveals about both Peirce and Buchler. Essentially, Buchler argues there is no "essence" to Peirce's system in the sense of a theme to which all of his views contribute and that we do a disservice to Peirce in trying to read him in this way.

5. I do not mean that this characterizes the historical development of Peirce's thought. That is, I do not believe that he set out to develop antirealist doctrines, then sought out a compatible form of realism. Peirce seems always to have been a realist, but a critical one. It would be more correct to say that his aim was always to save realism from the faulty doctrines with which it had often been associated.

6. One other great thinker used the concept of the sign to reformulate Kant: Ernst Cassirer. Peirce and Cassirer represent two versions of *semiotic* Kantianism.

7. Murray Murphey makes an interesting point that the denial of intuition means that for Peirce the limits of consciousness are not in consciousness. See Murray Murphey, *The Development of Peirce's Philosophy* (Cambridge, Mass.: Harvard University Press, 1961), p. 68.

8. This is reminiscent of Kant's description of the imagination as "a blind but indispensable function of the soul, without which we should have no knowledge whatsoever, but of which we are scarcely ever conscious." *Critique of Pure Reason*, trans. Norman Kemp Smith (New York: St. Martin's Press, 1965), B103.

9. Justus Buchler, *Charles Peirce's Empiricism* (New York: Octagon, 1966), p. 261.

10. "Questions" also contains a most interesting comparison of Peirce's aims to those of his great teacher, Kant. Peirce remarks that his views are compatible with Kant's in that, although Kant's aim is to make space and

time intuitions produced by a synthesis, Peirce' theory is "merely an account of this synthesis." Kant's Transcendental Aesthetic had proposed two principles, Peirce says. First, that universal and necessary propositions—meaning for Peirce, propositions true of "all of a sphere" and those true of "every possible state of things," respectively—are not derived from experience. Peirce says this is true if we restrict 'experience' to sense impressions, the consciousness of them, and their deductive implications. But that would rule out empirical induction, too. Induction is, by definition, the inference of universal and necessary propositions from experience. Kant would exclude induction because of its uncertainty; he speaks only of the a priori. But, Peirce insists, the uncertainty of induction is merely a quantitative matter; as the number of observations approaches infinity, true universality and necessity are "inferable."

Kant's second principle was, in Peirce's words, that "universal and necessary facts are determined by the conditions of experience. . . ." This is, Peirce claims, nothing but the principle of induction! Induction presupposes that what is true of a set of observations drawn from a certain sphere is determined by the conditions that characterize the sphere, thereby justifying an inference from the observations to the universal and necessary conditions of the sphere. "Apply induction not to any limited experience," Peirce says, "but to all human experience and you have the Kantian philosophy, so far as it is correctly developed." As Peirce would later remark, the real question in philosophy is not, how are synthetic a priori judgments possible, but, how are *synthetic* judgments possible? We will see Peirce's answer later.

11. In 1892, referring to this passage, Peirce remarks, "my views were, then, too nominalistic to enable me to see that every general idea has the unified living feeling of a person" (CP, 6.270). That is, signs are like persons.

12. See Vincent Colapietro, *Peirce's Approach to the Self: A Semiotic Perspective on Human Subjectivity* (Albany: State University of New York Press, 1989).

13. Peirce reminds us that "there is the most positive historic proof that innate truths are particularly uncertain and mixed up with error. . . ." (CP, 1.144).

14. Note that Peirce goes further than Neurath's famous metaphor that we are in the position of rebuilding the boat we are sailing in. Peirce puts us *in* the water, without a boat.

15. Another doctrine is related to fallibilism in Peirce. Although he insists that we know real things as they really are, Peirce claims that the belief in reality, in the existence of things independent of our experience and belief, is an hypothesis characteristic of a particular method of fixing belief, the scientific method. Although the claim that reality is hypothetical certainly smacks of fallibilism, its explication would involve a discussion of

the attenuated and critical nature of Peirce's realism, and so it will be left to the next section.

16. Although he later wondered whether he or James had first used the term. See his 1990 letter to James (CP, 8.253).

17. Kant, *Critique of Pure Reason*, B828.

18. Ibid., B852–3. We can imagine that Peirce took this as a Kantian certification of his own view that, in a sense, human life is all about betting, or hypothetical judgments. See, for example, Peirce's statement that "Each of us is an insurance company" (CP, 5.354). In this sense, pragmatism is the interpretation of all human judgment as gambling.

19. For a description of the club by Peirce, see CP, 5.11–13.

20. Alexander Bain (1818–1903) was a Scottish philosopher, a late representative of the common-sense school of Reid, and an associate of John Stuart Mill.

21. William James, *Collected Essays and Reviews* (New York: Russell and Russell, 1969), pp. 406–437.

22. It is not entirely certain, at least in my mind, whether James means to refer to "How to Make Our Ideas Clear" alone or to "The Fixation of Belief" as well. He mentions a Peirce essay of January 1878, which would be the former. But some of the ideas he attributes to that essay appear to be from "Fixation," which dates from November 1877. Peirce regarded the January 1878 essay as the one that formulated the doctrine for the first time (CP, 5.13, n. 1).

23. I will use 'pragmatism' to mean Peirce's doctrine (that is, pragmaticism), and what became of it. The context will make clear what components of the doctrine are at issue.

24. Peirce had introduced this idea in 1868, in "Some Consequences of Four Incapacities" (CP, 5.297).

25. These he conceived in 1883 and 1906, respectively. Peirce evidently footnoted the preceding quotation, "Then, our conception of these effects is the whole of our conception of the object" (CP, 5.402), with the phrase "Long addition refuting what comes next." The editors of the CP have added the later material as notes to that paragraph.

26. This is necessarily so in Peirce because of the following argument (presented, for example, in "Some Consequences of Four Incapacities," CP, 5.311–312). All cognitions have been logically derived (inferred) from previous cognitions. The thing in itself that is the "ideal first" in the series of cognitions cannot be an immediate object of consciousness (because cognition is continuous). Therefore the real cannot be known via immediate consciousness. The definition of the real (pragmatically speaking) must be the object

of the opinions that stand in the long run, which is independent of the idiosyncrasies of myself and the moment. It makes no sense to speak of a proposition whose error is incognizable or undiscoverable. Whatever is thought in propositions that the community fails to disconfirm in the long run is the real. Hence the object of such thoughts is reality itself (not phenomena). But all thoughts are partly indeterminate, that is, partly general and vague. Hence reality itself is partly general and vague. That is, generals or generality and vagueness are real. Real things are not fully determinate.

27. See Wittgenstein's remark against the possibility of a private language: "Here I should like to say: a wheel that can be turned though nothing else moves with it, is not part of the mechanism" (PI 271).

28. Buchler adds that the pragmatic principle must not only be limited to the logical interpretants of "intellectual concepts," but can be applied only to descriptive signs and synthetic sentences, and so not, for example, to logical connectives. Buchler, *Charles Peirce's Empiricism*, p. 105.

29. Ibid., pp. 157–160.

30. This is reaffirmed two pages after the passage in question, where Peirce objects to Schiller's claim that "the meaning of a rule lies in its application," because this would "make the 'meaning' consist in the energetic interpretant and would ignore the logical interpretant. . . ."(CP, 5.494)

31. Peirce writes that this compulsion "is evidently the reason of the dichotomy of the true and the false. For it takes two to make a quarrel, and a compulsion involves as large a dose of quarrel as is requisite to make it quite impossible that there should be compulsion without resistance" (CP, 5.554). This connects the notion of truth to Peirce's Secondness, which is otherness or resistance, hence duality. This could also be said of good and bad. In other words, our binary norms are Seconds.

32. Buchler refers to these as the "two kinds of statements" of pragmatism, and he—at least in his Peirce book, last issued in 1966—regarded the statement in terms of action vague and derivative.

33. Peirce adds a note here: "Let us not, however, be cocksure that natural selection is the only factor of evolution. . . ."

34. Peirce implies as much earlier in the same paragraph: "in the absence of facts. . . . Where hope is unchecked by experience, it is likely our optimism is extravagant" (CP, 5.366).

35. This is Nietzsche's question, from *The Genealogy of Morals*.

36. Peirce does remark that inquiry can be seen in terms of a fundamental biological drive. While opposing the reduction of truth to satisfaction of need or desire, Peirce admits that inquiry, like all purposive action, is accompanied by feeling, so that it operates *as if* it were directed to stimulate a certain feeling. This derives from the "fundamental properties of pro-

toplasm" (CP, 3.154), whereby "purposive action must be *virtually* directed" to remove stimulation (CP, 5.563).

37. Making his attribution of scientific method potential rather than actual—so that all people are potential followers of scientific method—does not ease the problem, because then those not actually scientists could fail (actually fail) to believe in reals, which is what he was seeking to deny in the first place.

38. Here I mean 'realism' in the epistemological sense, as I have been using it, not Scholastic realism, which asserts that generals are real. Peirce is both a Scholastic realist and an epistemological realist.

39. This must mean *intensionally* specifiable. The relevant community is a specific one; it is the community of scientific inquirers, who share an aim and a method. So the community *is* specifiable intensionally. The only sense in which the relevant set of minds is not specified is its extension: we cannot ennumerate the individuals in the community.

40. I take the second sentence ("there is . . . to every question a true answer") to be contradicted by the remark just mentioned from 1906, that we cannot know there is any truth on any given question.

41. I would offer apologies to the practitioners or advocates of this aesthetic movement for appropriating its name if I could, in the contemporary geopolitical environment, find such a person. The use of the term *socialism* in relation to Peirce evidently was earlier suggested by G. Wartenberg in his dissertation at Frankfurt, *"Logischer Sozialismus"* (1971). I have not seen this work. Karl-Otto Apel refers to it in his *Towards a Transformation of Philosophy*, trans. Glyn Adey and David Frisby (London: Routledge, 1980), p. 92.

42. John Smith, "Community and Reality," in Richard Bernstein, *Perspectives on Peirce* (New Haven, Conn.: Yale University Press, 1965), pp. 92–119, passage on pp. 96–97.

43. Buchler, *Charles Peirce's Empiricism*, p. 148.

44. I take this to be an acceptance, by Peirce, of the legitimacy of circular arguments at the foundational level. What matters is that every claim be reasoned, and this is possible only if, at some point, the condition that makes all the preceding phenomena intelligible is itself made intelligible by reference to those phenomena.

45. I believe that the class of indubitables for Peirce includes the following: (a) perceptions or perceptual judgments, (b) feelings, (c) aesthetic values, (d) certain general beliefs (like the uniformity of nature), (e) certain natural and social demands that our cognitive apparatus must serve (as presented in the doubt-belief theory), and (f) the fact that we know.

46. The first two-thirds of "Grounds," which roots deduction in the semiotic analysis of cognition, we will pass over to reach Peirce's explanation of probable reasoning or induction.

47. This same point is made in CP, 2.654.

48. See Hilary Putnam, *The Many Faces of Realism* (LaSalle, Ill.: Open Court Press, 1987), p. 82.

49. Peirce admitted to having been infected with "some benignant form" of the Concord transcendentalism of Emerson (CP, 6.102).

50. Immanuel Kant, *Fundamental Principle of the Metaphysic of Morals*, trans. T. K. Abbott (Buffalo, N.Y.: Prometheus Books, 1987).

Chapter Four. Nonfoundational Realism

1. W. V. O. Quine, "Epistemology Naturalized," in *Ontological Relativity and Other Essays* (New York: Columbia University Press, 1968), pp. 82–83.

2. Ibid., pp. 83–84.

3. See Shimony's "Introduction" and "Integral Epistemology" in Abner Shimony and Debra Nails, *Naturalistic Epistemology: A Symposium of Two Decades* (Dordrecht Reidel, 1987), pp. 1–13 and 299–318.

4. I am selecting from and paraphrasing Neville's criteria. See Robert Neville, *The High Road Around Postmodernism* (Albany: State University of New York Press, 1992), pp. 147–148. I appreciate Professor Neville's generosity in giving me a copy of his book so that I might criticize it.

5. Sir Karl Popper, *Objective Knowledge: An Evolutionary Approach* (Oxford: Clarendon Press, 1972), and W. W. Bartley III, "Theories of Rationality," in Gerrard Radnitzky and W.W. Bartley III, *Evolutionary Epistemology, Rationality, and the Sociology of Knowledge* (LaSalle, Ill.: Open Court Press, 1987).

6. On "Comprehensive Critical Rationality" see W. W. Bartley III, "Theories of Rationality," in Radnitzky and Bartley, pp. 205–214.

7. Ibid., pp. 211–212.

8. "I would have done better to call it simply *pragmatic* realism. . . ." Hilary Putnam, *Representation and Reality* (Cambridge, Mass.: MIT Press, 1988), p. 114.

9. Hilary Putnam, *The Many Faces of Realism* (LaSall, Ill.: Open Court Press, 1987), p. 17.

10. Hilary Putnam, *Reason, Truth and History* (Cambridge: Cambridge University Press, 1981), p. 54.

11. Ibid., p. 49.

12. *The Many Faces of Realism*, p. 36.

13. *Reason, Truth and History*, p. 48.

14. *The Many Faces of Realism*, p. 33.

15. Ibid., p. 121.

16. Ibid., p. 122.

17. *Reason, Truth and History*, p. 201.

18. Ibid., p. 215.

19. *The Many Faces of Realism*, p. 18. The single quotes indicate that this was an example Carnap used, which Putnam is turning to his own purpose.

20. *Representation and Reality*, p. 110.

21. *The Many Faces of Realism*, p. 19.

22. *Representation and Reality*, p. 113.

23. Ibid., p. 114.

24. The only way is through more pragmatism, e.g., the description we call scientific is better for guiding engineering, the description we call religious is better for thinking about the meaning of life, etc. To believe this is to go further down the antirealist road, hence this strategy cannot fend off the threat of antirealism.

25. That is, the two people are not in the room unless 'nothing' is meant to exclude only nonhuman things. But if so, then Putnam's description leaves it open whether the room is also full of people!

26. Joseph Margolis, *Pragmatism Without Foundations* (New York: Basil Blackwell, 1986), p. 214.

27. Ibid., p. 17.

28. Ibid., p. 175.

29. Ibid., p. 260.

30. Ibid., p. 48.

31. Ibid., p. 76.

32. Ibid., p. 164. This will be one of my objections to Rorty.

33. Ibid., p. 1.

Chapter Five. Nietzsche's Naturalistic Epistemology

1. The epigraph is from Nietzsche's *Thus Spoke Zarathustra* (TSZ, p. 328). In my references to Nietzsche's works, wherever passages are numbered in those works, the references will be to the numbered passage (e.g., WP, 55 indicates passage number 55 in WP). Wherever passage numbers are not available or where the division of the text makes unique identification of a passage cumbersome, the reference will be to a page number (e.g., GM, p. 55). The date for starting work on his first book comes from a letter to Georg Brandes, in SL, p. 338.

2. No one has confronted this question, in my estimation, more directly and tenaciously than Nietzsche. Nietzsche's literary career can be divided into four periods: an early phase, a transitional phase, and a final phase which itself can be divided in two. The early phase, extending from the summer of 1870 (at age twenty-five) to 1875, includes *The Birth of Tragedy*, the four *Untimely Meditations* (the most important for present concerns being "On the Advantage and Disadvantage of History for Life" and "Schopenhauer as Educator"), and his unpublished pieces on philosophy and truth, most important, "On the Truth and Lies in a Nonmoral Sense." The second or transitional phase, roughly from 1875 to 1879, was the nadir of Nietzsche's health, his least productive period (relative to the huge output of his later years), and the time of his break from Richard Wagner. He resigned his university post in 1879. *Human, All Too Human*, which he wrote during the summers from 1876 to 1879, is the chief work of this time.

The third period, the beginning of his mature philosophy, might be traced from the writing of *The Dawn* in 1880 or from his first conceiving the idea of the eternal recurrence in August 1881, which appeared in the *Gay Science*, a book written in January 1882. This was followed by what Nietzsche regarded as his greatest work, *Thus Spoke Zarathustra*, the four parts of which were written in four ten-day eruptions in 1883–1885.

Nietzsche wrote that his 1880s works could be divided into the "yes-saying" and the "no-saying," or the positive and the polemical. *The Gay Science* and *Zarathustra* represent the former. Most of Nietzsche's remaining books, during his final period from 1886 to January 1889, when he lost his mind, are polemics directed at morality, idealism, Wagner, and Christianity above all: *Beyond Good and Evil* (written summer 1885), the *Genealogy of Morals* (July 1887), *The Case of Wagner, The Twilight of the Idols, The Antichrist*, and *Nietzsche Contra Wagner* (all 1888). *Ecce Homo* (also 1888) is a commentary on himself, his books, and their significance.

3. The passage continues: "the very same symptoms could point to *decline* and to strength" (WP, 110).

4. At that early point in his career Nietzsche saw continuity between Kant and Schopenhauer, making Kant his own predecessor. But soon his differences with Kant would outweigh any complicity. For Nietzsche's path was to "oppose knowledge with art," not with morality (PT, p. 12). And, of

course, with Nietzsche's increasingly violent attack on Christianity, Kant would eventually come under almost uniformly harsh criticism. Nietzsche remained closer to Schopenhauer. Schopenhauer made the will the thing in itself, the reality to knowledge's appearance, thus creating a kind of irrationalist idealism. Nietzsche also shared Schopenhauer's pessimism. But two features of Schopenhauer's philosophy would cause Nietzsche to move on, always to regard the former as his one-time "educator," nevertheless as his "antipode" (NW, pp. 669–671). They were Schopenhauer's metaphysical idealism of the will, which led him to view the natural world of experience as illusion, and his deep asceticism, his longing to escape from the will and the will's world. Nietzsche eventually saw these as the powerful remnants of Christianity in Schopenhauer's thought.

5. After noting relevant remarks in *The Birth of Tragedy*, we will examine the essay, "On the Truth and Lies in a Nonmoral Sense," then passages in *The Gay Science, Beyond Good and Evil*, the conclusion of *The Genealogy of Morals*, and a number of interesting sections in *The Will to Power*.

6. "Crush the infamy." Nietzsche felt an affinity to Voltaire, which was evident in *Human, All Too Human*, in several passages (e.g., vol. 1, 221) and in the fact that Nietzsche wanted the book to appear during the centenary of Voltaire's death (1878). This felt affinity continued throughout Nietzsche's career.

7. I am tempted to repeat a line from the American television series "Taxi" to the effect that "meaningless superstition and pointless ritual is all that separates us from the animals."

8. The empiricist flavor of this is unmistakable, despite Nietzsche's intentions. Remember Hume's distinction between impressions and ideas, in which ideas are faint copies of impressions.

9. This is essentially one of the arguments George Berkeley used to deny that matter can be represented, hence known to exist.

10. There is a strong resemblance to Freud's related distinctions between the pleasure and reality principles, and between primary and secondary process.

11. The 1874 essay "The Advantage and Disadvantage of History for Life" is wholly concerned with it.

12. Nietzsche will repeat this formulation in *The Genealogy of Morals* (1887), pp. 297–298.

13. Peirce adopts this view, calling logic a "normative science," and the term appears in Wittgenstein's *Philosophical Investigations* (PI, 81) ascribed to Frank Ramsey, who was familiar with Peirce.

14. That there are echoes of Peirce here should be no surprise. That logic is normative and associated with conduct and self-control and that the indubitability of its rules is no evidence of their truth are part of Peirce's pragmatism, commonsensism, and naturalism, doctrines that Nietzsche is at least flirting with.

15. This remark appears in a section of WP entitled by Nietzsche's friend Peter Gast "Recapitulation," that is, of Book Three.

16. The date is in question. See Kaufman's note to p. 451, section 853, of WP.

17. I presume Nietzsche is referring to *The Birth of Tragedy*.

18. Note that the judgment that truth is dissimulative must be made from a perspective that accepts truth as a norm. The idea of dissimulation presumes truth as its opposite. Nietzsche did not abandon the idea of truth; if he had done so the ideas of falsehood, lie, illusion, dissimulation, etc., would be absent from his work.

19. This is reminiscent of Thrasymachus's equivocation of 'just' in Plato's *Republic*. Thrasymachus defines *justice* as the interest of the stronger—a very radical, counterintuitive definition. But later he says that the unjust life is the better, stronger life. This is a lapse, for it assumes the usual acceptation of justice. What he has done is to criticize the usual notion of justice in two contradictory ways: first by saying that the facts people usually refer to as just are utterly different than they think; second by saying that people are wrong in the value they place on facts they correctly know to be just. Socrates destroys him with this self-contradiction.

20. Maudemarie Clark, *Nietzsche on Truth and Philosophy* (Cambridge: Cambridge University Press, 1990).

21. Ibid., p. 61.

22. It is in this same sense, as we will see, that Wittgenstein is less radical than Russell. Wittgenstein cannot tolerate the existence of unsolved or unsolvable problems. Of course, one may deny that such tolerance is "radical." Perhaps radicalism is intolerant by definition. Nevertheless, a kind of purification of tradition is operative in both Nietzsche and Wittgenstein, as if they were young men who, having inherited the family business, pursued their work with a rational, ruthless disregard that would have horrified their cautious, traditionalist fathers, thereby driving their enterprizes into bankruptcy.

23. Clark suggests that we ought to defer to Nietzsche's published writings over the unpublished, a principle with which I generally agree. However, she quotes passages from *The Will to Power* to bolster her interpretation, so it seems only fair that the following passages ought to be taken into account as well.

24. Clark, p. 158.

25. Ibid., pp. 138–144.

26. Ibid., p. 149.

27. As we will see in Buchler, in Chapter Seven.

28. See Heidegger's discussion of Nietzsche's "biologism," in his *Nietzsche*, ed. David Farrell Krell (San Francisco: Harper Books, 1982–1987), vol. 3, lectures six and sixteen.

29. Angela Livingstone, *Salome: Her Life and Work* (Mount Kisco, N.Y.: Moyer Bell, 1984), p. 37. We could easily imagine this label applied to Peirce. Both Peirce and Nietzsche locate human being within a natural order conceived in a nondeterministic fashion. It is interesting to remember that the two were both influenced by Ralph Waldo Emerson, hence by Concord transcendentalism. Nietzsche thought so highly of Emerson that he reproduced a quotation from him as the epigraph for *The Gay Science*. At various times in the 1840s, Emerson used the phrase "Joyous Science" and referred to Zoroaster (the historical Persian prophet for whom 'Zarathustra' is another name). See, for example, Walter Kaufman's Introduction to his translation of *The Gay Science*.

30. The eternal recurrence is Nietzsche's *natural* myth.

31. There are interesting and, I believe, significant similarities between Nietzsche and Dewey. Both are naturalists, both are irreligious, both are philosophers of process and evolution, and both find a special place for art within a naturalistic view of the world. Dewey could accurately be called an *aesthetic naturalist*, which term might fit Nietzsche as well. To be sure, they differ, most notably in their evaluations of democracy, and hence of modernity.

32. Arthur Danto, *Nietzsche as Philosopher* (New York: Columbia University Press, 1965), p. 80.

33. The qualification "generally" covers the problem of how Nietzsche can consider his own view true, a problem to be discussed shortly.

34. Except that for Schopenhauer there is yet a second escape or betrayal, by which the other truly ceases to serve the will; namely, in art and metaphysical knowledge. It is this idealistic-ascetic escape that Nietzsche rejects.

35. This does not mean that there is no cooperation among living things nor that the competition among them is a zero-sum game.

36. Peirce also claimed that aesthetic values were the highest, but never worked out the implications of this claim for naturalism. Dewey on the other hand, explicitly tries to integrate aesthetic experience into his

anthropology as the culmination of human experience and into his naturalistic metaphysics as the actualization of nature.

37. For the moment we will assume that Nietzsche believes what he says is true; this assumption will be questioned in responding to the next question.

38. Kant's own knowledge cannot be analytic, that is, true by definition, nor true based on experience, for then it would be probable at best. But neither can it be synthetic a priori, because the categories, principles, and forms of intuition presumably exhaust such knowledge. Or more simply, what is synthetic a priori is the set of conditions for the objects of possible experience. The *Critique*, as the justification and explanation *of* the synthetic a priori, cannot itself *be* synthetic a priori.

39. Danto refers to a passage (BGE, 22) that reads, "Supposing that this, too, is only an interpretation—and one will be eager enough to raise this objection. Well—so much the better" (Danto's translation, p. 230). But this comes at the end of a section discussing nature's conformity to law, in which Nietzsche suggests that there is no such conformity (at least in the realist's sense). Consequently, the "this" that is "only an interpretation" appears to refer to the local claim that nature does not conform to law, rather than, as Danto seems to suggest, to Nietzsche's perspectivism. That Nietzsche could claim that his skeptical alternative to a realist's view of nature's conformity to law is 'just' an interpretation does not mean that he would admit that perspectivism is only perspectively true. Nietzsche may indeed admit this, but the passage in question does not, I believe, amount to such an admission.

40. Danto, *Nietzsche as Philosopher*, p. 80.

41. My use of *active*, unless otherwise indicated by context, is Buchlerian, and not to be understood in terms of either Nietzsche's use of that term or Giles Deleuze's interpretation of it.

42. Gilles Deleuze, *Nietzsche and Philosophy*, trans. Hugh Tomlinson (New York: Columbia University Press, 1983) p. 99.

43. Ibid., p. 100.

44. Ibid., p. 103.

45. Ibid., p. 104.

46. Ibid., p. 107.

47. Whatever its virtues, the remark about "free men" seems to indicate that this reading finds in Nietzsche certain political aspirations characteristic of the Parisian Left of the postwar era, which I find dubious. Nevertheless, I could accept Deleuze's remark if he were to add that Nietzsche would regard it as unconscionable to try to make "free men" out of

any more than a tiny elite of persons. What is noble cannot be given to the base, and the vast majority will always be base. We cannot at once appropriate Nietzsche's aristocratic temperament in epistemology (e.g. substitute "high" for "true') and hesitate before its antiegalitarian political implications.

48. Alexander Nehamas, *Nietzsche: Life as Literature* (Cambridge, Mass.: Harvard University Press, 1985).

49. Alisdair MacIntyre, *Three Rival Versions of Moral Enquiry: Encyclopedia, Genealogy, and Tradition* (Notre Dame, Ind.: Notre Dame University Press, 1990), pp. 48–49.

50. Later, MacIntyre accepts that Nietzschean genealogy is self-undermining, but not with respect to the notion of truth, rather in the impossibility of conceiving of the self of the genalogist. See ibid., p. 213.

51. This is more or less what Kant claimed about the boundary of reason, that it partakes both of the knowable (the inside) and the unknowable (the outside).

52. Heidegger, *Nietzsche*, vol. 3, pp. 139–141.

53. Ibid., p. 144.

54. Ibid., p. 149.

55. This idea, which is his most fundamental attack on modernity, finds its clearest expression in *The Antichrist* (A, 56–58).

Chapter Six. Wittgenstein's Social Relativism

1. The epigraph is from VC, p. 118.

2. This is, more or less, the view of Burton Dreben. Much of this chapter is inspired by Dreben's provocative reading of Wittgenstein, although the reader ought not take any of the views presented as an adequate representation of Dreben's view.

3. K. T. Fann asks the same question—what is he doing?—but comes to somewhat different conclusions in *Wittgenstein's Conception of Philosophy* (Berkeley: University of California Press, 1969), p. 105.

4. My inquiry will operate within the usual distinction of Wittgenstein's work into two phases, an early period dominated the *Tractatus Logico-Philosophicus* and a later dominated by the *Philosophical Investigations*. It is not at all clear that this binary picture is adequate; the question of how many Wittgensteins there are has been raised. But for my purposes the customary error, to paraphrase Nietzsche, will have to do. For a more nuanced account, see Anthony Kenny, *The Legacy of Wittgenstein*

(Oxford: Basil Blackwell, 1984), also Merrill Hintikka and Jaakko Hintikka, *Investigating Wittgenstein* (Oxford: Basil Blackwell, 1986), p. 137. Also, Steven Gerrard has argued that Wittgenstein's middle period represents not a mere transitional phase on the way to the views expressed in the *Investigations*, but a distinct view that Wittgenstein eventually rejected. In this sense, the middle and late views represent alternative solutions to the problems for which Wittgenstein no longer saw the *Tractatus* as an adequate answer. Wittgenstein tried one alternative, the "calculus" conception, found it wanting, then turned to the "language game" conception of the *Investigations*. See Steven Gerrard, "Two Ways of Grounding Meaning," *Philosophical Investigations* 14; no. 2 (April 1991): 95–114; and "Wittgenstein's Philosophies of Mathematics," *Synthese* 87 (1991): 125–142.

5. So goes the story that Wittgenstein told G .H. von Wright, about reading in September 1914 a newspaper account of the use of a model of a car accident in a Paris courtroom. See von Wright's "Biographical Sketch" in Norman Malcolm's *Ludwig Wittgenstein: A Memoir* (London: Oxford University Press, 1958), pp. 7–8.

6. It is tempting to use Heideggerian language here. For Heidegger, the world is the horizon or context of possible experience. Human being is being *in* the world (*In-der-Welt-Sein*) in the sense that it experiences itself as worldly. But human being is not, in Heidegger's terminology, "intraworldly" (*innerweltlich*); that term characterizes nonhuman beings. Nonhuman things are *within* the world and are encountered by human beings as such. Human beings project the world as the "horizon" of experience, and so humans cannot be said to be located "within" the world in the way that things are.

7. See Ray Monk's marvellous biography, *Ludwig Wittgenstein: The Duty of Genius* (New York: The Free Press, 1990), p. 18.

8. The world is characterized by *mineness*. This is also Heidegger's point in the opening sections of *Being and Time*.

9. This remark appeared in the *Notebooks* about a month before the passage concerning idealism was written. Only the former was included in the *Tractatus*. Wittgenstein further remarked about solipsism that "what the solipsist *means* is quite correct; only it cannot be *said*, but makes itself manifest" (T, 5.62). What is correct about solipsism? It is the idea that the world is mine. Wittgenstein implies that the "world" he means is not the natural or public world, but a personal world. So that, for example, "at death the world does not alter, but comes to an end" (T, 6.431), which can only indicate that Wittgenstein means the "mineness" of the world quite rigorously. At this point Wittgenstein is an idealist.

10. Monk, *Ludwig Wittgenstein*, p. 178.

11. Ludwig Wittgenstein, "Lecture on Ethics," *The Philosophical Review* 74 (January 1965): 3–12. We are told in an introductory note that the lecture was delivered to a Cambridge audience sometime between September 1929 and December 1930. Monk says that Wittgenstein accepted the invitation in November 1929 (ibid., p. 276).

12. For a more complete discussion, see Chapter Three of James Edwards, *Ethics Without Philosophy: Wittgenstein and the Moral Life* (Tampa: South Florida University Press, 1985).

13. This is reminiscent of Nietzsche's use of metaphor, metonymy, and various mistaken similarities to explain how we think we know what in fact cannot be known. It is also reminiscent of Hume's point against the argument that God must exist because the orderliness of the universe is evidence of design. The notion of design has meaning only among the manifold relations of our world; it cannot be legitimately extended to apply to the world as a whole, and the world's relation to something outside. Notions like 'order' and 'design' are part of the world and have meaning only in terms of the relations of parts of the world to each other. They cannot be applied to the whole of which they are parts.

14. Wittgenstein likens this to the problem of miracles. The scientific interest in facts cannot countenance miracles by its very nature. Science cannot prove that there are no miracles; rather, "the scientific way of looking at a fact is not the way to look at it as a miracle."
This also reminds us of Hume, specifically of his argument against miracles, that there can never be sufficient evidence to justify belief in a miracle, because a miracle is by definition that which violates the laws of nature, and the latter summarize the evidence amassed by the human race. The difference is that Wittgenstein reduces all this to the consequence of a perspective, which cannot falsify the religious perspective. Kant makes the similar point that even if theological arguments about the origin and limit of the universe were available, science is prohibited from making use of them. In short, as Hilary Putnam points out, the religious and scientific perspectives "talk past each other" and do not contradict. See Hilary Putnam, "Wittgenstein on Religious Belief," *On Community: Boston University Studies in the Philosophy of Religion*, ed. Leroy Rouner (Notre Dame, Ind.: Notre Dame University Press, 1991), pp. 56–75.

15. And his views of Nietzsche and Heidegger as well. Regarding Heidegger and Kierkegaard, see Monk, *Ludwig Wittgenstein*, pp. 283–284; regarding Kierkegaard alone, see also p.383. See James Edwards's book as well.

16. There is a sense in which Nietzsche, Kierkegaard, and Wittgenstein are all part of an anti-Hegelian movement—self-consciously anti-Hegelian only in the case of Kierkegaard—that rejects the all-inclusive nature of rationality. This would be consistent with a Kantian inheritance.

17. There is a question whether *language game* refers only to Wittgenstein's hypothetical textual examples and not to actual linguistic practice. For my purposes, it is enough to note that he certainly does not consistently restrict himself to the former. His later work is strewn with the broader use of *language game* as a term for something actually occuring in the world. See, e.g., OC, 554, 559, 599.

18. Wittgenstein had read James's *Varieties of Religious Experience* as early as 1912. He remarked of James in 1930 that "what makes him a good philosopher [is that] he was a real human being" (Rush Shees editor, *Ludwig Wittgenstein: Personal Recollections* [Totowa, N.J.: Rowman and Littlefield, 1981]). James's *Principles of Psychology* was at one point the only philosophical book "visible" on Wittgenstein's bookshelves (John Passmore, *A Hundred Years of Philosophy* [Middlesex: Penguin, 1970], p. 592, n. 4, based on the report of student A. C. Jackson). Wittgenstein report-edly spent whole classes in the postwar period discussing James (see Passmore, and Goodman, below). Wittgenstein's *Remarks on the Philosophy of Psychology* refer to James more than to any other figure. This connection is documented and discussed by Russell B. Goodman in his unpublished manuscript, "Experience, Meaning, Pragmatism: James and Wittgenstein." I am indebted to Professor Goodman for pointing out rele-vant passages, especially paragraph 266 in RPP, discussed below.

19. C. K. Ogden and I. A. Richards, *The Meaning of Meaning* (London: Kegan Paul, 1923). Wittgenstein was sent a copy by Ogden in 1923. Wittgenstein evidently discussed the book with Ramsey, who reviewed it, during the winter of 1923–1924. The book not only refers to Peirce several times (including on page 1), but contains a twelve-page appendix devoted to explaining Peirce's theory and typology of signs. This, along with Ramsey's enthusiasm, makes it highly unlikely that Wittgenstein did not at least know of Peirce. Yet given his apparent disapproval of Ogden and Richards and his ambivalent opinion of Ramsey, this does not show that he consid-ered Peirce important or congenial. See S. Stephen Hilmy, *The Later Wittgenstein: Emergence of a New Philosophical Method* (Cambridge: Basil Blackwell, 1987).

20. In thinking about this matter I have benefited from discussions with Jaakko Hintikka and Burton Dreben.

21. Frank Ramsey, *Foundations: Essays in Philosophy, Logic, Mathematics and Economics*, ed. D. H. Mellor (Atlantic Highlands, N.J.: Humanities Press, 1978), p. 100. All my references to Ramsey are to this edition. Some useful information can also be had from looking at the origi-nal edition, *The Foundations of Mathematics and Other Logical Essays* (London: Kegan Paul, 1931), which includes an Introduction by R. B. Braithwaite.

22. The other two are his January 1924 review of Ogden and Richards and an unpublished essay written in the summer of 1929 entitled "General Propositions and Causality." In the former, Ramsey praises the authors' "excellent appendix on C. S. Peirce," which "deserves special mention." See *Mind* 33, (January 1924): 108–109. The latter refers to Peirce's convergence theory. See Ramsey, *Foundations*, p. 129.

23. Ramsey, *Foundations*, p. 96, n. 2. We may wonder regarding Ramsey's knowledge of Peirce, what did he know and when did he know it? By January 1924 Ramsey must have known of Peirce. In "Truth and Probability" (written late 1926) he refers to a collection of Peirce's essays, *Chance, Love, and Logic* (New York: Harcourt, 1923), ed. Morris Cohen. The collection contains two series of Peirce's published essays: the 1877–1878 series on pragmatism and probable reasoning published in *Popular Science Monthly*; and the 1891–1893 series on metaphysics published in *The Monist*. There is also a three-page selection from the beginning of "Some Consequences of Four Incapacities." From these essays Ramsey could have gotten most of Peirce's early pragmatism, his convergence theory, the doubt-belief theory, his theory of induction and probable reasoning, Peirce's panpsychist metaphysics, synechism, tychism and notion of evolution, and a bit of his critique of Cartesianism. I do not believe the term 'normative science' appears in those essays, so it would seem that Ramsey read some of Peirce's post-1903 work. If Ramsey's approval of Ogden and Richards' presentation of Peirce's semiotics indicates that he knew something of the latter firsthand, then he must have read still more than the Cohen collection, because nothing of the theory of signs is contained in it.

24. From August 1925 to July 1927 they apparently had no contact because of a quarrel (Monk, *Ludwig Wittgenstein*, p. 245). If Ramsey and Wittgenstein did not speak of pragmatism or Peirce before 1925 (when Ramsey was only twenty), then only two and one half years would have remained for verbal communication on these subjects. Certainly Wittgenstein could have read the relevant essays anytime after Ramsey's death.

25. In PI, 81, Wittgenstein writes, "F. P. Ramsey once emphasized in conversation with me that logic was a 'normative science'. I do not know exactly what he had in mind. . . ." Peirce used exactly these words; for him, logic, ethics, and aesthetics are the three "normative sciences." Although we cannot be absolutely sure that the phrase came from Peirce, it seems very likely. For a discussion of Wittgenstein's response to this point, see Hilmy, *The Later Wittgenstein*, pp. 318–319, n. 510. This passage does suggest that if Ramsey got the term from Peirce, he must have read Peirce's later work, beyond the 1870s papers on pragmatism and the 1890s papers on metaphysics that are contained in *Chance, Love, and Logic*.

26. K. T. Fann, in *Wittgenstein's Conception of Philosophy*, claims that "The indirect (through Ramsey) influence of Peirce's pragmatism on

Wittgenstein is apparent in all of his [Wittgenstein's] later writings . . ." (p. 46, n. 1). Almost nothing would make me happier, but I see no evidence to support this conclusion in Fann's book. Fann refers to Wittgenstein's incipient pragmatism, to Ramsey's explicit pragmatism, and to Wittgenstein's use of the term *normative science*. But this is insufficient evidence that Wittgenstein adopted or was positively influence by Peircean ideas.

27. Monk, *Ludwig Wittgenstein*, p. 246.

28. See the 1931 edition of Ramsey, *Foundations*, "Epilogue," pp. 291–292.

29. In the summer of 1929, in a brief essay titled "Philosophy," Ramsey wrote regarding Wittgenstein's view of philosophy: "Philosophy must be of some use and we must take it seriously. . . . Or else it is a disposition we have to check . . . i.e. the chief proposition of philosophy is that philosophy is nonsense. And again we must then take seriously that it is nonsense, and not pretend, as Wittgenstein does, that it is important nonsense!" (1931 edition of Ramsey, *Foundations*, p. 263).

30. See Monk's excellent biography.

31. Russell, for example, said just this. "The later Wittgenstein," he wrote, ". . . seems to have grown tired of serious thinking and to have invented a doctrine which would make such an activity unnecessary" (Monk, *Ludwig Wittgenstein*, p. 472).

32. Peirce concludes from this that we must accept the hypothesis that the laws of nature evolved over time.

33. One thinks of Socrates's remark in the Phaedo: "What else can one do in the time before sunset?"(61e).

34. This implies that the claim that meaning is use must really signify that meaning is *possible* use.

35. Water, again. Much could be written about the role of fluid metaphors in epistemology and metaphysics, beginning with Thales. Wittgenstein's river could be compared with Heraclitus's river and with Neurath's ship, Peirce swimming in a continuum of indeterminacy, etc.

36. Hanfling also argues that Wittgenstein rejects realism, hence transcends the opposing philosophical positions. Oswald Hanfling, *Wittgenstein's Later Philosophy* (Albany: State University of New York Press, 1989).

37. Ibid., p. 143.

38. Ibid., p. 145.

39. Ibid., p. 146.

40. Juliet Floyd, "Wittgenstein on 2,2,2. . . . : The Opening of Remarks On The Foundations of Mathematics," *Synthese* 87: 143–180 (1991), p. 159.

41. Steven Gerrard's essay, "Is Wittgenstein a Relativist?" has informed the ensuing discussion. Gerrard is right in making the point that Wittgenstein roots language games in forms of life, which prevents them from being arbitrary. The final paragraph of his essay begins, "The point is that our language games have purposes and are embedded in our form of life, and thus not everything goes" (Gerrard, p. 26). Agreed. But my question is, does that justify the following sentence: "What must go is interpreting Wittgenstein as a relativist"? Gerrard admits that it is unclear whether this denial of relativism holds outside Wittgenstein's philosophy of mathematics: "How far, however, this account can be extended beyond the mathematical examples remains to be seen." His essay is in *Wittgenstein - Towards a Re-Evaluation: Proceedings of the Fourteenth International Wittgenstein-Symposium*, ed. Rudolf Haller and Johannes Brandl (Vienna: Verlag Holder-Pichler-Tempsky, 1990), pp. 163–173.

42. My view bears comparison to the related claim of Jaakko and Merrill Hintikka that, for Wittgenstein, because language is a universal medium, semantics is "ineffable." I do not disagree with this. In my interpretation as well Wittgenstein believes no valid philosophical claims can be made about semantics in general. I am suggesting that the reason is that he accepts an account of language and philosophy that is an at least implicitly antirealist account, and no universal antirealism can be consistently asserted. See Merril B. Hintikka and Jaakko Hintikka, *Investigating Wittgenstein* (New York: Basil Blackwell, 1986), especially Chapter One.

43. This last phrase can also be translated, "I *still* cannot say what I really want to say"—"*ich das noch nicht sagan kann, was ich eigentlich sagen will.*"

44. See also PI, 111 and PI, 112.

Chapter Seven. Buchler's Objective Relativism

1. The epigraph is from TGT, p. 127. A few words of introduction are in order. Justus Buchler (1914–1991) received his Ph.D. in philosophy from Columbia University in 1939, writing a thesis on Peirce under Ernest Nagel (published as *Charles Peirce's Empiricism*). He taught at Columbia from 1937 to 1971, where he collaborated with John Herman Randall, Jr., and was a colleague of Ernst Cassirer. He taught at the State University of New York at Stony Brook from 1971 to 1981. His interests ranged over the history of philosophy, and among contemporary figures Peirce, Whitehead, Santayana, Royce, Dewey, and Cassirer received his special attention. He worked in epistemology, metaphysics, philosophical anthropology, had an abiding interest in the aesthetics of poetry, and a brief "flirtation" with logi-

cal positivism. Most significant was his work in undergraduate education as a prime mover of Columbia's Contemporary Civilization program from 1942 to 1956, which Buchler regarded as "the most fundamental intellectual experience" of his life (see Armen Marsoobian, Kathleen Wallace, and Robert Corrington, *Nature's Perspectives: Prospects for an Ordinal Metahphysics* [Albany: State University of New York Press, 1991], p. 13).

His distinctive perspective on human "utterance" or "judgment" was developed in the late 1940s and first formulated in 1951 in *Toward a General Theory of Human Judgment.* This perspective was expanded and situated in a philosophical system developed over the next two decades in four more books: *Nature and Judgment* (1955), *The Concept of Method* (1961), *Metaphysics of Natural Complexes* (1966), and *The Main of Light* (1974). Also important for my purposes are two essays published in 1978, "On the Concept of 'The World'" and "Probing the Idea of Nature."

2. Marsoobian et al., ibid., pp. 13–14. In 1951, attempting to write a new introduction to his seminal *Experience and Nature* (published in 1925), John Dewey remarked, "Were I to write (or rewrite) *Experience and Nature* today I would entitle the book *Culture and Nature....* I would abandon the term 'experience' because of my growing realization that the historical obstacles which prevented understanding of my use of 'experience' are . . . insurmountable. I would substitute the term 'culture' because with its meanings as now firmly established it can fully carry my philosophy of experience." See John Dewey, *The Later Works: 1925–1953*, vol. 1, ed. Jo Ann Boydston (Carbondale: Southern Illinois University Press, 1981), p. 361. It is possible to regard the meaning of query in Buchler as tantamount to 'culture' for Dewey.

3. This characterization comes from Sidney Gelber and Kathleen Wallace, "Justus Buchler: Nature, Power, and Prospect," *Process Studies* 15, no. 2 (Summer 1986): 108.

4. See "Notes on the Contour of a Natural Comples," in the new edition of MNC, ed. Kathleen Wallace and Armen Marsoobian, with Robert S. Corrington (Albany: State University of New York Press, 1990), pp. 215–223. See also Kathleen Wallace's Introduction in that edition, pp. xvii–xxix.

5. See Thomas Nagel, *The View From Nowhere* (New York: Oxford University Press, 1986).

6. Such as Stephen Pepper associates with William James in *World Hypotheses* (Berkeley: University of California Press, 1942).

7. Heidegger uses the same term—in German, *Geschichtlichkeit.* And the meanings are remarkably close. I do not know whether Buchler was familiar with its use by Heidegger.

8. There is a problem of consistency here, inasmuch as Buchler else-where makes it a difference between assertive and exhibitive judgment that, whereas the former seeks "acceptance or rejection," the latter is open to "degrees of assimilability" (TGT, p. 157). Either Buchler means that assertive judgment seeks a particular kind of acceptance, e.g., a simple yes versus no, or he has misspoken. I tend to think he has misspoken, because I do not believe that, upon reflection, he would want to deny a qualified, "degrees of assimilability" validation to assertive judgments.

9. It is important to note a difference between Buchler and almost all of the classical American philosophers (Peirce, Mead, Royce, Dewey, less so James); namely, that Buchler's notion of community is not a "eulogistic" one. Community is as likely to be bad as good: the notion has no moral valence. See James Campbell, "Buchler's Conception of Community," in Marsoobian et al., *Nature's Perspectives*, pp. 315–334.

10. The qualification ("by and large") because Buchler allows there to be elements of validation that are private, by which he means, unique to the proceiver. The fact of privacy does not entail its necessity; for Buchler nothing is private in principle. Hence nothing is in principle incommunicable. For Buchler the very self is already social or multiple. Reflexive communication or thought is made possible by the fact that the self is not simple.

11. This does not mean that Buchler is a "process philosopher." Unlike Peirce, Dewey, and Whitehead, Buchler explicitly denies that we can regard everything as a process or as part of a process. Human beings, however, are processes for Buchler, and derivatively, validity and its various norms (truth, success or goodness, exhibitive quality or beauty) must be under-stood within the context of that human process.

12. Marsoobian et al., *Nature's Perspectives*, p. 51. As mentioned in Chapter Two, the problem with this definition is that it would hold equally for idealism.

13. See Kathleen Wallace's discussion of the meaning of *natural* in relation to 'natural complexes' in her Introduction to the 1990 State University of New York Press edition of MNC, pp. xvii–xxix.

14. Another comparison to Heidegger is not out of place. Providingness would seem to be at home in Heidegger's interpretation of Being in terms of "*es gibt*" ("it gives"). See Heidegger's 1962 lecture, "Time and Being," in *On Time and Being*, trans. Joan Stambaugh (New York: Harper Books, 1972), pp. 1–24.

15. Philosophy can also function actively; see NJ, p. 77, and *The Southern Journal of Philosophy* 14, no. 1 (Spring 1976): 103 and 140. But this mode is less prominent for Buchler in understanding philosophy than are exhibition and assertion.

16. Buchler was familiar with Wittgenstein's work, early and late. He refers to the *Tractatus* in OCW (p. 560), and to the *Philosophical Investigations*, directly in NJ (p. 41, n. 4) and obliquely in ML (p. 161). I am told by John Ryder that Buchler was no happier with the later than with the earlier Wittgenstein. The passage from NJ bears this out; there Buchler criticizes the view of language as "instrument." But I see no indication that Buchler was critical of what I am calling Wittgenstein's *contextualism*.

17. Buchler does claim that it is impossible to "be deaf to the eloquence of experimental decision." We cannot "disagree" with science, for science "is a formalization of our own proceptive demand for guidance among the complexes of fact" (TGT, p. 73). The reason is that attention to "fact" is requisite for the rational control of action, hence survival. So science is granted a kind of invulnerable status in Buchler, but only because of the priority of action aimed at survival. The validity of scientific judgment remains contextual, even if the context that validates it is a necessary one.

18. I hear the echo of Peirce here. Buchler has used a formulation similar to Peirce's definition of a sign as that which stimulates the development of more signs.

19. This is reminiscent of Derrida.

20. My favorite example is the remark of Heisenberg about Schrödinger's wave mechanics. "The more I ponder about the physical part of Schrödinger's theory," he wrote to Wolfgang Pauli, "the more disgusting it appears to me." See Gerald Holton, *Thematic Origins of Modern Science: Kepler to Einstein* (Cambridge, Mass.: Harvard University Press, 1973), p. 133.

21. Others have raised this issue, or its kind. See, for example, Robert Neville, "Metaphysics," *Social Research* 47, no. 4 (Winter 1980): 689 and 693, n. 9. Of course, we must remember the level at which this objection is being made. Buchler never claimed that his system satisfied all cognitive interests, only that it adequately *accounted for* all such interests, that they could be described by his theory.

Chapter Eight. Derrida's Semiotic Relativism

1. The epigraph is from "Toward an Ethic of Discussion," in L, p. 136.

2. I will not claim to present a complete picture of Derrida's work in what follows. I have concerned myself only with his more obviously philosophical writings and, even then, only with a distillation of his program rather than with his applications of that program to the reading of philosophers. To some, this will no doubt mean that I have stacked my deck in favor of a certain kind of interpretation of Derrida. My only defense against

that charge is that the Derrida I will present is, I believe, a true one, although it may not be the only true one.

3. I agree with the main premise of Staten's book, that the later Wittgenstein and Derrida are engaged in similar projects. Staten's work is groundbreaking, and deserves careful study. What Staten and I disagree on is the finer points of how to characterize what both Derrida and Wittgenstein are doing. See Henry Staten, *Wittgenstein and Derrida* (Lincoln: University of Nebraska Press, 1984). The reference is on p. 12.

4. I especially appreciate Len Lawlor's criticisms in this connection.

5. See Jacques Derrida, *Of Spirit: Heidegger and the Question*, trans. Geoffrey Bennington and Rachel Bowlby (Chicago: University of Chicago Press, 1989), originally given as a lecture in 1987.

6. This manner of interpreting phenomenology is exemplified in Erazim Kohák's work, for example, his *The Embers and the Stars: A Philosophical Inquiry into the Moral Sense of Nature* (Chicago: University of Chicago Press, 1984).

7. An investigation of which Husserl remarked that it affected him so deeply that his career was "dominated" by it. See Edmund Husserl, *The Crisis of the European Sciences and Transcendental Phenomenology*, trans. David Carr (Evanston, Ill.: Northwestern University Press, 1970), p. 166, author's note.

8. Derrida has said of it that, among his early (1959–1972) works, "It is perhaps the essay which I like the most" (P, p. 4). Among his first four books (with *Of Grammatology, Writing and Difference, The Origin of Geometry)*, "in a classical philosophical architecture, *Speech* . . . would come first . . ." (P, p.5). And rightly so, because in this fascinating essay the critique of Husserl develops into a discussion of presence and the voice, which naturally leads into grammatology.

9. Edmund Husserl, *Logical Investigations*, trans. J. N. Findlay (New York: Routledge, 1970), Investigation II, Chapter One, section one, "An Ambiguity in the Term 'Sign'," p. 269. Volume One of the English translation includes Investigations I and II.

10. Not freedom "from" the tradition, which Derrida thinks is as impossible as does Heidegger. But Derrida aims to make room for freedom, so to speak, within the tradition by handling it in a new way.

11. For an examination of Heidegger's notion of destruction and its relation to deconstruction, see Rodolphe Gasché, *The Tain of the Mirror: Derrida and the Philosophy of Reflection* (Cambridge, Mass.: Harvard University Press, 1986).

12. See especially his "Letter on Humanism" (1947), in Martin Heidegger, *Basic Writings*, ed. David Krell (New York: Harper Books, 1987), pp. 193–242.

13. *Being and Time*, trans. John Macquarrie and Edward Robinson (New York: Harper and Row, 1962), p. 67.

14. For example, Jean-Paul Sartre, in his popular lecture "Existentialism," asserted: "Atheistic existentialism . . . states that if God does not exist, there is at least one being in whom existence precedes essence . . . and that this being is man. . . ." (*Existentialism and Human Emotions*, trans. Bernard Frechtman, [New York: Citadel Press, 1957], p. 15).

15. This does not mean, however, that Heidegger denies all such oppositions, as Derrida knows and as I tried to show in my *The Dilemma of Modernity: Philosophy, Culture, and Anti-Culture* (Albany: State University of New York Press, 1988), Chapter Six.

16. Martin Heidegger, *The Question Concerning Technology and Other Essays*, trans. William Lovitt (New York: Harper Books, 1977), pp. 136 and 154, respectively.

17. See Heidegger's 1929 lecture, "What Is Metaphysics?" in *Basic Writings*, pp. 95–112.

18. Martin Heidegger, *On the Question of Being*, trans. William Kluback and Jean T. Wilde (New York: Twayne, 1958), p. 81.

19. Martin Heidegger, "The Onto-Theo-Logical Constitution of Metaphysics," in *Identity and Difference*, trans. Joan Stambaugh (New York: Harper Books, 1957), p. 70.

20. Ibid., p .63.

21. Ibid., p. 65.

22. Martin Heidegger, *Early Greek Thinking*, trans. David F. Krell and Frank A. Capuzzi (San Francisco: Harper Books, 1984), p. 50.

23. Ibid., p. 51.

24. The qualification *a priori* applied to iterability occurs in "Signature Event Context," in *Margins*, p. 326: "The iteration which structures [utterance] a priori introduces an essential dehiscence and demarcation."

25. Peirce's version of this might be better than the term *ideal*, namely, that signs are intrinsically *general*.

26 Edmund Husserl, *Ideas*, vol. 1, trans. W. R. Boyce Gibson (New York: Collier Books, 1962), sec. 100, p. 279.

27. The lecture was given on January 27 to La Société française de philosophie at the Sorbonne. The complete lecture appears in English as an appendix to David Allison's translation of *Speech and Phenomena* (pp. 129–160). A translation of the ensuing discussion is published in *Derrida and Différance*, ed. David Wood and Robert Bernasconi (Evanston, Ill.: Northwestern University Press, 1988), pp. 83–95. The lecture also appears in the collection *Margins* (pp. 3–27), but without the first five introductory paragraphs. My references will all be to the Allison translation in SP.

28. As translator David Allison explains, this term refers to the facilitation of the excitatory process in Freud.

29. Also in "The Double Session," he makes the point that, "If polysemy is infinite, if it cannot be mastered as such, this is thus not because a finite reading or a finite writing remains incapable of exhausting a superabundance of meaning. Not . . . unless one displaces the philosophical concept of finitude and reconstitutes it according to the law and structure of the text: according as the blank, like the hymen, re-marks itself forever as disappearance, erasure, non-sense" (D, p. 253).

30. That is, a Hegelian totality or a Peircean convergence is possible.

31. Interestingly, Derrida is not the first person to use this term. Henry Sheffer, in his 1926 review of the second edition of volume one of Russell and Whitehead's *Principia Mathematica*, wrote of the "logocentric predicament." Sheffer remarked, "Just as the proof of certain theories in metaphysics is made difficult, if not hopeless, because of the 'egocentric' predicament, so the attempt to formulate the foundations of logic is rendered arduous by a corresponding 'logocentric' predicament. *In order to give an account of logic, we must presuppose and employ logic.*" *Isis* 8 (1926): 226–231; see pp. 227–228 for the quotation. I thank Burton Dreben for his mention (and use) of Sheffer's remark. It is referred to in print in Burton Dreben, "Quine," in Robert Barrett and Roger Gibson, *Perspectives on Quine* (New York: Basil Blackwell, 1990), p. 83.

32. I presume that Derrida is referring to the everyday language (or languages) of the West only.

33. Derrida first employed the term *undecidable* in the context of his discussion of Husserl in *Edmund Husserl's "The Origin of Geometry": An Introduction*, trans. John Leavey (Stony Brook, N.Y.: Nicholas Hays, 1978). He refers the term to Kurt Gödel (pp. 53–56).

34. As we will see later, Derrida is engaged in inquiry, that is, in that form of query that functions assertively and is governed by truth, consistency, etc. There is certainly an exhibitive component to his work. And most of all, he is questioning the conditions of the possibility of inquiry, e.g., the nature of truth, the distinction of assertion from exhibition, the structure of

inference, etc. Derrida's work is, in my reading, inquiry questioning itself, not the abandonment of inquiry.

35. There appears to be a problem here, in that Derrida sometimes seems to allow meaning to be coextensive with language, thereby making nonlinguistic judgments nonmeaningful.

36. Derrida repeats this point in *Dissemination*, writing that "any *full, absolute* presence of what *is* . . . any full intuition of truth, any truth-filled intuition is impossible. . . ." (DS, p. 166).

37. Derrida also makes a brief reference to Peirce in the lecture "The Principle of Reason: The University in the Eyes of Its Pupils," in the context of a discussion of Heidegger and the problem of the apparent circularity of any attempt by reason to ground itself. Derrida's view of Peirce, as expressed in this lecture, is discussed by Christopher Norris in his *Derrida* (Cambridge, Mass.: Harvard University Press, 1987), pp. 160–161. Derrida quotes a passage from Philip P. Weiner's selection of Peirce, *Values in a Universe of Chance* (New York: Dover Books, 1958), p. 332. It is from Peirce's 1900 review of Clark University (*Science* [April 20, 1900]: 620–622). As a Clark alumnus I find myself unable to refrain from noting Peirce's remark in that review that, "the Clark University . . . has perhaps the most elevated ideal of any university in the world. . . ." How Derrida could have overlooked this crucial passage, I cannot say. Resisting temptation, I will spare the reader further exploration of Clark's imputed ideality and its grammatological place in the series: Peirce, Derrida, Harvard, Cornell, Heidegger, Freiburg, E.N.S., etc.

38. Ironically, Derrida's (and Spivak's) references to Peirce are variously incorrect. The reference in the English translation of *Of Grammatology* (OG, p. 326, n. 13) is wrong. The note, which correctly refers to "Elements of Logic," the second volume of Peirce's *Collected Papers*, then reads "Bk. I, 2, p. 302." The passage is actually in Book II, 3, paragraph 303 (page 169). The French original (Paris: Minuit, 1967) is slightly off as well; it correctly refers to Book II, but then to "p. 302." Also, Derrida puts the whole first sentence in emphasis, whereas only three terms are emphasized in the original. I might add that in regard to the immediately preceding reference (n. 12), in the text Derrida refers to a Peircean text called "*Principles of Phenomenology*" (in the French text it is plural; Spivak has made it "Principle"). That title is not Peirce's; it is Buchler's title for a chapter in his *Philosophical Writings of Peirce* (to which Derrida refers in notes 11 and 12), where Buchler has drawn together passages from several of Peirce's manuscripts. Derrida has written Buchler's sign for a rearrangement of Peirce's text into Peirce's text. The fragment Derrida quotes ("the idea of *manifestation* is the idea of a sign") is from a draft of Peirce's 1903 Lowell lectures ("Lowell Lectures of 1903"), and appears in CP, 1.346.

39. What I am unable to explain is why Derrida, after these passages published in 1967, rarely referred to Peirce again. If one thinks of Derrida's relation to Husserl, by comparison, Husserl seems to serve more as the raw material of critique for Derrida, whereas with Peirce there is real similarity at crucial points (to be sure, only *up to* a point). Yet Derrida wrote two books on Husserl and three pages on Peirce. I might imagine two possibilities: either Derrida perceived that his differences with Peirce, primarily in relation to the latter's nonsemiotic work, were too great; or precisely the similarity between them made a discussion of Peirce's semiotics—which, after all, would be Derrida's main interest—unfruitful as a vehicle and occasion for Derrida's deconstructionist writing. In other words, Husserl is a better vehicle because he is more wrong.

40. Peirce does also refer to the fact that "every thought is an *external* sign" (CP, 5.314).

41. A last, minor point is that both Derrida and Peirce deny that we can find a necessary starting point for inquiry. Derrida comments, "We must begin *wherever we are* and the thought of the trace, which cannot not take the scent into account, has already taught us that it was impossible to justify a point of departure absolutely. *Wherever we are*: in a text where we already believe ourselves to be" (OG, p. 162). As we have already seen, Peirce writes, "in truth, there is but one state of mind from which you can 'set out,' namely the very state of mind in which you actually find yourself at the time you do 'set out'—a state in which you are laden with an immense mass of cognition already formed, of which you cannot divest yourself if you would . . . (CP, 5.416).

42. Although empiricism has often mitigated this tendency with naturalism; that is, it has located experience within a scientific conception of nature as the cause of experience. This is most obvious in Locke. Berkeley, of course, contextualizes experience in a different way, with God. That is why, as a nonnaturalist empiricist, Berkeley exhibits some interesting comparisons to the German tradition of idealism and phenomenology (e.g., Heidegger).

43. There is one exception, a touch of naturalism in Derrida, as we will see.

44. In "Toward an Ethic of Discussion," Derrida does accept that inquiry constitutes a community with norms (for example, 'truth') that are legitimately constitutive; that is, norms that he recognizes as binding. But Derrida makes this context and community of inquiry one context among other possible contexts!

45. Derrida wrote approvingly, "Leroi-Gourhan . . . describes the unity of man and the human adventure . . . as a stage or an articulation in the history of life—of what I have called *différance*—as the history of the *grammè* [trace, mark]. Instead of having recourse to the concepts that habitually

serve to distinguish man from other living beings (instinct and intelligence, absence or presence of speech, of society, of economy, etc. etc.), the notion of *program* is invoked. . . . This movement goes far beyond the possibilities of the 'intentional consciousness'. . . . Since 'genetic inscription' and the 'short programmatic chains' regulating the behavior of the amoeba or the annelid up to the passage beyond alphabetic writing to the orders of the logos and of a certain *homo sapiens*, the possibility of the *grammè* structures the movement of its history according to rigorously original levels, types, and rhythms" (OG, p. 84).

46. If Derrida means only to say that nonhuman events can function as signs for humans, then no naturalism is implied. But the passage in question does not indicate that. If Derrida means that nonhuman events can inscribe, write, mean, independent of any relation between those events and human beings, then the notion of writing or semiosis is being radically expanded into some kind of continuity with typically naturalistic categories (e.g., "cause").

47. See Jacques Derrida, "Declarations of Independence," *New Political Science* 15 (Summer 1986): 7–15.

48. The material in quotation marks is from "My Chances/*Mes chances*: A Rendezvous with Some Epicurean Stereophonies," trans. Irene Harvey and Avital Ronell, in *Taking Chances*, ed. Joseph Smith and William Kerrigan (Baltimore: Johns Hopkins University Press, 1984), p. 27.

49. Derrida certainly has other objections to speech act theory in "Signature Event Context" (printed in *Margins* and in *Limited, Inc.*), but only these three seem relevant to the question of contextualism per se.

50. This is not the first time Derrida has made this point. For example, in a note to the interview "Positions" he wrote that "it goes without saying that in no case is it a question of a *discourse against truth*. . . ." (P, p. 105, n. 32).

51. Derrida does not, in my estimation, subordinate assertion to exhibition, logic to rhetoric, and inquiry to art. He makes this clear in a scathing response to Habermas (L, pp. 156–158, n. 9). Derrida *questions* the distinction, shows that it is problematic, that its occurrences contain undecidable elements, as he does with all other fundamental distinctions. See also the 1971 essay "White Mythology," in *Margins*, pp. 207–271.

52. This does not mean Wittgenstein agrees with Reid, only that he is closer to commonsensism than is Derrida. G. E. Moore, who Wittgenstein criticizes in *On Certainty*, is closer still; both he and Reid provide a philosophical defense of common sense. Wittgenstein would presumably have responded to Reid as he did to Moore, that such a defense cannot make assertive sense.

53. It is this misreading that irritates Derrida so much in "Toward an Ethic of Discussion."

Chapter Nine. Rorty's Antphilosophical Pragmatism

1. My title is a reference to the medieval classic, *The Consolation of Philosophy*, composed by Boethius about 524 A.D., while awaiting execution.

2. David Hiley, *Philosophy In Question: Essays on a Pyrrhonian Theme* (Chicago: University of Chicago Press, 1988).

3. Sextus Empiricus, *Outlines of Pyrrhonism*, trans. R. G. Bury (Cambridge, Mass.: Harvard University Press, 1961), vol. 1, part of the Loeb Classical Library series. References to Sextus will be made in the standard manner, where PH refers to *Outlines of Pyrrhonism*, the Roman numeral to Part I, II or III, and the number to the right of the decimal is the paragraph number.

4. Here I have used the more contemporary translation by Sanford Etheridge in *Selections from the Major Writings on Skepticism, Man, and God* (Indianapolis: Hackett, 1985), p. 96. The reason is that Etheridge's translation of the Greek *adoxastos* as "without opinions" or "without beliefs"—rather than Bury's "undogmatically"—seems to make matters more clear. It also conforms to discussions by contemporary scholars, e.g., Myles Burnyeat, "Can the Skeptic Live His Skepticism?," in Malcolm Schofield et al., *Doubt and Dogmatism: Studies in Hellenistic Epistemology* (Oxford: Clarendon Press, 1980), p. 43.

5. Sextus refers to a later period in the history of Plato's academy, during the time of Carneades (c. 213–128 B.C.). See PH, I.226-227.

6. There are two senses of *dogma* among the skeptics, a broad one and a narrow one. In its broad meaning *dogma* refers to whatever we think, any beliefs, including reports of experiences (e.g. "I was warmed"). Narrowly, it refers to claims about the "nonevident." I will use *dogma* only in the latter sense, restricted to the kinds of beliefs from which the skeptic abstains. Regarding the two meanings of *dogma*, see M. F. Burnyeat, "Can the Skeptic Live His Skepticism?" pp. 45–46.

7. Michael Frede, "The Skeptic's Two Kinds of Assent and the Question of the Possibility of Knowledge," in Richard Rorty et al., *Philosophy in History: Essays on the Historiography of Philosophy* (Cambridge: Cambridge University Press, 1984), pp. 255–278.

8. Ibid., p. 266.

9. Unless of course the question being discussed was something like "Do paintings exist?"

10. Even before *Philosophy and the Mirror* of Nature Rorty was an influential philosopher (e.g. see his *The Linguistic Turn: Recent Essays in Philosophical Method* [Chicago: University of Chicago Press, 1967]). This early work is, however, not especially relevant to my theme nor to his current reputation.

11. A more elaborate analysis of Rorty's argument appeared in my "Relativism and Metaphysics: On Justus Buchler and Richard Rorty," in Armen Marsoobian, Kathleen Wallace and Robert Corrington, *Nature's Perspectives: Prospects for an Ordinal Metaphysics* (Albany: State University of New York Press, 1990), pp. 235–252. That analysis was written without any knowledge of Rorty's *Contingency, Irony, and Solidarity* (1989), in which he introduced the term, *final vocabulary*. (CIS, p. 73). This term seems to confirm my analysis, at least in part.

12. Although I will occasionally resort to the upper case *Philosophy* for emphasis, I will usually employ the lower case *philosophy* to refer both to the kind of philosophy Rorty criticizes and the kind he accepts, leaving it to context to make my meaning clear.

13. Rorty has at various times emphasized the common sense nature of the form of philosophical discourse to which the denial of transcendence returns us, whereas at others he has endorsed irony, in opposition to common sense, to open the way for creative "redescription" and social change (CIS, p. 74). In the latter moments he wants to avoid the apparent conservatism of Sextus's acceptance of the guidance of custom and law. At the former times he emphasizes our inevitable ethnocentrism and recognizes that this emphasis may dampen radical ardor by denying the validity of transcendentalist justifications of social reform. See, for example, COP, pp. 169–175, ORT, pp. 203–210, and Rorty's address to the Inter-American Congress in Guadalajara, "From Logic to Language to Play," *Proceedings of the American Philosophical Association* 59, no. 5 (June 1986): 747–753.

14. Ray Monk, *Ludwig Wittgenstein: The Duty of Genius* (New York: Macmillan, 1990), p. 325.

15. I have argued that we could never identify a final vocabulary in "Relativism and Metaphysics: On Justus Buchler and Richard Rorty."

16. For example, in CIS (1989), he declared affinity with the "romanticist" project of constructing culture via "redescription," for which truth is "made" rather than "found."

17. In the 1986 essay "Pragmatism, Davidson and Truth," Rorty lists the legitimate uses of the term 'truth' so as to exclude any "explanatory" use. 'Truth' is primarily an "endorsement" of beliefs, but it also has a "disquotational" use in metalinguistic statements about truth and an important "cautionary" use, such that it makes sense to say that a belief is "perfectly" justified, but perhaps *not* "true." Rorty says that James's neglect

of this cautionary use "led to the association of pragmatism with relativism" (ORT, p. 128).

18. John Rawls, "Justice as Fairness: Political not Metaphysical," *Philosophy and Public Affairs* 14, no. 3 (Summer 1985): 223–251, see pp. 231 and 240, n. 22.

19. Arthur Fine, "The Natural Ontological Attitude," in Jarrett Leplin, *Scientific Realism* (Berkeley: University of California Press, 1984), pp. 83–107.

20. Ibid., p. 95.

21. Ibid., p. 101.

22. Ibid., p. 99.

23. Ibid., p. 101.

24. Arthur Fine, "And Not Anti-Realism Either," *Nous* 13, no. 1 (March 1984): 51–65, reference on p. 53.

25. Ibid., p. 54.

26. Jean François Lyotard, *The Postmodern Condition: A Report on Knowledge*, trans. Geoff Bennington and Brian Massumi (Minneapolis: University of Minnesota Press, 1984). See Rorty's 1984 essay, "Habermas and Lyotard on Postmodernity," EHO, pp. 164–176.

27. To me, this idea seems tantamount to trying to say what in our perception of things "goes beyond the facts."

28. Ibid., p. 62.

29. It is neither common nor intuitive.

30. The only way to avoid the second horn of my dilemma would be to deny contradiction on the basis of the context-dependency, hence incommensurability, of the meanings of beliefs in science and outside it. But this incommensurability has, of course, its own problems, famously attacked by Davidson, which Fine would presumably wish to avoid.

31. Fine, "And Not Anti-Realism Either," p. 61. This is another example of the method of avoidance, coupled with the therapeutic image. Although I agree that some questions are wrongheaded and so ought not be asked or answered, one ought to be able to say what is wrong with such questions and justify that response. Mere avoidance coupled with therapeutic metaphorics seems to import into philosophical discussion attitudes more appropriate to psychiatric treatment. One begins to imagine that Prozac would be the proper response to most philosophical questions.

32. The contextualist metaphor of "games" is reminiscent of Wittgenstein—I do not know if Fine intends this reference. But, as Steven Gerrard

points out, for Wittgenstein every language game has a point, which is its contribution to a form of life. See Gerrard's "Is Wittgenstein a Relativist?" in *Wittgenstein - Towards a Re-Evaluation: Proceedings for the Fourteenth International Wittgenstein-Symposium*, ed. Rudolf Haller and Johannes Brandl (Vienna: Verlag Holder-Pichler-Tempsky, 1990), pp. 163–173.

33. See Christopher Norris, *Derrida* (Cambridge, Mass.: Harvard University Press, 1987); and Rodolphe Gasché, *The Tain of the Mirror: Derrida and the Philosophy of Reflection* (Cambridge, Mass.: Harvard University Press, 1986).

34. Despite the denial that Derrida makes arguments, holds positions, or does philosophy, Rorty frequently ascribes to Derrida philosophical "points," philosophical "theses," and even a philosophical position, "nominalism." These are, respectively, "Derrida's revival of Peirce's anti-Cartesian point" (EHO, p. 115); "the familiar Peircean-Wittgensteinian anti-Cartesian thesis that meaning is a function of context" (EHO, p. 125); and, Derrida is either a transcendental philosopher or "a much-misunderstood nominalist" (EHO, p. 128).

35. In this respect Rorty, despite his turnings toward continental and classical pragmatic philosophy, remains a student of Reichenbach and Carnap. See Hans Reichenbach, *The Rise of Scientific Philosophy* (Berkeley: University of California Press, 1962)—and Rorty on Reichenbach, COP, pp. 211–230—and Rudolf Carnap, "Pseudoproblems in Philosophy," with *The Logical Structure of the World*, trans. Rolf George (Berkeley: University of California Press, 1967).

36. He is in good company, because, as we have seen, Wittgenstein's work is nonsense on his own account, just as Derrida admits that deconstruction can be deconstructed. See the last page of Wittgenstein's *Tractatus*, and Derrida's "Le Nouvel Observateur" interview, in David Wood and Robert Bernasconi, *Derrida and Différance*, (Evanston, Ill.: Northwestern University Press, 1988), p. 68.

Chapter Ten. The Ends of Philosophy

1. This distinction is from Kant, although I am, to be sure, changing Kant's usage. For him the limitation of science is its essential incompleteness, an incompleteness determined by bounds that science never encounters. Philosophy then seeks to know those bounds, which entails knowing the relationship between the knowable and the unknowable (the border between the two). I am using *limit* and *bound* to characterize two ways of explaining *philosophy's* incompleteness in principle. I am using *limits* quite differently from Kant's *Schranken*. When I say that philosophy is unlimited inquiry I do not mean that it is complete, rather that its *task* is unlimited,

hence every philosophical work is incomplete. See Chapter Two, the section "Answering Hume."

2. One of my favorite examples comes from a lecture by Marx Wartofsky at Clark University in, I believe, 1976. He meant it comically, so I do not mean to imply that he was accepting my view or anything like it. Wartofsky said, in effect, "If you told me I would die in five minutes, and demanded that I define science, I would say, 'It is the search for truth.' If you then asked me what truth is, I would say, 'Please, I'm dying!'"

3. Joseph Margolis, *Pragmatism Without Foundations: Reconciling Realism and Relativism* (Oxford: Basil Blackwell, 1986), p. 1.

4. I am not referring to logical theories of propositional truth, but to the prior question of what kinds of things can be called *true*.

5. See Jürgen Habermas's explication of Weber in Habermas's *The Theory of Communicative Action*, trans. Thomas McCarthy (Boston: Beacon Press, 1984), vol. 1, Chapter Two. Also, see Max Weber, for example, his "Science as a Vocation," in *From Max Weber*, trans. H. H. Gerth and C. Wright Mills (New York: Oxford University Press, 1946), pp. 129–158. The classical presentation of the rationalization theme is in the Introduction to Weber's *The Protestant Ethic and the Spirit of Capitalism*, trans. Talcott Parsons (London: Charles Scribner's & Sons, 1958).

6. See Buchler's marvelous discussion in NJ, pp. 187–191.

7. Here I am distinguishing types of philosophical method, not primarily philosophical objects. Nevertheless, differences in philosophy's method—i.e., in aim, norm, or criteria—certainly make for differences in philosophy's objects; that is, differences in what the objects of philosophy are taken to be, whether these are best described as differences between aspects of one set objects, or different foci of philosophical attention.

8. Truth is in quotes here because for Heidegger things are both concealing and revealing and the task of thinking is to attend to both, which is to say, to untruth as well as truth.

9. The importance of the notion of *poiesis*, making, was brought home to me by Thomas Thorp's very interesting dissertation on Habermas, Heidegger, and Derrida. See Thomas Thorp, "Politology," Ph.D. dissertation, State University of New York at Stony Brook, 1993.

10. This is a distinction between the language of Husserlian and Heideggerian phenomenology.

11. As Erazim Kohák claims in *Ideas and Experience: Edmund Husserl's Project of Phenomenology in Ideas I* (Chicago: University of Chicago Press, 1978), for example, on pp.xi and 143–147.

12. This last term, although common, should actually be: "Anglo-American except for the American pragmatists and process philosophers."

13. Husserl (at least, as of 1900) and Frege each reacted against psychologism, but differently, and the difference is significant for the traditions they inaugurated. For Frege, psychologism's greatest sin was its *subjectivism*, the reduction of logical and mathematical objects to individual minds and their private acts. For Husserl, its sin was *naturalism*, the reduction of ideality to psychic reality, hence to natural, biological, contingent fact.

14. Historically it would be more accurate to say that this second rebellion had three strains: first existentialism, then pragmatism, then phenomenology. Existentialism in Kierkegaard and Nietzsche explicitly linked truth with subjective expressiveness and art. Pragmatism linked truth with action. Phenomenology began (in Husserl) by demanding a return to experience; that is, to descriptive inquiry into experience. But Husserlian phenomenology, after having early spawned a huge field of interesting research, soon was impregnated by Heidegger with the Nietzschean artistic impulse, so that the offspring of its middle age bear the mark of non-assertive, nonrepresentational philosophic query.

15. One could add Wittgenstein in at least one phase of his work, according to Jaakko Hintikka and Merrrill Hintikka. See their *Investigating Wittgenstein* (New York: Basil Blackwell, 1986), Chapter Six.

16. This does not necessarily make philosophy utterly nonreferential. Art can be valued not only for its own sake but also for what it shows about something nonartistic.

17. A further twist to the story would involve trying to distinguish the career of process philosophy from pragmatism. Peirce and Dewey were certainly process philosophers, but contemporary process philosophers are especially indebted to Whitehead. To the extent that neoWhiteheadian process philosophy is not pragmatic, it appears more continuous with the traditional philosophy (the ancien régime, so to speak). At least one pragmatic element always remains, however: the metaphilosophical view that each process philosophy is a hypothesis aimed to satisfy our need to form a consistent picture of the whole of things, to build the best *weltanschauung*.

18. I acknowledge that my story is vaguely Weberian.

19. Pragmatists and process philosophers have consistently ascribed an essential continuity to things. For Peirce, Whitehead, Dewey, and Mead, things are more continuous than discontinuous. This is not so for Buchler.

20. William James's famous essay (1896), "The Will to Believe" (in William James, *Essays in Pragmatism* [New York: Hafner, 1969], pp. 88–109) is a response to W. K. Clifford's essay, "The Ethics of Belief," in

which Clifford had argued that it is ethically wrong to accept a belief "upon insufficient evidence."

21. I am concerned primarily with methodology, with some human interest or energy that has been left out of the practice, interest, and aim of philosophy; e.g., artistic creativity, personal expressiveness, the improvement of humanity, personal religious salvation. Presumably, concomitant with each of these would be something objective that had been left out; either a set of objects that philosophy as inquiry had ignored or, better, objects seen from a certain perspective, a certain aspect or dimension or ordinal integrity of things (to use Buchler's term). Philosophy as ultimate inquiry is interested in everything, it wishes to leave nothing out. It can inquire into everything, including other modes of query and their vicissitudes. But that can mean only that it treats everything in its way, through its method, in its perspective (e.g., for me, as a potential object of publicly valid assertion). This, despite its unlimited scope, may be seen as a limitation that neglects other human interests methodologically and hence neglects other senses or meanings of the things of the world.

22. It is implicit in this discussion that continental and American philosophy are in principle more open to the demand that philosophy encompass life and that analytic philosophy tends to dismiss this demand. This is, I think, generally, but only generally, true. There are analytic philosophers who clearly regard their philosophical work as morally virtuous, e.g., as a pursuit of honesty, intellectual humility, and heightened self-knowledge, and as continuous with political ideals, e.g. the critique of social mystifications that support antidemocratic forces. But the role of non-assertive values in inquiry for American and continental philosophers is more substantive than this.

23. This echoes Nietzsche's analysis of the role of the ascetic ideal vis-à-vis life in *The Genealogy of Morals*.

BIBLIOGRAPHY

Albert, Hans. *Treatise on Critical Reason*, tran. Mary Varney Rorty. Princeton: Princeton University, 1985.

Apel, Karl-Otto. "The Problem of Philosophical Foundations in Light of a Transcendental Pragmatics of Language," Kenneth Baynes et al., *After Philosophy: End or Transformation*. Cambridge: MIT, 1987, pp. 250–90.

———. *Towards a Transformation of Philosophy*, tran. Glyn Adey and David Frisby. London: Routledge, 1980.

The Bhagavad Gita, tran. Juan Mascaró. Baltimore: Penguin, 1962.

Brent, Joseph. *Charles Sanders Peirce: A Life*. Bloomington: Indiana University, 1993.

Buchler, Justus. "The Accidents of Peirce's System." *The Journal of Philosophy*, vol. 37, no. 10, May 9, 1940, pp. 264–69.

———. *Charles Peirce's Empiricism*. New York: Octagon, 1966.

———. *The Concept of Method*. Lanham: University of America, 1985.

———. *The Main of Light: On the Concept of Poetry*. New York: Oxford University, 1974.

———. *Metaphysics of Natural Complexes*. New York: Columbia University, 1966.

———. *Nature and Judgment*. New York: Grosset, 1966.

———. "On the Concept of 'The World'." *The Review of Metaphysics*, vol. 31, no. 4, June 1978, pp. 555–79.

——— *Philosophical Writings of Peirce*. New York: Dover, 1955.

——— "Probing the Idea of Nature." *Process Studies*, vol. 8, no. 3, fall 1978, pp. 157–68.

403

——— "Reply to Ross." *The Southern Journal of Philosophy*, vol. xiv, no. 1, spring 1976, pp. 103–09.

———. *Toward a General Theory of Human Judgment*. New York: Dover, 1979.

Burnyeat, Myles. "Can the Sceptic Live His Scepticism?" in Malcolm Schofield, et al., *Doubt and Dogmatism: Studies in Hellenistic Epistemology*. Oxford: Clarendon, 1980, pp. 20–53.

Cahoone, Lawrence. *The Dilemma of Modernity: Philosophy, Culture, and Anticulture*. Albany: State University of New York Press, 1988.

Carnap, Rudolf. "Pseudoproblems in Philosophy," in *The Logical Structure of the World*, tran. Rolf George. Berkeley: University of California, 1967, pp. 305–43.

Clark, Maudemarie. *Nietzsche on Truth and Philosophy*. Cambridge: Cambridge University, 1990.

Colapietro, Vincent. *Peirce's Approach to the Self: A Semiotic Perspective on Human Subjectivity*. Albany: State University of New York Press, 1989.

Crosser, Paul. *The Nihilism of John Dewey*. New York: Philosophical Library, 1955.

Danto, Arthur. *Nietzsche as Philosopher*. New York: Columbia University, 1965.

Davidson, Donald. "A Coherence Theory of Truth and Knowledge," in Ernest LePore, *Truth and Interpretation: Perspectives on the Philosophy of Donald Davidson*. Oxford: Basil Blackwell, 1986, pp. 307–19.

———. "The Method of Truth in Metaphysics," in *Inquiries into Truth and Interpretation*. Oxford: Clarendon, 1984, pp. 199–214.

———. "On the Very Idea of a Conceptual Scheme," in *Inquiries into Truth and Interpretation*. Oxford: Clarendon, 1984, pp. 183–98.

Deleuze, Gilles. *Nietzsche and Philosophy*, tran. Hugh Tomlinson. New York: Columbia University, 1983.

Derrida, Jacques. "Declarations of Independence." *New Political Science*, vol. 15, summer 1986, pp. 7–15.

———. "Differance," in *Speech and Phenomena and Other Essays on Husserl's Theory of Signs*, pp. 129–60.

———. *Dissemination*, tran. Barbara Johnson. Chicago: University of Chicago Press, 1981.

——. *The Ear of the Other*, tran. Peggy Kamuf. Lincoln: Nebraska, 1985.

——. *Edmund Husserl's The Origin of Geometry: An Introduction*, tran. John Leavey. Stony Brook: Nicholas Hays, 1978.

——. *Limited, Inc.*, tran. Sam Weber. Baltimore: Hopkins, 1977.

——. *Margins*, tran. Alan Bass. Chicago: University of Chicago Press, 1982.

——. "An Interview with Derrida," tran. David Wood and Robert Bernasconi, in *Derrida and Différence*. Evanston: Northwestern University, 1988, pp. 71–81.

——. *Of Grammatology*, tran. G.C. Spivak. Baltimore: Johns Hopkins University, 1976.

——. *Of Spirit: Heidegger and the Question*, tran. Geoffrey Bennington and Rachel Bowlby. Chicago: University of Chicago Press, 1989.

——. *Positions*, tran. Alan Bass. Chicago: University of Chicago Press, 1981.

——. "The Principle of Reason: The University in the Eyes of its Pupils," tran. Catherine Porter and Edward P. Morris, *Diacritics*, vol. 13, fall 1983, pp. 3–20.

——. *Spurs*, tran. Barbara Harlow. Chicago: University of Chicago Press, 1978.

——. *Speech and Phenomena and Other Essays on Husserl's Theory of Signs*, tran. David Allison. Evanston: Northwestern University, 1973.

——. *Writing and Difference*, tran. Alan Bass. Chicago: University of Chicago Press, 1978.

Dewey, John *Experience and Nature*. New York: Dover, 1958, p. 358.

——. *Logic: The Theory of Inquiry*, vol. twelve of *The Later Works, 1925–1953*, ed. Jo Ann Boydston. Carbondale: University of Southern Illinois, 1991.

——. *The Later Works: 1925–1953*, vol. 1, ed. Jo Ann Boydston. Carbondale: University of Southern Illinois, 1981.

Dreben, Burton. "Quine," in Robert Barrett and Roger Gibson, *Perspectives On Quine*. New York: Basil Blackwell, 1990.

Dummett, Michael. *Truth and Other Enigmas*. Cambridge: Harvard University, 1978.

Edwards, James. *Ethics Without Philosophy: Wittgenstein and the Moral Life*. Tampa: University of South Florida, 1985.

Fann, K.T. *Wittgenstein's Conception of Philosophy*. Berkeley: University of California, 1969.

Fine, Arthur. "And Not Anti-Realism Either." *Nous*, vol. XVIII, no. 1, March 1984, pp. 51–65.

———. "The Natural Ontological Attitude," in Leplin, *Scientific Realism*. Berkeley: University of California, 1984, pp. 83–107.

Floyd, Juliet. "Wittgenstein on 2,2,2 . . . : The Opening of Remarks On The Foundations of Mathematics." *Synthese* 87:23–49, 1991.

Foucault, Michel. *Power/Knowledge*, tran. by Colin Gordon, Leo Marshall, Hohn Mepham, Kate Soper. New York: Pantheon, 1980.

Frede, Michael. "The sceptic's two kinds of assent and the question of the possibility of knowledge," in Richard Rorty, et al., *Philosophy in History: Essays on the Historiography of Philosophy*. Cambridge: Cambridge University, 1984, pp. 255–78.

Frege, Gottlob. *The Foundations of Arithmetic*, tran. J.L. Austin. Evanston: Northwestern University, 1980.

Gasché, Rodolphe. *The Tain of the Mirror: Derrida and the Philosophy of Reflection*. Cambridge: Harvard University, 1986.

Gelber, Sidney and Kathleen Wallace. "Nature, Power and Prospect: Justus Buchler's System of Philosophy," in Armen Marsoobian, Kathleen Wallace, and Robert Corrington, *Nature's Perspectives: Prospects for Ordinal Metaphysics*. Albany: State University of New York Press, 1991, pp. 49–63.

Gerrard, Steven. "Is Wittgenstein a Relativist?" *Wittgenstein—Towards a Re-Evaluation: Proceedings of the 14th International Wittgenstein-Symposium*, ed. Rudolf Haller and Johannes Brandl. Vienna: Verlag Holder-Pichler-Tempsky, 1990, pp. 163–73.

———. "Two Ways of Grounding Meaning." *Philosophical Investigations* 14:2, April 1991, pp. 95–114.

———. "Wittgenstein's Philosophies of Mathematics." *Synthese* 87, 1991, pp. 125–42.

Habermas, Jürgen. "Discourse Ethics: Notes on a Program of Philosophical Justification," in *Moral Consciousness and Communicative Action*, tran. Christian Lenhardt and S. W. Nicholsen. Cambridge: MIT, 1990, pp. 43–115.

———. *The Theory of Communicative Action*, vol. one, tran. Thomas McCarthy. Boston: Beacon, 1984.

Hanfling, Oswald. *Wittgenstein's Later Philosophy*. Albany: State University of New York Press, 1989.

Heidegger, Martin. *Early Greek Thinking*, tran. David F. Kress and Frank A. Capuzzi. San Francisco: Harper, 1984.

———. "The End of Philosophy and the Task of Thinking," in *Basic Writings*, ed. by David Krell. New York: Harper, 1987, pp. 373–92.

———. "Letter on Humanism," in *Basic Writings*, pp. 193–242.

———. *Nietzsche*, vol. three, tran. Joan Stambaugh, David Krell, and Frank Capuzzi. New York: Harper, 1987.

———. "The Onto-Theo-Logical Constitution of Metaphysics," in *Identity and Difference*, tran. Joan Stambaugh. New York: Harper, 1957, pp. 42–74.

———. *On the Question of Being*, tran. William Kluback and Jean T. Wilde. New York: Twayne, 1958.

———. *The Question Concerning Technology and Other Essays*, tran. William Lovitt. New York: Harper, 1977.

———. "Time and Being," in *On Time and Being*, tran. Joan Stambaugh. New York: Harper, 1972, pp. 1–24.

———. "What is Metaphysics?" in *Basic Writings*, pp. 95–112.

Hiley, David. *Philosophy In Question: Essays on a Pyrrhonian Theme.* Chicago: University of Chicago Press, 1988.

Hilmy, S. Stephen. *The Later Wittgenstein: Emergence of a New Philosophical Method.* Cambridge: Basil Blackwell, 1987.

Hintikka, Jaakko. "C.S. Peirce's 'First Real Discovery' and Its Contemporary Relevance." *The Monist*, vol. 63, no. 3, July 1980, pp. 304–15.

Hintikka, Merrill and Jaakko Hintikka. *Investigating Wittgenstein.* Oxford: Basil Blackwell, 1986.

Holton, Gerald. *Thematic Origins of Modern Science: Kepler to Einstein.* Cambridge: Harvard University, 1973.

Hume, David, *Dialogues Concerning Natural Religion.* New York: Hafner, 1948.

———. *A Treatise of Human Nature.* Oxford: Oxford University 1975.

———. *An Inquiry Concerning Human Understanding.* New York: Liberal Arts, 1955.

Husserl, Edmund. *Ideas: General Introduction to Pure Phenomenology*, vol. one, tran. W.R. Boyce Gibson. New York: Collier, 1962.

———. *Logical Investigations*, tran. J.N. Findlay. New York: Routledge, 1970.

———. *The Crisis of the European Sciences and Transcendental Phenomenology*, tran. David Carr. Evanston: Northwestern University, 1970.

James, William. *Collected Essays and Reviews*. New York: Russell and Russell, 1969.

———. *Pragmatism*. Indianapolis: Hackett, 1981.

———. "The Will to Believe." *Essays in Pragmatism*. New York: Hafner, 1969.

Kant, Immanuel. *Critique of Pure Reason*, tran. Norman Kemp Smith. New York: St. Martin's, 1965.

———. *Fundamental Principle of the Metaphysic of Morals*, tran. T.K. Abbott. Buffalo: Prometheus, 1987.

———. *Prolegomena to Any Future Metaphysics*, tran. James W. Ellington. Indianapolis: Hackett, 1977.

Kenny, Anthony. *The Legacy of Wittgenstein*. Oxford: Basil Blackwell, 1984.

Kohák, Erazim. *Ideas and Experience: Edmund Husserl's Project of Phenomenology in Ideas I*. Chicago: University of Chicago Press, 1978.

———. *The Embers and the Stars: A Philosophical Inquiry into the Moral Sense of Nature*. Chicago: University of Chicago Press, 1984.

Leplin, Jarrett. *Scientific Realism*. Berkeley: University of California, 1984.

Livingstone, Angela. *Salome: Her Life and Work*. Mount Kisco: Moyer Bell, 1984.

Lyotard, Jean-François. *The Postmodern Condition: A Report on Knowledge*, tran. Geoff Bennington and Brian Massumi. Minneapolis: University of Minnesota, 1984.

MacIntyre, Alisdair. *Three Rival Versions of Moral Enquiry: Encyclopedia, Genealogy, and Tradition*. Notre Dame: University of Notre Dame, 1990.

Margolis, Joseph. *Pragmatism Without Foundations*. New York: Basil Blackwell, 1986.

Marsoobian, Armen, Kathleen Wallace, and Robert Corrington. *Nature's Perspectives: Prospects for an Ordinal Metaphysics*. Albany: State University of New York Press, 1991.

Monk, Ray. *Ludwig Wittgenstein: The Duty of Genius.* New York: Free Press, 1990.

Murphey, Murray. *The Development of Peirce's Philosophy.* Cambridge: Harvard University, 1961.

Nagel, Thomas. *The View From Nowhere.* New York: Oxford University, 1986.

Nehamas, Alexander. *Nietzsche: Life as Literature.* Cambridge: Harvard University, 1985.

Neville, Robert. *The High Road Around Postmodernism.* Albany: State University of New York Press, 1992.

———. "Metaphysics." *Social Research*, winter 1980, vol. 47, no. 4, pp. 686–703.

———. *Recovery of the Measure: Interpretation and Nature.* Albany: State University of New York Press, 1989.

Nietzsche, Friedrich. *The Antichrist*, in *The Portable Nietzsche*, ed. Walter Kaufman. New York: Viking, 1968, pp. 568–656.

———. *Beyond Good and Evil*, tran. Walter Kaufman. New York: Vintage, 1966.

———. *The Birth of Tragedy*, tran. Walter Kaufman. New York: Vintage. 1966.

———. *Ecce Home*, tran. Walter Kaufman. New York: Vintage, 1967.

———. *The Genealogy of Morals*, tran. Francis Golffing. Garden City: Anchor, 1956.

———. *The Gay Science*, tran. Walter Kaufman. New York: Vintage, 1974.

———. *Human. All Too Human*, tran. R.J. Hollingdale. Cambridge: 1986.

———. *Philosophy and Truth: Selections from Nietzsche's Notebooks of the Early 1870's*, tran. Daniel Brazeale. Atlantic Highlands: Humanities, 1979.

———. *Selected Letters*, tran. A.N. Ludovici. London: Soho, 1985.

———. *Twilight of the Idols*, tran. Walter Kaufman, in *The Portable Nietzsche.*

———. *The Will to Power*, tran. Walter Kaufman and R.J. Hollingdale. New York: Vintage, 1986.

———. *Thus Spoke Zarathustra*, tran. Walter Kaufman, in *The Portable Nietzsche.*

Norris, Christopher. *What's Wrong With Postmodernism: Critical Theory and the Ends of Philosophy.* Baltimore: Johns Hopkins University, 1990.

Ogden, C.K. and I.A. Richards. *The Meaning of Meaning.* London: Kegan Paul, 1923.

Peirce, Charles S. *Chance, Love, and Logic,* ed. Morris Cohen. New York: Harcourt, 1923.

———. *Collected Papers of Charles Sanders Peirce,* vol. one to six ed. by Charles Hartshorne and Paul Weiss; volumes seven and eight ed. by Arthur Burks. Cambridge: Harvard University, 1931–58.

———. *Values in a Universe of Chance,* ed. Philip Weiner. New York: Dover, 1958.

———. *The Writings of Charles S. Peirce: A Chronological Edition,* vol. one. Bloomington: Indiana University, 1982.

Pepper, Stephen. *World Hypotheses.* Berkeley: University of California, 1942.

Plato. *Meno,* in *Great Dialogues of Plato,* tran. W.H.D. Rouse. New York: Mentor, 1956.

———. *Theaetetus,* in G.S. Kirk and J.E. Raven, *The Presocratic Philosophers.* Cambridge: Cambridge University, 1957.

Popper, Sir Karl. *Objective Knowledge: An Evolutionary Approach.* Oxford: Clarendon, 1972.

Putnam, Hilary. *The Many Faces of Realism.* LaSalle: Open Court, 1987.

———. *Reason, Truth and History.* Cambridge: Cambridge University, 1981.

———. *Representation and Reality.* Cambridge: MIT, 1988.

———. "Wittgenstein on Religious Belief." *On Community: Boston University Studies in the Philosophy of Religion,* ed. Leroy Rouner. Notre Dame: University of Notre Dame, 1991, pp. 56–75.

Quine, W.V.O. "Epistemology Naturalized," in *Ontological Relativity and Other Essays.* New York: Columbia University, 1968, pp. 69–90.

———. "Natural Kinds," in *Ontological Relativity and Other Essays.* New York: Columbia University, 1968, pp. 114–38.

———. "What Price Bivalence?" *The Journal of Philosophy* 98:90–95, 1981.

Radnitzky, Gerrard and W.W. Bartley III. *Evolutionary Epistemology, Rationality, and the Sociology of Knowledge.* LaSalle: Open Court, 1987.

Ramsey, Frank. *Foundations: Essays in Philosophy, Logic, Mathematics and Economics*, ed. D.H. Mellor. Atlantic Highlands: Humanities, 1978.

———. *The Foundations of Mathematics and Other Logical Essays.* London: Kegan Paul, 1931.

———. Review of Ogden and Richards' *The Meaning of Meaning*. *Mind*, vol. 33, Jan. 1924, pp. 108–09.

Randall, John Herman. *The Career of Philosophy*, vol. two. New York: Columbia University, 1965.

Rawls, John. "Justice as Fairness: Political not Metaphysical," *Philosophy and Public Affairs*, 14:223–251, summer 1985.

Reichenbach, Hans. *The Rise of Scientific Philosophy.* Berkeley: University of California, 1962.

Reid, Thomas. *Inquiry and Essays*, ed. Ronald Beanblossom and Keith Lehrer. Indianapolis: Hackett, 1983.

Rorty, Richard. *Consequences of Pragmatism.* Minneapolis: University of Minnesota, 1982.

———. *Contingency, Irony, and Solidarity.* Cambridge: Cambridge University, 1989.

———. *Essays on Heidegger and Others.* Cambridge: Cambridge University, 1991.

———. *The Linguistic Turn: Recent Essays in Philosophical Method.* Chicago: University of Chicago, 1967.

———. "From Logic to Language to Play." in *Proceedings of the American Philosophical Association*, vol. 59, no. 5, June 1986. pp. 747–53.

———. *Philosophy and the Mirror of Nature.* Princeton: Princeton University, 1979.

———. *Objectivity, Relativism, and Truth.* Cambridge: Cambridge University, 1991.

Sartre, Jean-Paul. "Existentialism," in *Existentialism and Human Emotions*, tran. Bernard Frechtman. New York: Citadel, 1957.

Schopenhauer, Arthur. *The World as Will and Representation*, tran. E.F.J. Payne. New York: Dover, 1969.

Sextus Empiricus. *Outlines of Pyrrhonism*, tran. R.G. Bury. Cambridge: Harvard University, 1961.

———. *Selections from the Major Writings on Scepticism, Man, and God*, tran. Sanford Etheridge. Indianapolis: Hackett, 1985.

Sheffer, Henry. Review of the second edition of volume one of *Principia Mathematica*. *Isis*, VIII, 1926, pp. 226–231.

Shimony, Abner. "Integral Epistemology" and "Introduction" in *Naturalistic Epistemology: A Symposium of Two Decades*, ed. Abner Shimony and Debra Nails. Dordrecht: Reidel, 1987, pp. 299–318 and 1–13.

———. "Reality, Causality, and Closing the Circle," in Abner Shimony, *Search for a Naturalistic World View*, vol. one. Cambridge: Cambridge University, 1993, pp. 21–61.

Smith, John. "Community and Reality," in Richard Bernstein, *Perspectives on Peirce*. New Haven: Yale University, 1965, pp. 92–119.

Staten, Henry. *Wittgenstein and Derrida*. Lincoln: University of Nebraska, 1984.

Stein, Howard. "Yes, But . . . : Some Thoughts on Realism." *Dialectica*, vol. 43, no. 1–2, 1989, pp. 47–65.

Tarski, Alfred. "The Concept of Truth in Formalized Languages," in *Logic, Semantics, Metamathematics*, tran. F.H. Woodger. Oxford: Clarendon, 1969.

Thorp, Thomas. *Politology*. Ph.D. thesis. State University of New York at Stony Brook, 1993.

von Wright, G.H. "Biographical Sketch," in Norman Malcolm's *Ludwig Wittgenstein: A Memoir*. London: Oxford University, 1958.

Weber, Max. *The Protestant Ethic and the Spirit of Capitalism*, tran. Talcott Parsons. London: Scribner, 1958.

———. "Religious Rejections of the World and their Directions," in *From Max Weber*, tran. H.H. Gerth and C. Wright Mills. New York: Oxford University, 1946.

———. "Science as a Vocation," in *From Max Weber*. New York: Oxford University, 1946, pp. 129–58.

Whitehead, Alfred North. *Process and Reality: An Essay in Cosmology*. New York: Free Press, 1978.

Wittgenstein, Ludwig. "Lecture on Ethics." *The Philosophical Review*, vol. 74, no. 1, January 1965, pp. 3–12.

———. *Letters to Russell, Keynes and Moore*, ed. G.H. von Wright and B.F. McGuinness. Oxford: Basil Blackwell, 1974.

———. *Notebooks: 1914–1916*, tran. G.E.M. Anscombe. London: University of Chicago Press, 1979.

———. *On Certainty*, tran. Denis Paul and G.E.M. Anscombe. New York: Harper, 1969.

———. *Philosophical Investigations*, tran. G.E.M. Anscombe. New York: Macmillan, 1958.

———. *Remarks on the Foundations of Mathematics*, tran. G.E.M. Anscombe. Cambridge: MIT, 1983.

———. *Tractatus Logico-Philosophicus*, tran. D.F. Pears and B.F. McGuinness. London: Routledge, 1961.

———. *Ludwig Wittgenstein and the Vienna Circle: Conversations with Friedrich Waisman*, ed. Brian F, McGuinness. Oxford: Basil Blackwell, 1967.

———. *Zettel*, tran. G.E.M. Anscombe. Berkeley and Los Angeles: University of California, 1970.

Wong, Hao. *Beyond Analytic Philosophy: Doing Justice to What We Know*. Cambridge: MIT, 1986.

INDEX

Aesthetic naturalism, 176–77
Albert, Hans, 74, 304
Aletheia, 48, 187, 266, 333, 336, 343
Antifoundationalism, 8, 24
Antirealism: and contemporary philosophy, 8–9, 23–24; definition of, 60–65; types of, 62–80. *See also* relativism, naturalism, pragmatism
Antiphilosophy, 5–12, 23–26; consolation of, 318–20; failure of, 320–25, 344
Apel, Karl-Otto, 75, 79
Avoidance, method of, 309

Bain, Alexander, 106
Bartley III, W.W., 142, 143
Berkeley, George, 55, 86, 107, 127, 283
Biotic naturalism, 239
Bivalence, 53, 273
Boethius, 396
Buchler, Justus, 229–60; and Derrida, 285, 294, 393; exhibitive dimension of philosophy, 255–57; and Heidegger, 387–88; and Nietzsche, 238–42, 254–55; parity, principle of, 230, 258–59; and pragmatism, 242– 45; objective relativism, 245–55; theory of judgment, 33–36; view from anywhere, versus view from "nowhere," 231
Burnyeat, Miles, 396

Cahoone, Lawrence, 366
Campbell, James, 388
Carnap, Rudolf, 147, 149, 318, 399

Cassirer, Ernst, 230, 367–68
Colapietro, Vincent, 369
Common sense (commonsensism), 85–86; antiphilosophical use of, 299–303, 313; continuity with philosophy, 314–320; the new commonsensism, 12. *See also* Peirce
Contextualism: in Buchler, 253–55; definition of, 63–64; in Derrida, 287–91; in Wittgenstein, 210–17
Conventionalism: definition of, 63–64; in Peirce, 125–29, 135–36; in Wittgenstein, 210–17
Convergence theory of truth. *See* Peirce
Correspondence, truth as, 55–56, 59
Critical common sensism. *See* Peirce
Crosser, Paul, 355

Danto, Arthur, 179, 184
Davidson, Donald, 57, 75–79, 313
Deconstruction, 276–80
Deleuze, Gilles, 4, 184–86
Derrida, Jacques, 261–96, 322–29; account of semiosis, 269–75; and Buchler, 393; contextualism (relativism) in, 284–91; and Peirce, 393–94; and philosophy, 291–96
De Saussure, Ferdinand, 264, 272, 280, 283
Descartes, Rene, 3, 212, 225
Dewey, John: and Buchler, 230, 232, 235; and the ends of philosophy, 345–46; and Nietzsche, 378; and pragmatism, 71–73
Différance, 272–73

415

8231297R0

Made in the USA
Lexington, KY
17 January 2011